The Vigorous Core of Our Nationality

PITT LATIN AMERICAN SERIES

John Charles Chasteen and Catherine M. Conaghan, Editors

The

RACE AND

Vigorous

REGIONAL

Core

IDENTITY IN

# of Our

NORTHEASTERN

Nationality

BRAZIL

Stanley E. Blake

UNIVERSITY OF PITTSBURGH PRESS

Published by the University of Pittsburgh Press, Pittsburgh, Pa., 15260

Copyright © 2011, University of Pittsburgh Press

Manufactured in the United States of America

Printed on acid-free paper

10 9 8 7 6 5 4 3 2 1

Library of Congress Cataloging-in-Publication Data

Blake, Stanley E.
   The vigorous core of our nationality : race and regional identity in northeastern
Brazil / Stanley E. Blake.
      p. cm. — (Pitt Latin American series)
   Includes bibliographical references and index.
   ISBN 13: 978-0-8229-6133-8 (alk. paper)
   ISBN 10: 0-8229-6133-4 (alk. paper)
   1. Brazil, Northeast—Civilization. 2. Regionalism—Brazil, Northeast. 3. Group
identity—Brazil, Northeast. 4. Brazil, Northeast—Race relations. 5. Brazil,
Northeast—Social conditions—19th century. 6. Brazil, Northeast—Social
conditions—20th century. 7. National characteristics, Brazilian. I. Title.
F2583.B53 2011
305.800981'3—dc22
                                    2010045625

CONTENTS

PREFACE

THIS WORK focuses on the origins and development of northeastern regional identity in the Brazilian state of Pernambuco from the middle of the nineteenth century through 1945. This identity reflected a century of social, economic, and political transformations as well as the contributions of intellectuals, urban professionals, civil servants, and politicians who utilized new social, political, racial, and biomedical ideas to formally define northeastern regional identity and to construct a modern state with the capacity to improve social and economic conditions in the region.

Recent scholarship on nation building, state building, and the formation of national and regional identities informs the way the development of the northeastern regional identity is presented here. This literature has largely focused on São Paulo and Rio de Janeiro, with less attention paid to areas outside the leading centers of political and economic power. This work instead examines the ways in which the development of northeastern regional identity shaped debates about Brazilian national identity, citizenship, and state power while also investigating transformations that took place in the Northeast. Northeastern regional identity did not simply reflect the declining economic and political status of the region within the nation but became an essential component of Brazilian national identity. The Northeast and *nordestinos* came to represent a social, racial, and political "other" that was contrasted with the supposedly more developed regions and populations of southern Brazil. The *nordestino* thus became a symbol of regional backwardness and Brazil's mixed racial heritage while the whiter and supposedly more progressive populations of the South became a symbol of Brazilian national identity and racial progress.

In both original scholarship and in critical approaches to the work of Gilberto Freyre, northeastern understandings of race are characterized as, at best, out of step with the mainstream beliefs and, at worst, as antiquated and racist—characteristic, so the argument goes, of an older, more traditional generation of intellectuals and social critics. This work thus examines the ways in which racial ideas in northeastern Brazil differed from mainstream ideas and the ways in which these unique regional understandings of race shaped the development of northeastern regional identity.

This work also documents the ways in which ideas about northeastern regional identity and *nordestinos* were put into practice in the process of state building and in the management of civil society. Special attention is directed to state-generated understandings of northeastern regional identity because, through the mid-1940s, *nordestinos* were defined primarily in terms of supposedly "objective" and "scientific" characteristics and their status as objects of state-sponsored development projects. This is not to discount the significance of literary and cultural definitions of northeastern regional identity, but cultural definitions of the Northeast would become more important politically in the 1940s and 1950s, only after state-sponsored "objective" constructions of northeastern regional identity had become firmly established. This work thus focuses on scientific and medical ideas and practices and argues that the historical processes that produced northeastern regional identity and the *nordestino* constitute an example of modernity.

While there are social and economic problems specific to the Northeast that are both real and legitimate, the populations of the region must be understood first as Brazilians and second as *nordestinos,* workers, students, or Afro-Brazilians in order to move beyond the notion of the Northeast and *nordestinos* as a region and people apart. Unfortunately, since the 1930s, *nordestinos* themselves have often been identified as the cause of regional backwardness, and many Brazilians believed, and indeed continue to believe (whether they would publicly admit it or not) that *nordestinos* constitute an impediment to both regional and national social and economic development. Readers will note that I do not offer a definition of the term *nordestino.* This is deliberate, as the focus of this book is on examining the multiple ways in which northeastern regional identity was understood in the nineteenth and twentieth centuries. To put it most succinctly, I would argue that *nordestinos* are Brazilians who hail from the nine states that make up the geopolitical region of northeastern Brazil. This simple definition obscures the myriad historical and contemporary difficulties inherent in defining *nordestinos* according to race, culture, class, and ideology and instead privileges the idea that *nordestinos* are first and foremost Brazilian citizens. It is this idealistic notion that inspired me to write this book.

THE MULTIPLE orthographic changes that Portuguese has undergone since the nineteenth century complicate the use of Portuguese terms. I have rendered Portuguese names as the historical figures themselves used them, even if modern usage suggests a different spelling. For example, I use Freyre rather than Freire, Agamemnon rather than Agamenon, and Euclydes rather than Euclides. I have used original Portuguese spellings in reference matter but have modernized the spelling of commonly used terms and place names.

The use of Portuguese racial terms is also problematic. Historians need to avoid injecting modern and foreign racial terminology into their analyses. I have therefore left original Portuguese racial terminology untranslated but provide upon the first use of each term an English equivalent. I employ the same strategy with regard to terminology used to describe the Northeast and *nordestinos*. Readers can also make use of the glossary at the end of the book.

I HAVE received a tremendous amount of help while researching and writing this book. I am forever thankful to Barbara Weinstein, whose guidance and advice shaped all aspects of this project. Both her scholarship and professionalism have served as an inspiration throughout my career. I would also like to thank Paul Gootenberg, Brooke Larson, Aisha Kahn, and Nancy Tomes. Allen Wells inspired me and found work for me early in my career. Beth De Wolfe became a great colleague and friend. I would also like to thank my colleagues at Ohio State in Lima, Allison Gilmore, Tom Ingersoll, Tryntje Helfferich, Brian Himebaugh, Roger Nimps, and Bill Ackerman, and my fellow Latin Americanists at Ohio State in Columbus, Ken Andrien, Donna Guy, and Stephanie Smith.

I received time off from teaching and funding for research and writing from the Ohio State University at Lima and research funding from the University of New England, the Rockefeller Foundation, and the Center for Latin American and Caribbean Studies at Stony Brook. I would like to thank Marcília Gama da Silva and Hildo Leal da Rosa at the Arquivo Público Estadual de Pernambuco, where the majority of the research for this book took place, as well as staffs at the Biblioteca Pública de Pernambuco, the Biblioteca Blanche Knopf at the Fundação Joaquim Nabuco, the Biblioteca da Faculdade de Direito do Recife, and the Rockefeller Archives. Kirsten Schultz showed me the ropes in Rio de Janeiro while Homero Costa and Edilson Souza did the same in Natal.

I would also like to thank the readers for the University of Pittsburgh Press, Peter Beattie and Jim Green, whose comments and suggestions made this a better book. Joshua Shanholtzer, Deborah Meade, and Maureen Bemko guided the editing and production of the book. Many colleagues, including Dain Borges, Jim Green, Kirsten Schultz, John French, Jeff Lesser, Seth Garfield, and Nancy Appelbaum, have given advice, suggestions, and comments on different aspects of the book. Ana Lima and Roberto Marques helped with translations. I thank the Academy of American Franciscan History for permission to reprint a previous version of chapter 4, which was published as "The Medicalization of *Nordestinos:* Public Health and Regional Identity in Northeastern Brazil, 1889–1930," *The Americas* 60:2 (2003): 217–48.

My deepest thanks go to Daisy Delogu. Without her this book would not exist. Her contributions went far beyond moral support and managing the chaos of a busy family life in order to facilitate research and writing—she read and commented on countless drafts of the manuscript while coping with the demands of her own academic career. Finally, thanks to Jonah and Ezra for being themselves and reminding me of what is most important in life.

The Vigorous Core of Our Nationality

1

Introduction

Nordeste and Nation

IN 1921, a future Brazilian bureaucrat named Agamemnon Magalhães asserted in a thesis written for an academic appointment that the northeastern region of Brazil was "a distinct 'habitat,' characterized by the rigor of
its ecological conditions. Nature is reflected in man, imprinting his features,
sculpting his form, forming his spirit."[1] Magalhães wrote about the Northeast
and *nordestinos,* as peoples of the region were called, as if they had long been
thought of as a distinct political and geographic region and people. This was
most certainly not the case. Just six years before, in 1915, Brazilian geographers
had gathered in Recife, the capital of the northeastern state of Pernambuco,
for the Fourth Brazilian Congress of Geography. In the official sessions and
papers presented there, geographers referred only to the "states of the North,"
the "problem of the North," and the "droughts of the North."[2] Magalhães also
employed climatic, geographic, and racial determinism to describe *nordestinos,*
calling them the product of interaction between rugged terrain, a harsh climate,
and European, Indian, and African cultural and racial influences. Furthermore, he considered the peoples of the region to be "the producers of Brazilian
nationality."[3] In other words, for Magalhães, the mixed-race *nordestino* was
the quintessential Brazilian.[4] This notion ran contrary to conventional wis-
dom. During Brazil's First Republic (1889–1930), intellectuals and politicians

advanced new understandings of Brazilian national identity that idealized European immigration and racial whitening.

In 1925, after returning to Brazil from the United States, where he completed degrees at Baylor and Columbia universities, Gilberto Freyre wrote two articles for a commemorative work entitled *O livro do nordeste* (The Book of the Northeast), which celebrated the centennial issue of Recife's daily *Diário de Pernambuco,* Latin America's oldest continuously published newspaper. The first piece, "Social Life in the Northeast: Aspects of a Century of Transition," examined what Freyre understood to be essential aspects of northeastern society and culture and how those traditions had changed in a century's time.[5] The second piece, "The Cultivation of Sugar Cane in the Northeast," examined the history of sugar cultivation in the region from the founding of the captaincy of Pernambuco in the 1530s through the transition from slave to free labor and the industrialization of sugar production in the late nineteenth century.[6] In both pieces, Freyre treated northeastern sugar society as the foundation of Brazil, downplaying three centuries of African slavery and instead celebrating the social, cultural, and intellectual achievements of elite planter society and popular culture, which he attributed to the sexual, social, and cultural intermixing of Africans and Europeans. Like Magalhães, Freyre asserted that the Northeast was, and would continue to be, "the most Brazilian part of Brazil; the most characteristic."[7] This was a remarkable position to take in 1925, given the economic and political decline of Pernambuco and other northeastern states and the concomitant rise of southern states such as São Paulo, Minas Gerais, and Rio Grande do Sul. In the 1930s, Freyre would further explore the role of race in the formation of Brazilian and northeastern society.[8] In *Nordeste* (1937), he argued that the mixed-race worker of the sugar-growing region was a "strong and capable type with the capacity for constant effort" and that in the future "it would be perhaps possible to speak of a Brazilian race or semi-race of the *moreno* (brown) man of the Northeast."[9] For Freyre, the *nordestino* personified the ideal of racial democracy, the idea that Brazil is a nation in which individuals of different racial identities compete equally in a society largely free from racial prejudice and discrimination. Freyre's understanding of Brazilian race relations, especially the notion of racial democracy, would become profoundly influential in Brazil during the postwar period.[10] While the Northeast and *nordestinos* would become closely associated with regional social and economic underdevelopment in the 1950s and 1960s, they would nonetheless remain at the center of debates over Brazilian national identity and whether or not *nordestinos* were authentically Brazilian.

From the second half of the nineteenth century through 1945, Brazilian intellectuals, urban professionals, reformers, and political elites invented a northeastern regional identity that was based on a complex and diverse array of sources. In the late colonial period and early national period, two political separatist movements gave rise to a distinct regional political identity. The Pernambucan Revolution of 1817, in which rural landowners, with the support of urban workers and the poor, called for independence from Portugal and the formation of a republican government, expanded to involve the provinces of Alagoas, Paraíba, and Rio Grande do Norte before it was brought under control by Portuguese troops. The Confederation of the Equator, which began as a rebellion against the Portuguese imperial government and the constitution promulgated by Pedro I in 1824, started in Pernambuco and expanded to include the same provinces as the 1817 revolution as well as the provinces of Ceará, Piauí, and Pará. While historians usually downplay the national significance of these separatist movements, they proved to be of lasting cultural and political importance within the region itself. Political restiveness continued with the Guerra dos Cabanos of 1832–1835, a popular uprising in rural Alagoas and Pernambuco, and the Praieira Revolution of 1848–1850, which pitted liberals against conservatives in Pernambuco. While neither of these later movements expressly advocated separatism, they nonetheless represented the ongoing spirit of political independence in the region and figured prominently in the civic imaginations of Pernambuco and other northeastern provinces. The revolutions of 1817 and 1824 were a source of regional pride and served to reinforce northeastern politicians' independence in national political conflicts during the last decades of the nineteenth century. Far from the capital city of Rio de Janeiro, northern economic and political elites, with some exceptions, were marginalized in national politics. In the second half of the nineteenth century, this sense of political exclusion constituted the basis of regional political grievances against the imperial government, which, according to northern politicians, favored southern planters.[11] This sense of marginalization was exacerbated with the overthrow of the monarchy and establishment of the republic in 1889. Reapportionment according to the 1890 census led to the further decline of northeastern political influence at the federal level.

By the beginning of the twentieth century, increasingly divergent regional economies were contributing to the sense that the North was a land apart from the rest of Brazil. As Barbara Weinstein and others have argued, regional identities reflect, in part, the unevenness of economic development.[12] During the colonial period and the nineteenth century, the North's most important economic activity was sugar production, especially in coastal areas, while cattle ranching dominated in the interior. Despite attempts to diversify and modernize the economy by promoting the cultivation of cotton and other export

crops, encouraging industrial manufacturing through tax breaks, modernizing sugar production, and transitioning from slavery to wage labor, northern-
ers witnessed few fundamental changes in the economy in the nineteenth
century. What did change, however, was the economy of southern Brazil. As
had been the case since the early colonial period, economic development remained regional in nature, and the rapid expansion of coffee production and
ancillary economic activity in southern provinces beginning in the middle of
the nineteenth century led to considerable economic disparities between North
and South. The reinvestment of coffee profits in industrial manufacturing in
São Paulo beginning in the late nineteenth century exacerbated this trend.
Northern sugar producers were well aware of these disparities, and when the
imperial government convened a "national" congress in 1878 to discuss problems facing agricultural producers, representatives from northern provinces
were not invited. Although sugar producers and government representatives
from Pernambuco, Ceará, Rio Grande do Norte, Paraíba, Alagoas, and Sergipe
would hold their own congress to discuss the same issues, they increasingly
believed that the imperial government favored the economic interests of southern coffee planters.[13] In the 1880s and 1890s, continuing legislative debates in
the Senado and Câmara over slavery, abolition, immigration, labor policy,
agricultural credit, the modernization of sugar production, transportation,
and taxation contributed to northern planters' and politicians' sense that the
imperial and federal governments ignored their concerns. Political and economic elites' sense of disenfranchisement from the political process does not
alone constitute a sense of regional identity, however. Still, it is clear that by
the last quarter of the nineteenth century the North constituted a region that
could be differentiated from the South based on both its distinct economy
and the way in which regional economic issues were represented and accommodated in Rio de Janeiro.

An additional source of northeastern distinctiveness was the region's cli-
mate and geography. With the founding of the imperial Instituto Histórico e
Geográfico Brasileiro in 1838 and of provincial geographic institutes (including the Instituto Archeológico e Geográphico Pernambucano in 1862), the
Brazilian government emphasized cartography and geography as essential tools
in promoting the demographic and economic development of the nation.
Ranging from the humid tropical coast to the arid interior highlands, the
North's geography and climate gave rise to distinct subregional economies
based on sugar, cacao, cotton, and cattle. For geographers and politicians, the
natural landscape offered possibilities limited only by the will to develop it.
From the late nineteenth century, geographic congresses, geographic and car-
tographic surveys of the region, and later, the founding of the Conselho

Map 1. Brazil, ca. 1930.

Nacional de Geografia and the Instituto Brasileiro de Geografia e Estatística and the publication of the *Revista Brasileira de Geografia* produced an extensive body of geographic information about the region.[14] Although geographic studies were intended to aid in the development of mining and agriculture, many geographers also investigated the racial, physical, and psychological characteristics of the populations of the region. Geographic and climatic determinism gave rise to the notion that regional populations were unique, shaped by telluric and climatic forces as well as the vagaries of race and history. Equally important, geographers posited, were the periodic droughts that affected the region, especially in the interior. Perhaps more than any other single event, the so-called Great Drought of 1877 to 1879, which caused an estimated 200,000 to 500,000 deaths, shaped intellectual, public, and political understandings of the region.[15]

The term *Nordeste* (Northeast) was first employed by federal authorities to designate those states that were affected by drought.[16] "*Nordeste*" was used interchangeably with "*Norte*" through the early 1920s, but by the mid-1920s, "*Nordeste*" was used almost exclusively, even though there was still disagreement about which states made up the region. In 1936, federal law identified the so-called *polígono das secas* (drought polygon), which ultimately included much of the states of Piauí, Ceará, Rio Grande do Norte, Paraíba, Pernambuco, Alagoas, Sergipe, and Bahia, as well as a small section of Minas Gerais.[17] In 1938, the Ministério da Agricultura provided a more limited definition of the Northeast, including only the states of Ceará, Rio Grande do Norte, Paraíba, Pernambuco, and Alagoas. In 1942, the Instituto Brasileiro de Geografia e Estatística (IBGE), in a report entitled "The Regional Division of Brazil," defined the Northeast as these same five states.[18] The official geographic definition of the region changed frequently, and the current IBGE definition of the Northeast includes nine states: Alagoas, Bahia, Ceará, Maranhão, Paraíba, Pernambuco, Piauí, Rio Grande do Norte, and Sergipe.

Official geographic and political divisions, while important administratively and politically, were only one way in which the region was defined, however. Beginning with the establishment of sugar production in the early colonial period and continuing with the extension of Portuguese colonization into the interior, the region became known for its unique social and cultural traditions. The Dutch occupation of Bahia and Pernambuco in the first half of the seventeenth century produced the notion, especially in Pernambuco, that the region had been positively influenced in terms of culture, urban architecture, and social and racial composition of the population, by a northern European nation. Sugar production exacted a terrible toll, however, on the Indians and Africans who were forced to labor in the fields and mills. The Indian presence in the region was considerable through the early seventeenth century, and several Indian *aldeias* (villages) survived in coastal areas through the end of the nineteenth century. After independence, Indians figured prominently in constructions of national and regional identity as Brazilian intellectuals and social critics wrote Indians into foundational narratives of the nation and the region.[19] In the twentieth century, the resilient *sertanejo*, the inhabitant of the arid *sertão* region of the northeastern interior, was constructed as the racial and cultural fusion of the European and Indian and became a popular figure in literary and political circles.[20]

This understanding of northeastern regional identity was as much anti-African as it was pro-Indian. African slaves, free Africans, and their descendants have played an ambiguous role in constructions of northeastern regional

Map 2. Northeastern Brazil, defined by the Instituto Brasileiro de Geografia e Estatística in 1942 as the states of Ceará, Rio Grande do Norte, Paraíba, Pernambuco, and Alagoas. Maranhão and Piauí were included after 1950, and Bahia and Sergipe after 1970.

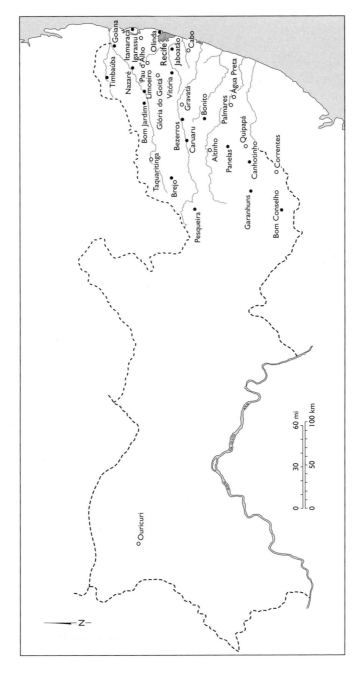

Map 3. Pernambuco in 1925, showing each *município* with a population greater than thirty thousand. Based on "Estado de Pernambuco," *Revista de Pernambuco* 2:9 (1925).

identity despite receiving considerable attention from Gilberto Freyre and other intellectuals. Constituting a majority of the population, especially in coastal sugar-growing areas, Afro-Brazilians nevertheless occupied a subservient role in northeastern society even after the abolition of slavery. While a few intellectuals of the period, including Sílvio Romero, questioned the widely accepted notion that Afro-Brazilians were inherently inferior, nineteenth-century and early-twentieth-century understandings of northeastern regional identity tended to ignore, deemphasize, or denigrate *nordestinos'* African heritage. By the 1920s, Brazilian intellectuals showed a greater interest in this aspect of northeastern regional identity. Gilberto Freyre's reimagining of northeastern and national identity was predicated on the intellectual and cultural rehabilitation of mixed-race Brazilians, and in the late 1920s and 1930s, Freyre and other intellectuals, including Arthur Ramos and Mário de Andrade, again advanced the notion that Afro-Brazilians and *nordestinos* were not inherently inferior to Brazilians of European origin. Some northeastern intellectuals, including modernist José Américo de Almeida, argued that coastal populations, due to the historical presence of African slaves, were biologically and socially inferior to interior populations, positing a fundamental division between the peoples and culture of the interior and the coast.[21]

Political and intellectual conservatives, both in the Northeast and nationally, rejected Freyre's position on race and continued to argue that Afro-Brazilians were inherently inferior, that they possessed physical and psychological qualities that corresponded to the demands of agricultural labor, and, perhaps most significantly, that race-based social and political movements had no place in Brazilian society and politics. Despite elite attempts at suppression, these popular social and political movements influenced understandings of northeastern regional identity. In these uprisings, Indians and slaves rose up against landowners; rural workers and sharecroppers attacked landowners and government offices, laborers organized and went on strike; and communists revolted, forcing northeastern ruling elites to confront the economic and political demands of the region's poor and working classes. Although ruling elites used force to put down rebellions, they also understood the necessity of addressing social and economic conditions in order to avoid future conflicts. Intellectual and elite constructions of northeastern regional identity did not directly reference these violent episodes, and the ideal *nordestino* was understood to be a docile, hardworking agriculturalist, not a runaway slave, rebel, bandit, or unionized worker who challenged the social and political status quo. Concern about popular rebellions was implicit in this idealized characterization, however, and regional elites understood the immediacy of the threats to their dominance.

These, then, are the core aspects of northeastern regional identity. More than an expression of the region's unique geography, climate, culture, and racial history, northeastern regional identity, personified in the *nordestino*, represents the broader social, economic, and political history of the region in which the poor and working classes were subjected to the demands of an elite class that sought to structure northeastern society according to its economic and political interests. The *nordestino* is thus both a social and a political construction, reflecting the objectives of the northeastern ruling classes, the popular and working class responses to the challenges of planter rule, and the changing economic, political, and symbolic position of the region within the nation.

There is a rich and varied historiography on the social, economic, and political development of northeastern Brazil between the mid-nineteenth and mid-twentieth centuries. Including economic histories of sugar and cotton production, social histories of slavery, banditry, millenarianism, and urban areas, as well as political histories of patronage networks and party politics, this historiography has placed the region firmly within broader historical narratives of nation building, state building, and social and economic development while highlighting the ways in which the region's historical development differed from that of other regions and nations.[22] Historians and literary scholars have examined the intellectual, artistic, and literary aspects of northeastern regional identity, especially the ways in which the northeastern modernist movement of the 1920s gave rise to a new cultural understanding of northeastern regional identity.[23] In his *A invenção do nordeste e outras artes,* Durval Muniz de Albuquerque Jr. focuses on the ways in which early-twentieth-century northeastern and national intellectuals, literary critics, novelists, poets, painters, sculptors, filmmakers, and musicians created an understanding of the region as simultaneously a "space of longing for times of glory" and a "region of misery and social injustice, the *locus* of the reaction to the revolutionary transformation of society."[24] The idea of the Northeast thus reflected broader political debates about the social and economic development of the region and the relationship between the region and the nation as a whole. Albuquerque's work focuses almost exclusively on intellectual, literary, and artistic understandings of northeastern regional identity. "The Northeast," he argues, "was created basically by a series of academic and artistic discourses."[25]

While literary and artistic constructions of northeastern identity succeeded in creating a set of literary narratives and cultural symbols that inspired continued reimaginings of the region, the idea of the Northeast and northeastern regional identity was also constructed in other, equally important, ways. Gerald

Greenfield and others have argued that a sense of northeastern regional identity arose first with elite understandings of the causes and effects of the region's Great Drought of 1877–1879.[26] Politicians, civil servants, urban professionals, scientists, and physicians participated in the process of creating a northeastern regional identity in order to advance their respective professional and political objectives and to improve social and economic conditions in the region. These groups exerted a profound influence on the economy, the legal environment, government, social services, education, medicine, and scientific research and ultimately shaped political, intellectual, and cultural understandings of the region and its peoples. The influence of these elite groups in the early twentieth century, a period of rapid social and economic transformations and changing expectations regarding the social and economic responsibilities of the state, has been well documented. Unfortunately, because of the region's economic position within the nation and its severe social and economic problems, academic assessments of the region have tended to conclude that the region's ruling elites, civil servants, and urban professionals have failed to improve social, economic, and political conditions in the region. An examination of social and labor legislation, social welfare programs, government responses to popular protests and rebellions, and the intellectual production and careers of academics and urban professionals, however, reveals that these groups took an active interest in improving social and economic conditions in the region and in shaping popular and elite perceptions of the region and its peoples.

Recent scholarship on the origins, development, and expansion of the nation-state in nineteenth- and twentieth-century Latin America has examined the ways in which changing understandings of the nation and citizenship are constituted through race, gender, and class, and advance the social, economic, and political objectives of the ruling classes. Gilbert Joseph and Daniel Nugent's *Everyday Forms of State Formation* has led historians to pay attention to the ways in which conceptions of the nation-state and citizenship reflect a continuous, and often contentious, dialogue between elite and popular understandings of race, citizenship, and national identity.[27] Interest in national identities has led historians to reexamine the origins and development of subnational regional identities and their relationship with national identities.[28] The continuing political, social, and cultural significance of regional identities in the era of the nation-state suggests that there is a fundamental relationship between regional and national identities. On one level, regional identities reflect continuing conflict over national identity and the sovereignty of the nation-state.[29]

Academic studies of Brazilian regionalism include a series published in the 1970s that focused on the economic and political dimensions of regionalism and state political machines' projection of political power at the federal level.[30] As Barbara Weinstein has pointed out, these studies defined "region" according to geopolitical borders, in this case state borders, and, with the exception of Robert Levine's study of Pernambuco, none of the studies considered the development of truly regional, or interstate, alliances.[31] At the same time, these studies focused almost exclusively on politics, defining regionalism as "political behavior that accepts the existence of a larger nation but that seeks economic favoritism and political patronage from the larger political unit."[32] Accordingly, the inability of less powerful states such as Pernambuco to influence national politics was interpreted as failure due to a lack of political coherence.[33] This interpretation did not take social and cultural aspects of regionalism into account.[34] More recent examinations of regionalism within Brazil have done precisely this. Barbara Weinstein's and James Woodard's studies of São Paulo regionalism in the late nineteenth and early twentieth centuries, including such topics as the intellectual and cultural origins of *paulista* regional identity and the political use of this identity as a justification for the São Paulo separatist revolt of 1932, emphasize the cultural, racial, and discursive aspects of regional identities.[35] Such an approach recognizes that regional identities represent much more than the region's relative economic and political power within the nation.

While regional identities represent distinct social, economic, and political practices, they both shape and provide content to understandings of the nation-state, citizenship, and national identity. Celia Applegate has argued that regional identities are either resistant, "taking shape around a claim to nationhood," or accommodating, "emphasizing a distinctiveness that can reinforce national markers of difference."[36] Over the course of the nineteenth and twentieth centuries, northeastern regional identity has been both resistant and accommodating. In the nineteenth century, Pernambucan-led separatist republican movements formed the basis of a resistant regional identity, while in the twentieth century, especially in the 1930s and 1940s, northeastern regional identity served to reinforce conceptions of Brazilian national identity, especially with regard to race and culture. Scholarship on the origins of the nation-state and national identity in Brazil has focused on the arrival of the Portuguese court in Brazil, independence, nineteenth-century state-building efforts, the transitions from slavery to wage labor and monarchy to republic, as well as the ways in which the social, economic, and political crises of the 1920s and 1930s led to new understandings of the relationship between the individual, the state and society, and the establishment of the nationalist and corporatist Vargas regime. This literature seldom addressed areas outside Rio de Janeiro and São Paulo.

Northeastern regional identity became an essential element of Brazilian national identity because it came to represent a social, racial, and political "other." As Thomas Skidmore and others have cogently argued, however, understandings of Brazilian national identity changed considerably in the 1930s as politicians and intellectuals embraced Afro-Brazilians as the archetype of Brazilian national identity.[37] With this shift, certain aspects of northeastern regional identity, especially culture in the form of folklore, music, and traditional religious practices, were identified as authentically Brazilian, and social and political conservatives exalted the *nordestino* as the quintessential hardworking Brazilian. During the populist Second Republic (1945–1964), the view of northeastern regional identity emphasizing regional culture and tradition would be replaced by economic-based assessments of the region and its peoples, which were less favorable. By the 1960s, *nordestinos* and the Northeast would become powerful symbols of the failures of developmentalism and the dangers of more radical approaches to social and economic development. Changing understandings of northeastern regional identity have thus reflected broader historical trends in Brazil and Latin America, and it is clear that the Northeast, far from being a region apart within the nation, is intimately linked —materially, politically, and symbolically—to the Brazilian nation as a whole.

Scholarship on race in Brazil and Latin America is also of critical importance with regard to northeastern regional identity. Much of the literature on race in twentieth-century Brazil has focused on the concept of racial democracy, the idea that Brazil is a nation in which individuals of different racial identities compete equally in a society largely free from racial prejudice and discrimination. Recent studies have focused not on whether the concept of racial democracy accurately describes Brazil (an approach that many scholars have rejected since the 1950s) but rather on the ways in which racial democracy has been appropriated by Brazilians as a racial ideal.[38] The ways in which intellectual and cultural understandings of race shaped understandings of the populations of northeastern Brazil from the middle of the nineteenth century through the 1930s are of particular importance here. Thomas Skidmore's work, in which he traces the relationship between understandings of race and national identity from the 1870s through the 1920s, is particularly relevant.[39] Since the publication of Skidmore's *Black into White* in 1974, historians of Brazil have acknowledged the ways in which ideas about race and nation were intertwined in the public and political imagination. There has been little work, however, on the origins and development of racial ideas in northeastern Brazil and the ways in which regional understandings of race differed from national and international racial ideas and theories.[40] Often, in both original scholarship and in critical approaches to Gilberto Freyre's work, northeastern understandings of race are characterized as, at best, out of step with the mainstream beliefs and, at worst, as antiquated and racist, characteristic, so the argument goes, of an older, more traditional generation of intellectuals and social critics. Thus, I examine the ways in which racial ideas in northeastern Brazil differed from mainstream ideas and how these unique regional understandings of race shaped the development of northeastern regional identity. At the same time, I show how northeastern ruling elites, civil servants, and urban professionals put these ideas into practice in governing the region and its peoples.

The ways in which the *nordestino* became a racial category in and of itself is another important topic. Scholarship on understandings of race in Brazil has revealed that individual and collective racial identities are socially and politically constructed and are historically specific, reflecting the changing racial demographics of the nation as well as the myriad social, cultural, and political upheavals that defined the First Republic and the Vargas era.[41] Racial classification schemes have changed considerably since the abolition of slavery. In the late nineteenth century, Brazilian intellectuals and politicians regularly employed a tripartite division of the black-white racial continuum to describe Brazilian populations, employing the terms *branco* (white), *negro* or *preto* (black), and *pardo* or *mulato* (brown). When necessary, they also used the category *índio* (Indian) to describe indigenous populations.[42] These categories were sufficiently flexible as to allow a degree of racial self-identification and limited mobility within the confines of Brazil's social and economic hierarchies.[43] In the late nineteenth and early twentieth centuries, foreign immigration forced a partial reconceptualization of racial categories to account for Asian, Jewish, and Middle Eastern immigrants who did not easily fit into standard racial classifications.[44] By the 1930s, the *nordestino* constituted a new racial category, one that simultaneously reinforced the dominant black-white racial continuum and embodied the new social and political ideal of racial mixing that undergirded new formulations of Brazilian national identity.[45]

While *nordestinos* were clearly nonwhite, the continuing social and cultural stigma associated with blackness suggested that personifications of regional and national identity, including the *nordestino*, should be nonblack. Despite being nonwhite, however, the *nordestino* became a constituent element of Brazilian national identity, a category that was at once both racialized and devoid of racial content. This changing position of the *nordestino* in Brazil's multiple racial taxonomies reflected the changing political ideals of the 1920s and 1930s. The *nordestino* emerged as a distinct regional and racial type in the 1920s, a period of social and political reforms designed to improve social and economic conditions in the Northeast. The *nordestino* became a national symbol during Getúlio Vargas's governments of the 1930s and 1940s, a period that saw the creation and expansion of social welfare programs, the implementation of nationalist economic development projects, and a fundamental transformation of the relationship between state and citizen. As a result of the suspension of individual political rights and party politics during Vargas's authoritarian Estado Novo, *nordestinos,* and indeed all Brazilians, were understood to be apolitical. The *nordestino* was thus stripped of both political and racial characteristics in order to conform to the nationalist corporatist ideals of Vargas's Estado Novo. Vargas applied the same strategy to all social, economic, and political interest groups, but at the time the *nordestino* was understood to be a "natural" category, one that reflected the racial, cultural, geographic, and climatic peculiarities of the region. In reality, northeastern regional identity reflected and advanced the political objectives of Brazilian elites as well as complex local and regional understandings of race and identity that are too often simplified for the sake of a cohesive national narrative.

Another important aspect of this study is the production and use of knowledge, an approach that owes much to cultural and intellectual history. Cultural theory, including the work of Michel Foucault, Pierre Bourdieu, and others, has exerted a profound influence in Latin American and Brazilian historical writing since the 1970s. The rise and dominance of military governments throughout Latin America from the 1960s through the 1980s led scholars to become increasingly focused on the expansion of the state and the surveillance and management of citizens as the objects of state power. In this context, Michel Foucault's notion of biopower and Antonio Gramsci's notion of hegemony became useful tools to historians, sociologists, and political scientists studying Latin America.[46] Since the return of democracy to Latin America in the 1980s, theorists and historians alike have come to recognize the ways in which popular understandings of identity, citizenship, and politics have both directly and indirectly challenged elites' attempts to impose their views on society.[47]

This work is not, however, intellectual history or cultural theory as such but rather focuses on the ways in which ideas about northeastern regional identity and *nordestinos* were put into practice in the process of state building and in the management of civil society. State-generated understandings of northeastern regional identity were especially important because *nordestinos* were defined primarily in terms of supposedly "objective" and "scientific" characteristics and their status as objects of state-sponsored development projects. It was not until the 1940s and 1950s that cultural definitions of the Northeast would become more important politically, when state-sponsored constructions of northeastern regional identity had become firmly established. The approach to northeastern regional identity here focuses on scientific and medical ideas and practices. Since the 1970s, scholarship on the history of science and medicine in Latin America and elsewhere has explored how scientific and medical ideas and practices are socially and culturally constructed and serve to advance the social and political objectives of modernizing elites.[48] Rather than show how northeastern scientists, physicians, public health officials, and their political interlocutors deviated from national and transnational scientific and medical paradigms, this work examines the way in which local and regional scientific and medical knowledge gave rise to uniquely regional understandings of nature, society, and the body.[49]

Another issue this book addresses is the fact that the historical processes that produced northeastern regional identity and the *nordestino* constitute an example of modernity. For both theorists and historians, the terms *modern, modernity, modernism*, and *modernization* are fraught with ambiguity.[50] Here modernity refers neither to cultural and aesthetic modernism nor to economic modernization but rather to the idea of modernity as a historical moment defined by a sharp rupture with a traditional, or premodern, past. Sociologists further define modernity as a historical period characterized by the predominance of a monetarized capitalistic economy and secular forms of political power and authority, as well as by the decline of traditional social relationships and a religious worldview.[51] The emergence of modernity in the more socially and economically developed centers of Brazil is well documented, but to argue that this process took place in a region of Brazil generally considered to be backward or underdeveloped is counterintuitive. As Néstor García Canclini and others have shown, however, in Latin America, modernity coexists with traditional, premodern institutions, social relationships, and systems of knowledge. The same can be said of northeastern Brazil.[52] A distinction must be made, however, between process and outcome. Although northeastern regional identity and the *nordestino* were ideas that developed concordantly with Brazilian modernity, in terms of Brazilian national identity, especially from the perspective of southern Brazil, the Northeast and its peoples remain symbols of traditional, premodern Brazil. What is significant, however, is that regional reformers and elites attempted to create a modern state that possessed the capacity to remake northeastern society and *nordestinos*.[53] That the

Northeast occupied an increasingly marginal position within the nation does not mean that the northeastern ruling classes did not attempt to improve social and economic conditions in the region and to redefine the relationship between the state and its citizens. Thus, northeastern Brazil was not unlike other regions in Latin America and the developing world where ruling elites attempted to gain and to maintain power by imposing on the public their own unique visions of modernity.

The focal point of this study of northeastern regional identity is the state of Pernambuco. Since the colonial period, Pernambuco had exercised considerable economic and political power over the neighboring provinces of Alagoas, Paraíba, Rio Grande do Norte, and Ceará, with its economic influence extending to the provinces of Piauí and Maranhão.[54] In the nineteenth century, Pernambuco emerged as the leading intellectual and cultural center within the region. Recife's publishing industry rapidly expanded, disseminating newspapers and books throughout the northeastern region, and the state's law school, the Faculdade de Direito, produced lawyers, judges, civil servants, and politicians who pursued careers in the region and throughout the Empire of Brazil.[55] Pernambucan politicians exercised considerable influence in the national legislature and government throughout the nineteenth century and during the First Republic.

There were, however, limits to this influence. The province of Bahia exerted economic and political influence over a wide area within the region, including the São Francisco river valley and the neighboring province of Sergipe. Bahia possessed a sugar economy rivaling that of Pernambuco, and Bahian planters successfully diversified agricultural production to include the cultivation of cacao and cotton. Salvador, Bahia's largest city and capital, served as the colonial capital from 1549 to 1763, and Bahian politicians were equally, if not more, influential in national politics than their Pernambucan counterparts. Despite their common social and economic history, Pernambuco and Bahia did not often cooperate politically; their respective political leaders proved content to carve out and protect spheres of influence at both the provincial and federal levels. Pernambuco and Bahia also disputed authority over several São Francisco valley *municípios* that had been transferred to Bahian control in the early nineteenth century.[56]

The ratification of the republic's constitution in 1891 and the ensuing decentralization of political power led the states of São Paulo, Minas Gerais, and Rio Grande do Sul to dominate the new federalist system. Northeastern states lost congressional seats as a result of reapportionment and were excluded from the so-called *café com leite* (literally, coffee with milk) alliance, in which the São Paulo and Minas Gerais republican machines controlled national elections. As they had during the nineteenth century, northeastern states competed rather than cooperated in their pursuit of federal largess. Northeastern politicians who challenged *paulista* and *mineiro* power were cowed and, if intransigent, removed from power by military force, as in the case of the 1911–1912 federal interventions in Ceará, Alagoas, Pernambuco, and Sergipe. Republican federalism also exacerbated state rivalries over territory and tax revenues.[57] States that had been subject to Pernambucan political and economic control during the empire period attempted to achieve a degree of economic and political autonomy. Most notable among these was Paraíba, which during the presidency of Epitácio Pessoa (1919–1922) attempted to make infrastructure and port improvements in order to decrease its economic dependence on Pernambuco.[58]

While federalism renewed long-standing political and economic rivalries within the region, paradoxically, the region's political and economic decline vis-à-vis southern states produced new intellectual and political interest in the region's common characteristics. Intellectuals and politicians took an active interest in studying the geographic, social, and cultural aspects of what they believed to be a distinct northeastern regional identity.[59] These multiple perspectives reflected not only the diversity within the region but also alternatives to Pernambucan dominance.

I take the position that by the 1920s, Pernambucan intellectuals and politicians, including Gilberto Freyre and Agamemnon Magalhães, were the leading intellectual voices of the region. The First Regionalist Congress of the Northeast (1926) marked the beginning of Gilberto Freyre's ascension to such a position, despite the fact that the Regionalist Congress was little known outside Recife and was criticized as a reactionary distortion of Brazilian modernism, which had inspired the original movement. After Freyre returned to Brazil from political exile in Europe and the United States and published *Casa-grande & senzala* in 1933, he actively promoted the idea that the colonial-era Pernambucan sugar society was the sine qua non of Brazilian national identity. This idea resonated with Brazilian political and intellectual elites, who were in the process of redefining Brazilian national identity in the face of a global economic crisis, declining foreign immigration, the São Paulo separatist movement, and the centralization of political power under Getúlio Vargas. While Freyre's regionalism found a national audience, his reception was less favorable within Pernambuco. Agamemnon Magalhães, perhaps the most conservative federal *interventor* (federally appointed state governor) to hold power during the Estado Novo, rejected Freyre's views on race and regional identity during his administration.

Racial politics did not unfold in the same way in every state in the region, however. In Bahia, *interventor* Juracy Magalhães (1905–2001) pursued policies that, according to Kim Butler, allowed a degree of protection for Afro-Brazilian culture and religion.[60] In Pernambuco, by contrast, the Magalhães administration attempted to eradicate the practice of Afro-Brazilian religion. It promoted a version of northeastern regional identity in which *nordestinos* were understood to be docile agricultural workers devoid of African racial characteristics. During the Estado Novo, the Magalhães administration's idealized *nordestino*, rather than Pernambucan or Bahian Afro-Brazilians, would become the personification of northeastern regional identity. This debate about northeastern regional identity reflected political and intellectual conflicts that were taking place primarily within Pernambuco. Although Pernambucan conservatives rejected Freyre's positions on race and northeastern regional identity, after Vargas was removed from power in 1945, Brazilians would embrace the ideal of racial democracy and Freyre would be regarded as the intellectual authority on Brazilian race relations. The big houses and slave quarters of Pernambucan sugar plantations, as imagined by Freyre, served as the crucible of the myth of racial democracy. Within the region, other social and racial identities would remain important, most significantly Bahian Afro-Brazilian identity and the distinct traditional culture of the arid northeastern interior. However, it was Gilberto Freyre's understanding of northeastern regional identity in Pernambuco that would dominate debates about the region and its peoples in the twentieth century.

2

The Nineteenth-Century Origins of the *Nordestino*, 1850–1870

AT THE 1878 Agricultural Congress of Recife, convened by the Pernambucan provincial government in response to the imperial government's exclusion of northern Brazilian states from an agricultural congress held in Rio de Janeiro in the same year, members of the Sociedade Auxiliadora da Agricultura de Pernambuco (SAAP) and representatives from five other northern states debated whether planters should rely on free native workers, *ingênuos* (children of slave mothers), or European immigrants to solve Pernambuco's impending labor crisis.[1] Henrique Augusto Milet, a French civil engineer who came to Pernambuco in 1840 to oversee the construction of public works, argued vehemently for the advantages of free native workers and lamented planters' negative opinions of native Pernambucans.[2] In a speech, Milet asserted that "workers exist, yes, but it is not the planter's preference, and for him it is as if they did not exist!"[3] While some planters took the position that migrant workers or "*braços nacionaes*" from the South would be more productive than Pernambucan workers, Milet argued that "the free national population offers us a sufficient source, an ample breeding ground, of manual labor."[4] At the conclusion of the congress, the Sociedade Auxiliadora formulated its own responses to questions that the imperial government had put to the Rio congress and affirmed Milet's position that in northern Brazil "laborers exist, and are even abundant."[5] This was, ultimately, the position Pernambucan planters and ruling elites adopted toward labor in the nineteenth century. The province did not want for workers. The challenge facing planters was instead the problem of turning the Pernambucan *povo*, comprising freed slaves, *ingênuos*, immigrants, Indians, drought refugees, sharecroppers, and subsistence farmers, into productive workers. To Pernambucan planters, it was essentially a political problem. Despite their growing disillusionment with the imperial government and its alleged favoritism toward southern planters, Pernambucan planters worked with the provincial government to develop labor policies that supported their efforts to create a work force that would meet their needs.

Slaves and Abolition

Until the second half of the nineteenth century, the production of sugar and cotton, Pernambuco's two most important commodities, depended almost entirely on slave labor.[6] Slaves constituted approximately 25 percent of Pernambuco's population prior to the end of the slave trade in 1850, 20 percent after 1850, 10 percent after the passage of the "Law of the Free Womb" in 1871, and 5 percent immediately prior to the abolition of slavery in 1888.[7]

African slavery was thus an integral aspect of Pernambucan society, as had been the case since the last quarter of the sixteenth century, when African slaves began to replace Indian slaves as the main source of labor building the sugar mills.[8] Despite slavery's prevalence in both urban and rural areas, its moral and ideological foundations went largely unexamined. Slavery was accepted as a necessary evil by Brazilian planters and political elites, one that was essential to economic production in both the North and the South. Prior to the abolition of slavery, slave owners' and ruling elites' attitudes toward slaves and the free population were infrequently articulated in public. The end of the slave trade and the transition to wage labor provided an opportunity for Pernambucan ruling elites to reexamine their attitudes and reformulate policy regarding slaves and the free population. Pernambucan political elites often expressed a deep sympathy for the plight of slaves, especially after the end of the slave trade caused a shortage of slaves, which resulted in more difficult working conditions. In 1855, Joaquim d'Aquino Fonseca, president of Pernambuco's Public Hygiene Commission, decried slaves' living conditions, which he argued had been steadily deteriorating since the end of the slave trade: "They are unhappy, poorly fed, poorly dressed, and obliged to work beyond their strength, they are not able to survive long, and because of this mortality is high

Table 2.1

Slave and free population of Pernambuco

Year	Slaves	Free	Total	Slaves as percentage of total
1819	97,633	273,832	371,465	26.3
1823	150,000	330,000	480,000	31.3
1829	80,265	208,832	287,140	28.0
1832			550,000	
1839	146,500	473,500	620,000	23.6
1842	146,398	498,526	644,924	22.7
1855	145,000	548,450	693,450	20.9
1872	89,028	752,511	841,539	10.6
1873	106,236			
1882	84,700			
1883	83,835			
1886	80,338			
1887	41,122			

Source: Eisenberg, *Sugar Industry in Pernambuco*, 147.

among *engenho* [sugar mill] slaves; without counting the many that succumb to the barbarous punishments that they suffer from."[9] A year later he reported that the conditions in which slaves lived and worked had not improved. He suggested, however, that "it would not be difficult to improve the luck of slaves, and even when this causes some expense, the results will compensate the excess." He suggested that the owners of slaves "should give them good treatment," offering them sufficient and appropriate food and clothing, excusing pregnant slaves from labor during the last three months of pregnancy, and providing space for the care of newborns, providing vaccinations, providing ill slaves with medical care and excusing them from labor, and eliminating labor for slaves younger than ten years old.[10] While Fonseca's suggestions were those of a physician who was, presumably, beholden to a sense of professional ethics and thus concerned with slaves' well-being as humans, he was also proposing these measures as a means of increasing slaves' productivity, longevity, fertility, and, ultimately, their economic usefulness to their masters. In the end, however, Pernambucan planters and political elites, like their southern counterparts, thought little of slaves' and *libertos'* (freed slaves) abilities as workers.[11]

From the abolition of the slave trade in 1850 through the outlawing of slavery in 1888, Pernambucan planters and political elites discussed slavery in the broader context of their ability to continue to control the labor market,

Table 2.2

Population of Pernambuco and Recife

Year	Pernambuco	Recife
1872	842,000	117,000
1890	1,050,000	112,000
1900	1,178,000	113,000
1920	2,155,000	239,000
1940	2,688,000	384,000
1960	4,137,000	797,000

Source: Levine, *Pernambuco,* 19.

linking the decline of slavery with the availability of land and free labor, including subsistence farmers, squatters, *libertos,* and immigrants.[12] Their concerns over the abolition of the slave trade and slavery itself lay primarily with the economic effects of abolition, rather than with slaves and *emancipados* as human beings or citizens. Planters slowly began to embrace the notion of paying wages to free workers. Several provincial presidents, the majority of whom were planters themselves, attempted to assuage planters' concerns by discussing and promoting the advantages of free labor. In 1857, provincial president Sergio Teixeira de Macedo pointed out that overall levels of sugar production in the province, as measured by exports, were increasing rather than decreasing, which he argued could be explained only by the "large number of free men who are beginning to work." The improved production, he suggested, indicated that planters had already begun to make a successful transition to free labor.[13] In 1866, provincial president João Lustosa da Cunha Paranaguá asserted that continuing annual increases in agricultural production prove "the truth of the economic principle that free labor, which is happily developing among us, is much more productive than slave labor."[14] A decade later, in 1875, the continuing decline in the slave population prompted Henrique Pereira de Lucena, a provincial supreme court justice serving as provincial president, to argue that planters were merely "affected by old habits" and did not yet "know how to take advantage of the new circumstances."[15] Slaves, Pernambucan political leaders argued, could be easily replaced by free labor, if only planters had the courage to do so. The declining number of slaves would soon enough make doing so a necessity.

Planters and their political allies' attempts to control the labor market were not universally successful. There were moments in which their dominance was challenged by both slaves and the free population.[16] Popular participation in numerous revolts and rebellions, including the Pernambucan Revolution (1817), the Confederation of the Equator (1824), the War of the Cabanos (1832–1835), the Praieira Revolution (1848–1850), the War of the Marimbondos (1851–1852), and the Quebra-Quilos Rebellion (1874–1875), challenged elites' control of labor, land, and politics and gave rise to new understandings of citizenship.[17] One often overlooked yet politically significant rebellion involved thousands of free blacks and mulattos attacking planters and government representatives in 1851 and 1852. Known as the "War of the Marimbondos" (War of the Hornets), that rebellion started in the towns of Nazareth, Pau d'Alho, and Limoeiro in the sugar-growing zone west of Recife, and it eventually spread to the entire sugar-growing area and parts of the interior. The Marimbondos rebellion had much in common with rebellions in the provinces of Alagoas, Paraíba, Sergipe, Ceará, and Minas Gerais.[18] It erupted in 1851 after passage of two imperial laws: the Regulamento do Registro dos Nascimentos e Óbitos, which required civil registry of births and deaths, and an act that established the first national census. The free population viewed the former, known popularly as the "Lei do Cativeiro" (Law of the Captive), as an attempt by the imperial government to "enslave men of color." Opponents of abolition believed the law was necessary, given that the slave trade had been abolished the previous year.[19] During the rebellion, bands of hundreds of *negros* and *mulatos* occupied small towns and *município* seats throughout the province. The resulting armed conflict included one pitched battle that killed twelve and wounded fifteen.[20] In early 1852, the army, national guard, and planters' militias quashed the rebellion and the provincial government suspended implementation of the Regulamento do Registro dos Nascimentos e Óbitos. Although the rebellion left few historical traces, Guillermo Palacios y Olivares has argued that not only the 1851 laws but also economic dislocations caused by sugar and cotton production, the Land Law of 1850, and forced military impressment motivated the rebels.[21] There is little doubt, however, that race was a motivating factor in the rebellion and that the rebels rejected what they perceived to be the state's attempt to enslave the free population. Although the rebellion was put down, the fundamental issues that gave rise to the revolt were not resolved. On January 1, 1854, the second anniversary of the armed conflict, provincial authorities found large numbers of the "most incautious population" gathered in interior towns, ostensibly to attend mass but who seemed likely to revolt again. Only through the "prudent actions" of local authorities was further conflict avoided.[22]

Lesser revolts also disrupted planters' tranquility. In August 1853, provincial authorities discovered that slaves in Pau d'Alho and Santo Amaro Jaboatão, the same area that gave rise to the Marimbondos rebellion, planned an insurrection.[23] A group of slaves revolted in Pau d'Alho and succeeded in "making a few robberies" before they were apprehended by local authorities. After provincial authorities sent out notices to local officials warning them of the potential for a coordinated revolt, another plot was discovered in Santo Amaro Jaboatão, led by a Muslim Nagô slave who possessed "some books written in Arabic" and amulets that "pertained to the ceremonies of the cult of which he was the priest."[24] The conspirators were arrested and sentenced to serve time at Fernando de Noronha, an island prison colony administered by the provincial government and the Imperial War Ministry. The landing of a slave ship at Barra do Sirinhaem and the sale of 200 to 240 slaves to nearby plantations in 1855—some five years after the slave trade became illegal—proved to be a considerable embarrassment for the provincial government, especially because some of the slaves were sold to government employees and the British accused government officials of colluding with slave traders.[25] The Pernambucan government asserted that only 4 slaves were sold and all were eventually located (it is unclear from the sources what became of these individuals). The government also took pains to prevent further trafficking in human "contraband," using flag-telegraph communication lines to coordinate additional coastal patrols. More importantly, these events prompted provincial authorities to address the problem of finding alternatives to slave labor.

The abolition of slavery was a drawn-out and difficult process due to the competing interests of abolitionists, planters, politicians, and the slaves themselves.[26] The British applied economic, military, and diplomatic pressure, which resulted in imperial legislation outlawing the slave trade in 1831. Slave traders, planters, and government officials largely ignored the measure, and the slave trade continued, with the expanding coffee sector increasing the demand for labor. External pressure again resulted in a ban on the slave trade, with the 1850 law effectively ending the importation of slaves from Africa, although a few slave ships made landfall in Brazil after this date. The end of the slave trade marked the beginning of the end of Brazilian slavery. Brazilian planters had historically taken little interest in the welfare of their slaves or in promoting slave reproduction, choosing instead to work slaves beyond their physical limits and to purchase new slaves to replace them. The economics of the labor market prompted Pernambucan planters to begin hiring free, native-born laborers.[27] They also entertained the idea of importing foreign agricultural laborers, although they would ultimately have much less success than their southern counterparts in this endeavor. At the same time, the growing labor demands of coffee production in southern provinces created an interprovincial market in slave labor. For Pernambucan planters, the decision to sell slaves to slave brokers and southern planters was purely economic. They could, as Peter Eisenberg has shown, sell their slaves and employ wage laborers or arrange contracts with sharecroppers and still turn a profit.[28] Even an 1853 provincial tax of one hundred *mil-réis* on slaves exported from the province could do little to stem the loss of slaves.[29] Some Pernambucan planters attempted to mitigate the effects of the transition from slavery to wage labor by forming associations such as the Sociedade Auxiliadora da Agricultura de Pernambuco, which sought to delay abolition as long as possible.[30] Despite planters' efforts, the slave population in Pernambuco declined steadily after 1850 due to the end of the international slave trade, the growth in the interprovincial slave trade, military impressment for the Paraguayan War, manumission, and deaths of slaves from working conditions and natural causes.[31] The 1871 national census counted 88,550 slaves and a total population of 810,540 in Pernambuco.[32] By 1887, the total number of slaves had been reduced to 41,122 (a number that provincial officials believed to be too high), plus 27,062 "*filhos livres*" or free children of slave mothers.[33] These figures indicate that not only did thousands of Brazilian slaves gain their freedom but also that Pernambucan planters had successfully managed the transition with relatively little disruption to production. While the transition was not easy, Peter Eisenberg has concluded that the long process of abolition in Pernambuco "did not create a labor crisis" thanks to the availability and low cost of wage laborers on which planters came to depend.[34] Because the transition to wage labor did not interrupt production, planters' paternalistic attitudes toward labor did not change significantly with abolition.

A final and poignant example of the ways in which planters and ruling elites viewed slaves and *libertos* came in September 1888, when the provincial president issued a circular that municipal judges were to post throughout the province. Coming four months after the last slaves, some forty thousand, were finally freed, the circular addressed planters' overzealous attempts to sign *emancipados* to labor contracts.[35] The circular suggested that because the "former slaves are used to work, and the life of the fields is a life of subsistence, it will be easy to gather them together on productive *fazendas* [estates], if the proprietors give them residences, as they have done before to their free *moradores* [tenant farmers], permitting them in the same manner to cultivate small plots aside from the labor they are obliged to do by contract, and to establish themselves as the zealous *protectors of their interests and rights*."[36] The circular not only suggested strategies for guaranteeing a steady supply of labor but also underscored the social and economic importance of the paternalistic relationship between property owners and workers. According to seignorial ideology, *libertos* were not capable of looking after their own interests—it was planters who were to ensure that the workers' "interests and rights," which were not fully enumerated, were protected.[37] The circular also suggested that it was planters' patriotic duty to ensure a smooth transition from slave to free labor: "If you proceed in this way, you will give *fazendeiros* examples of the faithful execution of contract . . . and avoid the great difficulties or misery that threatens many, and, saving your own interests, come together for the calm and pacific transition from slave labor to free labor; which will constitute the grand title of glory for your fatherland." The circular also acknowledged that *emancipados* might be unwilling to sign contracts with their former masters and perhaps would view the labor contract as "a new and odious subjection." The circular suggested, however, that if planters proceeded slowly and gently, then the *emancipados* would come to recognize "the advantages of an act that will best guarantee their *rights and obligations*."[38] It was clear that Pernambucan planters and ruling elites believed that *emancipados* were obliged to continue serving their former masters. This belief, born of an era in which slavery shaped elites' understandings of social and economic relationships, was also applied to the population that had never been enslaved. While Pernambucan elites argued that they were protecting workers' rights and interests, at the same time they utilized all the means at their disposal, including regulating the labor market, coercion, and rhetoric to ensure the compliance of Pernambuco's working classes.

The Povo

Planters and government officials also took a paternalistic approach toward Pernambuco's free agricultural workers, subsistence farmers, and sharecroppers. An examination of government labor policies and nascent social services in the second half of the nineteenth century makes it possible to reconstruct planters' and elites' attitudes toward the *povo*, or free population, as well as their understandings of citizenship and government responsibility. What is most striking is how elites' attitudes toward slaves differed so little from their views of the free population. Put simply, the social function of slaves, workers, and the poor was to serve the elite as laborers. According to the Pernambucan ruling classes, Brazilian society was an organic whole comprising two groups of vastly different social and economic status; the elite and the *povo* were dependent on one other and worked together to maintain social harmony.

Accordingly, from the elite perspective, the *povo* were to willingly subject themselves to the control of the ruling classes. In an 1865 report to the provincial legislature, Pernambucan vice president Antonio Borges Leal Castello Branco addressed the problem of maintaining public tranquility, writing that "the *povo* is, in almost every location, docile and easy to direct." Castello Branco believed that this was easily accomplished because the elite directed the *povo* "toward happiness with good examples and advice, with tenderness and, above all, with the law. We convince them practically that [the law] exists and governs, supporting the good citizen and punishing the bad." At the same time, he wrote, "It is established in them that [the law] is to be loved and respected as a power superior to all others, to which influences bow and for which the authorities are mere agents."[39] The law, Castello Branco concluded, provided ruling elites with a means of controlling the *povo*, while allowing them to appear to be the disinterested agents of a higher moral authority embodied in the Empire's legal system. Castello Branco suggested that the legal system should be used only as a last resort, as planters and civil authorities should rely on traditional paternalistic methods of controlling the *povo*.

Paternalism was also evident in the rudimentary social services offered by the provincial government to improve the health, education, and productivity of the *povo*, if not their social and economic status. Among the offerings were public health services, public and parochial education, and charitable works administered by Recife's Santa Casa da Misericórdia with the financial support of the provincial government. Charity for the less fortunate, including alms for the indigent poor, sick, disabled, and abandoned and orphaned children, was an essential aspect of Catholic culture and Brazilian society in the nineteenth century.[40] The Pernambucan provincial government provided significant financial support for Santa Casa da Misericórdia, which in the 1860s administered the state's only public hospital, plus a hospital for lepers, an insane asylum, a home for abandoned children, and sex-segregated *colegios* for orphans.[41] Recife's indigent poor, whom officials often noted were ubiquitous, especially near churches and in the central commercial district, drew particular attention from government officials. In 1855, the provincial commissioner of public hygiene expressed his concern about the indigent poor, suggesting that poor houses (*depositos de medincidade*) be constructed to house the mendicants; he then argued that they should be assigned "jobs appropriate to their capabilities" and put to work.[42] Even according to Pernambucan elites' understandings of charity, the *povo* were to work.

In Brazil, orphans attracted considerable attention because they existed outside the fundamental Brazilian social institution of the family. In addition to placing orphans in private homes under the tutelage of a guardian,

Pernambucan public officials also placed orphans in institutions that, rather than function as mere holding pens for minors, were designed to provide a moral education and job training so that orphans could become productive members of society.[43] In other words, orphans were also forced to conform to elites' conception of the *povo* as workers. The ideal for orphans was to learn a trade and enter a profession. The Santa Casa de Misericórdia administered two orphans' *colegios,* one for boys and one for girls, which placed an emphasis on the "practical and theoretical teaching of certain industries, especially of agriculture."[44] In 1857, the Pernambucan provincial president wrote that, "in order to introduce new rules, new ideas, and new practices and to create a new element of morality," it was necessary to disabuse orphan girls of the notion that the only way that they could escape hunger was by "waiting for the chance to be married." Instead, boys and girls alike were to be "inculcated with the habits of work, conveniently and adequately instructed in industry, and to seek out manual labor."[45]

In the second half of the nineteenth century, Pernambucan government officials also began to emphasize the social and economic benefits of public education that they believed should provide the *povo* with rudimentary education, jobs skills, and respect for authority. Provincial legislation stipulated that public education was to consist of "moral and religious instruction; reading and writing; the essential notions of National Grammar; the elementary principles of Arithmetic . . . ; [and] the system of Provincial weights and measures."[46] In addition to these basic skills, students were to be taught "the writings of the Evangels," "Sacred History," basic history and geography, and the principles of physical sciences. Provincial officials stressed the importance of religious instruction in instilling a sense of morality among the *povo.* In an 1857 report, the Pernambucan provincial president wrote that "religion is the primary moralizing element of societies."[47] He lamented, however, that "the *povo* in general have little instruction and almost no comprehension of the essential points of Christian doctrine. Neither the virtues to follow nor the vices to avoid are inculcated in frequent practice."[48] In June 1873, the imperial government passed Law 1124, which provided free, obligatory public education to all Brazilians. In discussing the implications of the law, Pernambucan provincial president Henrique Pereira de Lucena emphasized the transformative effects of education: "The poor class, . . . is accustomed to see the child simply as an auxiliary to the animal life of the family; the legitimate directors of society strive to teach them to value a moral life, which is only acquired by the means of instruction."[49] By the 1880s, government officials were also arguing that public education played a role in reducing crime, suggesting that education led to the "adoption of customs and thus the diminution of criminal statistics."[50] The function of public education was thus not only to provide a basic education but also to instill a healthy respect for authority and the law.

In the 1860s, in a tightening labor market, Pernambucan officials began to stress the importance of vocational training in public education. In 1866, the provincial president wrote that "among a *povo* like ours, inhabiting an extensive zone of opulent lands, and master of the richest natural products, it is to be deplored that nothing or almost nothing has been done since we have emancipated ourselves to remove from the social classes the pernicious downward slope of functionalism, and incline them toward useful arts, employment of first necessity, and above all the exercise of agriculture, which ought to be naturally our primary source of wealth." The provincial government initiated the construction of new "houses of education," which, in addition to instilling moral values, would "considerably augment the productive force and with it the riches of the State and of individuals." These new schools were to educate orphans and the indigent, who would "acquire the indispensable instruction more in harmony with the functions to which they are destined" and would lead ultimately to a "complete transfiguration of public customs" and a "spectacular economy of an intelligent and active *povo* regenerated by work."[51]

Pernambucan political leaders viewed vocational training as a solution to the shortage of trained workers. In 1870, government officials proposed the creation of an agricultural school and colony to be administered by the Santa Casa da Misericórdia.[52] The provincial president wrote in 1876 that professional and technical education would "produce general effects on the production of national wealth, promoting the expansion of our nascent industries, as well as the creation of others, and on the exploration and the utilization of our natural resources."[53]

While gymnastics and sports had been included in curriculums since the inauguration of Pernambuco's public education system in the 1840s, in the last decades of the nineteenth century, educators and public officials began placing greater emphasis on developing students' physical fitness. The author of an 1883 report on education wrote that "there is no one who presently writes about . . . pedagogy who leaves physical exercise out of the schools; gymnastics, swimming and equitation, which build a strong and developed physique, allow the education of intelligence and other psychological faculties."[54] What was implied but not overtly stated was that robust students would make better and more productive workers. Throughout the nineteenth century, it was almost impossible for educators to realize these ideals in an era of inadequate budgetary outlays for public education and a shortage of qualified personnel. Educators faced almost insurmountable difficulties in opening, equipping, and staffing new schools, especially in the interior. What these debates about educating the *povo* reveal, however, is that the Pernambucan ruling classes viewed the *povo* first and foremost in terms of their usefulness as workers. Through education and charitable works, the Pernambucan elite were able to realize their goal of providing planters with skilled workers to replace slaves.

Indians

In the middle of the nineteenth century, Pernambuco's indigenous population was quite small. An 1858 provincial census, which did not count *índios* as a separate racial or social category, showed that *índios* constituted less than 1 percent of recorded marriages and baptisms, which suggests that out of a total provincial population of 246,120 there were approximately 2,000 Indians in the province.[55] The majority of the province's *índios* lived in eight *aldeias*, which were Indian communities founded in the colonial era by the Jesuits.[56] Despite their small numbers, *índios* attracted a surprising degree of attention from planters and provincial authorities, the majority of whom argued that *índios* should be assimilated into Brazilian society. Provincial government officials regarded the assimilation of *índios* to be a moral and religious duty to be carried out by the provincial government in collaboration with the Catholic Church. In 1844, the provincial president wrote that "the catechization of the Natives is, in my view, one of the most urgent charges that falls to [the legislature] and one of the matters that most needs to be addressed, due to the neglect of this duty up to the present." The mission of the *aldeias*, as he understood it, was "to better the luck of errant and barbarous Indigenes who are abundant in the *sertões* of this province."[57] He lauded the Pernambucan legislature's appropriation of funds to "give clothing, habitation, and agricultural instruments to these individuals" and emphasized that the goal of such funding was "to turn them into workers, allowing them to enter civilized life."[58] The administration of the *aldeias* left much to be desired, however, and an 1852 report noted that "the *índios* have been seen in almost total abandon, at times being persecuted, and having their land taken from them."[59] A new director was appointed to oversee the *aldeias* and was charged with "giving good direction to the *índios* in order to make them useful to themselves and to the Province . . . until population growth and the progress of civilization makes the *aldeiamento* disappear."[60] Provincial authorities clearly believed that the proper strategy should be the integration of *índios* into civilized society. In 1857, the provincial president noted that "it seems to me that our plan should not be, like that of the United States, to segregate the natives from the European race; rather we should understand how they ought to be mixed, and in the future it would be more convenient to include *índios* in the general system of national colonization, and I believe that in this way they will win, and the population will march toward the homogeneity that we should thus long for."[61] While the provincial government faced numerous challenges in administering the *aldeias*, it was clear that *índios* were regarded first and foremost as another source of labor for planters.

In the 1860s, however, the provincial government paid little attention to *índios*, noting only in 1869 that seven *aldeias* continued to function and that one, located in Escada in the heart of the southern sugar zone, had been disbanded due to the assimilation of its inhabitants. The few remaining *índios* were given the choice of relocating to another *aldeia* (Riacho do Matto) or receiving plots of land.[62] Officials offered no explanation for their reduced interest in the province's indigenous population, but it is clear that planters and their political representatives had little need for *índios* as workers once these elites had successfully managed the disruptions in the labor market caused by the abolition of the slave trade. The 1871 passage of the Rio Branco Law (under which children born to slave mothers were no longer considered slaves but remained in their master's service until the age of twenty-one) rekindled planters' concerns about labor, and *índios* again attracted the attention of the provincial government. In 1875, an engineer contracted to survey *aldeias* reported that the majority had been abandoned and thus "lost their reason for existing."[63] In 1877, only three *aldeias* remained, and in 1878 the last two, located in the *sertão municípios* of Aguas Bellas and Tacaratú, disbanded, and plots of land were distributed outright to the few remaining *índios*.[64] Although *índios* were only a small percentage of the population, their assimilation into the general population and the disbanding of the *aldeias* represented a small triumph for provincial officials. They understood and treated the province's indigenous population in the same way they regarded slaves, *emancipados,* and the *povo:* as a source of labor. The provincial government's objective, couched in terms of pacification and catechization, was to turn Pernambucan *índios* into agricultural workers, and in this it succeeded.

Agricultural Colonies

Another way that the Pernambucan provincial government addressed the labor problem was by creating several agricultural colonies. Over the seventy-five years of their existence, they functioned variously as penal colonies, orphans' *colegios,* agricultural schools, refugee camps, and sugar mills. The first of these colonies was located in the sugar-growing region south of Recife, and at its zenith it accommodated more than four thousand colonists and supplied workers to nearby sugar mills. A second colony, located nearby on the grounds of the disbanded Indian *aldeia* of Riacho do Matto, operated for three years as a drought relief camp and housed more than nine thousand refugees. Pernambuco's agricultural colonies were also important symbolically in that they provided an idealized model of agricultural production and labor relations. Pernambucan economic and political elites intended these colonies to function as an inspiration and model for planters throughout the province as they coped with economic and labor upheavals in the second half of the nineteenth century.

Pernambuco's most important agricultural colony was founded as a prison colony by the imperial government in 1852 some 125 kilometers (80 miles) southwest of Recife near the boundary with the province of Alagoas. The Colonia Militar de Pimenteiras was created in order to quell rural unrest in the southern *zona da mata* (coastal sugar-growing zone) in the wake of the War of the Cabanos rebellion of 1832 to 1835.[65] The leader of the rebellion, Vicente Ferreira de Paula, a former army sergeant and son of a priest, led a popular uprising of Indians, runaway slaves, and free agricultural laborers in protest against economic conditions, the abdication and death of Pedro I, and the liberal reforms enacted during the succeeding regency. Imperial and provincial military forces used scorched earth tactics to put an end to the armed rebellion in 1835, although de Paula and a small group of his followers survived. Even after his death in the 1840s, de Paula's followers continued to defy authorities. Acknowledging that the military approach to controlling the rebels was not succeeding, the imperial government changed tactics and attempted to pacify the region by establishing two military penal colonies, Pimenteiras in Pernambuco and a second, named Leopoldina after Pedro II's daughter, located in Alagoas at the cemetery where de Paula was buried. The colonies were created in order to rid the region, as a Pernambucan administrator put it, of "criminals and vagrants" and the "evil influence of Vicente de Paula."[66]

The Pernambucan colony consisted of agricultural land, a regiment of fifty enlisted men, a church, agricultural processing equipment, and a small settlement that included about a dozen administrative buildings. Despite the fact that the colony suffered from almost continuous financial and supply problems, by 1857 there were more than four thousand colonists and one hundred slaves living at the colony and growing cotton, sugar, beans, corn, rice, and manioc.[67] Pernambucan politicians and administrators praised the colony in their reports, with the provincial president writing in 1857 that "this establishment, whose progress and importance will grow considerably when the railroad passes through the regions near it, is a great element of order, civilization, and progress."[68] Officials' enthusiasm for the colony was short lived, however. The shortage of soldiers to fight the Paraguayan War (1864–1870) led the imperial government to order all enlisted men stationed at Pimenteiras to return to Recife. In 1866, provincial officials conceded that the political conditions that had prompted the creation of the colony in the first place no longer existed, and the imperial government ordered the colony closed, stipulating that its lands be surveyed, divided into lots, and distributed to remaining colonists.[69] Despite an inspection by the emperor and empress in 1860, the imperial government also closed the Leopoldina colony in Alagoas in 1863.[70]

Although Pernambucan government officials lamented the imperial government's decision to close the colony, they worked out a plan to keep the colony open. Beginning in 1864, several plans were developed to bring foreign, preferably European, workers to Pernambuco. The plan included placing immigrants at Pimenteiras and Riacho do Matto, the recently disbanded Indian *aldeia* located twenty kilometers (twelve miles) down the Jacuípe River from Pimenteiras. However, by 1874, fewer than one thousand immigrants had arrived in the entire province, and most of these were craftsmen rather than agricultural workers.[71]

Provincial officials were undeterred, however, and developed yet another plan for Pimenteiras. In 1874, the provincial government decided to reform orphans' education, which had previously consisted of the two *colegios* in Recife run by the Santa Casa de Misericórdia. In place of these urban *colegios,* the provincial government established a new agricultural colony on the grounds of Pimenteiras and named it the Colonia Orphanologica Isabel, after the emperor's daughter and regent. The colony's purpose was to provide, as the provincial president put it, "moral and religious training, on par with that of arts and professions that will prepare [orphans] to later enter in social communication, worthy of themselves as citizens and worthy of us as a free, moral, and growing nation."[72] Although the repurposed colony also suffered from supply and financial problems, within a year it housed more than 100 orphans, who worked, attended school, and received religious instruction. The colony was administered by an Italian Capuchin friar, Fidelis Maria de Fognano, who subjected the colony's 100 male orphans to a rigorous daily regimen in which they rose before dawn, attended mass, worked from six to nine in the morning and from three to five-thirty in the afternoon, attended classes from ten to two, and studied from seven to eight in the evening before retiring at eight-thirty.[73] Fognano noted that the children, "returning after this daily toil, do not show any tiredness, boredom, and . . . are not affected by the climate of indolence that is unhappily to be observed among a certain class of workers," a rather thinly veiled reference to *libertos* and free workers, whom Fognano apparently believed were not enterprising and given over to vice.[74] The daily regimen at the Colonia Isabel, not dissimilar from the daily routine of a monk, or of *índios* at the remaining *aldeias*, which were also administered by the Capuchins, provided an opportunity to forge ideal workers in a period in which there was considerable uncertainty about the availability of labor. Thus, the Colonia Isabel, despite the fact that it never housed more than 150 orphans, received an extraordinary amount of attention from the provincial government. Father Fognano submitted lengthy annual reports that discussed in excruciating detail all aspects of life at the colony, including education, agricultural production, religious instruction, medical services, finances, and capital improvements. In this sense, the colony was a microcosm of the province as a whole. At the same time, it was an idealized religious community that sought to create Christian subjects who possessed a hearty work ethic, a strong sense of morality, and a healthy respect for God and paternalistic authority. The colony was also notable for what it did not include. Although an 1885 provincial census counted 41,122 slaves and 27,062 *ingênuos* in the state, the colony's administrators recorded accommodating but one *ingênuo*.[75] In this sense, Colonia Isabel constituted an ideal agricultural colony populated by workers unencumbered by the legacy of three centuries of African slavery.

In 1880, the provincial legislature decided that agricultural work at Colonia Isabel would focus exclusively on sugar production, and the provincial government imported and installed modern milling and processing equipment from Europe and extended a branch line of the Great Western railroad to serve the colony.[76] Budgetary and supply problems as well as frequent crop failures limited the financial impact of the colony. It did, however, produce harvests that compared favorably to several other government-subsidized central mills, and it even managed in some years to produce a small profit.[77] The colony's shift in focus from vocational and professional training to sugar production engendered a certain degree of discontent among the colony's orphans. Father Fognano noted that students, on more than one occasion, had told him that agricultural work was "only for slaves."[78] He observed that orphans from Recife wanted to learn a trade, while orphans from rural areas seemed content with agricultural work. In response to students' complaints, Fognano decided that while the colony would continue to focus on agriculture, students would be allowed to choose their own vocation, "as long as it is honest."[79] By 1883, colony orphans were being trained as cabinetmakers, blacksmiths, masons, locksmiths, shoemakers, cooks, and bakers, although approximately half of all students chose training in agriculture.[80] The colony's purpose changed little over the last two decades of its existence. In 1894, the Pernambucan governor stated that the mission of the colony was to provide students with "theoretical and practical studies for the diverse work of large and small scale agriculture and industrial production," which he hoped would lead to the "transformation of our agricultural production and the improvement of agricultural conditions in our State."[81] Unfortunately, the Escola Industrial, as it had been renamed, never lived up to the governor's expectations. The colony limped along until 1905, when the orphans' school was relocated to Recife to be administered once again by the Santa Casa de Misericórdia.[82] The Pernambucan state government rented out the property to a sugar mill operator until it was finally sold in 1927.[83]

Thus ended Pernambuco's experimentation with large-scale agricultural colonies. The state government continued to operate two small agricultural penal colonies, one on the island of Itamaracá north of Recife and a second on the archipelago of Fernando de Noronha, located 360 kilometers (220 miles) off the northeastern coast.[84] By the end of the nineteenth century, the transition from slavery to new forms of labor had been successfully completed and the sugar industry had been modernized; the agricultural colony at Pimenteiras had thus served its purpose. Although the nineteenth-century Pernambucan agricultural colonies at their peak had had only 4,000 agricultural workers, 100 slaves, and 150 orphans, they were significant nonetheless in that they provided a model of agricultural labor during these transitions. The abandonment of regimented agricultural labor in the early twentieth century did not in any way mark the end of the state's active involvement in managing labor, however. There were other sources of labor that would prove to be both readily available and less costly to manage.

Immigrants

In the 1850s, Pernambucan planters and political elites began to entertain the idea of promoting foreign immigration to satisfy their labor needs. Early discussions of foreign immigration identified a need for both skilled labor, including mechanics and artisans, and manual labor.[85] There were significant challenges facing the proponents of immigration in Pernambuco, however. Government officials worried about the climate and public health conditions, especially epidemics of yellow fever and smallpox and Recife's reputation as an unhealthy city, which they feared would lead immigrants to more salubrious ports of call. While nineteenth-century medicine could do little to improve sanitary and public health conditions, there were still bigger obstacles to foreign immigration. Provincial officials readily admitted that they had not yet put in place a system for surveying and auctioning public lands, which had been authorized in the imperial Land Law of 1850, and that there was no land available to distribute to potential immigrants.[86] Contract and wage prices were also low compared to those offered to immigrants on coffee plantations in the South. Despite these shortcomings, officials remained optimistic about the potential for foreign immigration. In 1857, provincial president Sergio Teixeira de Macedo suggested that the imperial government should purchase land in Pernambuco in order to create an immigrant agricultural colony modeled on the Colonia Militar de Pimenteiras and the penal colony on Fernando de Noronha. In addition to encouraging "colonies of national and foreign volunteers," the president proposed modifying the provincial criminal code in order to force vagrants and mendicants to work "under a severe regimen" at the state's agricultural penal colonies.[87] In 1857, a group of Portuguese merchants formed the Associação de Colonisação para as Provincias de Pernambuco, Parahiba e Alagôas to promote immigration.[88] Provincial political leaders lauded the association's plans, believing that increased immigration would lead to the "complete annihilation of the hopes of the slavers [negreiros] and the immoral commerce which was a shame on our civilization," and thus to wage labor and industrial growth in the province.[89] Despite the almost universal enthusiasm for immigration, few immigrants actually arrived in Pernambuco. An 1866 provincial report on immigration noted that 450 foreign immigrants had arrived in Pernambuco (including four families from the United States who had been recruited to plant cotton adjacent to the Colonia Militar de Pimenteiras), but relatively few of the immigrants were classified as agriculturalists.[90] The imperial government supplied the colonos (colonists) with "land and money for initial expenses," hoping for "good results" from this "partnership."[91] The American colonos were actually far less than "partners" because provincial authorities conceived of them "as equals to slaves working on behalf of landowning farmers." North American immigration proved especially attractive to Pernambucan planters and politicians, who believed that Americans' supposedly superior work ethic would transform agricultural production and spur economic growth. In 1866, the provincial president wrote that "that energetic and enterprising race . . . will encounter [in the interior] conditions to employ its indefatigable activity on the natural elements of wealth and prosperity, which when explored by means of perfected processes of cultivation and intelligent labor, will provide them with excess compensation and limit their longing for their *patria* in the heart of a country that is no less free and hospitable."[92] In 1868, the provincial government employed one of the immigrants, William Graham, to return to the United States to promote further immigration. It also contemplated sending a steamship to provide passage for immigrants and even purchased a building in Recife to serve as a hostel for new arrivals.[93] By 1869, however, the provincial government's attempts to promote immigration from the United States had failed, and the four families had left Brazil.[94]

Interest in immigration was rekindled in 1871 with the passage of the Rio Branco Law. In the same year, provincial president Diogo Velho Cavalcanti de Albuquerque addressed legislators' and planters' concerns about labor in his annual address to the state legislature, in which he proposed two strategies to counter the impending shortage of agricultural laborers. The first and most desirable, he wrote, was "the requisition of workers from outside the country." Cavalcanti recognized the difficulties that the provincial government had encountered in trying to attract foreign immigrants, so he also proposed the recruitment of "free national labor," which, he argued, would have the added benefit of "moralizing the inferior classes of the population."[95] Cavalcanti acknowledged planters' doubts about native workers: "Some interject that our people are lazy, given to the practice of vices and crime, incapable of agricultural labor. There is in this, disgracefully, much truth. . . . Realistically there is a part of our population profoundly demoralized, even lost, but from among the masses one can find useful laborers."[96] At the same time, he called a meeting of leading planters and politicians in order to create the Sociedade Auxiliadora da Immigração e Colonização para a Provincia de Pernambuco, which raised capital for the purchase of land for immigrants. The society was involved in several attempts to promote foreign immigration in the 1870s, including one plan to place immigrants at Pimenteiras, but the efforts were unsuccessful.[97] In 1876, provincial president João Pedro Carvalho de Moraes reflected on the reasons that the province had been unable to attract foreign immigrants, pointing out that "in this province where *terras devolutas* [government-controlled public lands] are held under private dominion and occupy small expanses, it is difficult to think about the creation of *nucleos coloniaes*." He went on to suggest that, upon arriving in Pernambuco, "the European worker does not have the occasion to exercise the specialty that they are obliged to dedicate themselves to in the division and organization of labor in their country."[98] In other words, in addition to a shortage of land, skilled European laborers simply did not want to grow sugar. At the 1878 Recife agricultural congress, planters and political representatives from Pernambuco, Ceará, Rio Grande do Norte, Paraíba, Alagoas, and Sergipe agreed, after considerable debate, that there was "no shortage" but rather an "abundance" of labor in the region, although many workers lived some distance from sugar mills and did not make themselves available to planters throughout the year.[99] At the same time, congress delegates resolved that native Pernambucan laborers should be augmented by "national laborers," "spontaneous foreign immigration," and *ingênuos* trained in public vocational schools.[100] Despite numerous failed attempts, Pernambucan planters continued to support the idea of foreign immigration, well aware of the transformations in labor practices that had taken place in southern provinces. In the end, however, they recognized that their fears about a labor shortage were largely unfounded and that they could rely on native Pernambucans to meet their labor needs.

Pernambucan planters and politicians seriously considered foreign immigration one last time as the long process of abolition was drawing to a close in the late 1880s. In February 1885, the provincial business and agriculture minister called a meeting of planters and mill owners to discuss labor and immigration, but no agreement was reached.[101] In 1887, the provincial president wrote that while there had been much discussion of immigration in previous years, the main complaint of sugar producers was not a "shortage of laborers" but "low prices" for the sugar produced.[102] Nevertheless, the provincial government hired an engineer to conduct a survey of available properties that would be suitable for agricultural colonies, and, in 1888, provincial president Joaquim José de Oliveira Andrade organized yet another commission to promote immigration and colonization, the Sociedade Promotora da Colonisação e Immigração de Pernambuco.[103] Commission members argued that both national and European *colonos* were desirable as workers but that what was most important in considering the establishment of agricultural colonies was to place *colonos* of the same nationality together so that "their development would not be hindered by any disturbances or divergence of customs, aptitudes, tendencies or rival traditions, of beliefs, of nationalities, or of races." It was necessary, commission members stated, "to obtain the assimilation of races, promoting the crossing of blood, of customs, and of ideas in a homogenous, ethnological product," and they hoped that *colonos* would work alongside native Pernambucans, displaying good work habits, sharing knowledge and skills, and, ultimately, "intermixing racially." According to the commission's plan, immigration agents were to choose foreign immigrants carefully, "obtaining in place of the vagrant, vagabond, and demoralized, the worker, the moralized, and the father of a family."[104] It was clear that Pernambucan planters continued to champion European immigrants because of the supposed transformative effects they would have on agricultural production and on local workers' attitudes. Engineer José Ozorio de Cerqueira's 1887 land survey identified lands adjacent to the Colonia Isabel and the Colonia Soccorro (a drought relief refugee camp founded in 1878) as appropriate for colonization. Cerqueira suggested that the provincial government should designate additional public land for immigration, which should be made ready for *colonos* by establishing legal titles, creating development plans, and constructing public amenities and housing.[105] The provincial government hoped to attract both *colonos* who would own land as well as contract laborers who would work on "*fazendas* or other establishments."[106] An announcement that a British mail agent had signed a contract to bring 100,000 immigrants to northern states provoked further activity, including the printing of 20,000 pamphlets that extolled the advantages of immigrating to Pernambuco, and the purchase of a property on which a *hospedaria* (inn) for immigrants would be constructed.[107] In 1889, the Pernambucan government also purchased the *fazenda* Suassuna in Jaboatão from the Barão de Muribeca and divided it into lots to be distributed to immigrants.[108] By 1891, however, fewer than 200 immigrants had passed through the *hospedaria,* and, in 1895, government officials acknowledged that the Colonia Suassuna was a failure and sold the property.[109]

There were several reasons that Pernambuco failed to attract foreign immigrants. Sugar planters simply could not compete with the contracts and wages that were being offered to immigrants in regions of the country undergoing economic expansion. Although the Pernambucan government received subsidies from the imperial government and later the federal government, it was unable to acquire and develop land for colonies or offer even the most rudimentary public amenities such as roads, rail service, and primary schools. Finally, the availability of native Pernambucans as a source of labor at low cost obviated European immigration. As Peter Eisenberg has shown in his examination of the Pernambucan sugar industry, wage labor rates declined during the last quarter of the nineteenth century and remained low after slavery's abolition in 1888.[110] As had been the case in the 1850s and 1870s, the Pernambucan government's failure to bring European immigrants to Pernambuco prompted a moment of reflection. In 1893, the governor, Alexandre José Barbosa Lima, criticized those who continued to favor European immigration, writing in a report to the state legislature that "those who leave their land disposed to adopt another nation . . . rarely adopt it; they belong to the declassified who, when placed in a dissolving cosmopolitan atmosphere, form a monstrous grouping of the rubbish of all races that certainly no one would wish to have as fellow citizens."[111] In contrast, he lauded native Brazilians, whom he described as "an ethnic type that results from the fusion of three races, descended from the European, crossed with the Indian and with the African, and is definitively constituted biologically, socially, and morally.[112] He added that those who were "preoccupied" by immigration did not desire a "more vigorous, more prosperous and always pacific Brazil" but favored a weakened Brazil in which immigrants "aspired to form a New Italy, a New Germany, in which they did not lose their traditions and customs." He concluded by imploring "*nortistas*" and Pernambucans to improve themselves "by their own forces," asserting that "this hospitable and generous Brazil does not have to be transformed into a vast encampment of the leftovers of all nationalities."[113] Given the inability of northern provinces to promote foreign immigration, Barbosa Lima adopted a nativist position toward labor and encouraged planters and industrialists to employ Pernambucan workers. They had little choice in the matter. Out of necessity, they made use of the workers who were available to them and were generally successful in dictating the terms of employment. As had been the case with slaves, however, it became clear that workers would, when necessary, challenge planters' dominance.

Quebra-Quilos

Elite attitudes toward the Pernambucan *povo* were shaped by two upheavals in the 1870s. First, in late 1874 and 1875, the northern provinces of Paraíba, Pernambuco, Rio Grande do Norte, and Alagoas were wracked by a popular revolt that started in Campina Grande, Paraíba.[114] Active primarily in the interior, small bands of rebels entered towns on market days, destroyed metric weights and measures (which had recently replaced traditional standards), and attacked tax collection offices (*coletorias*), registry offices (*cartórios*), and municipal *câmaras* (city halls), destroying tax records, contracts, and deeds. The participants in the revolt were agricultural workers, sharecroppers, and subsistence farmers from the interior, although they were aided at times by priests, landowners, and, occasionally, sympathetic local government officials. Within a month, the uprising had spread from Pernambucan *municípios* bordering Paraíba to every *município* in the Pernambucan *agreste*. By late December 1874, the revolt had expanded to include *municípios* of Itapissuma, Itamaracá, and Igaraçu in the sugar-growing region north of Recife. Provincial officials scrambled to mobilize national guard troops and local police in an attempt to quell the rapidly spreading unrest. The rebels often attacked towns in force; there were several cases of hundreds of rebels attacking towns defended by a combined national guard and police force of fewer than ten men. The rebels' objectives generally included denouncing new market taxes and destroying weights, measures, and notary records, although in a few cases they denounced local landowners and Freemasons, or made pronouncements in favor of the clergy and Pedro II. In most cases, the rebels quickly dispersed after attacking and briefly occupying a town, only to later regroup and attack a different town on its market day. By early 1875, the frequency of attacks had declined as provincial officials, aided by landowners, sent detachments of troops into the interior, capturing and imprisoning some and impressing others into military service. Market activity soon returned to normal, and Recife newspapers triumphantly announced that the revolt was over.[115] The conservative politicians who controlled the Pernambucan provincial government wasted little time in blaming liberals and Jesuit missionaries for fomenting the rebellion.[116] In his annual report to the provincial legislature, provincial president Henrique Pereira de Lucena asserted that "agents of fanaticism and anarchy, . . . in sowing and circulating false and pernicious rumors, succeeded in tricking the less sensible people of the *povo* and inciting them to seditious acts."[117] Liberals had not been in power in Pernambuco since the failed Praieira Revolution of 1848–1850, and while they were critical of the conservative government, both the liberal and conservative legislative rank-and-file publicly disavowed involvement in the revolt and conservative legislators absolved liberals of any blame.[118]

The question of Jesuit involvement was more complex but no less an attempt on the part of the Lucena government to blame its political enemies for the revolt. The Church-state conflict, also known as the Questão Religiosa, which unfolded in 1874 and 1875 pitted Olinda's ultramontaine bishop Dom Vital of Olinda against Pernambuco's political elite, many of whom had been excluded from lay religious brotherhoods because they were Freemasons.[119] Jesuit missionaries, expelled by the crown in 1759 and allowed to return in 1866, supported Dom Vital in his standoff with the conservative provincial government. As a result, in what Armando Souto Maior has called an ironic twist of politics, Jesuits became allies of Pernambucan liberals.[120] Authorities intercepted and published several letters written by Jesuits purporting to demonstrate the order's participation and leadership in the revolt, and Lucena used the letters as a justification for expelling all foreign-born Jesuits from the province in 1874.[121] While several Jesuits did support the rebels, contemporary observers, including French engineer Henrique Augusto Milet, who published a series of articles on the rebellion in the *Jornal do Recife*, argued that Jesuit participation was only a minor factor in the revolt and played down the importance of popular resistance to the Recruitment Law of 1874.[122]

What these two explanations for the Quebra-Quilos revolt had in common was the notion that the causes of the revolt were elite political conflicts rather than economic and political grievances and that the Pernambucan *povo* were incapable of rebelling on their own. Pernambucan planters were unwilling to admit that their labor practices created economic hardship, and they believed that the *povo* were incapable of contributing positively to society, much less organizing and carrying out a revolt, without paternalistic guidance. In December 1874, Lucena issued a circular to local police and judicial authorities singling out "citizens" who "dragged the ignorant and uncultured part of the population, inspiring in them ideas subversive to the social order." He condemned their attempts "to instill in the spirit of the *povo* the idea that, in order to avoid the announcement of imagined and new taxes . . . it is necessary to rebel against law and to subtract from them the contribution that society demands from each citizen" as a "plan of maximum perversity."[123] The essential problem, Lucena argued, was that the rebels had challenged governmental authority: "To deny the State the small quota that it demands, . . . which has to be applied to the immense and diverse charge of maintaining order, guaranteeing liberty, and . . . ensuring the regular exercise of the political and civil institutions from which the redeeming principles of personal and property rights result, is to deprive the social body of its indispensable and only element of life and to foster its complete destruction."[124] While Lucena understood that the revolt represented a challenge to government authority, he could not admit that this challenge originated with the Pernambucan *povo*. To suggest that the *povo* were capable of questioning the economic and political status quo would have been tantamount to recognizing the legitimacy of their grievances.

Henrique Augusto Milet argued instead that the primary cause of the revolt was economic, specifically, a collapse in the agricultural sector that resulted in declining wages for workers and declining prices for sharecroppers. The economic crisis was exacerbated, Milet argued, by excessive tax rates and government indifference toward the concerns of planters. In discussing the causes of the revolt, Milet took a wider perspective than had Pernambucan political leaders, addressing landholding patterns, labor markets, the availability of capital, transportation, and technological improvements. He offered a realistic, and pessimistic, assessment of the problems provincial leaders faced as they attempted to modernize sugar production. Milet was the only contemporary observer to emphasize economic factors as a cause of the revolt. However, he discussed rebels' collective rather than individual motivations, which resulted in a view of the *povo* that was as one-dimensional as that proffered by the Lucena government. Both Milet and Lucena believed that the Quebra-Quilos revolt was caused by the elite—Lucena argued that irresponsible priests and liberals had incited the *povo* to revolt, while Milet argued that planter and government negligence and incompetence led to economic stagnation, low wages, and popular unrest. In neither view was the *povo* responsible for their own actions. Aside from Milet's articles, the Quebra-Quilos revolt prompted little introspection on the part of Pernambucan planters and political rulers. Once the revolt was suppressed and its leaders tried, convicted, and sentenced, the Pernambucan interior again became a political afterthought. The 1880 presidential report to the provincial legislature noted in passing that seven interior *municípios* had adopted the metric system, while six had not, making no mention of the rebellion whatsoever.[125] The events of 1874 and 1875 were quickly forgotten as a new crisis of epic proportions overwhelmed the provincial government.

Seca

In 1876, the annual winter rains never came to the vast, arid interior of northern Brazil, and the result was crop failure, starvation, and the migration of tens of thousands of peasants, sharecroppers, and farm hands to the coast, the Amazon basin, and southern provinces.[126] In 1878, the Pernambucan president wrote that the "scourge of the drought" had "expelled thousands of emigrants from the interior of this and other provinces" and that a "foreign population, uncultivated and exhausted by misery and by hunger," had gathered on the coast.[127] The imperial and provincial governments both provided funding for relief efforts, and Minister of the Empire Antônio da Costa Pinto e Silva coordinated relief efforts from Rio de Janeiro, while the Central Commission for Aid to the Indigent Victims of Drought directed relief efforts from Recife.[128] Pernambuco's provincial president appointed prominent landowners to local commissions to direct relief efforts at the *município* level, including distributing food from regional warehouses and organizing temporary housing and employment for refugees. Relief commissioners regarded their efforts to provide aid to drought victims as charity, consistent with their sense of Catholic responsibility, and noted enthusiastically that the Italian Capuchin friars who had been engaged to provide religious services throughout the province "had been invited to assist authorities in the work of aiding the victims of the drought."[129] At the same time, officials understood that charity alone was insufficient; one official pointed out that "aid does not consist only of alms and donations for the unsheltered." While some drought relief commissioners argued that drought victims were "incapable of work," the provincial government claimed that "robust" drought victims were "in the position to be helped and employed in paid service."[130] Drought victims housed at refugee camps throughout the province were put to work constructing dams, cemeteries, churches, roads, jails, and public squares.[131] Relief officials found it increasingly difficult to find work for the steadily growing number of refugees, however, especially in the more densely populated areas in and near Recife. In 1878, three Recife shelters housed 15,000 refugees, and thirteen rural camps in the coastal sugar-growing region housed more than 40,000 refugees.[132] Provincial officials also placed drought victims at the Colonia Isabel, which by December 1878 had taken in 725 refugees.[133] In September 1879, during the second year of the drought, the provincial government estimated that there were more than 70,000 refugees from Pernambuco and other provinces seeking relief in Recife and its suburbs.[134]

In April 1878, in an attempt to relieve the growing pressure on Recife, provincial officials created a new agricultural colony specifically for drought victims, the Colonia Agricola Soccorro, located on *terras devolutas* on the grounds of the disbanded Indian *aldeia* of Riacho do Matto. The purpose of the colony was not only to provide shelter and work for refugees but also, as the provincial president put it, to "remove from this city [Recife] the greatest possible number of immigrants, creating a colony . . . where it would be easier to audit the public monies spent on the aid of the unprotected [*desvalidos*], and to take from the work of the emigrants a result that within a short time would be able to be counted against the enormous expenses [of the colony]."[135] A June 1879 telegram from the provincial finance minister suggested that "starving *retirantes* [drought refugees]" located at agricultural colonies should be "applied to agricultural work [where] they will no longer be sterile consumers."[136] There were only 385 refugees placed at the colony when it first opened, but it expanded rapidly. Within a month, 262 houses had been constructed, and the number of refugees had grown to more than 4,000.[137] In June 1879, the colony housed 9,000 refugees who had, without any assistance from the provincial government or relief agencies, constructed a school, a chapel, and an infirmary. One relief commissioner noted enthusiastically that the colony possessed a thriving market and that work was rapidly progressing on the construction of a forty-kilometer (twenty-five-mile) road that would provide a link with the nearby commercial center and *município* seat of Panelas.[138] As the numbers of refugees at the Colonia Soccorro swelled, a crucial transformation took place. Relief commissioners and provincial administrators began to refer to drought refugees as "*colonos*" rather than "*emigrantes*" or "*retirantes*," the two terms most commonly used for refugees. Once refugees were relocated to agricultural colonies, they became workers and, most importantly, a potential source of labor for sugar mill owners. While officials believed that most refugees would return to the interior once the rains returned the following winter, one official opined that "it was almost certain that there would remain at the Colonia Soccorro a first-rate nucleus of workers" after the crisis passed.[139]

The passage from drought victim to worker did not take place only at the Colonia Soccorro. In 1878, provincial president Adolpho de Barros Cavalcante de Lacerda ordered that "single emigrants or those who were capable of working" were to be dismissed from government shelters. Lacerda, who also directed the Central Commission for Aid to the Indigent Victims of Drought, approved a plan that turned refugees dismissed from relief camps over to sugar mill owners.[140] Refugees were to sign contracts stipulating that mill owners supply, free of charge, "land sufficient and appropriate to the growing of cane and cereals," a house, seed and tools, clothing, medical treatment and food in the case of illness, and food for the first three months of the contract, in return for labor. Significantly, refugees retained the right "to work [for themselves] for three days each week, with the other days dedicated to the service of the owner."[141] In 1878, the Central Commission reported that fourteen mill owners had signed contracts with 2,100 refugees, for an average of 161 workers per mill.[142] The following year, a provincial minister lamented that the plan had not been as successful as was hoped because the contracts placed a heavy burden on owners and because, as he put it, "the *retirantes* do not seem to be good workers."[143] Still, he noted that despite these problems, many *retirantes* had left government relief camps to work for mill owners.

Not all government officials were optimistic about refugees' potential as workers. Perhaps the most pessimistic assessment came in 1878 from Pernambuco's inspector of public health, Pedro de Attahyde Lobo Moscoso, who described *retirantes* as "thousands of ambulant mummies covered in tattered rags."[144] The populations of the *sertão*, he argued, were "indolent, without the pretensions of wealth, did not experiment with incentives that would better their luck, lived in an atmosphere in which ambition and necessity are unknown, which cause underdevelopment of the social state, [and] are not stimulated by work because they encounter a superabundance produced by favorable harvests that are larger than they require for their subsistence."[145] Moscoso, like many government officials who did not have significant experience with the interior, believed that the *sertão* was a veritable garden of Eden, free from the unfavorable tropical climate and endemic diseases of the coast. He nonetheless concluded that *sertanejos* were not strong and were not able to resist the forces of drought and hunger. Weakened by a lack of food, he wrote, "many of these ambulant mummies exhaled their last breath in the moment that they arrived, so to speak, at the door of their salvation."[146] Those who did not die of starvation were weak and susceptible to the diseases racing through government relief camps, and they too succumbed in large numbers. Moscoso's objective, of course, was to determine the causes of epidemic diseases among *retirantes,* and his assessments were consistent with nineteenth-century understandings of disease and public health. In describing the *sertão* populations as indolent, however, Moscoso substituted a reasoned assessment of conditions in the interior with Pernambucan planters' complaints about *sertanejos'* potential as workers. Moscoso's appraisal of *sertanejos* found a ready audience at the highest levels of the provincial government as Central Commission officials attempted to justify their attempts to relocate drought victims away from coastal cities and prime agricultural areas, which were certainly not suffering from a shortage of labor. Mill owners who needed workers were free, of course, to take advantage of *retirante* labor, but this was not the case for the majority of owners. Drought refugees were thus seen by both sugar planters and government officials as a scourge rather than a resource.

The first sign that the crisis was passing came with the return of winter rains in 1879. Imperial officials rapidly cut spending on relief efforts in order to appease the complaints of southern lawmakers and conservatives who had argued that liberal drought relief efforts had been costly and subject to graft and corruption.[147] The Central Commission and government officials hoped that refugees would return quickly and willingly to the interior, which they did in large numbers.[148] In 1881, the provincial government withdrew financial support for the Colonia Soccorro despite the fact that eight thousand colonists still lived in the area, and the colony was never again mentioned in annual provincial reports.[149] Although it is unclear why the colony was abandoned so abruptly, the presence of tens of thousands of drought refugees throughout the *zona da mata* did create a labor surplus, so the colonists were not all needed by nearby mill owners. That mill owners were not clamoring to sign refugees to labor contracts indicates the degree to which they had successfully managed the transition from slavery to wage labor. Simply put, agricultural laborers were plentiful, and planters had little difficulty in meeting their labor needs.

Thus, the refugees of the Great Drought of 1877 to 1879 were understood to be an anomaly—something like foreigners who were to return to their land of origin as soon as the crisis passed.

THE SOCIAL, economic, and political upheavals of the nineteenth century gave rise to new understandings of the working class and poor populations of Pernambuco and northern Brazil. Political and economic elites held that Pernambucans were, first and foremost, agricultural laborers whose social and moral duty was to serve the economic and political interests of Pernambuco's ruling elite. It was a view that was unapologetically one-dimensional. Although liberal ideals influenced both the form and content of nineteenth-century Brazilian politics and notions of citizenship, the Pernambucan *povo* were not considered to be either citizens or political actors but rather apolitical dependents of the ruling elite.[150] The popular uprisings of the nineteenth century that contained at their core specific political and economic grievances and demands did little to alter elite attitudes toward the *povo*. These movements were dismissed as either discontented elites' self-interested manipulation of the *povo* or isolated acts of violence rather than recognized as evidence of widespread economic and political discontent or a rejection of elite rule. This particular form of political myopia was, of course, not unique in this period. It was, however, a fundamental aspect of the way in which Pernambucan elites understood the *povo*.

3

Racial Science in Pernambuco, 1870–1910

THE SOCIAL, economic, and political pressures that resulted in the abolition of slavery in 1888, the end of the Brazilian Empire, and the establishment of the republic in 1889 prompted a reexamination of nineteenth-century understandings of citizenship and Brazilian national identity. In addition, the gradual decline of the institution of slavery, which culminated in 1888 with the granting of unconditional freedom to 750,000 slaves (of which 40,000 were Pernambucan) necessitated a reexamination of understandings of race.[1] The military coup d'état that in 1889 brought down the Bragança imperial dynasty led by Pedro II produced a federal republic that introduced a new legal system, new electoral system, and new notions of citizenship.[2] The advent of the republic also marked the beginning of a period of social and political instability in the nation, including rural millenarian movements at Canudos and Juazeiro do Norte in the states of Bahia and Ceará, popular political protests in the sugar-growing zone of Pernambuco, and urban protests in Recife, both in support of and against the republic. Historical treatments of the establishment of the republic in Pernambuco have focused on the political struggle among liberals, conservatives, and republicans for control of state government, a struggle settled in 1892 with President Floriano Peixoto's appointment of Alexandre José Barbosa Lima as federal *interventor* of Pernambuco and the emerging political dominance of the Partido Republicano Federal de Pernambuco (PRF) under the leadership of Francisco de Assis Rosa e Silva.[3] By the mid-1890s, Pernambucan politics had stabilized into a system of single-party rule that depended on the ability of rural *coronéis* (rural political bosses) and oligarchies to deliver votes in return for political patronage.[4] In focusing on political conflicts among the Pernambucan elite and the political upheavals of the early republic, historians have paid less attention to the ways in which the abolition of slavery and the establishment of the republic engendered new understandings of citizenship, political participation, and government responsibility in Pernambuco and the Northeast.

Central to these discussions was the issue of race. As discussed in the previous chapter, Pernambucan planters and politicians debated whether recently freed *libertos* or European immigrants were the most desirable type of workers.[5] During the republic, Brazilian intellectuals and elites almost without exception came to embrace the racial ideal of *branqueamento,* or whitening, which posited that the Brazilian population was rapidly becoming whiter due to the influx of white Europeans and the decline of nonwhite Brazilians. More than three centuries of African slavery had led planters to conclude that Brazil's *negros* and *mulatos* were inferior workers and that European immigrants were the key to the nation's social and economic future.[6] Studies of race and national identity during the First Republic have focused specifically on intellectual approaches to race, labor practices, and foreign immigration, and they have centered mostly on Rio de Janeiro and São Paulo.[7] There has been much less discussion of these issues as they related to areas outside Rio de Janeiro and São Paulo, which reflects the widely held notion that northeastern intellectuals and economic and political leaders either viewed race in the same way or were more overtly racist and discriminatory than were their southern counterparts.[8] However, northeastern politicians and intellectuals took a unique approach to the questions of race, citizenship, and national and regional identity, one that reflected their belief that the region was racially, socially, and culturally different from the rest of the nation.

In the context of the abolition of slavery, the Paraguayan War, electoral reforms, and rising interest in republicanism, Recife's Faculdade de Direito faculty began in the 1870s to examine the problems of citizenship and legal responsibility. In the 1890s, a new cohort of young intellectuals launched their own studies of racial theories and regional identity. In Bahia, physician Raymundo Nina Rodrigues undertook the medical and anthropological study of race, addressing differences in resistance to diseases as well as mental disorders and Afro-Brazilian culture and religion. Euclydes da Cunha, a positivist engineer from Rio de Janeiro, was hired by a São Paulo newspaper to report on a rebellion in Canudos in the remote Bahian interior, and his reports captured the imagination of a nation that knew little about the region and its peoples. His best-selling book, *Os sertões*, employed racial and geographic determinism to explain the origins of the rebellion and the characteristics of the region. These individuals employed racial science to create a body of knowledge about the physical and mental characteristics of northeastern peoples. Their observations were not scientific research in the modern sense of the word, but they worked in the spirit of scientific inquiry—they examined northeastern peoples and social problems with a self-conscious "objectivity" and utilized scientific theories and methods in their explorations of northeastern identity. Their contributions, especially da Cunha's *Os sertões*, exerted a tremendous influence on popular and elite understandings of the region, going well beyond the relatively small scientific, legal, and intellectual communities to which these men belonged. Federal and Pernambucan government officials incorporated racial science into new notions of citizenship and government responsibility that were taking shape in the first years of the republic. Government services, including education, social welfare, immigration, and agricultural and industrial development, reflected the notion that race was a significant social and political problem. Racial science, including criminal anthropology and legal medicine, was used by government authorities to identify individuals and groups deemed to be a threat to social and political stability. Far from being an unreflective, mechanistic application of European racial theory or a second-rate imitation of intellectual trends and government programs in Rio de Janeiro and São Paulo, the scientific study of race in northeastern Brazil constituted an attempt to explain the apparent differences between *nordestinos* and other Brazilians and, ultimately, between the modern, developed Brazil and the backward Northeast.

The Recife Law School and Racial Science

By the late nineteenth century, Recife's Faculdade de Direito had become one of the most important centers of intellectual thought in Brazil. Founded in 1828 and originally located in Olinda, it was one of four Brazilian schools of higher education, which also included a law school in São Paulo and medical schools in Rio de Janeiro and Salvador. While the purpose of the law schools was to provide the newly independent nation with trained magistrates for an understaffed judicial system decimated by the departure of Portuguese judges, the schools also played an important social and political function, providing educations for the sons of prominent families who hoped to secure a position among the political elite.[9] In addition to serving as the gateways to political power, the law schools became centers of intellectual inquiry. After relocation to Recife in 1854 and a major overhaul of the curriculum, the law school's increasingly professionalized faculty began to show an interest in German philosophy and scientific thought, including biological evolution and positivism.[10] Several faculty members, along with other Recife intellectuals and artists, came to be known as the "Escola do Recife."[11] Following the lead of North American and European philosophers and social critics who applied scientific theories to the study of race, Tobias Barreto, who taught at the law school from 1882 to 1889, and his students Sílvio Romero, José Isidoro Martins Júnior, and Clóvis Beviláqua, began to address the social and legal status of nonwhite Brazilians.[12] Romero, like his cohort, was a positivist and applied scientific theories in his analyses of Brazilian society and literature. In a volume on Brazilian poetry, Romero wrote that "the *negro* is not only an economic machine, he is, above all else, and despite his ignorance, an object of science."[13] Marshall Eakin has convincingly argued that Romero's legacy was "an appreciation of the role miscegenation had played in the formation of Brazilian society."[14] By the 1890s, scientific racial theories had become an integral aspect of the law school curriculum.[15] The willingness of the law school faculty and the Escola do Recife to address race was unusual because most Brazilian intellectuals did not give race serious intellectual attention prior to the abolition of slavery in 1888. As long social and legal distinctions between slave and citizen remained, intellectuals and elites had little to gain from contemplating the meaning of race. In Pernambuco, however, sugar planters made the transition to wage labor earlier than did their counterparts in São Paulo and Rio de Janeiro, and thus the racial question took on added urgency.

In addition to scientific understandings of race, positivism played an important role in shaping social and political thought at the Faculdade de Direito. Brazilian positivists believed that scientific observations of social and economic problems should be used to design reforms that would fundamentally restructure society. Brazil's leading positivist was Benjamin Constant de Magalhães (1831–1891), a professor of mathematics at the Praia Vermelha Military School in Rio de Janeiro, founder of the Rio de Janeiro's Club Militar, and perhaps most significantly, a leader of the military coup d'état that overthrew the Brazilian monarchy in 1889. After the establishment of the republic, many Brazilian politicians, including prominent legislators, governors, and presidents adopted positivism and used it in governing the nation.[16] While

Brazilian positivists differed in their level of commitment, which reflected the differences between orthodox practitioners who treated positivism as a religion and those who rejected its religious aspects, positivism nevertheless played an important role in shaping understandings of Brazilian society and informing public policy during the early years of the republic.[17] In Recife, positivism underpinned the Escola do Recife's approaches to understanding Brazilian society and law. In the first issue of the Faculdade de Direito's academic journal, the editors wrote that the study of law should be transformed, substituting "the ugly practice of philosophy with the art of guiding and judging processes by science in which we seek to understand the laws or natural uniformities to which juridical phenomena are subjected."[18] The so-called science practiced by Brazilian intellectuals was not, as Lilia Moritz Schwarcz has pointed out, scientific research in the modern sense. "What was valued in this moment," she writes, "was not scientific advancement, understood at that time as the impulse for original research, as much as a certain scientific ethic, an indiscriminate and 'diffuse scientism.'"[19] This spirit of scientific inquiry pervaded the writing of Brazilian intellectuals in the late nineteenth and early twentieth centuries, and the "scientific method" and "objective inquiry" were applied in several fields of intellectual and academic inquiry, including literature, music, history, law, and the natural sciences.

The degree to which the law school faculty embraced science as a means of understanding Brazilian society became manifest in the pages of the law school's academic journal, the *Revista Academica da Faculdade de Direito do Recife* (*RAFDR*), which was first published in 1891 after a law sponsored by Benjamin Constant de Magalhães in the federal legislature authorized a curricular reform and funded the journal's publication.[20] In an editorial in the first issue, the law school's director argued that the curricular reform would produce good results because "it will spread exact notions about all of science ... [and] because it will awaken a mental drive for scientific investigation."[21] Clóvis Beviláqua (1859–1944), a student of Tobias Barreto, faculty member, and editor of the *RAFDR*, wrote in 1899 that "all who hope in their hearts for the intellectual and moral aggrandizement of the country, a better future, [and] the raising of their prestige in the cultured world must sincerely applaud the great work and dedication [of positive science]." He added that the adoption of positivism was "not a small thing for a people in which climate produces indolence and weakness."[22] In embracing positivism, Beviláqua and his colleagues rejected what they viewed as the traditional, "a priori, subjective method" of their predecessors. They instead argued for an approach that sought knowledge from "induction, searching history and changing the limits of tradition;

penetrating paleontology and particularly paleo-ethnology, asking for verification from experimental psychology, biology, linguistics, anthropology, ethnology, sociology, [and] from all the sciences that are concerned with human beings."[23]

The law school faculty wholeheartedly embraced the theories of European and North American natural and social scientists, quoting liberally from Charles Darwin, Herbert Spencer, Ernst Haeckel, Gustave Le Bon, Cesare Lombroso, and Ludwig Gumplowicz. In the *RAFDR*, authors often invoked Darwin's theory of evolution and Spencer's social Darwinism in their analyses of Brazilian society. Individual differences, political competitions, racial differences, and international conflicts were all recast as the "survival of the fittest." In an 1897 article, Laurindo Leão, a faculty member, argued that the "struggle for survival" (*lucta pela vida*) was not unique to the animal kingdom but that it encompassed "all social conflict, for existence, for rights, for morals, for religion, for culture, for economics, for aesthetics, and even for caprice, royal and immoral extravagances and insanity, and dynastic wars and universal empires. It also describes the conflicts of all social groups, individuals, families, associations, peoples, States, actions, and races."[24] Beviláqua, Leão, and their colleagues posited that this struggle was an essential aspect of all human societies and that it was the driving force behind social and political change in Brazil. They essentialized differences between social classes, races, and political parties and argued that these groups should have different legal rights and privileges to reflect their respective "natural" rights. The most important distinction to be made, they argued, was based on race. Beviláqua argued that race determined social status and was the fundamental cause of crime and social conflict.[25] He also wrote that racial differences became manifest as atavisms, individual physical and mental characteristics that supposedly represented previous stages in human evolution. Atavisms, he wrote, were "the chains of heredity that are seen in an individual and that fix one to its immediate superior, . . . and this speaks of the return to more remote times."[26] Beviláqua went on to construct a theory in which he placed the "primitive," "savage," and "retarded" races of Africa at the bottom of a strict racial hierarchy dominated by Europeans.[27] Beviláqua's deterministic understanding of race was typical of late-nineteenth-century intellectuals and represented a willingness on their part to adopt European and North American racial theories without question, despite the fact that Brazil had large numbers of Africans, Indians, and *mestiços* (people of mixed race).

Beginning in the 1870s, some Brazilian intellectuals and social critics, including Sílvio Romero, began to question the notion that Brazilians were racially inferior.[28] Brazilians struggled to reconcile European and North American racial theories with Brazilian social reality, and Pernambucan intellectuals were no exception. Clóvis Beviláqua, while generally accepting of the notion of a racial hierarchy, also believed that inheritable physical and psychological characteristics played an important role in the formation of national races. He did not believe that these characteristics were entirely deterministic, however. Rather, they were "acquired and perfected, in the manner of becoming constant and progressively accentuating the abilities of each people in each nation." He believed on the one hand that climate and geography played an essential role in determining individual and national character: "The geography of a country, the contents of its soil, its climate, its flora and its fauna, etc., are necessary elements for those who endeavor to comprehend civilization and the future destiny of a nation."[29] On the other hand, he questioned the notion that Brazilians were inherently inferior to Europeans due to the influence of climate, geography, and race. While the law school faculty made use of received racial and social theory, their interest in race also showed a genuine, reflective interest in social and political problems and regional and national identity in the immediate aftermath of the abolition of slavery and establishment of the republic.

Beviláqua soon became an outspoken critic of racial determinism. In the introduction to his *Esboços e fragmentos* (1899), T. A. Araripe Júnior argued that the *mestiço* inhabitants of the northern *sertão* were not degenerate and that they compared favorably to São Paulo's legendary *bandeirantes* (colonial-era pioneers), who, he pointed out, were also of mixed racial ancestry.[30] Beviláqua took the notion of *mestiço* degeneracy, which informed the thinking of most Brazilian racial theorists, and turned it on its head. He argued instead that "*mestiçagem* has permitted incontestable intellectual adaptations, as the elements of the black or red races have done forcefully in the sense of the coloring of the skin. Among our men of letters, artists, and notable politicians how many are pure *brancos?*"[31] To Beviláqua, Brazilian *mestiços'* ascent to the upper echelons of the arts, letters, and politics constituted scientific "proof" that they were not inherently degenerate.[32] Criticizing the racial determinism of European racial theorists such as Le Bon and Gumplowicz, he argued that "the falsity of Le Bonian theory has appeared suddenly from several sources. With race there is value only in character, to intelligence it is more than a hindrance, it comes to be the most powerful element of ruin."[33] Beviláqua suggested that race did not determine individual character but that civil society, government, and religion tempered the effects of race. "It is not possible," he boldly stated, "for Le Bon to succeed in the venture of discovering the *psychological laws of the evolution of peoples.*" Beviláqua went on to criticize Gumplowicz's belief that race relations should be interpreted as a Spencerian struggle for survival, instead arguing that if social Darwinism were applicable to Brazilian society, then racial conflict would be "more preponderant among the social classes, among capitalists, industrialists, and large landowners on one side and workers in general on the other[,] . . . among the governors and the governed, among the weak and humble of all classes and the predominant and powerful of any standard."[34] The relatively harmonious quotidian interactions among the races indicated to him that racial conflict was not at the root of Brazilian society. One should be careful not to cast Beviláqua as a proponent of racial democracy or as an intellectual who believed that race was meaningless, however. Beviláqua's beliefs on race were typical for his era: he proved flexible and adapted useful racial theories and rejected others. What was most significant was his willingness to examine the meaning of race in Brazil in a period of social and political change.[35]

The Recife law school faculty also embraced the teachings of the Italian school of criminology. In the 1870s, Italian physician Cesare Lombroso outlined a theory positing that crime was an integral aspect of human society and that trained medical professionals could determine an individual's predisposition to crime by cataloging specific physical and psychological characteristics.[36] According to Lombroso, the "lower races" were more likely to commit crimes, an idea that provided Brazilian legal theorists with a plausible explanation for crime and social disorder. Criminal anthropology also proved attractive to the law school faculty because it gave the study of law and crime a scientific foundation. Beviláqua was one of the first faculty members to embrace the Italian school, utilizing criminal anthropology in a study of crime in the neighboring northern state of Ceará. While Beviláqua contended that Ceará was socially, economically, and politically quite similar to Pernambuco, he argued that crime was more common in Ceará because a higher percentage of the state's population consisted of *índios* and *mestiços*. Crime was thus "a product of the survival of savage life, a phenomenon [that is] very characteristic of atavisms." Beviláqua's methodology consisted of pointing out that "the ethnic elements that constitute the population of the state are the same in all *comarcas*, varying only in the amount of each of these elements." He then "attempted to see if the preponderance of the indigenous race elevated the number of crimes," which, if true, he argued, would constitute "indirect evidence of Lombrosian theory."[37] Beviláqua found a higher number of property crimes in rural areas and a higher number of personal crimes in urban areas, which he attributed to the higher concentrations of *índios* and *mestiços* in rural areas. It is revealing that Beviláqua focused on the allegedly pronounced indigenous background of Ceará's population, or *cearenses,* given that a high percentage of *pernambucanos* were of African descent. It was likely easier for Beviláqua to discuss the relationship between race and crime in Ceará because a discussion of these issues in Pernambuco would have created too much political controversy. In fact, the law school faculty generally did not discuss race in Pernambuco, and Beviláqua's article on Ceará was one of only a handful of articles that expressly treated the relationship between race and crime. What was most significant about Beviláqua's discussion of crime in Ceará was his willingness to apply criminal anthropology to the study of social and political issues.

His colleagues adopted a similar approach. In 1913, Laurindo Leão, a member of the law school faculty, posited the existence of a "born criminal type" displaying specific physical attributes. He also argued that there was a close relationship between race and crime and that "the criminal is a savage, or better a barbarian, and because barbarity reflects the . . . sentiments of savagery persistent in civilizations, it seems that . . . the persistence of crime is a natural phenomenon." He concluded that Brazil was awash in "an ocean of crimes caused by the customs of primitive savagery."[38] While Leão argued that there were "here and there in this ocean, islands of morality that have ascended beyond the race and climate," he concluded that because Brazil was a nation in which a significant percentage of the population had descended from "barbarians," crime had become an integral aspect of "the social environment in all its forms: war, religious persecution, despotism, slavery, hostility to foreigners, the subjugation of women, crime itself, and the death penalty."[39] In 1915, Augusto Lins e Silva revisited the issue of the relationship between race and crime in Ceará in a speech delivered at a national congress on geography. Lins e Silva argued that drought-prone areas of Ceará were also prone to "an unmistakable mesological struggle [between] different types of men, different in stature, weight, color, robustness, cerebral constitution, vivacity, moral energy, and ability to work, [which constitutes] . . . a rude contrast with men who are guaranteed and covered under the arch of a common nation."[40] He believed that the combination of *cearenses'* racial background and the influence of environment produced an inferior sub-race. He further argued that "climate and tropical nosology" had produced a "typical, distinct, unmistakable differentiation between the anthropological formation of the types of the North and the South."[41] Lins e Silva was the only faculty member to suggest that the racial differences between North and South had given rise to separate racial groups. The faculty collectively, however, believed not only that race was an essential aspect of Brazilians' identity but also that the social, political, and criminal importance of race should be recognized in the Brazilian legal system, in contradiction to classical liberalism.

The Faculdade de Direito's particular contribution to society's discussion of race lay in its utilization of scientific approaches to intellectual and social problems. As was common in the late nineteenth century, their analyses focused on the supposed shortcomings of Indians, Africans, and *mestiços*. While the law school faculty did not use racial and scientific theories uncritically, they nevertheless viewed race as problematic and spent considerable energy contemplating the social, political, and legal consequences of racial miscegenation. It is perhaps puzzling that the law school faculty could criticize Le Bon's and Gumplowicz's overtly racist theories and at the same time accept Lombroso's criminal anthropology, which was no less racist. As many historians and literary critics have pointed out, however, there were many such inconsistencies in the thought of nineteenth-century Brazilian intellectuals. Torn by an almost insatiable appetite for North American and European ideas, Brazilian intellectuals faced the difficulty of reconciling scientific and racial theories that condemned Brazilians because of their supposedly inferior racial background with their own sense of national identity and national pride. The law school faculty also contemplated the importance of national and, in a more limited fashion, regional identity. They posited that geographic and climatic differences, patterns of immigration from both Africa and Europe, and differing degrees of racial miscegenation had produced significant racial and cultural differences within Brazil. While they did not explicitly state that there was a distinct northern racial type, they did conclude that there were significant social, cultural, and racial differences between North and South. The law school faculty were naturally most concerned with law and how the country's seemingly antiquated legal system should be reformed in order to better reflect modern Brazilian society.

The impact of the Faculdade de Direito faculty was not limited to the pages of the *RAFDR* or to classroom lectures. Law school graduates went on to secure civil service positions as judges, prosecutors, and police officers and to pursue political careers that contributed to a sense of both regional and professional identity.[42] The theories of race, crime, and society taught at the Faculdade de Direito thus shaped government officials' approach to the pressing intellectual, social, and political problems of the late empire and early republic and also laid the groundwork for a new generation of scholars, most importantly Raymundo Nina Rodrigues and Euclydes da Cunha, who began to take an interest in the social, racial, and cultural foundations of northeastern regional identity.

Raymundo Nina Rodrigues and the Negro

Raymundo Nina Rodrigues (1862–1906) was undoubtedly one of the most influential intellectuals of the early republican period, and his medical and anthropological studies of race and Afro-Brazilian culture proved crucial to the development of northeastern regional identity. Born in Maranhão and educated at the Faculdade de Medicina in Salvador before graduating from the Faculdade de Medicina in Rio de Janeiro, Nina Rodrigues worked in a number of fields, including medicine, public health, criminology, legal medicine, psychology, and anthropology.[43] Early in his career, Nina Rodrigues became inspired by the innovative approach to medicine and public health taken by the Bahian *tropicalistas*, a diverse group of physicians and medical researchers who came to prominence in the 1870s and 1880s at the Faculdade de Medicina in Salvador.[44] In the 1880s, Nina Rodrigues began to study the relationship between race and diseases, including leprosy, in the state of Maranhão. By the mid-1890s, after securing a teaching chair at the medical school in Bahia, he turned to the study of Afro-Brazilian culture and religion and of legal medicine. He made the first detailed descriptions and interpretations of African religions in Brazil, and prior to his premature death at the age of forty-four in 1906, Nina Rodrigues had almost single-handedly founded the study of anthropology and legal medicine in Brazil.[45] As did many of his contemporaries and the scholars who followed them, Nina Rodrigues adopted a strict racial hierarchy, essentialized Afro-Brazilians, and argued that nonwhites within Brazil should not enjoy full citizenship. He also believed that the *mestiço*, a generic term applied to any individual who was the product of racial mixing, was inherently flawed because, as he argued, racial crossing generally resulted in the genetic and cultural transfer of the worst qualities of the supposedly inferior race to their offspring. In short, Nina Rodrigues believed that Brazilians were racially inferior and that it was scientists' responsibility to determine how racial degeneracy manifested itself in both individuals and society.

Like the Recife law school faculty, Nina Rodrigues found criminal anthropology to be an especially appealing and applicable theory. Unlike his Pernambucan counterparts, however, he conducted his own research in order to verify whether European racial theories were applicable to Brazil. In the introduction to a posthumously published collection of articles, Nina Rodrigues outlined the scope of his research on race: "we consider the immediate or long-term supremacy of the *Raça Negra* harmful to our nationality, and that its influence is prejudicial in all cases, restraining the progress and culture of our people."[46] He devoted himself to studying what he called "the problem of the ethnologic pathology of our country," which, he believed, "required the more or less rigorous determination of the pure and crossed races, which necessarily precedes the demonstration of the pathological modifications demonstrated by each."[47] He employed this methodology in his early work, first categorizing individuals according to race, then collecting data on physical and psychological characteristics, culture, religion, and susceptibility to diseases, and finally comparing his data across racial groups.[48] Based on this research, he believed he could trace specific physical, psychological, social, and cultural pathologies to the racial group from which they supposedly originated.

According to this methodology, the delineation and classification of individual racial characteristics was crucial. Nina Rodrigues thus proposed a new racial classification system that consisted of six racial groups: *branco, negro, mulato, mameluco, cafuso,* and *pardo. Brancos* and *negros* were the "pure" races of white and black, respectively (interestingly, he did not define *índios* as a pure racial category). He defined *mulato* as the racial mixture of *branco* and *negro, mameluco* as the mixture of *índio* and *branco, cafuso* as the mixture of *negro* and *índio,* and *pardo* as "complex *mestiço* in which the characteristics of three races were present."[49] These racial terms were already in common usage in the late nineteenth century, but Nina Rodrigues defined them more rigorously and used them more consistently than did his counterparts. Accepting the notion of a racial hierarchy, he described *negros* and *índios* as "primitive races" and argued that the presence of both "primitive" and "civilized" races constituted a "duality" in Brazilian society in spite of the "political and constitutional equalities" that made the races equivalent under the law.[50] At the same time, he believed that certain individuals and races could be improved through education, public health campaigns, and laws designed to compensate for supposed racial deficiencies. For example, he argued that African Muslims could be improved, while he argued that more "primitive" racial subgroups, such as non-Muslim Africans and Indians, were "atavistic" and would disappear over time as their descendants failed to reproduce in sufficient numbers. In the end, he did not believe that race wholly determined an individual's status and place in society. He conceived of race relations in Brazilian society as a conflict—racial groups could be civilized by government social and racial projects or through the process of natural selection.

Nina Rodrigues's painstaking research on *negros* and *mestiços* included investigating their alleged physical and psychological pathologies. In an 1889 article in the *Gazeta Medica da Bahia,* he examined the relationship between leprosy and race in Maranhão. Physicians and public health officials had long noted the high rates of leprosy in the region, and Nina Rodrigues hoped to determine if leprosy was more common there because *índios* and *mamelucos* constituted a higher percentage of Maranhão's population than was the case in other northern states. He started from the premise that *negros* and *brancos* were "naturally" prone to contract leprosy, which implied that *maranhenses* should have been less rather than more likely to contract leprosy. However, because he took the position that there were few supposedly "pure" races in Brazil due to extensive racial miscegenation, he argued that *maranhenses* were as likely to contract leprosy as any other group, despite the alleged racial immunity that their *índio* background should have provided. He concluded, in fact, that racial miscegenation had conferred immunity to leprosy to *maranhenses*, thus explaining differing rates of disease to be the result of race. What was most significant about this piece was that Nina Rodrigues had defined a new field of research—the medical and scientific investigation of the connections between race and disease. In the 1870s and 1880s, the Bahian *tropicalistas* had labored to disprove European notions of climatic and racial degeneracy and thus chose to ignore race as a factor in their discussions of the origins of tropical diseases. Nina Rodrigues's research again legitimized this approach, and race became an essential aspect of medical and public health research in the early twentieth century.[51]

In the mid-1890s, Nina Rodrigues turned his attention to the relationship between race and psychological disorders. He had become increasingly dissatisfied with examining physical racial characteristics, likely because his results were inconclusive.[52] His particular interest was Afro-Brazilian religions, which he characterized as the individual and collective manifestation of psychological disorders. Prior to Nina Rodrigues, Afro-Brazilian religions had received little attention from Brazilian intellectuals. He justified his interest by arguing that the study of Afro-Brazilian religions would permit the "medical-legal evaluation of the mental state of the *raça negra*," along with a more precise legal definition of insanity and more effective policing of Brazil's Afro-Brazilian populations.[53] He was especially interested in spirit possession, which was an integral aspect of Candomblé and other Afro-Brazilian religions. Utilizing nineteenth-century psychiatric terminology, Nina Rodrigues called spirit possession "epidemic choreaic abasement" and described the disease as a "contagion [that results from] the imitation of a foreign nervous syndrome," which was ultimately caused by "meteorological, ethnic, social-political, and pathological" factors. Thus, the "epidemic nervous manifestations" of spirit possession had a "rational and scientific explanation" in racial miscegenation.[54] He further contended that, because there were large numbers of Afro-Brazilians in northern Brazil, the "disorder" existed throughout the region in a "very benign epidemic form."[55] Nina Rodrigues's pathologization of spirit possession would shape the way that successive generations of Brazilian psychiatrists, ethnologists, and anthropologists approached Afro-

Brazilian religions. In 1934, Arthur Ramos, perhaps Brazil's most influential and prolific anthropologist, described "fetishistic spirit possession" as "a very complicated phenomenon, linked to various morbid states," and argued that its origins were similar to "hysteria, with symptoms or motor mechanisms of ancestral origins . . . , hypnotic forms of thought, magical and catathymic, common to hysteria, of somnambulant states, dreamlike hypnoses, and schizophrenic with changes in consciousness and personality."[56] As recently as the 1940s, Brazilian psychiatrists and anthropologists claimed that spirit possession was a mental disease rather than a legitimate religious practice.[57]

In addition to investigating the relationship between race and diseases, Nina Rodrigues contemplated the origins and implications of regional differences within Brazil. Not surprisingly, he saw race as the most important factor in determining regional character, although he acknowledged that climate and geography also played a role. He cautioned against drawing too sharp a racial contrast between North and South, however, writing in 1905 that "for the most incautious and improvident Brazilian it is not possible to speak of the possibility of a different future, already partially realized, between a white nation, strong and powerful, probably of Teutonic origins, which consists of the states of the South where climate and civilization will eliminate the *Raça Negra*, [and] the states of the North, *mestiço*, vegetating in the sterile turbulence of a ready and vivid intelligence but associated with the most resolute inertia and indolence."[58]

Nina Rodrigues instead took the position that the process of racial mixing produced regional populations that were capable of readily adapting to climate and geography; thus, with the addition of European blood, Africans could live in the more temperate South, and with the addition of African blood, Europeans could live in the equatorial North. At the same time, he believed that racial miscegenation was "a degenerative process that progresses chronically and is therefore very slow."[59] Nina Rodrigues concluded that the North was populated by *mestiços* who lived in conditions unfavorable to progress and civilization, and he believed that little could be done to improve the region. Thus, while race was not wholly deterministic, the preponderance of African ancestry, geography, and the region's climate dictated that the North was inferior to the South.

Beyond offering general observations about the racial divide between North and South, Nina Rodrigues contributed to understandings of northern Brazil in his writings on the Canudos rebellion (1893–1897), a millenarian movement of an estimated thirty-five thousand poor, rural peasants from Bahia and neighboring states led by folk healer and mystic Antônio Conselheiro. While Euclydes da Cunha's 1902 account of the rebellion, *Os sertões*, would become the best-known and most influential account of the rebellion, da Cunha's discussion of the psychological and religious aspects of the rebellion bear a striking resemblance to the content of an article Nina Rodrigues published in 1897, one in which he interpreted the rebellion an example of "epidemic insanity." Nina Rodrigues focused on Conselheiro, whom he described as an "anachronistic figure" and "madman" who was "surely simply crazy."[60] As was common among psychiatrists of his era, Nina Rodrigues sought to explain Conselheiro's "progressive psychosis" through an examination of key events in his life. Explaining the actions of Conselheiro's followers was more problematic, however. Lacking any direct evidence or firsthand accounts, Nina Rodrigues argued, not surprisingly, that race accounted for the rebels' mental instability and their willingness to follow Conselheiro and participate in the rebellion. Nina Rodrigues believed that the rebels possessed a "primitive mentality" because they were predominantly *mestiços*. He described the rebels as a "population of childlike and uncultured spirits who are tormented by unsatisfied religious aspirations."[61] All that was required to spark a rebellion was a charismatic leader who could take advantage of their psychological inclinations. Conselheiro's "mystic insanity," Nina Rodrigues wrote, was reflected in the rebels' "rebellious, atavistic instincts, [which are] not extinct or at least tolerated in the socially hybrid surroundings of our *sertões* to the degree that the insanity to which the infected are loyal are legitimate creations. In fact, here are found, admirably realized, all the conditions for an epidemic constitution of insanity."[62]

Nina Rodrigues described not only the rebels' psychology but also their racial characteristics. He argued that the *jagunço*, a term both he and Euclydes da Cunha used to describe the rebels, was a "physically mixed product that reproduces the combined anthropological characteristics of races from which it is constituted, very much hybrid in its social manifestations, which represent the almost not viable fusion of very unequal civilizations."[63] While Nina Rodrigues generally argued that racial miscegenation was undesirable, he believed that *jagunços* compared favorably to coastal *mestiços*, whom he described as "worthless and sterile types who come from inferior degenerates, true pathological products." Coastal *mestiços'* inferiority, he concluded, was due to the effects of alcohol, the "ambience of the cities," and "a struggle for survival that is more intellectual than physical."[64] *Jagunços* instead revealed "an indomitable character of the jungle Indian, love of the life of a vagabond and nomad, resistance to physical sufferings, hunger, thirst, and bad weather, and a decided proclivity to the adventure of war."[65] Nina Rodrigues believed that the *jagunço* was an example of a virile hybrid that had successfully adapted to the harsh geography and climate of the northern *sertão*. This idea, as well as the distinction he made between *mestiços* of the coast and of the interior, became key components of later constructions of northeastern identity. Nina Rodrigues's discussions of *jagunços'* racial qualities were contradictory, however. While he portrayed them as a strong rather than degenerate racial subtype, his discussion of *jagunços'* supposed "primitive mentality" and propensity for "religious fanaticism" reinforced common popular myths and stereotypes about the peoples of the region.

Nina Rodrigues later refined his interpretations of the Canudos rebellion based on Le Bon's theory of crowd psychology.[66] Rather than attributing the rebels' actions to their purported "primitive mentality," he outlined a more complex mechanism by which rebellions take shape. He believed that the origins of rebellions and deviant religious movements were to be found in crowd psychology, defined as "a psychological association" in which "differences, inequalities, [and] individualities disappear in the formation of a psychological unity where the uneven and impulsive character of the primitive dominates." In Canudos, Nina Rodrigues argued, one could find "all the morbid manifestations of mental instability, from neuropathia, simple temperamental nervousness, to larger neuroses, neurasthenia, hysteria, epilepsy, and at the same time sustained mental insanity." Conselheiro, through charismatic leadership, "provoked a collective delirious state of a political and religious character, endowed with such intensity that he was able to impel the faithful to all sacrifices."[67] The rebellion was thus "a contagion, a communication of true mental insanity that is reflected in each member of the *seita* [sect]."[68] Nina Rodrigues provided one final piece of evidence to support his interpretation of Canudos as a collective mental disturbance. He and a colleague were asked by federal authorities to examine the decapitated head of Antônio Conselheiro, which had been sent from Canudos to the Faculdade de Medicina in Salvador. They subjected it to the rigors of a biometric examination following the accepted practices of late-nineteenth-century craniometry. Somewhat surprisingly, they found that Conselheiro's cranium "did not present any anomaly that indicated any sign of degeneracy: it is a cranium of *mestiço* origin that is associated with anthropological characteristics of different races." They concluded, in fact, that Conselheiro's cranium was entirely "normal" aside from the fact that it was no longer attached to his body. Despite a lack of physical evidence, they nonetheless concluded that, "in accordance with the information gathered about the history of the insane, [it] confirms the diagnosis of the systematic evolution of chronic delirium."[69] In other words, Conselheiro's insanity was confirmed as the primary cause of the rebellion.[70]

Nina Rodrigues used his analysis of the Canudos rebellion as the basis for interpreting an earlier example of religious fanaticism, that took place at

Pedra Bonita in the interior of Pernambuco. In 1838, a small group of Sebastianists, believers in the millenarian return of "lost" Portuguese king Sebastião I, who was killed fighting the Moors in Morocco in 1578, were sacrificed by their leader João Santos, who believed that the offerings would hasten Sebastião's return. In his analysis of the episode, Nina Rodrigues pointed out that Santos and his followers were *mestiços,* and he concluded that religious fanaticism and hereditary tendencies "awakened the worst tendencies and instincts of cruelty."[71] For Nina Rodrigues, Canudos and Pedra Bonita constituted examples of the consequences of racial miscegenation. He suggested that the "practical conclusion" of his analyses of these rebellions was that "juridical responsibility of the multitudes disappears completely in cases where there is an unquestionable or true collective delirium."[72] Thus, he reasoned, rebels were not legally responsible for their actions because of their racial background. They were not full citizens of the nation. That Nina Rodrigues explained the Canudos and Pedra Bonita events by using racial psychology rather than by discussing economic or political factors, as Henrique Augusto Milet had done in discussing the Quebra-Quilos revolt, made the rebellions symbolically less dangerous to federal and state political and economic elites. To have discussed Canudos and Pedra Bonita as justified, if not rational, responses to the social, economic, and political marginalization of the rural peasantry would have constituted a radical criticism of the republic. While Nina Rodrigues willingly established notions of regional and national identity, he was not willing to criticize the young republic.

Raymundo Nina Rodrigues's body of work was significant in several ways. First, he studied race and Afro-Brazilian culture and religion at a time when most Brazilian intellectuals and social critics did not. Despite his essentialist and deterministic approach, his pioneering investigations of Afro-Brazilian culture and religion remained a starting point for scholars through the middle of the twentieth century. As Julyan Peard has argued, Nina Rodrigues's interest in Afro-Brazilian populations "in the long run . . . laid the foundation for a whole new way of evaluating the African contribution to the Brazilian nation."[73] Later studies of race, including the study of northeastern identity initiated by Gilberto Freyre and other intellectuals in the 1920s, raised the same issues that had occupied Nina Rodrigues's attention in the 1890s. Although Freyre and his contemporaries rejected Nina Rodrigues's characterizations of *mestiços* and *negros* as deterministic and racist, they relied on both his findings and his methods, and their work was more similar to his than they were willing to admit. Second, Nina Rodrigues initiated the intellectual study of northeastern regional identity by contemplating the racial divide between the North and the South. He argued that racial miscegenation, in combination with the enervating effects of climate and geography, had produced an inferior people in the North. His investigations of diseases and rebellions served to confirm his characterizations of the region. He was one of the first Brazilian intellectuals to describe the populations of the North as degenerate and pathological. His interpretations of Afro-Brazilian religions and millenarian Catholicism as psychological disorders were to become key components of constructions of northeastern regional identity in the 1920s and 1930s. Third, and perhaps most importantly, was the way in which Nina Rodrigues addressed the most pressing social and political issue of the early republic—the question of whether or not Brazil's substantial numbers of Afro-Brazilians were full citizens.[74] He approached the issue as a technical question to be answered by qualified professionals, which, at the turn of the century, included physicians and jurists.[75] The answer, which many of his colleagues affirmed and continued to believe well into the twentieth century, was that all Brazilians were not, in fact, equal citizens. Nina Rodrigues believed that the origins of this inequality were racial and that it was the responsibility of the state to determine, both individually and collectively, the social and political rights and duties of the nation's citizens. The Brazilian republican constitution of 1891, which was more restrictive with regard to voting rights than the constitution of 1824 had been, outlined two categories of political citizenship, characterized by José Murilo de Carvalho as "active" and "inactive," based on income and literacy.[76] To accept the political exclusion of individuals based on race, as Nina Rodrigues proposed, would not have been considered exceptional. Finally, Nina Rodrigues spoke with an authority that reflected the continuing prestige of liberal professionals as well the burgeoning power of the republican state. Euclydes da Cunha, who was neither physician nor lawyer but rather a positivist, engineer, and journalist, would offer his own interpretations of the Canudos rebellion. His views would have an even greater impact on understandings of northeastern regional identity.

Euclydes da Cunha and the Sertanejo

Within four years of the establishment of the Brazilian republic, the millenarian Canudos rebellion erupted in the interior of the northern state of Bahia. It was of unprecedented size and scope, and at the time of the rebellion's greatest intensity, the rebels' stronghold of Canudos was Bahia's second largest city, with some thirty-five thousand inhabitants. Rebellion leader Antônio Conselheiro was a celebrated and influential itinerant lay preacher who migrated from *sertão* town to town preaching and tending to the spiritual and medical needs of a dispersed population that had little contact with either the Catholic Church or the Brazilian state. At Canudos, an abandoned ranch located in a remote fertile valley 350 kilometers (220 miles) north of Salvador, Conselheiro established a pious, egalitarian community to which he preached moral and social redemption. Conselheiro also criticized the republic and the separation of church and state, both consecrated in the new constitution of 1891. The community rapidly attracted thousands of *sertanejos* from the surrounding region.[77] The migration of rural workers to Canudos had a significant economic impact on the region and drew objections from local ranchers, landowners, and political officials. At the same time, Conselheiro's unorthodox Catholicism drew unwanted attention and criticism from Catholic officials.[78] A dispute over delivery of lumber that was to be used in the construction of a new church for the growing community led to a confrontation with local authorities that rapidly escalated into an armed conflict between Bahian and federal military forces and Conselheiro and his followers, who tenaciously defended Canudos. It would take four military campaigns and a five-month siege before the rebels were finally defeated in October 1897.

In 1902, Euclydes da Cunha published his account of the Canudos rebellion, *Os sertões*.[79] Despite his publisher's concerns about potential sales, the initial printing of two thousand copies, which da Cunha personally subsidized, sold out in two months. By 1911, the book was in its fourth edition and had come to be regarded as a classic of Brazilian literature.[80] Da Cunha's rise to literary fame was unlikely. He had studied with Brazil's leading positivist, Benjamin Constant Botelho de Magalhães, and pursued careers as an army lieutenant and civil engineer before being hired by a São Paulo newspaper, *Estado de São Paulo,* to accompany and report on a federal military detachment sent to put down the rebellion. Da Cunha kept a journal of his journey and posted some two dozen dispatches, which were published in the *Estado de São Paulo* from August to October 1897.[81] *Os sertões* was only one of several accounts of the rebellion, however, and the majority of them were published shortly after the conclusion of the rebellion. *Os sertões*, however, captured the public's imagination because it not only detailed the vicissitudes of the military campaign but also described the people and the setting in painstaking detail.[82] For readers, especially those in southern Brazil who had no firsthand knowledge of the region, it was at once adventure epic, scientific treatise, and republican foundational myth.[83]

While Brazilian intellectuals would eventually reject the more overtly racist and deterministic explanations of the rebellion, scholars accepted through the 1950s the notion that the rebels were religious fanatics with no legitimate political or economic grievances. In the 1960s and 1970s, scholars such as Rui Facó adopted a Marxist approach and analyzed about landholding patterns and labor markets to explain rebel behavior.[84] Recent scholarship has successfully incorporated the often discounted religious aspects of the rebellion to develop a nuanced materialist theory of millenarian revolts.[85] Little attention has been given, however, to da Cunha's impact on understandings of northeastern regional identity. His descriptions of regional human and physical geography were widely accepted in subsequent portrayals of the region. To urban Brazilians, the region portrayed in *Os sertões* represented traditional, rural life and stood in stark contrast to modern, developing Brazil. Da Cunha's portrayals of the people of the region, *sertanejos* and the *jagunços* who took part in the armed rebellion, became as real as the rebellion itself.

Da Cunha originally intended *Os sertões* to be a timely account of the Canudos rebellion, but after significant additional writing and delays in publication, he understood the work to be a scientific study of *sertanejos*. He wrote that his purpose was to "sketch in, however inadequately, for the gaze of future historians, the most significant present-day characteristics of the *sertanejan* sub-races of Brazil."[86] Throughout *Os sertões*, da Cunha described the various racial types of the region in great detail because, he argued, the racial types of the interior were destined to disappear: "The fearless *jagunço* [rural northeastern rebel], the ingenuous *tabaréu* [military recruit or rural northeasterner], and the stolid *caipira* [rural southerner] are types that will soon be relegated to the realm of evanescent or extinct traditions. . . . Backward races today, tomorrow these types will be wholly extinguished. Civilization is destined to continue its advance in the *sertão*." The disappearance of these distinct racial types would be caused by "the growing exigencies of civilization" and "the stream of immigrants that is already beginning to invade our land."[87] The tone da Cunha adopted throughout *Os sertões* was that of a naturalist describing the extinction of a species or that of an anthropologist witnessing the assimilation of a primitive tribe.

Da Cunha's understanding of race, like that of the Faculdade de Direito faculty and Raymundo Nina Rodrigues, was based on European and North American racial science, and he believed in the "inevitable crushing of weak races by the strong." He argued that northern *sertanejos* would not survive their encounter with modern society, embodied in republican Brazil, whether that encounter would take the form of a military campaign or the gradual extension of civilization into the hinterlands. He also believed, like Nina Rodrigues, that it was essential to study Brazilian racial types scientifically.

He pointed out that there were few formal studies of race in Brazil and that almost nothing was known about northern racial types. He warned that Brazilian scientists had not considered "all the alternatives and all the intermediary phases of this admixture of anthropological types, of varying degrees of development as regards their physical and psychic attributes."[88] Da Cunha's task, as he envisioned it, was to study *sertanejos* and to catalog their physical and psychological characteristics.

Da Cunha did not believe, like some Brazilian racial theorists who feared racial mixing, that Brazilians were in the process of becoming one homogenous racial type. He argued instead that racial miscegenation had given rise to many racial types, and he concluded that "there is no such thing as a Brazilian anthropological type."[89] He posited the existence of several Brazilian racial types, including *jagunços, bandeirantes, gaúchos,* and *vaqueiros,* and argued that each arose in a specific region, the product of distinct racial ancestry, geography, and climate. Unlike Nina Rodrigues, who believed that distinct racial types were defined more by race, da Cunha's theory gave more weight to the influence of environmental factors. This difference was significant. Da Cunha and Brazilian intellectuals and politicians who adopted his perspective believed that *sertanejos* and other northern "sub-races" could ultimately be improved through the manipulation of geography and climate. Inherent biological differences, including race, were less malleable.

Despite his acceptance of most aspects of racial science, da Cunha, like many other Brazilian intellectuals, rejected the notion that all *mestiços* were inherently degenerate.[90] He criticized the "conclusions of evolutionism," which posited that the *mestiço* "lack[ed] the physical energy of his savage ancestors and [was] without the intellectual elevation of his ancestors on the other side." He argued instead that northern *mestiços* displayed a "moral hybridism: a brilliant mind at times, but unstable, restless, inconstant, flaring one moment and the next moment extinguished, a victim of the fatality of biologic laws, weighted down to the lower plane of the less favored race."[91] *Mestiços* thus displayed the characteristics of both of their racial progenitors—they were simultaneously brilliant and flawed. Like the Faculdade de Direito faculty and Nina Rodrigues, da Cunha struggled to interpret European racial science in a way that reflected favorably on Brazilians. He challenged the notion of racial evolution, arguing that, "if all this is true, how then account for the normality of an anthropologic type that suddenly makes its appearance, combining tendencies that are so opposed," referring specifically to *sertanejos*. Not all *mestiços* were worthy of praise, however. He claimed that *sertanejos* did not "display the debilitating rachitic tendencies of neurasthenic *mestiços* of the coast."[92] He contrasted the allegedly weak, degenerate coastal *mulato* with the strong, robust *sertanejo,* arguing that, in the *sertão,* "the situation is the reverse of that to be observed in the cities of the seaboard, where an extravagant inversion prevails, highly compressing and atrophying them before they have attained their full development." In the *sertanejo* da Cunha found "the robust organic integrity of the *mestiço,*" whom he believed was "capable of evolving and differentiating himself in accommodation to new and loftier destinies."[93] Da Cunha explained this apparent paradox by suggesting that *sertanejos* were a "retrograde" rather than a "degenerate" racial type. He argued that geographic and cultural isolation had "freed [*sertanejos*] from a highly painful adaptation to a superior social state and at the same time prevented their slipping backward through the aberrations and vices of a more advanced milieu."[94] At the same time, he believed that social and geographic conditions in the *sertão* brought out atavistic characteristics in *sertanejos.* "The retrograde type of the *sertão,*" he wrote, "reproduces the aspect presented by mystics of the past. Viewing [Antônio Conselheiro], one has the marvelous impression of a perspective down the centuries. He is a being out of time." The Canudos rebellion thus represented a previous stage in human development: "It was a parenthesis, a hiatus. It was a vacuum. It did not exist."[95]

Da Cunha's belief in the primacy of geography and climate in the formation of racial types meant that individuals were shaped by their environment, and, through the transmission of acquired characteristics, physiological deficiencies were passed to successive generations.[96] Although da Cunha believed that effects of environmental factors were primarily physiological rather than psychological, he argued that, through the process of natural selection, "the central functions of the brain, in a most prejudicial inverse progression between intellectual and physical development, [ensure] . . . a maximum of organic energy and a minimum of moral fortitude." In the case of the Amazon, da Cunha argued that individual acclimatization resulted in "regressive evolution," "constant decline," and, ultimately, "total extinction" of non-natives.[97] In contrast, da Cunha argued that the physical environment of the northern interior exerted a positive influence on *sertanejos:* "the inhabitant of the *sertão* has in large degree taken from the savage the latter's intimacy with his physical surroundings, and this, instead of acting as a depressing influence, has enriched his potent organism." Thus, the *sertanejo* adapted to, and even thrived in, the arid conditions common to the region. In *Os sertões,* da Cunha repeatedly described *sertanejos'* effective adaptations to conditions that caused considerable difficulties for federal troops. *Sertanejos* possessed an intimate knowledge of the land, which they used to their advantage. In the heat of battle it was as if *sertanejos* materialized at will out of the seemingly barren landscape or thick undergrowth to attack federal troops and then retreated to their hiding places as quickly and easily as they had appeared. Their guerrilla tactics, and indeed their entire manner of living, were in perfect harmony with the land and climate. Da Cunha wrote that "nature protects the *sertanejo* [and] renders him an indomitable Antaeus," referring to the mythological Greek god who drew his physical strength from physical contact with the Earth (Gaia), his mother.[98] Da Cunha warned his readers not to be deceived by initial impressions of *sertanejos* who might seem weak and debilitated: "His appearance, it is true, at first glance would lead one to think that this was not the case. He does not have the flawless features, the graceful bearing, the correct build of the athlete. He is ugly, awkward, stooped. Hercules-Quasimodo reflects in his bearing the typical unprepossessing attributes of the weak. His unsteady, slightly swaying sinuous gait conveys the impression of loose-jointedness. His normal downtrodden mien is aggravated by a dour look which gives him an air of depressing humility." But other characteristics were revealed as necessary. Da Cunha likened this change to the transformation of the arid *sertão* with the return of annual rains. When pressed, the *sertanejo* displayed "an instantaneous discharge of nervous energy, he at once corrects all the faults that come from the habitual relaxation of his organs; and the awkward rustic unexpectedly assumes the dominating aspect of a powerful, copper-hued Titan, an amazingly different being, capable of extraordinary feats of strength and agility." Da Cunha saw in the *sertanejo* what he observed in the flora and fauna of the region— the ability to conserve resources and use them only when needed. During the dry season, the *sertão* and *sertanejo* alike displayed the "physiological possibility of a virtual existence where no life seems to be, with all energies pent up, lulled to sleep simply, and ready to break out again of a sudden when favorable conditions return, giving rise to unforeseen and amazing resurrections."[99] He concluded that the *sertanejo* had "served an arduous apprenticeship in the school of adversity, and he has quickly learned to face his troubles squarely and to react to them promptly."[100] To da Cunha, the *sertanejo* was the quintessential "natural man."

Da Cunha's vivid descriptions of *sertanejos* remain one of the most striking aspects of *Os sertões*. While many Brazilian intellectuals, including Nina Rodrigues, had begun to emphasize psychological rather than physiological characteristics in their description of Brazilians, da Cunha provided his readers with detailed physiognomic descriptions of *sertanejos* reminiscent of those penned by Balzac and Dickens. Da Cunha described the typical *jagunço* as "lighter than the musket that he bore; lean, dried up, fantastic, melting into a sprite, weighing less than a child, his bronzed skin stretched tautly over his bones, rough as the epidermis of a mummy." During the siege, the rebels' tenacious resistance produced increasing frustration and bewilderment among the federal troops. Da Cunha chided the troops, who had begun to view the rebels as "a being apart, teratological and monstrous, half-man, and half-goblin; violating all biological laws by displaying an inconceivable power of resistance." Da Cunha wrote that troops' imaginations "ran riot, in a drunken delirium of stupendous happenings, woven out of fantasies."[101] As the siege drew to a close, federal troops came face to face with an enemy that had proven elusive. The capture of prisoners allowed the closer inspection of *jagunços*, whom da Cunha described collectively as "an ugly cluster of ragged, repulsive-looking human bodies."[102] One *negro* prisoner captured da Cunha's imagination more than any other:

> Tall and lean in appearance, his gaunt and slightly stooping frame showed all the rigors of hunger and of battle, his emaciation causing him to seem even taller than he was. His inordinately long hair afforded but a glimpse of his narrow brow, and his markedly prognathous face, all but lost in his cottony beard, was a bruised and filthy mask. He reeled as he walked; and his tottering, infirm step, his woolly head, the scant bit of his countenance that was to be seen, his flattened nose, thick lips, his crookedly protruding teeth, his tiny eyes sparklingly brightly in their deep sockets, his long, bare, dangling arms—all this gave him the wizened appearance of a sickly orangutan.[103]

Da Cunha's description of the prisoner was not inconsistent with his belief that *mulatos* were inherently degenerate—the prisoner was inferior because he was black, not because he was a rebel. At the same time, the prisoner underwent a remarkable physical transformation after he had been judged and sentenced to a summary execution:

> That begrimed and filthy body, barely supported by the long, withered limbs beneath, now of a sudden took on admirably—and terribly—sculpturesque lines, exhibiting a plasticity that was nothing less than stupendous. It was a statuesque masterpiece, modeled out of the mire. The *negro's* stooping frame was now rigid and erect, striking a pose that was exceedingly beautiful in the pride of bearing it expressed: head up, shoulders thrown back, chest out, with all the defiant hauteur of a nobleman of old, as a pair of flashing eyes lighted up the manly face. . . . Truly, he was a statue, an ancient statue of Titan, buried four centuries ago and now exhumed, blackened and mutilated, in that enormous ruin heap of Canudos.[104]

The transformation of the prisoner from orangutan to Titan reveals da Cunha's belief that race was not wholly deterministic. If the *negro* prisoner, whom da Cunha believed was racially inferior and further debased by geography and climate, could be transformed by circumstance into an exemplar, then surely the republican government could subdue and civilize *sertanejos*.

Throughout *Os sertões*, da Cunha pointed out unusual physical and racial characteristics among the rebels. The Dutch occupation of Bahia from 1624 to 1625 and of Pernambuco from 1630 to 1654 brought northern European settlers to the northern interior, and these settlers' supposed descendants provided da Cunha with an opportunity to nuance his portraits of *sertanejos*. One rebel, he wrote, "gave the impression of being Flemish," with "big manly blue eyes" and "a flat, energetic-looking head," which da Cunha construed as evidence of "his credentials, as coming from a higher racial stock."[105] He described a second rebel, who "did not, like the others, show the effects of the privations they had endured," as "sturdily built, of medium height and broad-shouldered—a perfect specimen of *sertanejan* Hercules of the kind to be seen at fairs, with a bony framework that was like iron, and gnarled and prominent joints."[106] Although the sun had darkened the second's features, da Cunha believed that the man was "primitively *branco*."[107] In two separate passages in *Os sertões*, da Cunha wrote about the "*tipo judaico*" (Jewish type), referring to the descendants of Jewish immigrants who settled in Pernambuco during the Dutch occupation from 1630 to 1654. He described the female "*tipo judaico*" as "repulsive-looking, with the hardened faces of old shrews and evil, squinting eyes."[108] One woman, however, stood out as an "Olympian beauty," with a "firm, impeccable line of that Judaic profile, disturbed now by the protuberance of the cheekbones in a countenance that, pale and ravaged by hunger, was lighted by big black eyes filled with a deep and sovereign melancholy."[109]

Despite these anomalies, da Cunha believed that there were few "pure" racial types in the *sertão*. He wrote, in fact, that *sertanejos* as a group possessed numerous physical similarities: "whoever today traverses these regions will observe a notable uniformity among the inhabitants: an appearance and stature that vary but slightly from a given model, conveying the impression of an unvarying anthropologic type." He added that the *sertanejo* "appears to have been run through one common mold, with the individuals exhibiting almost identical physical characteristics: the same complexion, . . . the same athletic build, the same moral characteristics, the same superstitions, the same vices, and the same virtues." He concluded that "there is no doubt about it, the *sertanejo* of the North represents an ethnic sub-category that had already been formed."[110] This is da Cunha's most significant observation about the region. Despite the similarities between the North and South—both regions depended on export-oriented agricultural production and slave labor and both experienced Portuguese colonial rule and the political upheavals of independence and its aftermath—da Cunha believed that *sertanejos* were so fundamentally different from other Brazilians that they constituted a separate race. Of course not all Brazilians, especially those from the North, would adopt this view, but this idea would form the foundation of northeastern regional identity as it took shape in the succeeding decades.

While da Cunha did not emphasize psychology in his descriptions of racial types, he did write about the rebels' psychological characteristics, focusing on Antônio Conselheiro's ability to garner such a large and devoted following. Da Cunha, like Nina Rodrigues, understood *sertanejos'* psychological characteristics to be the result of racial miscegenation and adaptation to the environment. He noted a certain sense of fatalism among *sertanejos*—their relationship with their environment produced a "strong and constant impulse to fall back upon the miraculous, representing the inferior mental state of the backward individual who feels himself the ward of divinity." As *sertanejos* waited for the annual rains, da Cunha observed, they also waited for a savior to deliver them from their earthly sufferings. *Sertanejos,* he concluded, were thus "readily . . . led astray by the most absurd superstitions," a psychological characteristic that Antônio Conselheiro exploited.[111] In discussing the causes of the rebellion, da Cunha adopted Nina Rodrigues's conclusion that it was a collective psychological disorder but was vague about its origins and the mechanism by which it spread.[112] Like Nina Rodrigues, he recounted episodes from Conselheiro's childhood and more recent past, which he presented as evidence of mental degeneration leading to fanaticism. His lack of medical training notwithstanding, da Cunha proclaimed mental illness to be at the root of Conselheiro's behavior, calling him an "indifferent paranoiac" who suffered from "intellectual degeneracy," "neurosis," and "mystical psychosis."[113] Never having met Conselheiro, who died before the final siege, da Cunha relied on other evidence to support his diagnosis. He saw the layout of Canudos itself as the manifestation of Conselheiro's insanity. The church that was under construction when the military conflict began provided the best evidence of Conselheiro's mental state: "there it stood facing the East, that stupendous disharmonious façade, without rule or proportion, with its gross friezes, its impossible volutes, its capering delirium of incorrect curves, its horrible ogives and embrasures, a brutish, shapeless hulk, something like an exhumed crypt, as if the builder had sought to objectivize in stone and cement the disorder of his own delirious mind." Da Cunha viewed the physical world as a representation of intrinsic truths that could be discerned through careful, objective observation. As he was able to discern *sertanejos'* essential nature by scrutinizing thousands of faces, so too was he able to understand Conselheiro's psychology by studying the world he had created. As for Nina Rodrigues, the final confirmation of Conselheiro's insanity came with the exhumation and examination of his body, when "that horrible face, sticky with scars and pus, once more appeared before the victor's gaze."[114] The head was put on public display, and Da Cunha, although disgusted by the public's interest in the gruesome artifact, exclaimed, "Let science here have the last word. Standing out in bold relief from all the significant circumvolutions were the essential outlines of crime and madness."[115]

While his characterizations of Antônio Conselheiro and his followers were impressionistic and at times inconsistent, da Cunha conceived of his work as both scientific and pragmatic—he believed that the Canudos rebellion posed a real and immediate threat to civilized society. He warned that "the moral environment of the region favored the contagion and spread of this particular form of neurasthenia, and this local disorder might well be the spark that would touch off a conflagration throughout the whole of the interior of the North." Herein lay the real danger of Canudos. While he argued that *sertanejos* were destined to racial extinction, as indeed the federal military campaign against Canudos had proven, he believed that the conditions that gave rise to Canudos were present throughout the region and that another rebellion was likely, if not inevitable. He argued that "the Canudos campaign must have a higher objective than the stupid and inglorious one of merely wiping out a backlands settlement." He warned, with the assurance of a devout positivist, that the "entire campaign would be a crime" if the republican state did not "[follow] up our cannon with a constant, stubborn, and persistent campaign of education, with the object of drawing these rude and backward fellow countrymen of ours into the current of our times and our own national life."[116] Da Cunha's solution to the problem of rural rebellions and religious fanaticism was to transform *sertanejos* into modern citizens of the Brazilian republic. Thus, the entire region, differentiated from the rest of Brazil by race, geography, and climate, was constructed as a problem to be addressed by the republican government. Although regional elites had asked for government assistance in economic development and in responding to drought, the problems were usually short lived, dependent on the vicissitudes of the weather or the market. Da Cunha, however, identified the people of the region, and indeed the region itself, as a problem.

It is not surprising that both Nina Rodrigues and da Cunha found the origins of the Canudos rebellion in race and racial psychology. These approaches reflected contemporary approaches in science, medicine, and understandings of human nature. More significantly, they found the origins of rural rebellions, religious fanaticism, and regional identity in the individual rather than in social and political structures. This view of the individual was fundamentally liberal and republican and more palatable to regional ruling elites than were explanations that brought attention to the deep social and economic inequalities of Brazilian society. To argue that the rebels' actions were a rational response to changing social and economic conditions would have constituted a radical critique of existing social and economic relationships and the republic. After Canudos and the publication of *Os sertões*, government officials and liberal professionals generally interpreted banditry, millenarian movements, and Afro-Brazilian religions as isolated episodes that reflected leaders' and participants' supposedly primitive mentalities. Not until the 1930s and 1940s would this interpretation be questioned. The Faculdade de Direito faculty, Raymundo Nina Rodrigues, and Euclydes da Cunha each used racial science and racial psychology to examine individual and group identities and to define the relationship between state and citizen. Pernambuco's political leaders, still reeling from the political upheavals of the 1890s, would use racial science and racial psychology to develop new approaches to social and economic problems within the state and the region.

Criminals and Vagrants

In the 1890s, the Pernambucan state government began to apply theories of race, racial psychology, and crime in government institutions, the workplace, and society. While these ideas had been utilized during the empire to manage the free workers of Pernambuco, they took on added significance with the founding of the republic and the development of new legal and political systems. Concerns about the breakdown of social order stemming from the abolition of slavery, the demise of the patriarchal family, urbanization, and nascent industrialization led Brazilian political elites to place considerable faith in positivist principles of rational government and the legal system as a means of governing. The Pernambucan state government in the 1890s embraced criminal anthropology in particular as a means of identifying and rehabilitating criminals, vagrants, mendicants, and otherwise unproductive citizens.

Antonio Pedro da Silva Marques, who served as the Pernambucan state government's minister of justice (*questor*) and later Recife's chief of police, cited Italian criminologist Raffaele Garofalo to argue that "crime, reducible . . . to the transgressions of the sentiments of compassion and probity, is a product of complex causes. It is recognized that physical and sociological factors, represented by climate, temperature, age, heredity, legislation, wealth, etc., are factors in crime."[117] Marques believed that race and heredity were the root causes of crime. He wrote that "crime is inherited capital" since "ascendants passed to their descendants their individual traits of organization and their physiological, moral, and intellectual aptitudes." He concluded that inherited atavistic qualities "produced in the criminal the psychological traces as well as the moral and intellectual tendencies of a remote ancestor."[118] His thoughts on the causes of crime echoed those of the Faculdade de Direito professors, but as a civil servant, Marques was in a position to influence public policy directly. While the state justice system was being reformed after the establishment of the republic, Marques, and indeed most Pernambucan politicians, legislators, and jurists, argued that the state should attempt to take a more active role in controlling and preventing crime. Marques wrote that "the entire exercise of public power depends on the adoption of measures that, [in order to] promote the expansion of wealth and the development of education, will drain the two most abundant fonts of crime: misery and ignorance."[119] Marques proposed the extensive use of agricultural penal colonies, which he argued would assist the state in "the task of promoting the rehabilitation of the criminal." He wrote that, "without these measures, we will struggle against vagrancy and feed the *negro* army of crime. The formerly condemned will return to society, without the habit of work, and fall back into their criminal career."[120] Marques maintained the belief that there was a clear correlation between crime and race, a belief that likely resulted from his perception that many of the 40,000 slaves freed in Pernambuco in 1888 had not secured gainful employment. Marques reported that, unfortunately, "the police do not have the means to effectively punish vagabonds" since the state did not yet possess agricultural penal colonies.[121] In 1898 alone, 750 "indigents" were sent to the Santa Casa de Misericórdia's asylum for beggars.[122] Marques advocated the creation of penal colonies similar to the Auburn state prison in New York. There, he wrote, prisoners were "obliged to work together in absolute silence, isolated in cells at night, and the sentenced would be taught, aside from religious and moral instruction, moralizing messages."[123]

At the same time, state legislators worked on a bill that would create a system of penal colonies in Pernambuco. In a speech to the state senate in 1898, Francisco Corrêa argued that penal colonies were necessary because "in great part the *libertos*, accustomed to the service regimen of the *fazenda*, shortly after they were set free, sought out populated centers where their lives were easier." He believed that *libertos* were inherently lazy, a trait he argued was characteristic of "countries where the climate is hot" and in which "the inhabitants only work for what is necessary." He argued that it was thus necessary to create "a correctional colony for vagabonds who infest the cities, stations, and all populated centers," plus "educational establishments for children" and "a penitentiary where we will pursue the regeneration of the criminal." Corrêa concluded that "it is cultivating the soil and forcing manual labor that will achieve regeneration."[124] In 1898, the state legislature passed a law creating two correctional colonies.[125] Five classes of individuals were singled out for placement at the colonies: (1) those who "did not possess a means of subsistence . . . or an honest and legal profession," (2) those who had "broken the terms of good living [*termos de bem viver*] in which they have been obliged to work, manifesting intentions to live inactively or in the exercise of illicit, immoral, or forbidden industry," (3) minors between the ages of nine and fourteen who had been convicted of crimes, (4) orphans and minors who were not subject to "*patrio poder*" (patriarchal control), and (5) those found to be "vagrants, beggars, or practicing disorder or vice."[126] In 1897, the state government had been given administrative control of the presidio of Fernando de Noronha, the island prison colony off the northeastern coast.[127] By 1900, the penal colony was receiving Pernambucans convicted of vagrancy and "*capoeiragem*," the practice of African martial arts.[128] According to Martha Knisely Huggins, a second penal colony was established at Colonia Suassuna, a state-owned agricultural colony, although its main purpose, as discussed in the previous chapter, was to attract European immigrants.[129]

It quickly became apparent to those advocating institutionalization of Pernambuco's poor and unemployed that the state simply did not have the resources to enforce the vagrancy laws passed in 1898. Recife's police chief, Leopoldo Marinho de Paula Lins, lamented to the governor that "unhappily, if you will permit me to tell you, up to this time we have done very little to satisfy these very noble and humanitarian aims." He declared that the creation of the agricultural correctional colony at Fernando de Noronha "will not be able to satisfy the requirements of the work that the police have done toward to the repression of vagrancy and recidivism of petty criminals."[130] He concluded that additional measures would be necessary if the police were to continue their work. By 1900, the Colonia Suassuna had been converted into an agricultural colony, but it was producing very little. Despite the Pernambucan government's efforts to encourage development of the property, including the sale of lots to private investors, the governor described the colony as "morose," and it was closed in 1902.[131] Wracked by budget crises beginning in 1900, the state government did not have sufficient funds to support primary education and basic public health measures. In this atmosphere, efforts to turn criminals and vagrants into productive workers proved to be a luxury the state government simply could not afford.

Criminal anthropology also influenced the development of Pernambuco's justice system, including sentencing guidelines, levels of criminal responsibility, and the legal definition of minors. In 1897, administrators at Recife's Casa de Detenção established an "anthropometric examination office" that would identify criminals utilizing *bertillonage,* the biometric system developed by French police statistician Alphonse Bertillon in the 1880s.[132] The Pernambucan governor admitted that there was insufficient funding for the service, but he nonetheless recognized "the utility that anthropometry lends to criminal anthropology and to the cause of Justice, principally in the punishment of relapsing criminals."[133] In 1900, the service was fully funded, and Recife's police chief reported using it to identify repeat offenders. Although *bertillonage* would prove less reliable than fingerprinting as a means of identifying criminals, Recife's police chief argued that the anthropometric identification of criminals was essential to ensuring public order.[134] While it is unlikely that criminal anthropology had much of an effect on crime in Pernambuco, the creation of anthropometric guidelines nevertheless reveals the Pernambucan elite's enthusiasm for scientific explanations of human behavior and their increasing interest in using scientific methods to control the Pernambucan *povo.*

In the 1890s, the Pernambucan government also adopted techniques for investigating crimes, collecting evidence, and determining legal competency. These techniques were constituent elements of "legal medicine," a concept that encompassed the medical and biological aspects of law and policing. The principles of legal medicine were most applied when determining official causes of death, collecting physical evidence in cases of rape and "deflowering," determining legal sanity, and identifying and categorizing criminals (which also involved the use of anthropometry). Corrheiro da Cunha, a Faculdade de Direito professor, visited medical-legal institutes and law schools in Germany, England, and France and proposed that the Pernambucan government establish a chemical laboratory "where verifications and falsifications of medical-legal analyses can be made," a legal medicine laboratory with a "section of anthropology and an anthropometry service, which is applicable to criminology," and a library for the acquisition of "books, maps, and plans, etc., that demonstrate the diverse branches of hygiene in its application in the various cities of Brazil."[135] Many of da Cunha's suggestions were followed, and by 1900, legal medicine was established as an essential tool in Pernambuco's judicial system.

Crime reports from the 1890s reveal the degree to which criminal anthropology and legal medicine had become accepted components of the state's justice system.[136] Physicians were called on to determine official causes of death, suspected poisons were sent to the chemical laboratory for analysis, and physicians were consulted in order to determine defendants' legal competency. An interesting case from 1898 reflected both the increasing professionalization of the criminal justice system as well as the ways in which recent conflicts at Canudos and Juazeiro do Norte had influenced the way in which public authorities responded to the threat of popular uprisings. José Guedes do Santos Barbosa, who resided in the *agreste município* of Bom Jardim, eighty-five kilometers (fifty miles) inland from Recife, had, according to authorities, declared himself "to have been sent by God" and thus garnered a "great number of proselytes who obey him blindly." Antonio Pedro da Silva Marques, as police chief, explained Guedes's popularity as "a repercussion of the religious neurosis of Padre Cícero in the state of Ceará, and of the accursed Antônio Conselheiro, of Bahia, a true product of the law of imitation." Based on the notion that "insanity of similar fanatics can result in serious disturbances to public order," Marques ordered Guedes held at the state asylum. Two "distinguished" psychiatrists examined him and "concluded that it was necessary to sequester José Guedes because he suffered from religious paranoia."[137] What is significant here, beyond Guedes's legal status (which is not revealed in the available historical record), is the way in which authorities responded to a perceived threat to public order. Guedes and his followers were innocuous enough—there were no formal charges levied against Guedes—he was merely a popular lay preacher. Yet the state government reacted by arresting and institutionalizing him, justifying their actions based on legal medicine and criminal anthropology. The state government's actions in the case of José Guedes exemplified how a state being built from the ground up began utilizing modern policing techniques during the initial years of the republic.

Historians have paid considerable attention to labor relations in Pernambuco during the late empire and early republic.[138] The broad consensus is that Pernambucan sugar planters made a successful transition from slavery, although there is disagreement about how smooth this transition was.[139] Nevertheless, the transition to free labor depended on an oversupply of agricultural workers, and while planters were anxious about the labor supply, especially when imperial legislation put an end to the slave trade and moved toward final abolition in stages, the labor market demographics continuously favored the planters' financial interests—workers were easy to find and they proved willing to work for minimal wages. As Robert Levine succinctly puts it, "The ability of landowners to keep a supply of cheap labor permanently available was the most efficient element in the noncompetitive agricultural system."[140] However, the Pernambucan government's efforts to criminalize vagrancy and poverty cannot be interpreted exclusively as a deliberate effort on the part of planters and their political representatives to create a pool of inexpensive labor.[141] While efforts to institutionalize nonregimented labor reflected concerns about social and economic development, there was no economic need to interfere in the labor market. The criminalization of vagrants and the indigent instead reflected changing understandings of citizenship and the role of the state. If the state's primary function during the empire was to allow the elite to pursue their own economic interests with little government interference, the positivist founders of the republic imagined a more interventionist role for the state. The poor, the unemployed, criminals, and former slaves were all to contribute to the social and economic development of the nation. Those unable or unwilling would be forced to do so. Unfortunately, Pernambucan republicans' idealistic attempts to create a new system of government and transform Brazilian society would give way to political infighting, patronage, and corruption. Their efforts nonetheless represented a new ideal of citizenship and government responsibility that would shape later reform efforts in the 1910s and 1920s.

By the second decade of the twentieth century, the study of *nordestinos'* racial qualities had become less important to Brazilian and northeastern intellectuals. Most national political and economic leaders believed that white European immigration was the only appropriate and feasible solution to Brazil's labor problem. *Nordestinos* were largely forgotten, and it was only when foreign immigration declined during and after World War I that government officials again became interested in studying and improving the populations of northeastern Brazil. It was at this point that national and regional intellectuals, urban professionals, reformers, and civil servants renewed their interest in *nordestinos'* racial, physical, and psychological characteristics. Their concerns with the "northeastern problem" began to be expressed in a new language, that of medicine and public health.

4

The Medicalization of *Nordestinos,* 1910–1925

In his annual report to the Pernambucan legislature in 1927, the state's governor, Estácio de Albuquerque Coimbra, wrote that "the economic, intellectual, moral, and civic value of the Nation and the State is shaped, with the expression of human activity, in the excellence of physical and moral robustness of its population." He argued that "man, healthy or sick, . . . ought to fall under the knowing gaze of the Governments, preserving or restoring him to health, to benefit the Nation."[1] Under Coimbra, who served as governor of Pernambuco from 1926 to 1930, the state government inaugurated new public health, assistance, and education programs designed to improve Pernambucans' material and physical well-being. This was no easy task. Regional economic underdevelopment and perennial budget crises threatened government-sponsored social programs. Implementing and administering public health programs in Recife and its immediate suburbs was relatively easy, but transportation difficulties and low population densities made the extension of public health services to the state's interior almost impossible. Despite these obstacles, Pernambucans' health became the state government's most important concern by the mid-1920s because political and economic elites believed that economic development and social progress depended on effective public health programs.

Interest in improving public health was growing worldwide in the 1910s and 1920s, and that interest extended into northeastern Brazil. In addition to services offered by the Pernambucan state government, the federal government created the Rural Preventive Health Service in 1918 and the National Department of Public Health in 1920. In addition, the Rockefeller Foundation, in consultation with federal and state governments, provided public health services in northeastern Brazil, administering rural health posts for the treatment of ancylostomiasis, or hookworm disease, and mosquito control programs designed to eliminate yellow fever and malaria. As several historians of Brazil's public health reforms of the early twentieth century have pointed out, these efforts represented an unprecedented expansion of government services and a significant change in the government's level of responsibility for its citizens' well-being.[2]

While the period from 1910 to 1925 saw significant gains in public health, especially a decline in the number of deaths attributable to epidemic diseases, northeastern Brazil was understood by both Brazilian and foreign experts to be one of the most unhealthy regions in Brazil and Latin America.[3] There was, however, significant disagreement on the origins and causes of the region's public health problems. Pernambucan, federal, and foreign public health officials each offered different explanations based on differing understandings of diseases and their treatments and the relative significance of race, climate, and geography.[4] Experts' opinions also reflected widely divergent opinions about the economic, social, and political position of the Northeast and *nordestinos* within the nation. In the late nineteenth and early twentieth centuries, Pernambucan reformers and public health officials' assessments of *nordestinos* were generally optimistic. While they found *nordestinos* to be unhealthy, they believed that public health programs could control diseases and improve their health. Conversely, national and foreign public health officials' understandings of the region reflected their negative assessments of the region's declining economic and political fortunes as well as the prevailing notion that *nordestinos* were racially inferior to other Brazilians.[5] Both federal and foreign public health officials believed that well-designed and properly administered public health programs would improve sanitary conditions and, ultimately, social and economic conditions. However, they did not believe that *nordestinos* could become the equals of Brazilians from developed regions of the nation. These beliefs shaped political debates about public health throughout the 1910s and 1920s. Ultimately, the notion that *nordestinos* were inherently unhealthy became widely accepted in medical, political, and intellectual circles, and ideas about diseases and their long-term effects on *nordestinos* became an essential component of constructions of northeastern regional identity. By 1920, northeastern and national reformers and politicians most often expressed their concerns about the region using the language of medicine and public health.

The development of Brazil's public health movement in the early twentieth century has received considerable attention from historians who have focused on changing understandings of disease, the dissemination and adoption of new medical and public health ideas and practices, and the political and institutional dimensions of what constituted the first social services offered by the Brazilian federal government. In the late 1910s and early 1920s, politicians and reformers, led by physicians associated with the Oswaldo Cruz Institute in Rio de Janeiro, succeeded in creating the Rural Preventive Health Service and the National Department of Public Health.[6] Many scholars have focused on the national significance of these programs and have shown how they constituted an integral part of national state-building efforts during Brazil's First Republic (1889–1930). Less attention has been paid, however, to the regional and local origins and development of public health programs and, more specifically, to the differences between national, regional, and local understandings of disease and public health.[7] Historians generally have argued that northeastern states were unable to create effective public health services in the early twentieth century because of inadequate technical expertise and financial support and a lack of political will. The historiographical consensus is that effective public health services arrived in the region only after the creation of the Rural Preventive Health Service and the National Department of Public Health. There were, however, some exceptions, including Pernambuco and Bahia, which created effective public health services without federal assistance.[8]

The Northeast is usually presented in comparison with São Paulo, which established effective public health programs with minimal assistance from the Brazilian federal government, and with Rio de Janeiro, which, as the nation's capital, received considerable political and financial attention from the federal government.[9] An examination of the development and institutionalization of public health at the state and regional level, however, reveals the ways in which the early-twentieth-century public health movement reflected local and regional debates about the relationship between the state and civil society as well as how medicine and public health generated ideas that were used in the construction of a northeastern regional identity. Although Pernambucan reformers and public health officials were far removed from the leading scientific and medical research centers in São Paulo and Rio de Janeiro and were hampered by perennial budget crises and a nativist pride (which led to a refusal of federal assistance), they were nonetheless able to create public health services that, far from being a cut-rate imitation of successful programs in more developed regions of the nation, effectively addressed local and regional public health concerns.[10]

Climate, Geography, and Disease

In the nineteenth century, Brazilian physicians and public health officials understood disease to be the result of complex interactions between humans and their environment. Because the etiology of most diseases was unknown, physicians focused instead on improving sanitary conditions and mitigating the effects of climate and geography. Understandings of diseases were based on seemingly contradictory theories of the nature and transmission of disease. Well into the twentieth century, Brazilian physicians and public health officials continued to refer to miasmas, poisonous gases emanating from polluted soil, and contagions, or infectious airborne particles transmitted from individual to individual. These references all indicated that older theories of disease transmission had not yet been superseded in Brazil by the germ theory of disease, which had already been accepted in Europe and the United States. Finding the origins of disease in miasmas and contagions was compatible with physicians' belief that environmental factors—climate and geography— were the primary causes of disease. In 1897, for example, low rainfall levels in coastal areas of Pernambuco created unusually dry conditions in Recife, which public health officials pointed to as the cause of a smallpox epidemic but a decrease in yellow fever cases.[11] At the same time, because rain was not washing human and animal waste from the streets, officials noted an increase in "disagreeable odors," or miasmas, emanating from the streets, and they feared these miasmas would cause outbreaks of so-called "filth" diseases.[12] Typical of nineteenth-century understandings of the relationship between disease, climate, and geography was an 1878 study of Pernambuco authored by Emilio Béringer, a French engineer the provincial government hired to study climatic conditions and mortality in Recife. Béringer found that the average life expectancy in Pernambuco was 26.8 years, compared to a European high of 48.0 years in Norway and a low of 31.2 years in Spain. Béringer argued that Pernambuco's high mortality rates were "attributable to the climate or telluric influences" and that the single most important factor was, as he put it, "the accidentally corrupted environment." Béringer also believed that race contributed to Pernambuco's high mortality rates, arguing that slaves and *pretos* were "fatally subjected to a much higher mortality than of the *raça branca*, whose life is happier."[13] However, because whites enjoyed lower mortality rates than blacks, Béringer argued, Pernambuco was well suited to European immigration, particularly of the "Latin race," which he believed could adapt rapidly to Pernambuco's tropical climate. Béringer concluded that "customs, like ideas, are transformed rapidly in the new continent; great progress has been made in few years, and it is certain that, notwithstanding some slow moments like the occasional real crisis, the province of Pernambuco is marching incessantly toward a more elevated level of culture and prosperity."[14] Although nineteenth-century physicians and public health officials lacked a comprehensive understanding of the causes of diseases and the ways in which they were transmitted, they remained optimistic that efforts to improve sanitary conditions would produce social and economic benefits.

By the turn of the century, understandings of diseases had begun to change as the germ theory of disease became more widely accepted among medical professionals and government officials. As physicians and public health officials learned of new research during their tours of foreign hospitals and laboratories and from medical journals, Pernambuco's Department of Public Health underwent a transformation, expanding to include a vaccination service, a biological research laboratory that utilized Pasteurian techniques, and a laboratory dedicated to producing vaccines and serums for smallpox and other diseases. José Octávio de Freitas, who graduated from Rio de Janeiro's Faculdade de Medicina in 1893 and served in a series of public health positions for the Pernambucan government from the 1890s through the 1920s, was a leading popularizer of the germ theory. In his earliest writings on public health, he combined the germ and environmental theories of disease transmission, however. In an epidemiological study of Recife published in 1905, Freitas argued that "the causes of our very exalted sanitary decadence reside almost entirely in the soil and subsoil of the city," a reference to the mangrove swamps that existed throughout the city.[15] Because waterborne diseases were not yet entirely understood, physicians and public health officials continued to believe that Recife's climatic and geographic features were to blame for the city's high mortality rates. The fact that Pernambucan officials did not see contradictions between miasmatic, contagion, and germ theories of disease was not particularly important in a state where basic sanitation and hygiene were lacking. With the older theory linking disease to environmental factors and the new germ theory pointing to biological causes, it was apparent to both scientists and public officials that humans could not be viewed as inherently unhealthy. Thus, effective sanitation and public health services could prevent diseases and control outbreaks.

Many historians consider the creation of public health and sanitation services in early-twentieth-century Brazil to have been the result of the expansion of capitalism; improvements in public health were deemed to be essential to the expansion of agriculture, industry, and commerce. More recent scholarship, which has built on the work of Luis Antonio de Castro Santos, has recognized that social and political progressivism, the professionalization of medicine, and state building also spurred the early public health movement in Brazil. Pernambuco was no exception.

In Pernambuco, federal public health authorities were responsible for disease control at Recife's port, while state and local governments were responsible for public health in the rest of the state.[16] Only in Recife, however, were effective sanitation and public health services created and maintained in the first two decades of the twentieth century. In urban areas, public health officials were concerned with epidemics of smallpox, plague, and yellow fever, which were commonplace in Pernambuco and its capital, Recife, well into the twentieth century.[17] In 1898, Rodolpho Galvão, Pernambuco's inspector general for hygiene, informed the state governor that "the causes of insalubrity in any urban agglomeration are complex. Some of these causes are intangible and cannot be modified by human will and force: some are meteorological accidents and cosmic fatalities. Others are dependent on topographical conditions and because of this they can be modified only at the cost of a great deal of work and time."[18] Public health officials were especially concerned with epidemic diseases because they could lead to the closure of Recife's port, which accounted for the majority of Pernambuco's imports and exports and most of the government's revenue. Public health officials recorded deaths from tuberculosis, malaria, ancylostomiasis, dysentery, trachoma, leishmaniasis, leprosy, and syphilis, but limited fiscal resources and the fact that these diseases were endemic rather than epidemic (which meant that they did not pose an immediate economic threat) allowed Pernambucan state public health officials to ignore them. Whether public health officials believed the cause of a specific disease was miasma, contagion, or germ, they responded in the same way. Strategies for controlling diseases included eliminating biological and environmental causes of disease by upgrading sewer, water, and sanitation services, isolating the sick, providing disinfection services, and conducting home visits, all of which were designed to "improve the sanitary interests of the population."[19]

Public health officials often expressed concern about Recife's urban slums (locally called *mocambos*). Rodolpho Galvão noted that "one of the worst causes of unhealthiness of this capital . . . is the humidity of the housing [of the lower classes]."[20] In the early twentieth century, public health officials and politicians set out to improve sanitary conditions in the city and thus prevent disease epidemics. However, workers' living conditions remained abysmal despite the fact that tax exemptions for industry had provided additional jobs and increased the availability of consumer items. In 1916, Pernambuco's governor, Manoel Antonio Pereira Borba, pointed out that "large urban zones are swampy and insalubrious and, in the midst of waters and near them, [there are] innumerable houses where an enormous population of poor people live prolifically, creating a generation that, from its inception, is weak, debilitated, and condemned to death by the inconvenient conditions in the environment in which they are born and live."[21] Public officials authorized the construction of workers' housing (*casas operarias*) in new neighborhoods outside the city center, suspended the collection of taxes on new buildings, and ordered the demolition of *mocambos*.[22] At the same time, the state legislature amended the public health code in an attempt to regulate the location, construction, and layout of lower-class housing, although these measures were largely ineffective because they could not be effectively enforced. Even with these efforts, it proved difficult for public health officials to improve sanitary conditions in Recife. Strategies for improving the living conditions of the urban poor and reducing the impact of diseases were predicated on the notion that inferior housing, public amenities, and wages rather than the poor themselves were the cause of high disease rates in poor and working-class neighborhoods. Pernambucan public health officials continued to believe that they could improve living conditions by controlling disease outbreaks.

For public health officials, the arid *sertão* constituted a stark geographic and climatic contrast to the humid coastal areas. Since the mid-nineteenth century, medical researchers associated with the Faculdade de Medicina in Bahia, including Raymundo Nina Rodrigues, had been attempting to determine whether diseases common to coastal regions took different clinical forms in the *sertão*.[23] By the early twentieth century, northeastern physicians and public health officials were arguing that the coastal area and the interior each produced unique forms of diseases and that specific treatments were required for these regional variations. While European tropical medicine influenced Brazilians' understandings of diseases, northeastern physicians formulated their own ideas about diseases based on their clinical and field observations. Most Pernambucan public health officials believed that the arid interior of the state was inherently more healthy than coastal regions due to low humidity levels and cooler temperatures.

The periodic droughts that afflicted the northeastern interior presented the greatest public health challenge. After the Great Drought of 1877–1879 and less severe droughts in the 1890s and 1910s, Pernambucan politicians and public health officials came to fear the epidemics that inevitably followed a drought. During and after a drought, which sometimes lasted two planting seasons, otherwise endemic and controllable diseases would spread quickly among the tens of thousands of *sertanejos* who sought relief in refugee camps and coastal cities. Drought victims were frequently hungry and weak, and the squalid conditions in the camps facilitated the transmission of disease. State and federal authorities responded to the public health crisis by distributing free vaccinations for smallpox and the bubonic plague and, if possible, by isolating victims. Public health officials argued that the periodic droughts had a profound impact on *sertanejos'* health. Drought victims were not only subject to epidemic diseases but also left permanently weakened by their sufferings. Government concern with the public health threat posed by periodic droughts in the interior was usually short lived, however. When the rains returned, drought victims returned to the interior and refugee camps emptied. The threat of epidemics subsided, and drought victims' health was no longer a pressing concern for public health officials.

Aside from providing emergency aid during droughts, government officials could do little to improve sanitary conditions in the interior. Transportation difficulties, perennial budget crises, and political resistance to promoting development in a region where few ballots were cast constituted insurmountable obstacles to improving social and economic conditions in the region. Beyond observations made during drought relief efforts, government officials had little firsthand knowledge of public health conditions in the interior. There were few practicing physicians in the region, and medical care was either unavailable or too expensive for most *sertanejos*, even in the larger towns and *município* seats. After the turn of the century, with improvements in transportation, more detailed reports of public health conditions in the interior made their way to public health officials in Recife. In 1905, one official reported an outbreak of "paludal fevers" in Pesqueira, located 200 kilometers (120 miles) inland from Recife; he warned the government that the situation required its immediate attention lest the outbreak spread to other towns.[24] With greater knowledge of public health conditions in the interior, the Pernambucan government responded by dividing the state into four public health zones and appointing to each zone physicians who were to report to local government officials and public health officials in Recife about specific public health concerns.[25] In 1910, some of these posts were filled, but the Department of Public Health's ability to respond to public health threats had not improved substantially. Outside of Recife and its suburbs, there were only four physicians practicing in the entire state, these being in the *município* seats of Nazareth, Caruaru, and Triumpho.[26] Despite the dearth of physicians and the almost complete lack of government-sponsored public health services in the interior, public health officials began to argue that it was in fact *sertanejos'* supposed ignorance of the most basic principles of hygiene that constituted the most important stumbling block to improvement of sanitary conditions in the interior. The improvement of public health conditions was thus linked to improvements in the public education system, which government officials argued should be "adapted to the conditions of the localities where they will be applied" and "limited to teaching the rudiments of reading, writing, and math, [and] . . . the elementary notions of agriculture and animal husbandry."[27] These well-intentioned calls for reform resulted in few measurable improvements, however. As the governor admitted to the state legislature in 1912, "In the *interior* of the State the Hygiene Service is almost nonexistent, given the impossibility that the commissaries encounter in simultaneously attending to the most distant points in an opportune fashion."[28] Thus, although public health conditions were improving in Recife and its suburbs, the Pernambucan state government simply lacked the material resources to create and administer effective public health services in the interior.

Controlling Diseases

The realization that existing public health services were largely ineffective, even in urban areas, led Pernambucan public health officials to call for the reorganization and expansion of public health services in 1905.[29] Nineteenth-century public health efforts were restricted to controlling epidemics of smallpox, yellow fever, and the plague, and little attention was paid to endemic diseases and Pernambucans' overall health. Another factor behind the call to expand services was that the state's political leaders increasingly saw improving public health services not only as a way of preventing disease but also as a means of improving the state's economy; controlling diseases helped to prevent disruptions in agricultural production and commerce.[30] A key factor in the growing interest in public health was that the state's role in it had been expanding since the late nineteenth century and the founding of Brazil's First Republic in 1889. The decentralization of political power that took place with the transition from empire to republic was instrumental in forcing the expansion of government services at the state level. Pernambucan political leaders negotiated the transfer of church-run hospitals and charities to state control, built new public hospitals, and appropriated funding for new public health services. By the second decade of the twentieth century, house-to-house visits by nurses, vaccination campaigns, disinfection services, sanitary policing, and improvements in urban sanitation had led to marked improvement public health. The state government more than tripled spending on public health in the 1910s, spending some 210 *contos* in 1912 and 709 *contos* by 1920.[31] Most of these efforts were limited to Recife and its immediate suburbs and thus benefited only a small percentage of the state's population. It would take decades for improvements in public health services to make a substantial impact on Pernambucans' health and mortality, but these initial efforts were significant in that they constituted an expansion of state-sponsored social services and led to a more thorough understanding of the public health and the social and economic problems facing government administrators and the populations of the region.

The most pressing public health problem in early-twentieth-century Pernambuco was the same as in the previous century: the potential for an outbreak of smallpox. Epidemics of the disease had killed thousands of Pernambucans in 1862, 1878, 1879, 1890, and 1896.[32] Vaccination campaigns became the most effective—and controversial—means of controlling the disease. The state's public health department operated a small laboratory, named the Pasteur Institute, to produce vaccine for free public distribution, and it employed nurses who conducted home visits to vaccinate citizens. On the heels of the 1896 epidemic, which resulted in 2,119 deaths in Pernambuco, public health officials considered the merits of an obligatory smallpox vaccination campaign, limited to students and the police, arguing that such a campaign would be easy to carry out and would produce little public resistance.[33] This proposal was not immediately taken up by the state legislature, and public health officials again proposed a vaccination campaign in the spring of 1904. However, in the same year, a revolt against a mandatory vaccination campaign in Rio de Janeiro persuaded Pernambucan public health officials and political leaders that a mandatory vaccination campaign would produce too much public resistance, and they abandoned their plans.[34] The human cost of this decision must have been only too apparent in the following year when a smallpox epidemic resulted in 3,965 deaths in the state.[35] As the death toll rose in late 1905, public health officials increased vaccine production and visiting nurses provided free vaccinations at health posts throughout the capital.

Although the etiology of smallpox was not understood, traditional inoculation techniques and Jennerian vaccination provided individual immunity to the disease.[36] To fight diseases for which there were no vaccines or effective treatments, public health officials employed "disinfection" techniques, which

Table 4.1
Annual Mortality Rates, Recife and Suburbs

Year	Population	Deaths	Deaths per thousand persons
1856	61,402	5,029	81.9
1857	62,976	2,047	32.5
1858	64,596	1,938	30.0
1859	66,246	1,789	27.0
1860	67,944	2,133	34.4
1861	69,686	2,412	34.6
1862	71,473	2,774	38.8
1863	73,305	2,639	36.0
1864	75,187	2,519	34.8
1865	77,112	2,707	35.1
1866	79,076	3,044	38.4
1867	81,118	2,921	36.0
1868	83,197	3,107	37.3
1869	85,330	2,979	34.9
1870	87,517	3,181	36.3
1871	89,761	3,564	40.6
1872	92,062	3,801	41.2
1873	94,363	3,480	36.9
1874	96,722	3,483	36.0
1875	99,140	3,444	34.7
1876	101,618	3,665	36.1
1877	104,158	3,627	34.7
1878	106,761	6,022	56.4
1879	109,430	5,330	48.7
1880	112,165	4,127	36.8
1881	114,914	3,939	33.3
1882	117,817	4,161	35.2
1883	120,762	3,648	30.2
1884	123,781	3,838	31.0
1885	126,786	3,694	29.1
1886	130,048	3,668	28.2
1887	133,299	3,826	28.7
1888	136,631	4,099	30.0
1889	140,047	4,034	28.8
1890	143,548	6,116	42.6
1891	147,136	4,232	28.7
1892	150,814	4,363	28.9
1893	154,584	4,829	31.2
1894	158,449	4,992	31.5

Table 4.1 (cont.)
Annual Mortality Rates, Recife and Suburbs

Year	Population	Deaths	Deaths per thousand persons
1895	162,410	5,793	35.1
1896	166,470	7,765	46.6
1897	170,632	5,264	30.8
1898	174,897	5,106	29.1
1899	179,270	5,713	31.8
1900	183,000	6,206	33.9
1901	186,000	6,498	34.6
1902	189,000	6,424	33.9
1903	192,000	6,148	32.0
1904	195,000	10,210	52.8
1905	—	—	—
1906	—	—	—
1907	—	—	—
1908	—	—	—
1909	—	—	—
1910	—	8,341	43.1
1911	200,000	10,254	51.2
1912	—	7,677	36.5
1913	—	6,894	29.9
1914	—	7,198	30.6
1915	—	8,167	34.0
1916	—	7,560	31.5
1917	—	6,347	25.9
1918	—	—	37.4
1919	—	8,641	34.5
1920	260,000	7,629	29.3
1921	—	—	28.7
1922	270,000	7,565	28.0
1923	313,150	7,936	25.3
1924	—	7,818	24.4
1925	—	7,388	20.7
1926	—	—	22.5
1927	—	—	19.8
1928	365,097	—	18.8
1929	420,090*	—	20.6

*Increase reflects annexation of Beberibe and Arruda (*Mensagem 1930*, 42).

Sources: Freitas, *O clima*, 55; *Mensagem 1912*, 7; *Mensagem 1913*, 17; *Mensagem 1914*, 12; *Mensagem 1915*, 14; *Mensagem 1916*, 26; *Mensagem 1917*, 29; *Mensagem 1918*, 19; *Mensagem 1920*, 20; *Mensagem 1921*, 25; *Mensagem 1922*, 22; *Mensagem 1923*, 16; *Mensagem 1924*, 12; *Mensagem 1926*, 64; *Mensagem 1929*, 45; *Mensagem 1930*, 42–43.

were designed to reduce or eliminate pathogenic materials from buildings and public spaces. The state's disinfection service was inaugurated in 1893 and used to cleanse and disinfect locations where individuals had contracted, convalesced from, or died from a disease. Pernambucan public health officials, like their national and foreign counterparts, placed considerable faith in disinfection, which was used to combat yellow fever, smallpox, measles, and tuberculosis.[37] In 1898, Pernambuco's inspector general for hygiene wrote that the "disinfectory," a horse-drawn disinfection unit that carried a small incinerator and a chemical sprayer, "is an optimal auxiliary to home disinfections." The official also told the state's political leadership that disinfection services were the most important tool of the public health department in the fight against disease.[38] By 1910, disinfection services constituted the largest single public health expenditure in Pernambuco.[39] The Disinfection Service, centrally located in Recife, was dispatched to disinfect buildings when cases of smallpox, yellow fever, or bubonic plague were reported to the public health department, as was required by law. Houses deemed unsanitary were "disinfected" by spraying or burning chemicals in affected rooms and removing and incinerating infected bedding and clothing. In rural areas, small houses were covered with canvas tents to facilitate the fumigation of germs and pests, and in some cases, especially in the *sertão*, where bubonic plague was endemic, houses were burned down as a so-called "sanitary measure."[40] The reported number of plague cases in rural *municípios* declined as the number of disinfections increased, but this decrease may have been a testament to local residents' fear of the Disinfection Service rather than its sanitary or medical effectiveness.

The Disinfection Service was also employed to prevent epidemics. Between 1912 and 1918, approximately 75 percent of the disinfections carried out in Pernambuco were classified as "preventive" rather than as responses to specific reports of disease, which indicates that public health officials had gone beyond attempting to control the spread of disease and were engaged in efforts to improve sanitary conditions and prevent diseases.[41] As Steven Williams has shown in his study of mosquito control measures in northeastern Brazil, public health services had political as well as health benefits; the disinfection and fumigation of houses and neighborhoods demonstrated that the government was responding to public health threats, regardless of whether their efforts actually provided any medical benefits.[42] The same was true for Recife's Disinfection Service. While the service may have done little to improve Pernambucans' general health or to prevent epidemics, citizens could take comfort in the fact that public health workers were out in the streets working on the problem.

By the turn of the century, the public health department had begun using "sanitary police," a cadre of public health officers charged with enforcing public health laws and controlling diseases. According to the state's public health code of 1905, the sanitary police were responsible for "removing any cause prejudicial to public health" and inspecting houses, places of business, and public spaces for infractions of the public health code.[43] By 1912, the sanitary police had evolved into a service dedicated to controlling mosquitoes, which by this time were known to be a disease vector for both malaria and yellow fever.[44] From 1852 to 1919, yellow fever had caused 2,757 deaths in Recife, with most coming during epidemics that struck in 1849, 1871 to 1873, 1895, 1901, 1909, and 1912. There were relatively few cases in other years, and the disease produced, on average, only 8.7 deaths per year between 1896 and 1918.[45] Nevertheless, the "mosquito police" became a highly visible presence throughout Recife and its suburbs. When the mosquito population increased to dangerous levels or when isolated cases of yellow fever produced concern about a potential outbreak, public health officials increased the frequency of visits, claiming that every building in Recife was inspected on a biweekly basis. Even in years when the number of deaths from the disease remained low, public health officials continued their inspections. The service recorded 571,483 actions in 1913 and 579,732 actions in 1914.[46] Although a budget crisis forced cutbacks and the service recorded only 45,100 actions in 1915, by 1919, funding had been partially restored and the service recorded 252,824 actions.[47] As with the Disinfection Service, citizens were comforted by the visible presence of mosquito police in the streets of the state capital.

Public and political interest in and support for public health efforts increased substantially with the founding of Recife's Faculdade de Medicina in 1915.[48] Classes were first held at the Faculdade do Direito, and in 1920 the medical school moved to a new location and matriculated its first class of fifteen students.[49] The Faculdade de Medicina soon offered courses in medicine, surgery, orthopedics, gynecology, pediatrics, psychiatry, and public medicine. At the inauguration of a course in public medicine, Edgar Altino Correia de Araújo, a faculty member in clinical medicine, spoke about "the true role of hygiene," arguing that, "effectively, deadly and varied endemics (paludism [malaria], Chagas disease [American sleeping sickness], and ancylostomiasis to cite only three of these deadly scourges) exist and spread out through our fields, making invalids of our people of the interior and preparing for Brazil a generation of physical and mental degenerates." The solution to the problem, Altino argued, was to utilize "prophylactic measures" to "destroy the diseases and restore our citizens' health, vigor, and pleasure in work that dignifies and encourages, preparing and executing the grand work of the incessant progress of our nation."[50]

The Faculdade de Medicina would contribute to the expansion of public health in Pernambuco in several important ways. First, although the graduating classes were small, Pernambuco's public health department could count on a pool of new physicians to fill its posts. This human resource was critical because, as the department's directors often noted, they had difficulty hiring physicians, especially in the interior of the state. The medical school was created, in part, to serve public interests. The school's first two directors, José Octávio de Freitas (1915–1920, 1921–1935) and Manoel Gouveia de Barros (1920–1921), both served simultaneously as directors of Pernambuco's public health department, and most faculty members held positions in state government in addition to attending to their private practices.[51] Second, the presence of a medical school reinforced growing public and government interest in medicine and public health as a valid approach to social and economic problems. Just as the faculty of the law school had been consulted in the reform and expansion of Pernambuco's legal system after the founding of the republic (and in fact the majority of elected officials had been trained at the law school), the Faculdade de Medicina's professors provided the technical expertise needed to support the state's expanding public health bureaucracy as well as professional validation of the increasingly popular notion that improvements in public health and economic progress were two sides of the same coin.

In the realm of ideas, the early-twentieth-century efforts to control diseases in Pernambuco produced a wealth of empirical data about the state's citizens. Faculdade de Medicina professors produced research on common local and regional diseases and public health problems, the results of which were published in a number of Pernambucan medical journals, theses written by graduate students, and *concurso* theses (submitted by prospective faculty competing for teaching positions). The *Jornal de Medicina de Pernambuco* (1905–) and later the *Revista Medica de Pernambuco* (1931–1948), among others, provided the Pernambucan medical community with a forum for not only publishing research but also discussing the social and political dimensions of medicine and public health.

In the first and only issue of *Archivos de Hygiene Publica e Medicina Tropical,* published in 1915 by Pernambuco's Directorate of Hygiene, Gouveia de Barros, the journal's editorial director, wrote that "the problem of sanitation in the State of Pernambuco, and with it, economic issues, involves the study of the more profound scientific questions connected with climatology, nosology, and medical geography." The journal's mission was to educate public health officials and physicians about "our NATURE," which, he argued, would "provide the most salient benefits to the State, in attempting to elucidate questions already important to the scientific study of orienting and systematizing administrative and legislative precautions and measures in relation to the most vital interests of our collective."[52] This rational, scientific approach to the problem of improving Pernambucans produced what were at times contradictory opinions about the economic value of the state's citizens. Local politicians and public health officials remained almost blindly optimistic about the prospects for improving Pernambucans. While poverty, unemployment, disease, and hunger were common among the lower and working classes, Pernambucan elites rarely expressed negative opinions about their own people. According to the positivist logic typical of the period, the Pernambucan masses were merely the victims of disease. If germs could be eliminated and epidemics controlled, so the reasoning went, then Pernambucans and, by extension, all *nordestinos*, could become healthy and productive citizens. In 1909, Pernambuco's governor, Herculano Bandeira de Mello, reflecting on improvements wrought by the state's public health services, wrote that he was "certain that in a short time, . . . Recife will become one of the most salubrious cities, in accordance with its climate and magnificent topographic location."[53] Thus, those who patiently applied modern medical techniques would be rewarded with a prosperous future.

Ironically, the expansion of public health services in the 1910s and 1920s also raised the alarm for those who were less optimistic about Pernambucans' potential. Epidemic diseases always returned, they reasoned, and as more and more Pernambucans took advantage of public health services, officials began to realize that most suffered from at least one, if not several, chronic debilitating diseases. By the late 1910s, it was apparent that the citizens of Pernambuco, and indeed the entire Northeast, were not as healthy as had previously been thought. Even José Octávio de Freitas bluntly stated in 1919 that Recife was "the city in Brazil *where more die*," and Pernambuco's governor admitted that the city's death rates were the highest in the nation.[54] In spite of free vaccinations, the Disinfection Service, and the sanitary police, little could be done to avoid epidemics of smallpox and yellow fever that could, in any given year, lead to thousands of deaths. Although medical researchers had discovered the causes of several epidemic diseases and public health campaigns had proven that these diseases could, under ideal conditions, be controlled, Pernambucan public health officials and politicians must have been frustrated to learn that mortality rates were higher in the 1910s than they had been in the 1880s. Public health officials' grave concerns about Pernambucans' health would soon be confirmed by federal and foreign public health authorities who carried out their own medical surveys of Pernambuco in the 1910s.

The Oswaldo Cruz Institute Surveys of the Northeast

Beginning in the 1910s, national and international public health organizations began to establish a presence in northeastern Brazil. There were several factors that prompted federal authorities to take an interest in public health in the region. The federal government's interest originated with efforts to mitigate the effects of the periodic droughts and to control the spread of yellow fever from port to port. Like their Pernambucan counterparts, federal authorities were concerned about epidemic diseases possibly spreading via commercial shipping or with refugees who were fleeing drought conditions. Federal and Pernambucan officials also kept an eye out for ways to provide the interior of the state with both new economic opportunities and employment for those who could not find jobs in the sugar industry. In 1914, federally appointed governor Emygdio Dantas Barreto wrote that "the exploration of land, an unending source of riches, deserves our most spirited attention."[55] There was, however, little scientific or practical information about the northeastern *sertão* that could be used to develop policies and reform projects. To remedy this, the Inspectoria Federal de Obras Contra as Secas (IFOCS) commissioned the Oswaldo Cruz Institute of Rio de Janeiro to conduct scientific surveys of the northern and northeastern *sertão*. From 1912 to 1914, three expeditions of physicians and scientists surveyed the region and produced detailed reports about geography, human populations, diseases, and economic activities.[56] As historians of the Brazilian public health movement have argued, the knowledge of medical and public health conditions in the interior contained in these reports proved instrumental to the development of federal public health services and Brazilian state-building efforts of the 1920s.[57] The reports of the expeditions were published in the *Memorias do Instituto Oswaldo Cruz*, Brazil's leading scientific journal, and later circulated among federal legislators. The reports were based on the expedition leaders' daily journal of their activities, with entries noting unique species of plants and animals, diseases, and general observations of life in the interior. In each village, the physicians examined the locals for signs of unusual and unknown diseases. Medical care was either nonexistent or beyond the means of most *sertanejos* who sought out the expedition physicians for a consultation upon hearing of their arrival. The physicians treated *sertanejos* as best they could, given their limited medical supplies, but they seemed more interested in compiling an inventory of epidemic and endemic diseases, and especially in verifying cases of the recently discovered Chagas disease. The physicians carefully noted diseases unique to the region, some quickly dismissed as mere folk superstition and others deemed worthy of further investigation.[58]

Although historians have emphasized the role that the Oswaldo Cruz Institute surveys played in focusing public and political attention on the considerable medical, social, and economic problems of the northeastern *sertão,* they have not adequately scrutinized the expedition leaders' consistent condemnation of *sertanejos* and the region as a whole. Arthur Neiva and Belisário Penna, the two physicians who led a survey of Bahia, Pernambuco, Piauí, and Goiás, concluded that they had "become acquainted with almost all the states of Brazil, and it saddens us to say that, with the exception of the states of the South, . . . almost all the others, excepting the capitals and some *municípios,* are vast abandoned territories, forgotten by rulers, with populations vegetating in misery and obscurantism . . . defeated by drought in central Brazil and by annihilating diseases."[59] The Oswaldo Cruz physicians believed that there were several reasons for the region's backwardness. Neiva and Penna wrote that *sertanejos'* weakened physical state, which they believed resulted from difficult living conditions produced by the drought and the depressed regional economy, led to a decreased resistance to disease. This weakened state was thus behind the high rates of epidemic and endemic diseases in the interior. The absence of rudimentary medical services, physicians, hospitals, and pharmacies contributed to the dire public health conditions to be found in the interior. Neiva and Penna also cited government indifference to the plight of *nordestinos* and to antiquated forms of labor, which demonstrated that "the North has shown itself incapable of progressing with free labor, the origin of the material development of the South."[60] In addition, they believed that low literacy levels, which they estimated at 95 percent in some isolated areas and attributed to the lack of even elementary public education, prevented *sertanejos* from becoming informed citizens:

> It is rare to find an individual who knows what Brazil is. Piauí is one land, Ceará another, Pernambuco another, and the same with the other states. The government is, for these pariahs, a person who rules the people, and they are aware of the existence of government because this *person* rules through the annual collection of taxes. Asked if these lands (Piauí, Ceará, Pernambuco, etc.) are connected with each other, constituting one nation, one country, they said that they did not understand any of this. We were, for them, *gringos,* lords (foreign fidalgos). The only flag they know is that of the Divine.[61]

In their survey reports, expedition leaders often made note of *sertanejos'* racial background, suggesting that race was a factor in the region's backwardness.[62] Neiva and Penna pointed out that there were many *negros* and *caboclos* (*mestiços* of African and Indian ancestry) in the interior, and they carefully recorded the presence or absence of whites in each town. In southern Goiás, they noted that "the white element already predominates and the inhabitants are more vigorous."[63] In their report on the São Francisco valley, Adolpho Lutz and Astrogildo Machado wrote that "in regard to the population, it is worth noting that the Indian element is almost zero. Nevertheless, the black race is present in large numbers, and is in many cases predominant. Among the natives, it is not rare to find places where there is a complete absence of the white element. This, naturally, greatly influences the characteristics of a population that generally lives in a very primitive fashion."[64]

The expeditions' leaders equated whiteness with health and economic progress and, conversely, blackness with disease and indolence. The physicians not only considered *sertanejos* racially inferior to the whiter populations of coastal areas and southern Brazil but also believed that the primitive social and cultural surroundings of the *sertão* itself produced atavistic characteristics and behaviors among *sertanejos*. They noted among local populations some traditional "African habits" such as tooth filing, which was offered as further evidence of regional backwardness.[65] Put simply, they believed that *sertanejos* had regressed to their primitive origins in the vast expanse of the *sertão*, beyond the civilizing influences of modern Brazilian society.[66]

Thus, to the physicians, *sertanejos*, especially those of African ancestry, symbolized the primitive while European immigrants represented progress. Neiva and Penna recounted the story of an Italian immigrant who worked for a *fazendeiro* in a drought-stricken area, transforming the arid land into a thriving garden. For Neiva and Penna, this one example constituted evidence of European immigrants' ability to improve the *sertão*, a task they believed native *sertanejos* incapable of completing. In their report, Neiva and Penna noted that they had encountered only eighteen foreigners in their travels and wrote that "for us this fact explains the overwhelming backwardness of these parts; the progress of Brazil is, in large part, due to foreigners."[67] Like most Brazilian intellectuals and scientists, Neiva and Penna accepted the notion of *branqueamento*, or whitening, the theory that a steady influx of white immigrants from Europe would lead to a gradual "whitening" of the nation's citizens through miscegenation and the natural decline of the nation's nonwhites.[68] *Branqueamento* was also explicitly linked to notions of social and economic progress. Neiva and Penna considered European immigration to be an indispensable aspect of plans to develop the *sertão* and suggested that federal and state authorities should endeavor to "intelligently explore the land, populate it with able and wise men, and give them . . . exact instructions and knowledge of the prophylaxis of regional diseases, all of which are avoidable with rational and continual assistance and with the learned laws of the careful perfection of the races."[69] They found it incomprehensible that northeastern political leaders had done so little to promote immigration and blamed those leaders for perpetuating the myth that the tropics were inhospitable to Europeans. While Penna later explicitly rejected race as a cause of *nordestino* inferiority in his *Saneamento do Brasil,* which was published in 1918 in order to strengthen public and political support for public health, his overall opinion of *nordestinos* did not change significantly from his original expedition report of 1916.[70] As part of his proposal for improving social and economic conditions in rural Brazil, Penna wrote that "the vast Brazilian territory cannot be populated without the cooperation of the foreign element."[71] Nísia Trindade Lima and Gilberto Hochman argue that Penna and Neiva rejected romantic portrayals of *sertanejos* and instead provided a "real description" of life in the interior based on their own observations. While Penna and Neiva were more objective in their portrayal of the *sertão* than those who had never traveled or visited the area, to argue that their assessment of the region and its peoples was free from the influence of contemporary social, cultural, and political ideologies is misleading. The pair believed that there was no place for the poor, diseased, uneducated, and racially inferior *sertanejo* in the region's or the nation's future.[72]

The public health surveys of the northeastern *sertão* had two important effects. First, the knowledge of sanitary conditions in the interior prompted officials to establish the federal Rural Preventive Health Service in 1918. Belisário Penna successfully raised public and political awareness of the plight of *sertanejos* in a series of newspaper articles that described the problems in the interior and proposed national legislation for new public health services.[73] The resulting Rural Preventive Health Service, which was funded by the federal government and received technical assistance from the Rockefeller Foundation, was given the task of improving sanitary and public health conditions rural areas of the nation.[74] The second and more important effect of the health surveys was the way in which the Oswaldo Cruz Institute expeditions shaped both popular and expert opinions about *nordestinos.* The survey reports and Penna's articles purported to offer incontrovertible scientific evidence that *sertanejos,* and by extension all *nordestinos,* were inferior to other Brazilians. What was novel about the Oswaldo Cruz Institute surveys' medical assessments of *nordestinos* was the notion that the most pressing public health issue was not epidemic diseases such as smallpox, yellow fever, and the plague but endemic diseases such as malaria and Chagas disease. Officials of the Rural Preventive Health Service designed programs that concentrated on treating these chronic, debilitating diseases, which Penna argued left workers in a physically weakened state. In *Saneamento do Brasil* he wrote that "seventy-five percent or more of the Brazilian population, rural and urban, consists of anemic individuals, with a level of hemoglobin and number of red cells in their blood below and far below normal, in addition to other abnormalities." Penna concluded that there was a "perfect relationship between general diseases . . . and the proclaimed indolence and incapacity of the indigenous worker."[75] In short, the problem was not that *sertanejos* were dying from epidemic diseases but that they were living with debilitating endemic diseases. This view was a significant departure from the view held by northeastern public health officials and politicians, and it indeed shattered the myth that the *sertão* was intrinsically healthy.

Historians have argued that the Oswaldo Cruz Institute surveys and Belisário Penna's advocacy fundamentally changed the ways in which *sertanejos* and *nordestinos* were viewed. One argument, which a close reading of the surveys contradicts, is that the surveys' authors rejected racial determinism in their explanations of *nordestinos'* apparent backwardness.[76] While the physicians rejected race as a factor in susceptibility to diseases, they clearly understood *nordestinos* to be racially inferior. Historians have also argued that the creation of the Rural Preventive Health Service and the National Department of Public Health constituted an attempt to integrate rural Brazil, including the Northeast, into the national collective. According to this view, public health reformers recognized and attempted to address the myriad medical, public, and social problems faced by rural northeastern populations. While understandings of national identity were changing rapidly in this period, especially because of heightened national pride during and after World War I, it cannot be argued that the Rural Preventive Health Service's mission was to prepare *nordestinos* for the labor markets of the South or that the diseased, backward *nordestino* (as portrayed in the Oswaldo Cruz Institute surveys) in any sense compared favorably to the idealized white European immigrant worker that was so prominent a feature of Brazilian national identity.[77]

Instead, the most significant concept to arise from the national public health movement of the 1910s was the medicalization of *nordestinos*. Penna's notion that *nordestinos* suffered long-term, debilitating effects from endemic diseases was novel and much more pessimistic than previous medical assessments of *nordestinos*. While northeastern public health officials regarded *nordestinos* to be victims of epidemic diseases that could be controlled, national public health officials saw *nordestinos* themselves as the fundamental problem. The widespread acceptance of this idea among national public health officials indicated the increasing inability of northeastern intellectuals, scientists, and politicians to shape national debates about northeastern regional identity and development. In the face of overwhelming scientific evidence of *nordestino* inferiority, northeastern physicians and public health officials found themselves in a difficult position. While they wanted to raise national awareness of social and economic problems in the region in order to receive financial support from the federal government, they took issue with the increasingly negative assessments of *nordestinos* expressed by federal reformers and public health officials. This bleak view of *nordestinos* would be reinforced by North American experts who arrived in the late 1910s on a philanthropic mission to rid Brazil of epidemic diseases.

The Rockefeller Foundation in Northeastern Brazil

As more than one historian has pointed out, the history of public health in northeastern Brazil in the early twentieth century cannot be told without including the efforts of the Rockefeller Foundation.[78] Considerable attention has been paid to the foundation's activities in Brazil, especially in Rio de Janeiro and São Paulo, but little light has been shed on its activities in northeastern Brazil. In addition to carrying out biomedical research and promoting medical education in Brazil, the Rockefeller Foundation conducted public health campaigns against hookworm disease, yellow fever, and malaria.[79] The foundation's public health officers introduced new medical ideas and practices that differed significantly from those of their Brazilian counterparts.

The most influential change wrought by the foundation was in the treatment of ancylostomiasis, which, despite substantial research carried out by Bahian researchers in the nineteenth century, received little clinical attention in the Northeast prior to the foundation's arrival in Brazil in 1916.[80] For Brazilian physicians and public health officials, ancylostomiasis represented a fundamentally different type of disease. The disease was not only common among the poor, especially rural agricultural workers, but also was understood to have lasting, debilitating effects on its victims. Physicians knew that hookworms entered their human hosts through the feet and that those most likely to acquire the parasite were the poor, who often could not afford to purchase shoes or construct latrines. Hookworms settled in the digestive tract and fed on their host's blood supply, reducing the volume of oxygen-carrying blood and thus diminishing the "vitality" of the victim. Rockefeller Foundation officials estimated that ancylostomiasis reduced victims' so-called productive capacity by 20 percent and argued that untreated individuals could sustain a hookworm infestation for years, struggling through life unable to reach their full economic potential. Officials also argued that the disease diminished resistance to other diseases and had a profound effect on the development of "future workers" because "infected children are known to be physically and intellectually retarded."[81] Several foundation officials stationed in Brazil had participated in efforts against hookworm in the southern United States between 1909 and 1915 and, in applying that experience to Brazil, argued that ancylostomiasis was a physically debilitating disease that seriously compromised the ability of rural workers to labor effectively.[82]

The Rockefeller Foundation's initial efforts to eliminate hookworm disease in southern Brazil proved to be a medical and political success. Pernambucan public health officials moved quickly to treat the disease. In 1918, state public health officials conducted independent surveys of two coastal islands located near Recife—Pina and Itamaracá. Results showed that 75 to 79 percent of the population was infected with hookworms. The Pernambucan Directorate of Hygiene then organized a treatment service, modeled on Rockefeller Foundation services, which they hoped would "combat ancylostomiasis, the terrible infestation that has already pauperized and annihilated the inhabitants of the state."[83] In its first year of operation, the hookworm service worked on Pina, close to Recife, and public health officers examined 1,402 individuals, of which 1,206, or 86 percent, tested positive for hookworms.[84] Of those who tested positive, 40 percent received treatment via purgatives. Only 4 individuals were declared cured after two treatments—a cure rate of 0.3 percent. Officials offered no explanation as to why so few who tested positive received treatment or why drug treatments failed. Their attempts to address hookworm disease were disappointing on two counts. First, their surveys and field work indicated that almost the entire rural population suffered from the disease, and second, they could do almost nothing about it.

In 1920, Pernambucan officials, realizing that their own efforts to control hookworm disease had failed to produce results, invited the Rockefeller Foundation to conduct a hookworm survey of the state. Foundation officials found that a staggering 93.4 percent of the population was infected with hookworms and that 97.1 percent showed some variety of parasitic worm infection.[85] Fred Soper, the author of the survey, speculated on the causes of these high rates of infection and wrote that the "lack of proper housing facilities and low standard of living are responsible for many of the health problems of Pernambuco." Although Soper found differences in infection rates among different racial groups, he noted that "there is a small but increasing difference in percentage of infection as we go from the white race to the Indian[,] who has less idea of hygiene and a lower standard of living than the other races."[86] In other words, differences in infection rates were attributable to economic and social conditions rather than racial susceptibility to disease. Soper's superiors proved more willing to attribute differing infection rates to race, especially when comparing São Paulo and Rio de Janeiro, which had lower rates, with Pernambuco. In a 1920 report, Wickliffe Rose, director of Rockefeller Foundation activities in Brazil, claimed that "the northern boundary of the State of São Paulo divides Brazil into two sections presenting contrasts, with respect to populations, as sharp as those between Mexico and the United States." He asserted that the populations of northeastern Brazil were "composed of shiftless blacks, parasitic whites of Portuguese origins, and a large percentage of their hybrid progeny, with traces here and there of Indian characteristics."[87] Rose's thoughts on race reflected not only his own racial biases but also the prevailing Brazilian racial ideologies. For Rockefeller Foundation officials, the geographies of race and disease were congruent. They believed that the high rates of infection in the Northeast were attributable, in part, to the racial background of the region's populations.

After the foundation's initial hookworm survey of Pernambuco, state officials contracted the Rockefeller Foundation to take over operation of the state's hookworm service. The state also established new public health posts in the sugar-growing region and the semiarid *agreste* region of the interior.[88] At the inauguration of the first post, Pernambucan governor José Rufino Bezerra Cavalcanti extolled the social and public health benefits of the service, stating that the state's rural workers should not be left to "the stratagems of paludism, hookworm disease, miasmic fevers, and other diseases."[89] He was concerned that ancylostomiasis could lead to a decline in agricultural production and eventually to "our ruin and, consequently, the depopulation of the fields, the congestion of the cities, the augmentation of the number of unemployed, and, finally, a threat to health of the race." Cavalcanti argued that the Rockefeller Foundation–run Postos de Profilaxia Rural would ensure a "rapid and systematic cure for a population attacked by verminosis and malaria," while Gouveia de Barros, Pernambuco's director of hygiene and public health, argued that the public health posts marked "the beginning of this highly human and national plan, to raise the moral and material level of our workers."[90]

Recife's medical and professional community rapidly assimilated Rockefeller Foundation officials' understanding of the disease. At a lecture delivered to Recife's Society of Medicine and Tropical Hygiene, Joaquim Pimenta suggested that hookworm disease "retards the growth of the child, predisposing it to rickets, tuberculosis, and syphilis, making it infected, wanting, and unfit for life; [and] in adults extinguishes the desire for work and courage, the spirit of initiative, the joy of life that is characteristic of healthy organisms." To mitigate the effects of ancylostomiasis, he deemed it essential "to cultivate and teach the best of life, to convince the most obtuse spirits that health and prosperity are one and the same; to remodel our people, physically, morally, and intellectually by rational and positive processes, to combat the microbes with the same vehemence that we destroy the preconceptions of those who disorient the mind."[91] Although Pernambucan elites were wary of the increasing influence of federal and foreign authority in the state, they nonetheless embraced the idea that the state's rural and urban workers suffered from debilitating diseases. As intellectuals, professionals, and government officials struggled to understand the causes of the region's economic decline, diseases and their cures offered an explanation of and remedy for the region's social and economic ills. The evidence of ancylostomiasis among a large percentage of Pernambucan workers provided a scientific explanation for the region's decline that avoided more complicated discussions of political economy.

In 1923, Rockefeller Foundation officials, satisfied with the results of the hookworm campaign, shifted their focus to conquering yellow fever in Brazil.[92] The foundation, in cooperation with the National Department of Public Health, created the Yellow Fever Commission and undertook a nationwide campaign against yellow fever until 1940.[93] Rockefeller Foundation officials utilized the so-called intensive method to control mosquito populations: instead of concentrating on controlling adult mosquitoes, the Yellow Fever Commission focused on killing mosquito larvae and eliminating deposits of standing water in which they matured.[94] The Yellow Fever Commission employed hundreds of workers, in both urban and rural areas, including North American and Brazilian physicians, *guardas* (inspectors), and support staff. In 1932, the commission carried a payroll of 502 and 374 employees in Pernambuco and Bahia, respectively, the two most populous states in the Northeast.[95]

Mosquito control efforts consisted of dividing urban areas into zones with inspection routes that *guardas* would follow on a weekly schedule. *Guardas* inspected houses for adult mosquitoes, mosquito larvae, and breeding places, which included any standing water in which mosquitoes could deposit their eggs. Because most houses were not connected to the public water supply, even in wealthy urban neighborhoods, citizens kept household water supplies in various storage containers, including cisterns, water boxes, barrels, and *jarras,* or earthenware jugs. *Guardas* were to eliminate breeding places using a variety of techniques, including dumping water from *jarras* that contained larvae, oiling containers (which deprived larvae of oxygen by producing an impermeable oil film on the water's surface), placing larvae-eating fish in cisterns, and summarily destroying unprotected *jarras* on second or third "offenses."[96] It was, of course, impossible to eliminate all standing water in a tropical climate. Rain could collect virtually anywhere—in a discarded tire, a plant pot, or the crook of a tree. In collaboration with municipal and state public health authorities, Yellow Fever Commission officials used Brazilian public health laws to lend legitimacy to their efforts, and they relied on the police, the military, and local magistrates to ensure compliance with their prescriptions. By the mid-1920s, Yellow Fever Commission *guardas* had became a common, if unwelcome, sight in urban and rural areas of Pernambuco.

It might seem that Brazilians should have welcomed the Yellow Fever Commission's efforts, but Brazil's physicians, public health officials, the press, and the general public questioned the foundation's objectives and methods. Popular resistance to the Yellow Fever Commission took several forms. Most numerous were complaints about the public comportment of the commission's *guardas.* The service diaries that commission officials were required to keep as part of their administrative duties were replete with complaints about rudeness, improper behavior toward women, petty theft, and the inconvenience of weekly visits. These types of complaints were neither uncommon nor unexpected—the Yellow Fever Commission employed hundreds of *guardas,* and disputes were bound to arise. In response to each complaint, a *guarda-chefe* (or chief inspector) was sent to investigate, and if complainants were still not satisfied, they could appeal to a Brazilian or North American administrator. Occasionally, encounters between *guardas* and citizens turned violent. Commission officials' service diaries provide numerous examples of citizens and *guardas* physically attacking each other, wielding razors, knives, and guns. One official noted that he had come to expect a certain degree of violent resistance to the commission's inspections, but he did not believe that "it was fair to instruct our *guardas* to enforce the state sanitary code if they ran the risk of being murdered for so doing."[97] Despite the frequency of violence, commission officials believed that the public, rather than the commission's own "intensive method," was to blame. They also believed the inflammatory local press was partly responsible because it portrayed the commission's work in a negative light. Commission officials believed their mission was morally, socially, and medically justified, and they adopted a surprisingly callous attitude when citizens who refused to comply with commission orders were accidentally injured or killed. In one incident in Recife, a young woman was badly burned while using alcohol to clean a *jarra* that had been oiled by a commission *guarda*. Lucian Smith, the commission director in Pernambuco, discussed the incident with Gouveia de Barros, Pernambuco's director of public health, who characterized it as a "merited castigation." Barros then told Smith of an incident he witnessed in which a woman who had repeatedly resisted a commission officer's instructions to cover an open well fell in and drowned. Smith wrote that the incident "looked very much like retribution for [an] offense against the sanitary code" and likened the episode to "childhood stories of swift, sudden, and devastating judgments from Heaven to 'fit the crime.'" Smith reasoned that "a little serious preaching of this doctrine might prove potential propaganda."[98]

Complaints and resistance raised questions of individual rights and social justice. Some citizens simply refused to allow *guardas* into their homes. Porter J. Crawford, the Yellow Fever Commission's director of Pernambucan operations in 1928, noted that, especially among the upper classes, "native Brazilians are found who have an inborn sense of individual rights—the home being supreme over State rights."[99] Foundation officials grudgingly admitted that many citizens did not appreciate *guardas* entering their homes and dispensing advice on how their households should be run.

Public resistance to the Yellow Fever Commission's campaign grew in 1927 when Gouveia de Barros decided that the campaign provided an opportunity to eliminate *jarras,* as he put it, "once and for all." The Yellow Fever Commission and Pernambuco's public health department used articles published in government newspapers and educational propaganda to make the public aware of the danger of *jarras*.[100] *Guardas* were ordered, on Barros's authority, to destroy all *jarras* containing mosquito larvae. The campaign produced considerable resistance among the general public because water storage containers, as well as the water in them, were expensive to replace. The Recife press was quick to criticize the campaign. One reporter asked a Pernambucan public health official what citizens should do to replace their *jarras,* and the official suggested that gasoline or kerosene cans, purchased from the Rockefeller Foundation or the local Standard Oil depot, could be used as replacements. When questioned about the suitability of fuel cans as water storage containers, the official admitted that they were not ideal: "They rust, to be sure 'but rust is good for health. Rust is iron . . . we need iron.'" The reporter emphasized the absurdity of this claim and clearly illustrated the predicament of those who had their *jarras* destroyed. Suitable replacements were difficult to locate and, for the poor, they were prohibitively expensive. He concluded by noting that "the fight against the striped stegomyia, transmitter of yellow fever, has been turned into a burlesque comedy, with humorous aspects."[101]

Resistance to the "broken jar" campaign was especially notable in poor and working-class neighborhoods. One commission official noted that "among the *mocambos* the time of visits is regular, as everywhere else, plus that when the *guarda* enters the zone for his regular visit, everyone knows it at once by some mysterious communication and the 'donors' have plenty of time to hide jars."[102] As the campaign progressed into its second year, officials began to realize the impossibility of eliminating *jarras* in a city where plumbed water was the exception rather than the rule. On October 5, 1930, as part of the revolution that brought Getúlio Vargas to power, the state government was overthrown and demonstrations were held throughout the city both for and against the provisional government. One group of demonstrators "sacked and burned" Gouveia de Barros's house while shouting "down with Doctor '*quebrajarras*' [broken jars]."[103] On October 13, presumably in order to avoid further antagonizing the public in what was already a volatile political atmosphere, the provisional governor, Julio Celso de Albuquerque Belo, asked Yellow Fever Commission officials to suspend the broken jar campaign, and they readily agreed.

Despite these episodes, the Yellow Fever Commission had some success in gaining the trust and, more importantly, the compliance of the general public. M. E. Connor, summarizing the Rockefeller Foundation's efforts against yellow fever in 1927, wrote that he was "reasonably certain that the average citizen in Brazil will come to the aid of any movement which gives a promise of raising the sanitary standards of his household or community. I have found the general public most responsive to our request and they have given intelligent and continued co-operation in the present campaign."[104] By the late 1920s, Rockefeller Foundation officials had considered the campaign against yellow fever a success.[105] While some Brazilian public health officials complained that American physicians were more concerned with mosquito larvae than victims of yellow fever and questioned whether such an expensive campaign against one disease that produced so few deaths in an average year was a prudent way to spend public funds, Pernambucan politicians and public health officials embraced the Yellow Fever Commission because it constituted an effective model of sanitary policing.[106]

The commission established a public health presence in every household in urban areas, with public health officials regularly inspecting households and scrutinizing Pernambucans' sanitary habits. While the Pernambucan public health department had relied on visiting nurses, disinfection services, and flying brigades of mosquito police in their own efforts to combat epidemic diseases in the 1910s and 1920s, they had not developed services that were as detail oriented and methodical as those of the Yellow Fever Commission. Rockefeller Foundation officials also proved effective in using educational propaganda, existing local public health regulations, the police, and political pressure to further their goals. Despite some resistance, the general public accepted their efforts, and the *guardas* became a highly visible and powerful symbol of government power. The Pernambucan government took advantage of the foundation's technical expertise and deep pockets to advance its own state-building efforts, while foundation officials were satisfied that they had successfully controlled, if not eliminated, two deadly and debilitating diseases in one of the most unhealthy regions of Latin America. Ultimately, the close congruence of Brazilian and Rockefeller Foundation interests explains the success of the Yellow Fever Commission. While there were occasional "refusals," most Pernambucans responded to the *guardas'* knock and request to "*dá licença para a hygiene*" (give permission to hygiene) with "*pode entrar*" (you may enter).[107]

The End of an Era

Within a year of the opening of the first Postos de Profilaxia Rural in Pernambuco in 1920, politicians and public health officials believed that the service had already succeeded in improving sanitary conditions in the region. This belief was based as much on perceived political gains attributed to the new service as on measurable improvements in *nordestinos'* health. In 1921, Gouveia de Barros, chief of the state's Directorate of Hygiene, declared,

> We have enjoyed . . . the benefits of a systematic cure . . . for a population affected by worm disease and malaria. . . . Within a few months we have seen all these people, jaundiced by hookworm and by malaria, permanently tired, without energy and vigor, humbled by their physical condition and enslaved by a moral incapacity that originates in a profound anemia that removes sentiment and intelligence, . . . return to their rude cabins with faces colored by blood rich in hemoglobin and the rays of an ardent sun, with minds satisfied and able to feel and think of a happy and more comfortable existence, which produces more human aspirations in their inferior lives.[108]

Despite his doubts about *nordestinos'* character, Barros expressed his complete faith in the ability of the Rural Preventive Health Service to improve public health and economic conditions in the Pernambucan interior. Joaquim Pimenta, the law school faculty member who had embraced hookworm disease as an explanation for regional backwardness, argued that effective public health and educational programs would "liberate us from degeneracy and death."[109] Public health officials and politicians argued that the considerable cost of funding the health posts, which was split among the Rockefeller Foundation, the federal government, and municipal governments, was justified.[110] They believed that public health programs were an effective means of slowing the region's economic decline, and unlike previous explanations of regional backwardness that focused on race, climate, and geography, diseases could more easily be treated, controlled or, ideally, eradicated through human and government action.

In spite of their initial enthusiasm, Pernambucan officials soon began to realize that there were limitations to the effectiveness of the Rural Preventive Health Service. Because the posts were run by the Rockefeller Foundation, their main focus was initially hookworm disease and then yellow fever rather than *nordestinos'* overall health. Gouveia de Barros argued that public health conditions in the interior required more comprehensive medical services, and he pointed out that the Rockefeller Foundation's preferred treatment for hookworm disease, two rounds of purgatives, provided only a temporary cure. *Nordestinos'* material position had not changed, and they were likely to become re-infected from the same sources because they still could not afford to purchase shoes or build sanitary latrines. Amaury de Medeiros, appointed director of Pernambuco's Department of Health and Assistance in 1923, argued that the posts were ineffective because they were not permanent.[111] Indeed, once drugs had been dispensed in a particular town or village, the post administrators would close shop and move on to a new location. While the number of posts had increased from two in 1922 to seventeen in 1923 to thirty-five in 1924, they were not permanent. Medeiros pointed out that local governments could not afford to underwrite the operation of the posts for more than a short period. When a certain percentage of the population had received treatment for hookworm disease, Rockefeller Foundation officials turned control of posts over to municipal authorities, who had neither the technical expertise nor resources to continue operating them. State support for public health was abruptly reduced in 1921 when a sharp decline in the price of sugar on international markets reduced tax revenues and forced the state government to abandon all but essential services. By 1923, Pernambuco's Department of Health and Assistance had been subjected to several deep budget cuts and was barely functioning. In his 1923 annual report, Pernambuco's governor lamented that "our sanitary organization gives a sad picture of our culture and our development."[112] In 1926, only one state-run health post remained open, in an "old and inappropriate building" in Recife, operating "infrequently and without action."[113] By the mid-1920s, the so-called heroic age of public health had drawn to a close.

Still, Pernambuco's Department of Health and Assistance had made significant gains in improving conditions in the state, if only in the capital and its suburbs. Mortality rates from epidemic diseases such as smallpox, the plague, and yellow fever had fallen significantly, and overall mortality rates in Recife had fallen from an average of 38.3 per thousand for the five-year period of 1910–1914 to 20.5 per thousand in 1926–1929, a 46 percent decline.[114] The situation in the interior was less encouraging, however. While public health services expanded significantly in the northeastern interior in the 1920s, federal and Rockefeller Foundation public health officials were fighting a battle they could not win with the resources they possessed. Unfortunately, the legacy of their efforts was the belief that *nordestinos* were intrinsically unhealthy. Pernambucan politicians and public health officials criticized negative portrayals of *nordestinos*, yet the medicalized *nordestino* justified the creation of public health and social reform programs and, more importantly, federal financial support. Even José Octávio de Freitas, who had consistently argued that climate, geography, and germs were the causes of the region's public health problems, began to believe that *nordestinos* themselves constituted a threat to public health. In 1919, he wrote that the cumulative effect of endemic diseases "had thus created, little by little, a population of weaklings, anemics, and individuals susceptible to all diseases."[115]

As several historians have argued, Brazil's public health movement, especially the creation of the National Department of Public Health and the Rural Preventive Health Service, served both to augment the role of the state in an era dominated by liberal social and political values and to strengthen the power of the centralized federal government in the final years of the federalist First Republic.[116] In the case of Pernambuco, however, the growth and institutionalization of public health took place in a way that reflected local and regional political and economic concerns and reinforced a sense of regional identity. Within Pernambuco, its significance went beyond national reformers' desire to sanitize the *sertão*, prepare workers for jobs in the South, or to create a more inclusive national identity, as some historians have argued. The Pernambucan public health movement also constituted something more than "conservative modernization," a term that has been used to describe economic modernization projects that did not seek a radical reordering of social and economic hierarchies.[117] In the turbulent intellectual and political atmosphere of the 1920s, Pernambucan intellectuals, reformers, and politicians recognized the need to respond to the new challenges of economic change, population growth, urbanization, and industrialization. In so doing, Pernambucan public officials created a model for government-sponsored social reform programs. Although the heroic age of public health had drawn to a close, interest in medicine and public health as a solution to social problems led Pernambucan reformers to embrace new scientific approaches, including social hygiene, eugenics, mental hygiene, and biotypology, which they used in their continuing efforts to improve *nordestinos* in the 1930s and 1940s.

5

Social Hygiene

The Science of Reform, 1925–1940

IN A LECTURE to Recife's Rotary Club in 1935, José Octávio de Freitas, who had served as Pernambuco's chief public health officer and as the director of Recife's Faculdade de Medicina, asserted that in order "to resolve the immense problem of the Healthy Man—the right to a long and normal life," it was necessary "not only to avoid the diseases that encircle Man from all sides and in all stages of life; not only to remove all the various factors of degeneracy, of decadence, and of weakening; but, above all, to seek to elevate him, to perfect him by selection, by eugenics, by complete health, and by the perfect reinvigoration of all of his anatomic organs, physiologically, and psychologically."[1] Late in his career, Freitas, like many Pernambucan physicians and public health officials, had embraced the pseudoscience of eugenics, which he believed would lead to the biological and racial improvement of Pernambucans.

In the mid-1920s, Pernambucan political leaders and reformers initiated a number of social and educational reform programs designed to ensure social and economic progress by improving living conditions, eliminating biological and social diseases, and assisting families in creating healthy and economically productive citizens. The Pernambucan Department of Health and Assistance and Department of Education became the primary vehicles for these reform efforts, which were not unlike those carried out in other Brazilian and foreign cities.[2] Pernambucan reformers were familiar with these efforts as a result of their professional training and postings in southern Brazilian cities and abroad. They did not merely imitate their counterparts, however. They adopted scientific and medical ideas and practices and used them to craft reform programs that addressed specific local and regional needs.

There has been considerable debate among historians about the origins of social reform movements in Brazil.[3] Several historians have asserted that Latin American scientists, physicians, reformers, and politicians unquestioningly followed trends in North American and European science, medicine, public health, and education either because of the weakness of local primary science or because of the degree to which Latin Americans valued Western ideas over local traditions.[4] More recent approaches have posited that national and local contexts, including political reform movements of the 1920s and the growing political importance of social welfare programs under the Vargas governments of the 1930s and 1940s, as well as institutional and professional concerns, contributed to the push for social and economic reform.[5] I take the position, however, that the impetus for the development of social welfare programs in Pernambuco in the late 1920s was local in origin and addressed local concerns. Thus, the study of local and regional social reform projects reveals more about local and regional social, economic, and political contexts than it does about ways in which scientific and medical ideas and practices were taken up in the periphery.[6]

Pernambucan reformers' concerns about social and economic development prompted the creation of reform programs to address the state's most pressing social problems, including workers' health, infant mortality, children's physical development, diet and hunger, and the living conditions of the poor and working classes. At the same time, these reforms advanced new understandings of the relationship between the state and the individual. The Pernambucan social hygiene movement in the 1920s and 1930s reflected the belief that the state possessed the right and the capacity to improve Brazilian society, specifically, to improve the physical development of Pernambucans. These reform projects also exonerated political and economic elites from blame for the state and region's social and economic underdevelopment. By concentrating on Pernambucans' individual deficiencies, politicians and reformers could avoid potentially divisive discussions of social, economic, and racial inequality. These concerns became paramount in the late 1930s, when Pernambucan *interventor* Agamemnon Magalhães used the social reform programs created by progressives to support the conservative social and political agenda of Getúlio

Vargas's regime, known as the Estado Novo. His strategy reveals the ways Pernambucan social reforms were used to advance new conceptions of the relationship between the state, society, and the individual.

The Origins of Social Hygiene

In 1923, Amaury de Medeiros, who had previously served as director of federal public health services in Pernambuco, was appointed director of Pernambuco's Department of Health and Assistance. In this capacity, he introduced a series of services that would transform the department, including prenatal and infant hygiene services, dietary assistance programs, an industrial hygiene service, a school hygiene service, an anthropometry service, a hygiene education and propaganda service, a social hygiene service, and a mental hygiene service. While Pernambucan public health officials remained concerned with controlling diseases and general hygiene and sanitation, the reforms of the late 1920s and 1930s constituted an attempt to remake Pernambucans according to the theories of eugenics, biotypology, and racial psychology.[7] In 1927, Pernambucan governor Estácio de Albuquerque Coimbra had written that "the economic, intellectual, moral, and civic value of the Nation and the State" depended on "the physical and moral robustness of its population."[8] Coimbra believed that the state government should do everything in its power to develop its citizens, who, he believed, through proper management and hard work, could strengthen the regional economy and "support and justify the legitimate aspirations of the greatness of the Nation and of our state." Coimbra presented a detailed reform plan, developed by Medeiros, that identified "three great social causes of public insalubrity: urbanism, industrialism, and pauperism."[9] These social problems, Coimbra argued, were the direct result of Pernambuco's rapid population growth and the increasing industrialization of the state capital and its suburbs. In order to better understand and to address these problems, the Department of Health and Assistance's new Social Hygiene Service was charged with studying "the anthropology and living conditions of different segments of the population," "the reciprocal relations that exist between public health disturbances and social factors and phenomena," and "the collective order, [studies of] which permit the reduction and prevention of the devastations caused by diseases of this origin, prolonging the existence of and bettering the race."[10] At the same time, Pernambucan political leaders authorized and funded social, educational, and economic reforms that they hoped would improve education and living conditions for the poor and the working classes and, ultimately, the state's economy.[11] These efforts were expanded and elaborated under the administrations of Pernambucan governor Coimbra (1926–1930) and federal *interventors* Carlos de Lima Cavalcanti (1930–1937) and Agamemnon Magalhães (1937–1945).

The Pernambucan government's interest in improving its citizens had several origins. First, the state's economic and political elite were concerned with the physical well-being and economic productivity of the working classes. As with the federal government's public health campaigns and drought relief efforts of the 1910s and 1920s, Pernambucan reformers attempted to come to terms with the state's considerable social and economic problems, including periodic droughts, debilitating endemic diseases, so-called social diseases including alcoholism, venereal diseases, malnutrition, and infant mortality, as well as unemployment, low wages, and inadequate housing. Pernambucan reformers were most concerned with agricultural workers. Although planters proved unwilling to increase wages to ensure an improved standard of living for workers, they lobbied the state government to do as much as possible to improve workers' health. In a 1920 report to the state legislature, Governor José Rufino Bezerra Cavalcanti gave voice to the ruling elite's concerns about agricultural production: "[agriculture's] decadence represents our ruin (and consequently, the depopulation of the fields [and] the overcrowding of the cities), augments the number of unemployed, and, in the end, threatens the health of the race." Cavalcanti believed the improvement of workers' health would ensure the further growth and development of the state's agricultural sector. He concluded that social welfare programs were necessary in order to "benefit populations, whose economic value, capacity for work, and social and moral progress have been diminished by disease, with evident and notable prejudice for the economy and the future of our State."[12] Gouveia de Barros, Pernambuco's director of public health, wrote that the state's hookworm service, initiated in 1921, constituted "the highly humanistic and national plan to raise the material and moral level of our workers."[13] The hookworm service constituted a significant shift in government involvement in labor relations. For most of the nineteenth century, the state did not interfere in the patron-client relationship in which employers assumed a certain degree of responsibility toward workers in return for labor and political loyalty. By the late nineteenth century, however, Pernambucan sugar producers' successful transition from slave to wage labor resulted in an erosion of the traditional patron-client relationship. Although many employers provided some health care for workers, in the 1920s the state began to assume a greater responsibility for workers.

Agricultural workers were not the only group to benefit from changing understandings of the "public good" and government responsibility. Pernambucan reformers and politicians took an interest in the living conditions and health of the urban poor and Recife's burgeoning industrial working class. Although elites generally believed that the urban poor held little economic potential, reformers confronted urban problems with the same determination they had shown toward agriculture, even though industrial workers were fewer in number. *Mocambos*, the self-help housing of the urban poor that accounted for almost 50 percent of all housing in Recife in 1923, had long been of concern.[14] In 1916, Pernambuco's governor had reported that "large urban zones are swampy and unhealthy."[15] Unfortunately, the Pernambucan government did not have the material resources to adequately address the structural social and economic inequalities that caused a significant percentage of Recife's population to live in abject poverty. The state government instead endeavored to improve living conditions for the urban poor and working classes by controlling diseases, offering free vaccinations, establishing free health clinics located in working-class neighborhoods, providing food and financial assistance to families, and regulating the location and construction of workers' housing. While the goal of these programs was to create healthy and productive workers, other factors, such as the founding of a Brazilian communist party in 1922, increasing worker activism, the formation of unions, the reformist *tenente* movement, and disillusionment with republican government, led Pernambucan elites to recognize the potential danger of ignoring the plight of the poor and working classes.

Pernambucan social hygiene was also informed by diverse, and at times contradictory, scientific and medical ideas, including social Darwinism, eugenics, biotypology, puericulture, and mental hygiene. As with José Octávio de Freitas and Amaury de Medeiros, eugenics practices, including prenuptial medical examinations, restrictions on immigration, and forced sterilization, proved to have a strong influence. The Brazilian eugenics movement originated with physician and pharmacist Renato Kehl, who founded the Sociedade Eugénica de São Paulo in 1918.[16] The society's membership quickly grew to 140 and included prominent figures in Brazilian medicine, public health, and education, such as Belisário Penna, Arthur Neiva, and Antônio Austregesilo Lima. While the São Paulo society disbanded after Kehl relocated to Rio de Janeiro, professional and political interest in eugenics led to the founding of Rio de Janeiro's Liga de Higiene Mental in 1922 under the leadership of psychiatrist Gustavo Reidel.[17] The organization proved instrumental in advocating for the reform of asylums and psychiatric care and for the application of eugenics in psychiatry and in treatment of the insane and mentally deficient.[18]

Over the course of the 1920s and 1930s, eugenics was widely adopted by Brazilian medical professionals, social reformers, educators, and government officials as a legitimate means of addressing public health and social problems.[19] In 1927, after stepping down as director of Pernambuco's Department of Health and Assistance to become a federal lawmaker, Amaury de Medeiros introduced legislation calling for voluntary prenuptial examinations as a means of promoting eugenic marriages and healthy offspring.[20] After the 1930 revolution that brought Getúlio Vargas to power, Brazilian eugenicists successfully lobbied lawmakers to include in the constitutions of 1934 and 1937 eugenic language that regulated marriage and restricted foreign immigration.[21] As several historians have pointed out, most Brazilian eugenicists did not favor "negative" eugenics, such as involuntary sterilization and euthanasia, which were integral aspects of the North American and European practice of eugenics, and instead favored "positive" eugenics, which emphasized individual and collective hygiene, education, and public health.[22] While eugenics in São Paulo and Rio de Janeiro was taking on overtly racial overtones, Pernambucan eugenicists were carefully avoiding the issue of race and endorsing a more inclusive eugenics that advocated improving all citizens, regardless of race.[23] Because the majority of nordestinos were nonwhite, Pernambucan reformers seldom referred explicitly to race. There was little point in referring to "superior" and "inferior" races if most nordestinos were, according to eugenic theory, racially inferior. Pernambucan reformers thus tailored eugenics to fit northeastern social and racial realities. Science, or, more properly speaking, pseudoscience in the case of eugenics, gained political legitimacy as a means of addressing the considerable social, economic, and political challenges of the 1920s and 1930s.

Another factor that prompted the development of Pernambucan social hygiene was a new view of government responsibility for citizens. The public health reforms of the 1910s and early 1920s were shaped by liberal republicanism and free-market capitalism—Pernambucans were generally treated as individual citizens rather than as members of a social collective. This is not to say that Pernambucan public health officials were not concerned with social dimensions of diseases—the heroic age of public health had taught them that diseases were dangerous because of their potential threat to labor and commerce, which are profoundly social activities—but that the treatment and prevention of diseases focused on the individual. Vaccination, isolation, and disinfection treated the individual rather than society as a whole. By the mid-1920s, growing intellectual, elite, and popular disenchantment with liberalism and the republic produced new social and political ideas, inspired by both Marxism and fascism, in which the individual was understood to be part of an integrated, organic, corporate whole.[24] Pernambucan social hygiene reflected these new political ideas. The historiography on republican politics of the 1920s and the 1930 revolution that brought Getúlio Vargas to power usually presents Pernambuco as disconnected from the main political currents of the era and Pernambucan politicians as being most concerned with maintaining oligarchic rule and the profitability of the sugar industry rather than with social and economic reforms.[25] It is clear, however, that the Pernambucan ruling classes continued to be concerned with improving the regional economy and addressing social problems.[26] The progressive reforms of the 1920s carried out by the Pernambucan state government have been largely forgotten, however, because they were eclipsed by the extensive social, educational, and economic reforms enacted by new federal agencies created during the Vargas era, most notably the Ministry of Labor, Industry, and Commerce and the Ministry of Education and Health. The Pernambucan reforms were significant, however, in that they preceded the 1930 revolution and reflected changing understandings of the nature of Brazilian society and of individual and government responsibility.

Assisting Mothers

Throughout Brazil, the early twentieth century marked the beginning of increased public and political interest in the family as rapidly changing social and economic conditions forced women into the workplace and the public spotlight. While Pernambucan women, especially agricultural workers, had long worked for wages out of economic necessity, urban growth and nascent industrialization created new social and economic opportunities for women that were perceived to be inconsistent with traditional gender roles. Faced with the decline of the patriarchal family, government officials, educators, physicians, employers, social commentators, and reformers blamed women for the decline of the traditional family and attempted to promote traditional roles for women.[27] Increasing government interest in women and the family also reflected the importance of gender and reproduction in understandings of the nation and national identity in the interwar period.[28] Nancy Stepan, in her study of Latin American eugenics, emphasizes the importance of women in the social reforms of the 1920s and 1930s because, as she puts it, "the social role of women was viewed as primarily reproductive."[29] Although there was less male anxiety about women entering the workplace and abandoning their families in Pernambuco than there was in Rio de Janeiro and São Paulo (primarily because there were fewer economic opportunities that were perceived as inconsistent with traditional gender roles), women and the family nevertheless became central concerns for social reformers.[30]

Pernambucan reformers believed that the goals of the Social Hygiene Service could be best achieved by protecting the family from biological, social, and moral diseases that they believed threatened to undermine the foundation of traditional society. Beginning in the nineteenth century, children attracted the attention of physicians and reformers who sought to medicalize childbirth and childrearing.[31] In the 1920s, the Pernambucan government increased funding for services that benefited the family and created new programs designed to provide preventive and clinical care for pregnant women, infants, and school-age children.[32] In 1926, Amaury de Medeiros wrote that "infant hygiene is without doubt the hygiene of the future. I foresee an epoch in which an extensive infant hygiene service will protect the entire new generation and this generation will come to replace the old, with a mentality entirely affected by sanitary questions; it will know where to live and how to live, defending itself against all the causes of insalubrity."[33] By the late 1920s, "infant hygiene" had become a popular cause among Pernambucan reformers and politicians. Governor Coimbra wrote that "the importance of the problems that relate to the child, from the medical, sanitary, and social point of view, must crystallize in the consciousness of the men of the Brazilian government, with the end of making the Brazilian child the object of a true national cult."[34] While political support for infant hygiene reflected a pronatalist nationalism of the 1920s, public health reformers were especially concerned about high infant mortality rates in Pernambuco. The public health campaigns of the 1910s and early 1920s had led public health officials to acknowledge that malnutrition and disease were the primary causes of infant mortality, especially among the poor and working classes. In 1928, Pernambucan public health officials set a goal of reducing infant mortality rates from 169 to 100 per thousand, which they believed could be achieved through a combination of preventive care, educational programs, and public assistance programs for children and families.[35] To this end, the Pernambucan government reorganized several services and created the Infant Hygiene Service, which provided prenuptial, prenatal, and postnatal medical services, a dispensary for food and medicine, and a hygiene education program.[36] In 1930, a supervisory council reported that the service's dispensaries, located in working- and lower-class neighborhoods in Recife, provided daily milk and meals to 100 infants and disbursed weekly cash payments to 150 "poor mothers" to assist them in purchasing food for their children.[37]

The problem of infant mortality was even more daunting outside the state capital. Public health officials realized the importance of improving public health and assistance services in rural areas, and, in 1929, the state legislature created the Pernambucan League against Infant Mortality (Liga Pernambucana contra Mortalidade Infantil), which was dedicated to "making the protection of and assistance for children in Pernambuco more extensive and efficient."[38] The league was funded by a special sales tax on meals and alcoholic beverages served at restaurants, bars, and hotels, in addition to private charitable donations.[39] The league's main concern became the prevention and elimination of so-called hereditary diseases, such as syphilis, tuberculosis, and alcoholism, which reformers and eugenicists believed adversely affected the health of children by way of genes passed down from afflicted parents. In its first year of operation, the league established a "methodological service to investigate hereditary syphilis" that tested both adults and children for the disease.[40] The low population densities of the Pernambucan interior made it impossible to offer permanent medical services in all areas, and prior to the development of antibiotics, little could be done to treat adults and children if they contracted tuberculosis or syphilis. League officials instead focused on education and propaganda and on providing direct assistance to families. By 1934, thirty-five milk stations (*lactários*) had been established in towns and villages where administrators had reported "very alarming" rates of infant mortality.[41] In addition, the league administered nutritional kitchens (*cozinhas dietéticas*) where mothers could receive free meals and information about diet and hygienic child-rearing techniques.[42] The league also took on a moralizing role, counseling rural populations about the supposed eugenic consequences of drinking and extramarital sex.

Pernambucan public health officials believed, however, that the single most important cause of infant deaths was mothers' ignorance about how to feed their infants, and they argued that mortality rates could be reduced if mothers were taught proper feeding techniques. Often their discussions centered on the dangers associated with the use of cow's or goat's milk, or *mingau*, a mixture of wheat or corn flour and water or powdered milk.[43] Physicians and public health officials were highly critical of so-called "artificial nourishment" and generally endorsed breastfeeding.[44] Celso Caldas, who administered a hygiene post in Limoeiro, studied infant mortality in the interior town of Bom Jardim and suggested that mortality rates would fall "if mothers breastfeed their little children, thus giving them specific nourishment, [instead of] substituting an artificial or mixed . . . milk that is frequently made worse by an improper, degraded, and dangerous diet."[45] Public health officials spent little time debating breastfeeding, however, because they were more concerned with whether children were receiving enough food. Officials' approach to infant mortality focused on direct assistance and advice to mothers rather than the implementation of broader social and economic reforms to improve the material well-being of the poor and working classes. The campaign to reduce infant mortality was thus shaped and limited by the political and economic ideals of the First Republic; reforms treated individuals rather than structural economic inequalities.

In addition to providing milk and meals to families, public health officials took an interest in public health education. They believed that a significant obstacle to improving public health was citizens' alleged ignorance regarding even the most basic principles of hygiene. In 1927, Governor Coimbra suggested that "only through systematic and amply disseminated sanitary education in urban centers as well as rural zones will we succeed in helping the population . . . to improve the factors that resist disease, . . . thus transforming each individual into an active collaborator with the sanitary service in the name of the sanitation of the State."[46] João Rodrigues, director of Recife's Children's Hospital, identified mothers' lack of education as a factor contributing to high infant mortality rates.[47] In 1927, the Department of Health and Assistance created a new program, the "School of Sanitary Education," which trained visiting nurses and "hygiene educators."[48] In effect, the government wanted women to pursue not only their traditional roles as wives, mothers, and caretakers of the family but also to transform Pernambucans into healthy, robust citizens. The hygiene educator, who would "leave the 'School of Sanitary Education' with scientific and moral preparation formed by an acquaintance with the real world," was to "organize sanitary services in the factories, schools, *fazendas*, hospitals, and towns."[49] The Department of Health and Assistance also expanded its *visitadora* (visiting nurse) service, which provided medical services and instruction for pregnant women and mothers in their homes, for students in public schools, and for workers in factories. In 1926, the service employed thirty-two *visitadoras*, and in 1932, with additional financial support from the federal government, the service was expanded, with *visitadoras* making 2,876 prenatal and 73,910 postnatal visits. The Department of Health and Assistance's Infant Hygiene Service kept detailed records of births and calculated that 17 percent of all infants were connected with the service and that each was visited, on average, thirty times per year.[50] Administrators admitted that this was a "positively inconceivable" number of visits per child and suggested that supervisors and *visitadoras* should be more concerned with the quality rather than frequency of visits. By 1940, the *visita-*

dora service also included the free distribution of milk, vaccinations for infants, and screening for syphilis and other diseases.[51] In public schools, visiting nurses offered free medical and dental examinations and compiled medical records for students. The collection of data allowed public health officials to measure individual health, physical, and psychological development and the effectiveness of the services they provided, although in their annual reports effectiveness was usually measured by whether more visits had been made than in the previous year.[52]

The significance of the Department of Health and Assistance's programs went far beyond their limited impact on Pernambucans' health. Reformers' efforts extended into the private sphere to treat the family at home. There were, however, limits to the effectiveness of this approach. Direct medical, dietary, and financial assistance to families at home could achieve only so much. What was required was a more comprehensive approach to improving Pernambucans' health, and reformers would soon shift their focus to public institutions, specifically, the state's public schools.

Educating the Masses

In 1920, the Pernambucan public education system was woefully inadequate, providing few educational opportunities for the state's school-age children. Pernambuco's wealthy and privileged families usually sent their children to private Catholic schools, while the children of the poor and working classes attended state-run schools for only a few years before entering the work force.[53] Historically, Pernambuco had school attendance rates considerably lower than those of other Brazilian states and, until the late 1920s, generally spent a smaller percentage of its budget on education than did any other state.[54] There were few public schools outside the capital, and most secondary schools were run by the Catholic Church, with the exception of the Ginásio Pernambucano and the Escola Normal, the latter serving as the state's teacher training institute. In 1921, Pernambucan governor José Rufino Bezerra Cavalcanti lamented the state of education, writing that "the problem of popular instruction continues to torment Brazilian administrators."[55] In 1923, Governor Sérgio Loreto reported that, due to a budget crisis and administrative incompetence, primary education was in a state of "complete and absolute anarchy."[56] The inadequacies of the educational system prompted reformers and politicians to call for the construction of new schools and sweeping curricular reforms that would reflect the latest North American and European research on education and incorporate principles of hygiene and eugenics in order to promote students' intellectual, physical, and moral development. In the reform-minded political climate of the 1920s, educational reform epitomized progress and modernity.[57] Further educational reforms came during the administration of Governor Coimbra, who in his 1926 election campaign proposed a new type of school that, "along with letters and arithmetic, will be able to awaken and strengthen the capacity for action, the love of work, moral integrity, and in sum, the formation of character."[58] Antônio Carneiro Leão, a Recife-born educator who served as director of Rio de Janeiro's public schools from 1922 to 1926 and was hired to evaluate and to design reforms for the Pernambucan educational system, wrote that "it is not possible to construct a lasting modern State without the diffusion of popular education. It is not merely enough to teach literacy; a true education has become necessary."[59] Pernambucan educators and reformers universally embraced this notion that education should do much more than teach basic skills. In 1928, the Pernambucan state legislature approved Carneiro's proposed reforms, which included the construction of new schools, administrative reforms, professional training for teachers and evaluations by pedagogy experts, medical and dental examinations for students, the creation of two technical-professional schools (one for men and one for women), and the creation of the Institute of Professional Selection and Orientation, which utilized psychological testing to evaluate students and assign appropriate courses of study.[60]

Educators and politicians agreed that the proper education of school-age children was essential to their efforts to create healthy citizens. The 1928 reforms specified that hygiene education was to be incorporated into the primary school curriculum. The editor of the state government's professional education journal wrote in 1931 that an important aspect of public education was to encourage the "love and care of the home, the comfort and happiness of life," and "not only to instruct the young in domestic secrets . . . but also to initiate them in the principles of infant hygiene, making them collaborators in the fight against infant mortality."[61] A 1937 report on primary education suggested that instruction in hygiene "ought to be offered persistently so that healthy habits take root in the child." In primary school, girls received special instruction in "postnatal puericulture," including bathing, dressing, and feeding infants.[62] In the first five years of primary school, boys and girls were lectured on the dangers of tobacco and alcohol use, on nutrition (*higiene alimentar*) and childhood diseases, as well as on the importance of "physical and mental vigor as a factor in racial progress."[63]

The 1928 reforms also specified that domestic education courses be incorporated into the primary school curriculum and offered at the technical-professional school for women and that a new four-year "Escola Domestica" be created.[64] Education officials argued that "domestic education" would encourage young women to "take root in the home, furnishing them with an education that has the capacity to make them housewives and knowledgeable in all the mysteries that concern the well-being of the family."[65] The curriculum at the Escola Domestica was to include traditional offerings of Portuguese, either French or English, mathematics and geometry, geography, physical and natural sciences, human anatomy, and physiology, as well as courses on "alimentary hygiene and chemistry," puericulture, music, handwork, drawing, gymnastics and games, culinary arts, washing and ironing, horticulture, pomiculture and gardening, housekeeping, sewing, home economics, and breastfeeding.[66] While the proposed Escola Domestica was never funded, domestic education was incorporated into the curriculum at existing schools.[67]

Educators and reformers justified these curricular changes by arguing that they would benefit both public health and the family. Publio Dias, the director of a hygiene post in the Pernambucan interior, believed that educating children was as important as educating mothers, especially with regard to diet. He argued that for girls, "propaganda regarding maternal diet could be begun without inconvenience in their own schools by the means of an institution called the school of little mothers [escola da mãezinhas]. This would serve to directly reduce infant mortality, which is almost always caused by the mother's ignorance."[68] In an article on "family hygiene," a Pernambucan physician wrote that education for women "ought to begin . . . in the schools in the teaching of puericulture, [as] the base of preparation for future mothers [who are] conscious of [motherhood's] obligations and its valor."[69]

In addition to domestic education, Pernambuco's Department of Education offered technical and professional instruction and training for Pernambucan students at the Escola Profissional Masculina and Escola Profissional Feminina. While instruction for men focused on learning trades, including mechanics, cabinet making, and graphic arts, instruction for women emphasized domestic education and trades that were consistent with traditional gender roles. The four-year program included sewing, handwork, embroidery, lacework, knitting, flower arranging, millinery, domestic arts (including cooking, washing, and ironing), agriculture and animal husbandry, industrial chemistry, domestic economy, shorthand and typing, and accounting.[70] Although research did not uncover evidence of women's motivations for enrolling, the courses were clearly popular; the school's enrollment doubled within a year of its opening.[71] The design of the curriculum reflected the belief that women were to be educated only inasmuch as it prepared them to fulfill traditional gender roles. Carlos de Lima Cavalcanti, appointed *interventor* by Getúlio

Vargas in 1930, summarized the state government's position on women's education when he wrote that it should be "dedicated to the preparation of women for the home, providing them with an education oriented toward an appreciation of the multiple functions that are part of directing family life."[72]

Pernambucan teachers, administrators, and politicians viewed the reform of the state's public education system as an opportunity to shape the moral and social attitudes of the state's school-age children by instilling principles of individual and social hygiene and emphasizing the social and political importance of motherhood and the family. They thus attempted to impose an idealized vision of the family on all Pernambucans, despite the fact that many women needed to work outside the home in order to support their families.[73] The social and educational reforms of the late 1920s and early 1930s were devised by social progressives who hoped to alter Pernambucan society by providing medical and social assistance and new educational opportunities for the poor and working classes. Not all Pernambucans embraced this model, however.

Weeding Out the Undesirables

In the 1920s, Pernambucan reformers and public health officials began to design and implement social, educational, and public health reforms they hoped would "protect future generations" and "improve the race" by regulating the family, marriage, education, and employment. These reforms reflected, in part, the growing influence of eugenics in Brazil, and by the 1920s, Pernambucan physicians and public health officials were increasingly discussing social and public health reforms using the language of eugenics.[74] At the same time, these reforms constituted a response to the economic, social, and political upheavals of the 1920s and 1930s, which included industrialization, urbanization, the collapse of export-led economic production, and the 1930 revolution. In this sense, Pernambucan reformers and political elites utilized eugenics and other so-called normative sciences, including biotypology, anthropometry, and intelligence testing, as a means of addressing contemporary economic, social, and political crises.[75]

While most Pernambucan reformers continued to champion the use of public health measures, public assistance, and educational reforms to improve *nordestinos*, there were those who believed that voluntary efforts to improve Pernambucans had been ineffective and argued that more forceful methods should be employed. They called for mandatory prenuptial medical examinations, selective birth control, and government regulation of professions that supposedly posed a threat to public and eugenic health. The most vocal proponent of eugenics in Pernambuco was Amaury de Medeiros, who implemented numerous reforms incorporating eugenics during his tenure as director of the Department of Health and Assistance. These included using intelligence testing to evaluate students and workers, expanding prenatal, postnatal, and school medical services, creating a directorate of sanitary education that disseminated public health and eugenic propaganda, and providing food aid and public housing to the lower and working classes.[76] Medeiros believed that these reforms would, as he put it, create "a strong race, healthy and intellectually and morally elevated, which will populate the lands of Brazil and lead it toward greatness."[77] Although Medeiros stepped down as director of the Department of Health and Assistance in 1926 when he was elected to the federal Câmara dos Deputados, as a legislator he advocated an even more interventionist approach to improving Brazilians' health. In 1927, he introduced a bill calling for voluntary prenuptial medical examinations, which he argued would prohibit individuals with "an irremediable physical defect or grave disease that is transmissible to the spouse or offspring" from receiving a marriage license.[78] Disqualifying diseases included "tuberculosis, leprosy, infectious syphilis, venereal cankers, epilepsy, idiocy, imbecilism, and mental alienation in all its forms."[79] Although the bill was debated in congress, it was dropped within a year due to Medeiros's death and legislators' opposition to a clause in the bill that would have allowed any "competent person" to denounce a marriage if they could provide evidence of an "irremediable physical defect" or a "grave disease" that could be transmitted to a spouse or child.[80] While Medeiros's bill never became law, it proved to be an inspiration to Pernambucan reformers who hoped to discourage and even prohibit certain allegedly unhealthy individuals and groups from reproducing what contemporary English eugenicists termed "negative eugenics."[81]

In 1928, Waldemar de Oliveira, a professor at Recife's Faculdade de Medicina and an inspector for the propaganda and education section of the Department of Health and Assistance, took Medeiros's bill a step further and proposed mandatory prenuptial medical examinations. He argued that such measures would "impede unions that could produce, due to the mercy of dysgenic factors, morbid results."[82] Oliveira believed that the "right to marry" implied the "right to defend mating and the lineage," and he argued that the government was justly "invested with the function of protecting and safeguarding the public."[83] He recognized that mandatory examinations would be impossible to enforce due to the shortage of qualified medical personnel outside major urban areas, the infrequency of civil marriages, and public resistance to any attempt by the state to interfere in a matter that, despite the formal separation of state and church outlined in the constitution of 1891, was still considered to be an institution under the domain of the Catholic Church. Oliveira nevertheless argued that eugenic legislation was necessary, and he believed that rural Pernambucans would be willing to accept mandatory medical screenings if they understood the social importance of sanitation, hygiene, and "personal cleanliness" by being subjected to the same "propaganda that had been handed out in the cities."[84]

The debate over prenuptial medical examinations continued into the 1930s. In 1934, João Aureliano, an appellate court justice (*desembargador*) and president of Pernambuco's Liga de Higiene Mental, wrote that obligatory prenuptial medical exams were compatible with the state's "coercive function [to regulate] citizens in order to benefit moral, intellectual, and even economic conditions of society." He concluded that the state was responsible for "the integrity and purity of the race."[85] Aureliano argued that the Pernambucan state government should pass legislation along the lines of Medeiros's 1927 bill, but as a judge, he recognized the difficulties in making prenuptial exams mandatory. Not all Pernambucan physicians supported prenuptial examinations, however. In 1935, Valdemir Miranda, a clinical dermatologist and member of the Liga de Higiene Mental, rejected prenuptial examinations because he believed they constituted an impediment to "the right of sexual union" and the "emancipation of women."[86] He reasoned that the challenge of improving individuals was complex and could not be addressed by simply creating legislation that promoted eugenic principles. Miranda concluded that the Brazilian government needed to do much more to support the family and motherhood.

A few Pernambucan physicians and public health officials proposed birth control as a means of controlling the state's growing population, and they invoked the theories of Charles Darwin, Herbert Spencer, and Thomas Malthus to support their belief that the fundamental cause of all Pernambucan social problems was overpopulation. In an article published in the *Jornal de Medicina de Pernambuco*, Celso Arcoverde de Freitas asserted that birth control was the most effective means of improving "the race." He argued that mandatory birth control measures would reduce the region's population, which would have "great social repercussions, because . . . future offspring will have a precise education, contributing to the moral, intellectual, and physical progress of the race and to the integration of positive elements in society, who augment the population, through the reduction of infant mortality." Freitas believed that selective reproduction and reduced birth rates would eliminate unwanted congenital diseases and reduce infant mortality, sexual precocity, "Don Juanism," prostitution, and crime. Freitas proposed that 75 percent of Brazilians be forced to use birth control and that literacy, regardless of social class, would be the standard that would be applied in determining whether couples would be allowed to reproduce. He concluded that birth control was "one of the methods of great efficiency for achieving the moral, physical, and intellectual purification of the people, increasing the splendor of the high star in the constellation of noble human ideas, Eugenics."[87]

The most restrictive eugenic proposal came from Pernambucan physician Jorge Lôbo, who in a 1933 lecture to Recife's Society of Interns argued that "crises of the moral, economic, and biological order" had led to a "lack of natural selection in our civilized life." He warned that "the domination of mediocrity . . . will grow if responsible doctors who are familiar with Mendelian laws do not urgently intervene."[88] In order to reintroduce "natural selection," Lôbo proposed the creation of a national "pedigree registry" that would be used in conjunction with prenuptial medical examinations to restrict marriage and reproduction. He also advocated the sterilization of "abnormals," the segregation of the "criminally deficient," birth control, eugenic education and propaganda, intelligence testing, restrictions on immigration, and public health campaigns against "degenerative" diseases such as syphilis, tuberculosis, leprosy, and alcoholism. Finally, Lôbo urged the creation of a "Pernambucan Eugenics Commission" that would coordinate its efforts with national eugenics organizations in order to fight for the "good cause" of eugenics in Pernambuco.[89] In essence, Lôbo believed that the state should become the proxy for natural selection and determine who was fit to reproduce and who was not.

These myriad proposals were never considered seriously by either state government officials or the medical establishment in Pernambuco. Public health officials and politicians understood eugenics to be a useful tool in their efforts to improve public health, especially as propaganda. There was, however, little political support for birth control and sterilization among Pernambucan lawmakers who believed that legal restrictions on marriage and the right to reproduce would have placed a heavy burden on the state's public health and legal systems, which were already stretched to their limits. In addition, social conservatives and the Catholic Church opposed eugenics on moral and religious grounds.[90]

Pernambucan public health officials also rejected eugenicists' view that individual heredity (rather than social and environmental factors) was the cause of the state's considerable social and economic problems.[91] Because professional ethics dissuaded physicians from publicly criticizing one another, it is often difficult to ascertain how the Pernambucan medical establishment received new scientific and medical ideas and techniques. Pernambucan professional medical journals occasionally included discussion and criticism of published articles, however. In an article published in *Revista Medica de Pernambuco* in 1931, Augusto Lins e Silva, a professor of legal medicine at Recife's Faculdade de Medicina, argued for the adoption of eugenic measures that he believed would reduce crime and degeneracy and permit the "moral and physical reconstruction of Man."[92] Lins e Silva argued that human heredity lay at the root of all crime and that eugenic principles should be incorporated into penal legislation. This could be achieved, he wrote, by "combating all the social diseases, which exaggerate illiteracy and pauperism—the two great factors in criminality." Like most Pernambucan eugenicists, Lins e Silva did not suggest how these goals could be achieved. What is significant about Lins e Silva's proposal is the reaction it produced. Psychiatrist Ulysses Pernambucano, who headed the Department of Education's Institute of Professional Orientation and Selection, suggested that "certain individual constitutions are exaggerations of normal constitutions, but it is understood that crime is motivated above all by social factors." He added, somewhat subversively, that it was in fact the 1930 revolution that "awoke conditions that increased crime." Edgar Altino, a physician and Lins e Silva's colleague at the Faculdade de Medicina, suggested that he should consider "the existence of constitutions that respond abnormally to the influence of their surroundings," not individual degeneracy.[93] In short, Lins e Silva's colleagues argued that social factors rather than heredity were the primary cause of crime. It was the position of the Pernambucan medical establishment that eugenicists' proposals were reductionist and did not take social factors into account.

Instead of adopting eugenicists' proposals to restrict reproduction, Pernambucan public health officials and legislators chose to regulate specific professions that were deemed to be a threat to public health. In 1928, as part of a reform of the Department of Health and Assistance, public health officials created the Inspectorate of Social Hygiene. This agency's charge was to investigate the "anthropology and living conditions of the different classes of the population" as well as the "reciprocal relations that exist between disturbances in health and other factors and social phenomena."[94] The group that received the most attention from public health officials was Recife's domestic workers.[95] In the first year of the inspectorate's operation, researchers conducted medical and anthropometric examinations of more than seven thousand domestic workers and compiled data cards (*fichas*) that contained personal, medical, racial, and anthropometric data.[96] *Fichas* were an indispensable tool that allowed researchers to compile statistics and establish a baseline against which individuals and groups could be measured. The state legislature passed a law requiring all domestic workers to submit to a medical examination and to carry an identity card (*carteira de domestico*) confirming that the bearer did not carry any transmissible diseases such as syphilis or tuberculosis. Public health officials were especially concerned with the possibility of disease transmission via close daily contact between employers and employees in the home.[97] What was implied but never overtly stated was that female domestic workers could spread sexually transmitted diseases to husbands and fathers, who would infect wives, who in turn would pass diseases on to the next generation.[98] Domestic workers judged to be unhealthy were to be "excluded from the profession," and officials recommended "the isolation and treatment of individuals who were the carriers of transmissible diseases and the reduction of sources of contagion that would result in the contamination of the social collective."[99] Public health officers prohibited only sixty-six out of seventy-four hundred domestics from working, however. There is little evidence of domestic workers' reactions and responses to these regulatory efforts, but it is likely that those who believed that they would not pass the medical examination would have avoided public health officials in order to continue working, even though they could not acquire an official identity card. The government's attempts to study and regulate domestic workers were short lived. The considerable difficulties in regulating a profession as ubiquitous as domestic service proved insurmountable—the Pernambucan government simply did not have the necessary resources.

The Inspectorate of Social Hygiene's work was significant, however, in that it constituted an attempt on the part of the state government to apply eugenics to the regulation of employment in the home, which historically had been considered a private rather than public affair. Public health officials justified this intrusion by arguing that it was the government's duty to protect society from the public health danger posed by the poor and the working classes, who often suffered high rates of infectious communicable diseases, often endemic in working-class neighborhoods. Geraldo de Andrade, inspector of general health in the Department of Health and Assistance, directed the department's research on domestic workers. Data collected for each individual included personal and medical history, "type of habitation," "habitual diet," racial data (including "paternal color, maternal color, race of the examined, type of racial mixing, . . . color, hair, [and] eyes"), anthropometric data (including height, weight, "cranial type," measurements of the thorax and abdomen, resistance to fatigue, and physical deformities), and finally, psychological data (including "mental state" and "level of culture").[100] The information collected, especially with regard to race, was exacting and detailed, especially compared to previous studies of the general population. After analyzing the data for five thousand subjects, Andrade concluded that "the domestic worker of Recife is not very robust" and constituted "a rickety type." Andrade wrote openly about the domestic workers' supposed "racial degeneration" and concluded that *mulatos* were the predominant racial type among domestic workers, although he carefully pointed out that his research did not "place the opprobrium of ethnic degeneration on all the Pernambucan people" because he was referring only to one social and economic class.[101] Although Andrade would later emphasize social and economic factors as the primary causes of anthropometric differences among human populations, his research on domestic workers constituted the first formal application of eugenics in the study of Pernambucans and provided a model for research on race carried out in the 1930s and 1940s.

The study and regulation of domestic workers proved to be the most ambitious application of eugenics in Pernambuco. Although a few Pernambucan eugenicists proposed regulating marriage and reproduction as a means of promoting eugenics, state legislators and public health officials never fully embraced the idea. The application of eugenics was limited by the political ethos of the era. During a period in which laissez-faire social and economic policies dominated federal and state politics, the eugenic regulation of domestic workers, while protecting the middle and upper classes from a supposed public health threat, was understood to be an attempt to regulate the private sphere, an area in which the state had no presumptive rights. Further attempts to transform civil society would be possible only after the 1930 revolution, after which the centralized Vargas state sought to remake the relationship between the state and civil society by incorporating Brazilian citizens into government institutions and social programs. Whereas the social reform programs of the 1920s provided educational and vocational training, direct social assistance, and public health services in which citizens could choose to participate, the Vargas state sought to remake society from the ground up. The question was no longer how society should treat dangerous or problematic individuals or groups but how all citizens would be integrated into a harmonious, corporate society.[102]

Conditioning the Body

Getúlio Vargas's ascension to power in 1930 marked the beginning of a period of government expansion at both the state and federal levels. New federal agencies, including the Ministry of Education and Health (Ministério da

Educação e Saúde, or MES), and the Ministry of Labor, Industry, and Commerce (Ministério do Trabalho, Indústria, e Comércio, or MTIC), were created to oversee social assistance, educational, and public health programs designed to improve social and economic conditions and to remake the relationship between the state, society, and citizen. These new federal programs and services often duplicated those offered by the Pernambucan state government and created friction and occasional conflict between state and federal officials. Federal control resulted in subtle but significant shifts in political objectives as officials discussed how to achieve the goal of creating social harmony by integrating the individual into state-controlled associations and institutions.[103] In their study of Gustavo Capanema and educational policy under Vargas, Simon Schwartzman, Helena Maria Bousquet Bomeny, and Vanda Maria Ribeiro Costa argues that "in truth, the model of Brazilian nationalism—in contrast to the liberal view, which understands the nation as a collection of individuals—sought to transform the nation into an organic whole, a moral, political and economic entity whose ends were realized in the State."[104] At the same time, continuing concern about regional economic development resulted in renewed calls for improving workers' health, skills, and productivity. The general public—especially the working classes—fell under greater scrutiny as politicians, reformers, educators, and public health officials sought to integrate individuals into state-controlled institutions and improve workers' health through cultivation of the body.

This interest in Pernambucans' physical development recalls earlier trends, like that which led to Euclydes da Cunha's turn-of-the-century descriptions of *jagunços* in *Os sertões*, which established a precedent for scientific interest in *nordestinos'* physical characteristics. Evidence of "primitive" or "advanced" characteristics placed individuals and groups within a racial and evolutionary hierarchy that served to reinforce Brazilian social and cultural norms. Arthur Lobo da Silva's 1928 anthropological study of the Brazilian army meticulously cataloged the racial and physical attributes of more than thirty-eight thousand soldiers, which allowed, as he put it, "the future and definitive determination of the anthropological types of the inhabitants of this great Brazil."[105] Whether or not they agreed with his conclusions—Lobo argued that Indians and "black Africans" were rapidly disappearing due to the "predominance of the white race"—Brazilian anthropologists and reformers widely cited Lobo's study because it provided a research model and a benchmark for their own investigations of race.

In Pernambuco, state-sponsored reform efforts focused on promoting "physical culture" and instilling interest in physical development among the general public. The Pernambucan government created two services to address Pernambucans' physical development: the Serviço de Hygiene Social and the Inspectoria de Hygiene do Trabalho. Geraldo de Andrade, after conducting his research on domestic workers, directed both services and organized them to facilitate the collection of anthropometric data. These programs elicited the praise of noted conservative social critic Oliveira Viana, who wrote in 1929 that "I think it is not erroneous to say that Pernambuco has founded [the first] regular anthropological measurement service in our nation."[106] Andrade and his assistants collected data on workers' physical and psychological characteristics and made recommendations regarding employment and the improvement of working conditions in factories. He justified the laborious and costly collection of data by arguing that "anthropology must be regarded more in the study of social questions" and that "in a country of intense racial mixture, populated by crossings of elements of various origins, rife with pauperism, Brazil needs to posses, in its principal cities, laboratories where we study the manner of living of the proletarian classes and practice somametrics."[107] He proposed that every Pernambucan worker be subjected to a physical and psychological examination, the results of which would be used to assign occupations that would take advantage of workers' abilities and minimize the potential effects of physical and mental defects.[108] In 1931, Andrade and his assistants completed a study of three hundred industrial workers, and he reached the conclusion that poverty and low wages produced physical underdevelopment among Pernambucan industrial workers. Significantly, Andrade used Marxist language to describe social and economic relationships and to explain the precarious economic position of Pernambucan workers.[109] Andrade's conclusions, acceptable in the more progressive political and social atmosphere of the late 1920s, proved too controversial for the Cavalcanti administration, and, in 1931, he was dismissed from his government posts and the Inspectoria de Hygiene do Trabalho was eliminated.[110]

The Pernambucan government then turned its attention to students' physical and psychological development, which allowed the government to maintain a greater degree of oversight—students in public schools were easier to monitor than workers in private employ—and to avoid politically charged discussions of workers' salaries and economic inequality. Pernambucan officials also realized that public schools provided an opportunity to influence a significant percentage of the state's children at a crucial stage in their physical and psychological development. Students, unlike adults, could be "improved" before they reached maturity and entered the work force. Beginning in 1931, state researchers collected data on students' physical development and used the data to design physical education programs that addressed the students' supposed shortcomings. Jurandyr Mamede, Pernambuco's secretary of education, justified the government's interest in physical education by arguing that "perhaps more than in any other people, it is pressing to seriously consider among us the physical origins of the race. If in [Pernambuco], the health [and] the physical capacity of the nation are considered to be the origin of all social progress, then much more attention should be paid to physical education in Brazil, where accumulated anti-hygienic factors create a sick race." Although local concerns about social and economic development were the primary reason for the interest in physical education, Mamede also acknowledged the federal government's role, noting that "the Government, understanding the elevated importance of measures that tend to encourage physical education, will oversee the organization, in a scientifically rigorous fashion, of this important area of education."[111]

By the mid-1930s, physical education dominated the educational agenda. In a 1933 report on state government activities since the 1930 revolution, *interventor* Carlos de Lima Cavalcanti wrote that, "given the importance of the problem of the physical improvement of the race in Brazil, the [Pernambucan] government has adopted a series of measures that place physical education . . . within a scientific framework."[112] A new biotypology service was given the task of conducting a "complete clinical and biometric study" of Pernambucan students that would involve collecting biometric data and recommending a specific regimen of physical training for each student in the public school system.[113] The Biotypology Service employed thirty-three physical education monitors who traveled from school to school to examine students and collect data. In 1936, monitors conducted nine hundred examinations and had compiled a total of sixty-eight hundred individual data cards.[114] Data included each student's weight, height, and other physical measurements used to calculate a "coefficient of robustness," "vital capacity," and "base metabolic rate."[115] Researchers used the data to produce standardized "growth curves" against which individual physical development was measured.[116] They concluded that Pernambucan children were shorter, weighed less, and were not as physically mature as their counterparts in southern Brazil. In order to correct these perceived shortcomings, physical education monitors calculated each student's "physiological age," and students were placed in physical education classes according to their calculated stage of physical development. Students with more serious physical deficiencies were placed in remedial classes and given a regimen of corrective exercises.

The Department of Education also organized activities such as games, team sports, calisthenics, and gymnastics. Public parks in Recife were used as playgrounds and exercise fields, and gymnasiums and athletic tracks were constructed to encourage physical activity.[117] Photographs of brigades of exercising students peppered the pages of government reports in the 1930s, and physical education was discussed more often than the content of the curriculum.[118] Pernambucan politicians and educators also promoted scouting as a means of improving boys' physical condition, arguing that camping trips and practical skills would "contribute to raising the index of physical culture and civic spirit of our young scholars."[119] Educators and politicians borrowed liberally from the corporatist rhetoric that dominated the Vargas era and emphasized the individual's place within the social collective and the role of the state in guiding students' social, intellectual, and moral development. The goal, as one Pernambucan educator put it, was to "develop their intelligence and shape their character."[120]

Educators and politicians almost immediately declared their efforts to improve Pernambucans' physical development to be a success. This claim was based more on the popularity of the programs among politicians than on any measurable improvements in students' physical condition. Researchers were less confident. Some argued that Pernambucan students compared favorably to students from southern Brazil and even to Europeans and North Americans, but most argued that Pernambucans were inferior physical specimens.[121] In one study, researchers found that Pernambucan students were shorter, thinner, and weaker than students of the same age in São Paulo. Another study, of four thousand Pernambucan student subjects, found, somewhat implausibly, only three whom researchers felt confident in describing as "almost entirely normal."[122] These doubts did not stop politicians and reformers from continuing to extol the virtues of physical education. If anything, comparisons with *paulistas* only encouraged Pernambucan reformers who saw plenty of room for improvement. Agamemnon Magalhães, who served as Pernambuco's federally appointed *interventor* during the Estado Novo, stressed the importance of physical education in his 1940 annual report to Getúlio Vargas, writing that "physical culture and sport are factors of purification and ennoblement of the body that create a combative spirit, the will to overcome obstacles, courage in the face of danger, and are a powerful aid in moral development."[123] The success of physical education in Pernambuco lay both in its reflection of corporatist ideals and in the symbolic potency of exercising students. While researchers debated the results of pseudoscientific research, no politician questioned the display of strength, endurance, and regimentation on display in mass exhibitions of jumping jacks and deep knee bends.

Encouraged by the success of the Department of Education's physical education programs, Pernambucan officials created two additional biotypology services: the Biotypology Service of the Military Brigade of Pernambuco, which studied soldiers' physical constitution in order to "elevate the level of physical resistance of enlisted men," and the Criminal Biotypology Laboratory, which provided prison officials with data to be used to determine the "professional orientation of delinquents, unmasking their principal psychophysical aptitudes."[124] Alvaro Ferraz, Miguel Ignacio de Andrade Lima Júnior, and Luiz Ignacio, who staffed the services and had written several anthropometric studies of Pernambucan students, adopted the methodology of Italian biotypologists Nicola Pende and Gacinto Viola.[125] Biotypology posited that there were six essential biotypes, each with specific physiological and psychological characteristics into which humans could be classified. The determination of an individual's biotype allowed researchers to discuss the causes of their subjects' physical and psychological shortcomings and to recommend appropriate exercise regimens, educational programs, job training, and employment without making explicit references to social, economic, or racial status. In their 1939 study, *A morfologia do homem do nordeste*, which cataloged the biotypological characteristics of fifteen hundred enlisted men in Pernambuco's Military Brigade, Alvaro Ferraz and Andrade Lima Júnior argued that biotypology was an indispensable tool. In their assessment, it would assist government officials in organizing education; students with similar levels of mental achievement could be grouped into the same classes. It would aid in the organization of work by determining an appropriate "distribution of labor, the selection of specialists, the determination of individuals predisposed, for morphological, sensory, mental, or whatever reason, to cause or be victims of accidents." They noted its use as well for organizing military forces and for conducting medical research "in which fundamental scientific data for preventive hygiene is based in the knowledge of constitutional characteristics that predispose one to diverse morbid afflictions." Finally, they wrote, biotypology could enhance "the mental hygiene of societies, where it is known that the study of different delinquent types . . . is the fundamental rationale of an effective criminal prophylaxis."[126] In short, Ferraz and Lima Júnior believed that there were few social and political problems that could not be addressed by the rational application of the principles of biotypology.

By 1940, researchers had accumulated data for more than two thousand enlisted men, a data set used as a baseline for further studies of prisoners carried out by the Criminal Biotypology Laboratory.[127] In these prison studies,

Ferraz, Lima Júnior, and Ignacio argued that there was a strong correlation between race and body type and that Pernambucans could be classified into three biotypes, which, not surprisingly, corresponded to the racial groups of *branco, negro,* and *mulato*—the racial categories into which Brazilians were usually divided. In other words, the researchers used biotypes as a substitute for racial categories and argued that race determined individual physical and psychological characteristics. At the same time, they argued that Pernambucans were less robust than other Brazilians, a circumstance they ascribed to the fact that the majority of Pernambucans had some degree of African ancestry. In one article, however, Ferraz attempted to assuage readers' concerns about Pernambucans' racial heritage: "who has not thought that we are irremediably burdened with the physical stigmas of degeneracy, attributed by some anthropologists to the *mestiços.* Nevertheless, we are able to affirm, with the modest results obtained . . . that there is no reason to worry."[128] He argued that Pernambucan *mulatos* were not "ethnically inferior" and instead suggested that *mulatos* were well suited to heavy agricultural labor because their arms were long in proportion to their bodies and were thus able to till the ground more easily, a conclusion he attempted to justify based on measurements of his subjects.[129] Ferraz's conclusion that the state's Afro-Brazilian populations should be engaged in agricultural labor was not terribly original given that Pernambuco was less industrialized than the states of southern Brazil. His conclusions about race were also consistent with government social and economic policy that marginalized the state's Afro-Brazilian populations.[130] Ferraz and his fellow researchers also avoided discussing controversial social, economic, and political issues, and they placed their policy suggestions firmly within a corporatist framework. Biotypology provided not only a means of measuring Pernambucans' individual and collective physiological and psychological development but also a supposedly scientifically rigorous confirmation that Pernambucans were physiologically different from, if not inferior to, other Brazilians.

That biotypology and its progenitor, eugenics, were used as justification for and as a means of improving Pernambucans in the 1920s and 1930s is not surprising. Reformers of all political stripes throughout the Americas and Europe utilized eugenics and other normative sciences in their efforts to improve humans and reorganize society. Ongoing concerns among elites about the region's economic decline and decreased worker productivity, coupled with new understandings of national identity that emphasized the role of the military, labor, and families in regenerating and reconstructing the nation, generated interest among reformers and politicians for aiding and improving Pernambucans' physical development. This approach was relatively short lived, however, due to an inability to ascertain whether their efforts were succeeding and, by the late 1930s, the growing realization that the causes of regional social and economic underdevelopment were more complex than previously thought. Researchers began to understand that Pernambucans' physical underdevelopment was a symptom, rather than a cause, of the region's decline.

Depoliticizing Hunger

As reformers devised various social programs to address Pernambucans' alleged shortcomings, there was little discussion of the fundamental causes of their supposed physical underdevelopment. The reasons for this lack of attention were primarily political. Hunger, which relatively few public health officials and reformers had acknowledged was widespread in Pernambuco and the Northeast, was considered a taboo subject.[131] In the reformist political atmosphere of the 1920s, however, reformers, physicians, and public health officials began to take an interest in the subject, a move that was consistent with Medeiros's and Coimbra's progressive reforms addressing the causes of "public insalubrity," including urban poverty.[132] The eugenic and biotypological research of the late 1920s and early 1930s also led researchers to believe that poor diet contributed to physical underdevelopment. Poor diet was initially construed as a medical rather than a social or an economic problem. Physicians and public health officials concentrated on the ways in which a lack of nutrients in the diet affected growth, physical development, and general health. By the turn of the century, medical research on the connection between diet and disease had revealed that nutritional deficiencies resulted in diseases such as beriberi, scurvy, rickets, and pellagra.[133] Brazilian researchers had already discovered that dietary deficiencies were the cause of night blindness, a condition that was common among rural populations of northeastern Brazil.[134] By the mid-1920s, researchers at Recife's Faculdade de Medicina were conducting medical research on diet and articles on the subject began to appear in local medical journals and the annual reports of the Department of Health and Assistance.

Pernambucan public health officials suspected that malnutrition was the leading cause of infant mortality and one of the causes of physical deformities among children in both the drought-ravaged interior and the poor and working-class neighborhoods of urban areas.[135] The connection between diet and infant mortality proved to be especially troubling to public health officials who were concerned with Pernambuco's high infant mortality rates.[136] Because of the emphasis placed on family and raising healthy children, the problem of infant mortality and children's physical development took on added significance. Although medical researchers pointed out that a proper diet was essential to physical and intellectual development, they, and state government officials, proved less willing to acknowledge that many infants and children simply did not have enough to eat.[137] The state government attempted to address the problem with the League against Infant Mortality, but by the time children reached the age when they were eligible to attend public schools, the prescribed remedy for physical underdevelopment was physical exercises, which did not address the question of whether students had enough to eat. In fact, in promoting physical education, education and public health officials made little or no mention of students' diets, because doing so would have constituted an acknowledgment that students' physical underdevelopment was at least partially caused by families' economic situation. The Coimbra administration did create a "popular meals service," which provided a limited number of *recifenses* with midday meals for five hundred *reis,* or about seven U.S. cents at 1926 conversion rates.[138] While this was a tacit acknowledgment that at least some Pernambucans did not have enough to eat because of low wages, public health officials usually argued that the main cause of dietary deficiencies was the general population's ignorance of what constituted a healthy diet.

On his travels through the Pernambucan *sertão* in his capacity as director of the Department of Health and Assistance, Medeiros questioned *sertanejos* in order to "gain an impression of their thinking" about diet. In one "small interior city," Medeiros recalled the situation of a worker who lived in a "small primitive house" that stood in stark contrast to a spacious and well-kept chicken coop that contained more than a dozen hens.[139] Medeiros recounted the conversation he had with the worker:

—How is it that you eat?
—Listen, Senhor Doutor, how is it that the poor eat?
—If I ask it's because I don't know.
—Fish and jerked beef with manioc flour.
—But don't you have more than enough hens in the backyard?
—I do, but I'm not going to eat the hens.
—And don't they lay eggs?
—They do, and that's why I don't eat them.
—And the eggs?
—I sell them.

Medeiros was incredulous that the worker did not eat the chickens, or at least the eggs, as doing so would have provided "a quantity of superior and useful nourishment." The worker instead sold the eggs at market and purchased "nutritionally inferior" food for his family. Medeiros was clearly frustrated with what he perceived as *nordestinos'* ignorance regarding what constituted a proper diet. He lamented that "it is not even worth discussing how much better fed they would be if they used the eggs in their own and their children's diet."[140] Medeiros and indeed the majority of Pernambucan physicians and public health officials believed that dietary habits could be improved through education and propaganda. If *nordestinos* were taught that eggs and chicken were better for them than dried fish and jerked beef, they reasoned, then they would surely adopt more sound dietary habits. In the late 1920s and early 1930s, the Pernambucan government regarded diet and nutrition to be a problem that originated with the individual. Thus, by teaching individuals how to make the right dietary choices, their health and physical development would improve.

As research continued in the 1930s, ideas about diet began to change as even more evidence about the connections between diet and disease came to light. The intellectual and professional trajectory of Josué de Castro, the author of numerous medical and geographic studies of northeastern Brazil and Latin America, including *Geografia da fome,* illustrates changing ideas about diet and hunger in this period.[141] De Castro was born in Pernambuco, and after receiving his medical degree from the Universidade do Brasil in Rio de Janeiro, he returned to Recife and was appointed to the faculty of the Faculdade de Medicina. While in Recife, de Castro conducted research on the biochemical and physiological aspects of diet, and like the majority of his colleagues, he initially believed that ignorance was the principal cause of dietary deficiencies among the populations of northeastern Brazil. In his 1932 Faculdade de Medicina *concurso,* he wrote that "among us, unhappily, the dietary problem has not received necessary attention, and [we have] the ignorance of the most elementary principles of a healthy diet among the *povo* as well as the wealthy classes." This ignorance was "lamentable," he argued, because "the dietary problem was basic and indispensable to the social and economic development of our nation." De Castro concluded that "as a eugenic problem, it cannot be forgotten that diet is one of the most important external factors in the constitution of vital biotypes and that it is by biotypological selection that the vital index of the race is raised."[142] De Castro clearly understood the "dietary problem" to be part of wider efforts to improve Brazilians via eugenics.

By the mid-1930s, de Castro had begun to place a greater emphasis on the social, economic, and racial dimensions of diet. De Castro's research revealed startling facts about the lives of the Pernambucan working classes. In 1935, after completing a survey of Pernambucans' living conditions and dietary habits, he suggested that hunger was widespread among the working classes and that there was a need for "urgent social assistance . . . in order to impede the progressive weakness, provoked by a chronic and hereditary inanition, true traditional hunger."[143] De Castro determined that agricultural workers consumed an average of 1,646 calories per day, and he estimated that between 3,000 and 4,000 calories a day were necessary for survival.[144] De Castro wrote that nutritional and dietary researchers would have only one question to ask of a worker who ate so little: "How is it that you can eat like this and not die of hunger?" The "more than a little disconcerting" response he provided: "How? I am dying of hunger."[145] De Castro's shock upon discovering the prevalence of hunger among Pernambucan workers was echoed in the writing of Antônio Carneiro Leão, the reformer and educator from Rio de Janeiro. He wrote that workers "never ever say 'I am going to eat lunch or dinner' but only—'I am going to trick hunger.'" Carneiro Leão concluded that "this is realistically what a large percentage of the poor population of rural zones in a good portion of Brazil do—'trick hunger.'"[146] De Castro's realization that Pernambucan agricultural workers were chronically malnourished went beyond the notion that they simply did not know how to eat. By the mid-1930s, he had concluded that the "dietary problem" was in fact a problem of hunger, a social and economic phenomenon rather than a question of education and individual choices. This crucial shift led to new insights into the causes of Pernambucans' apparent physical deficiencies. Although hunger and even starvation had long been recognized as a social consequence of the periodic droughts that affected the northeastern interior, de Castro argued that endemic, chronic hunger was the single most important public health problem in both the coast and the interior and that hunger was the primary cause of elevated mortality rates in both children and adults.[147]

De Castro also believed that hunger, rather than inherent biological and racial qualities, "translated into the inferiority of the anthropo-sociological characteristics" of the working and lower classes. Aware of the declining currency of scientific racism, de Castro argued that "today no one still conscientiously believes that *mestiçagem* would be the true cause of the lessened vitality of our people. The crossing of *índio, negro,* and Portuguese did not generate a debilitated, anemic, and rachitic *mestiço* because of fatal heredity. If the majority of *mulatos* are composed of debilitated souls, with mental 'deficit' and physical incapacity, it is not because of the effect of a racial defect, it is because of an empty stomach. It is not the misfortune of race, it is the misfortune of hunger."[148] In a 1935 study of Pernambucan workers, de Castro concluded that "if the majority of *mulatos* are aestivated souls . . . it is because of their empty stomachs. It is not a racial sickness, but it is sickness of hunger."[149] Like most intellectuals who were concerned with the racial dimensions of social problems in the 1930s, de Castro was influenced by the work of Gilberto Freyre. In *Casa-grande & senzala* (1933), Freyre weighed in on the problem of nutrition, writing that "most of the physical inferiority of the Brazilian is in general completely attributed to race, or . . . climate, derived from the poor use of our natural resources or nutrition."[150] While Freyre and de Castro took similar approaches to race, arguing that apparent racial inferiority was in fact due to social and economic rather than biological and racial factors, they disagreed on the causes of malnutrition. Freyre argued that "nutritional food" was not readily available to northeastern workers because of Brazilian planters' historical preference for growing sugarcane rather than market crops, while de Castro argued that all the elements of healthy diet were available but that economic conditions made them prohibitively expensive for the poor and working classes.[151]

De Castro also maintained that diet rather than race explained the physical differences between the peoples of southern and northeastern Brazil and between *nordestinos* of the *litoral* and the *sertão*.[152] As late as 1946, when most Brazilian intellectuals and scientists had abandoned biotypology as a legitimate research methodology, de Castro cited Alvaro Ferraz and Andrade Lima Júnior's 1939 *A morfologia do homem do nordeste*, arguing that there were two essential northeastern biotypes (hailing from the *sertão* and the *litoral*) and claiming that diet played a role in the divergence of the two biotypes.[153] De Castro's research reflected the intellectual debates of his era: although he held that dietary habits produced differences among distinct populations (which constituted a disavowal of racial determinism), he nevertheless argued that *sertanejos* were a primitive people, concluding that the study of their diet had made it "possible to attain a more just understanding of the mystery of *sertanejo* barbarity, of intolerance, and of the bravery of the man of the Northeast, of their arrogance and of their medieval mysticism."[154] De Castro's characterizations of *sertanejos* were not inconsistent with contemporary assessments of the northeastern interior, and, indeed, although *sertanejos* were held up as the "core" of the nation, they were still understood to be socially and culturally inferior to the populations of more developed coastal and urban areas. De Castro's contention that physical differences among the races was due to diet rather than inheritable biological characteristics nonetheless constituted a repudiation of prevailing scientific understandings of race and supported the positivistic notion that individuals and Brazilian society as a whole could be improved through government intervention.

By the mid-1930s, de Castro had also begun to consider economic factors to be an important cause of chronic malnutrition and hunger, and in 1936 he published *Alimentação e raça*, his study of the relationship between diet and race. In considering the causes of hunger, he argued that "the economic factor becomes clear: we have come to realize that with these miserable salaries, workers are not able to acquire a sufficient quantity of necessary foods for their families' consumption." De Castro criticized employer labor practices that did not provide workers with salaries sufficient to meet their families' basic needs. Like Geraldo de Andrade, de Castro used Marxist language, including "capitalist regime," "bourgeois classes," and "proletariat" to describe class and labor relations in Pernambuco and to criticize employers' indifference toward workers.[155] He carefully constructed his criticisms to be consistent with nationalist discourses of economic progress and development, however.[156] De Castro believed that Brazil was rich in both natural and human resources, and he argued that "many naturally rich agricultural zones are exploited without bettering the economic level of the people, and without this natural wealth contributing as a direct cause of economic prosperity."[157] In short, the solution to hunger and economic underdevelopment in northeastern Brazil was reform rather than revolution. In *Geografia da fome*, de Castro argued that the federal government should take steps to reform agricultural production, including limiting the size of the *latifundium* (large estate), ending monoculture, reorienting agricultural production toward local markets, and mechanizing and collectivizing production.[158] De Castro stopped short of calling for land reform, as this would have proven too controversial and likely would have led to his professional marginalization. De Castro concluded *Geografia da fome* by reiterating that the problem of diet was "troubling," while emphasizing that appropriate social and cultural reforms could "change the fundamental biological characteristics of our people, who had become diminished exclusively by the degrading action of a defective social and economic organization."[159]

Although de Castro's investigations of the human, economic, and political dimensions of hunger would later prove to be an inspiration and a model for reformers, especially after the end of the Estado Novo, few government officials in the 1930s were willing to admit that hunger was part of Brazilians' daily life. During the Estado Novo, the Pernambucan government's engagement with the issue was predictably limited. The state government did not acknowledge the existence of hunger among adults. This would have been an admission that state-sponsored social welfare programs were ineffective, so government officials concentrated instead on poor diet and maternal ignorance as a cause of infant mortality.[160] In the early 1940s, government officials first acknowledged that malnutrition and hunger existed in rural areas, especially in the *sertão*.[161] The government adopted the same approach to malnutrition in the *sertão* as it did to infant mortality, however. Since government officials understood the causes hunger to be ignorance and agricultural issues rather than low wages and economic inequality, the approaches they adopted were technical rather than political. State and federal authorities provided direct aid to families, encouraged crop diversification, funded irrigation and dam projects, and, as a last resort, relocated families to reputedly more fertile land in the Amazon region.[162] None of these approaches attempted to address larger questions of social and economic inequality.

The Pernambucan government's treatment of the "dietary problem" was part of a broader strategy that sought to limit the ways in which the social and economic situation of the poor and working classes were addressed. Financial constraints restricted the state's ability to deal effectively with social and economic problems, and political considerations shaped public policy, especially with regard to the government's efforts to suppress the political Left after the Intentona Comunista of 1935, an attempted coup d'état by the Partido Comunista Brasileiro in Natal, Recife, and Rio de Janeiro. Urbanism, industrialism, and pauperism, identified by Medeiros in 1926 as the state's most pressing social problems, were addressed neither directly nor effectively by the Pernambucan government during the Estado Novo. The Industrial Hygiene Service was limited to studying workers' physiological and psychological characteristics without confronting larger issues of wages and working conditions.[163] Hunger was constructed as a "dietary problem" to be solved by educating the public rather than ensuring that the working and lower classes had enough to eat. Pernambucans' physical underdevelopment reflected a lack of exercise and individual initiative rather than chronic malnutrition. The state, in collusion with intellectuals and economic elites, had succeeded in depoliticizing hunger.

During the Estado Novo, the Pernambucan government's approach to social problems focused on *mocambos*, the seemingly ubiquitous self-help housing of the poor and working classes, where one-third of Recife's population lived, according to official estimates.[164] Twentieth-century efforts to address the problem of workers' housing began with the Pernambucan government's attempts to encourage industrialization during World War I.[165] Legislation offering tax relief to manufacturers resulted in a significant expansion in industrial production and employment for hundreds of workers and a severe shortage of workers' housing. In his 1917 annual report to the state legislature, Governor Manuel Antônio Pereira Borba acknowledged that the government needed to provide additional workers' housing, but the government never took action. Medeiros revived the issue in the 1920s, pointing out that *mocambos* constituted a grave threat to public health and that they were produced by macroeconomic factors, specifically "the useless latifundio," rather than individual "pauperism."[166] During Medeiros's tenure as director of the Department of Health and Assistance, little was done to directly address the problem of workers' housing because the department's limited budget was applied primarily to sanitation and disease prevention. The issue was again raised during the Estado Novo, when the government created the Social League against the Mocambo in 1939.[167] League officials and reformers argued that *mocambos,* most often located on swampy land without running water or sewers, were a breeding ground for epidemic, endemic, and social diseases, including yellow fever, malaria, hookworm disease, alcoholism, idleness, gambling, and prostitution.[168] Living conditions within *mocambos,* they concluded, created a population that was physically, psychologically, and morally incapacitated and incapable of contributing to society. The solution to the problem was to build hygienic "popular housing" in new working-class neighborhoods and to demolish existing *mocambos.* By 1942, ten thousand new houses had been constructed and nine thousand *mocambos* had been razed.[169] The league oversaw the construction of schools, which offered primary education and job training, in an attempt, as one official put it, "to impose a measure of moral cleansing" because "the *mocambo* is not only a problem of hygiene and health but also a problem of the renovation of man and of his standards of life."[170]

Although government officials were discouraged by how quickly *mocambos* were rebuilt—a reflection of the city's rapidly expanding population and the influx of rural migrants—the campaign against the *mocambo* became the centerpiece of efforts to improve the lives of the poor and working classes during the Estado Novo. The political benefits of such an approach were clear to Pernambucan political leaders, who could measure progress in numbers of houses constructed and shacks demolished rather than the obscure metrics of eugenics and biotypology. Agamemnon Magalhães outlined the government's approach in a 1941 radio address: "In order to defeat pauperism, it is necessary to impose, first, the redistribution of the excess of our urban population."[171] For Magalhães the problem was technical, to be solved by relocating "excess" urban populations out of the city center. It also constituted an authoritarian approach to social problems. The state government quite literally attempted to erase all evidence of poverty from the urban landscape by employing large-scale social engineering.[172]

Although the scientific study of hunger shed light on a long-standing and deeply troubling aspect of northeastern society, reformers and government officials invoked established explanations of what was wrong with the region and its peoples in their approach to the problem. Hunger and poverty were understood to be the result of a lack of individual initiative and social and environmental causes rather than an exploitive economic system. Constructing malnutrition and hunger as a medical problem allowed Pernambucan reformers and government officials to avoid discussing divisive social and political issues. Although Josué de Castro recognized the importance of the economic causes of hunger, until the fall of the Vargas administration and the Estado Novo in 1945, Pernambucan officials and researchers focused on *nordestinos'* supposed ignorance of the basic principles of "alimentary hygiene" rather than the economic and political causes of poverty. Alimentary education, milk stations, nutritional kitchens, and the campaign against *mocambos* constituted attempts to treat the symptoms rather than the causes of hunger and poverty among the Pernambucan poor and working classes.

The rise and development of social hygiene in Pernambuco in many ways conforms to similar developments in other Brazilian cities and Latin American nations.[173] There were several ways, however, in which Pernambucan social hygiene was unique. Perhaps the most surprising aspect of Pernambuco's social hygiene movement was its existence in a region of Latin America that historically has been considered to be reactionary rather than progressive in its treatment of social problems. Histories of Brazilian social medicine and social welfare programs often ignore Pernambuco and the Northeast because the region was, by the early twentieth century, at the nation's economic and political periphery. But several key factors led Pernambucan reformers and politicians to embrace social hygiene programs, including concern with economic development and the successes of public health and social medicine in cities across Brazil and abroad. Historians of medicine and public health must be careful, however, not to overemphasize the influence of one particular set of medical ideas and practices. Eugenics was an essential aspect of government-funded Brazilian social reforms in the 1920s and 1930s, and in Brazil eugenics was understood and practiced primarily as a means of social reform rather than a means of social and racial exclusion.[174] It is clear, however, that eugenics had limited political appeal in Pernambuco and in Brazil as a whole. North American and European eugenics championed a racialized, white ideal that conformed to neither Latin American social and racial realities nor new understandings of national identity that idealized mixed-race, native Brazilians.

The Pernambucan social hygiene movement was most decisively shaped by politics. In the 1920s, public health and social hygiene became an essential aspect of progressive social and educational reforms that sought to redress the shortcomings of liberal capitalism. The political upheavals that culminated in the fascist-inspired Estado Novo emphasized the integration of healthy, robust workers and citizens into a corporatist society. Social hygiene thus reflected changing notions of the political as the state became an important social actor in a process that Alexandra Minna Stern has described as "the introduction of a series of behavioral and normative codes designed to produce new kinds of citizens and national subjects."[175]

6

Mental Hygiene

The Science of Character, 1925–1940

IN THE MID-1920s, reformers and politicians in Pernambuco began to take an interest in Pernambucans' psychological characteristics.[1] The state government's rapidly expanding Department of Health and Assistance took over the operation of the Santa Casa de Misericórdia's Hospício de Alienados (Lunatic Hospice) in 1924, and, by the early 1930s, the state had created additional services for the mentally ill and mentally deficient, including the Assistance for Psychopaths Service, the Mental Hygiene Service, and the Institute of Psychology. Public health officials and reformers embraced mental hygiene both as a means of diagnosing, treating, and preventing mental diseases and as a means of studying *nordestinos'* supposed psychological deficiencies. According to early-twentieth-century psychiatry and psychology, those deficiencies included the practice of Afro-Brazilian religions and popular millenarian Catholicism. The state government's mental hygiene services were understood to be an outgrowth of, and complement to, the state's social hygiene movement, which focused on Pernambucans' physical development. Pernambuco's mental hygiene movement instead focused on Pernambucans' psychological development, including education, in an attempt to improve care for the state's mentally ill and mentally deficient and to prepare citizens for the rigors of modern society.

In the mid-1920s, reformers' and politicians' concerns about the poor, the working classes, Afro-Brazilians, and the potentially restive populations of the interior began to be expressed using the language of psychology, psychiatry, and mental hygiene. They embraced mental hygiene as an effective means of ensuring *nordestinos'* intellectual and psychological development and as integral part of their efforts to expand the role of the state. By the end of the 1930s, the precepts of mental hygiene were being used extensively in education, prison management, industrial hygiene, and the social control of Afro-Brazilians. Mental hygiene constituted a new approach to addressing social and political problems, but in some respects it was used for a less progressive purpose: to reinforce Pernambuco's social and economic status quo. The precepts of mental health and education conformed to political and economic elites' idealized understandings of *nordestinos* as hard-working, well-trained workers who did not challenge elites' hold on power.

The extensive use of mental hygiene principles in public institutions allowed Pernambucan public health officials and political leaders to define individuals and groups as psychologically "normal" or "abnormal," which served to either reinforce or redefine existing conceptions of regional identity. Mental hygiene focused more directly on race than any other social reform effort in Pernambuco since the 1890s. Pernambucan psychiatrists endeavored to determine whether race constituted a predisposing factor in mental disorders, which led to investigations of Afro-Brazilian culture, including the first detailed studies of the practice of Candomblé in Pernambuco. These concerns about racial psychology were reflected in renewed interest in national and regional identity. Mariza Corrêa argues that "the definition of the country and its peoples had been the principal preoccupation of our intellectuals" in both the 1890s and the 1930s.[2] This was certainly the case in Pernambuco as reformers and political leaders, concerned with rural migration, urbanization, industrialization, and the control of labor, as well as increasing economic disparities between North and South, endeavored to better understand Pernambucans' racial and psychological characteristics.[3]

The origins and development of Pernambuco's mental hygiene movement reflected elites' concerns about northeastern social and economic development and their attempts to resolve questions about race and northeastern regional identity. Although I place the Mental Hygiene Service in an institutional and political context, I am less concerned with outlining the ways in which it differed from similar reforms in Brazil and abroad or whether it represented the incomplete institutionalization or misguided reception of European and North American science in a regional "backwater" of a nation already regarded as being on the scientific periphery. Instead I focus on how the Pernambucan mental hygiene movement reflected concerns about local and regional social and economic development and how it was used to formally define northeastern regional identity.

From Asylums to Mental Hygiene

For more than four decades after its establishment in 1883, the Hospício de Alienados was Pernambuco's sole treatment facility for the mentally ill and mentally deficient.[4] Administered by the Santa Casa de Misericórdia, a Catholic charitable organization, the *hospício* received almost no public funding, and it had the reputation, especially among physicians, of being a moribund institution whose personnel were more concerned with keeping patients locked up than attending to their needs. As late as the 1920s, the *hospício* remained the only institution devoted to the care of the mentally ill in northeastern Brazil.[5] In 1924, as part of the transfer of Santa Casa charities to the state government, the *hospício* was placed under the administration of the Department of Health and Assistance, whose director, Amaury de Medeiros, had been given the task of modernizing the state's public health system.[6] The *hospício* was renamed the Hospital of Nervous and Mental Diseases (Hospital de Doenças Nervosas e Mentais), and Medeiros appointed Ulysses Pernambucano de Melo, a cousin of Gilberto Freyre, as its director.[7] Pernambucano, who would prove to be one of the most progressive and successful reformers in Pernambuco during the 1920s and 1930s, received his medical degree in 1912 from the Faculdade de Medicina in Rio de Janeiro, completed a residency in Paraná, and tended a private practice in the Pernambucan interior before returning to Recife in 1916 to take a post at the *hospício*. As a result of his clinical work in the *hospício*, Pernambucano proposed several changes in patient care, including eliminating the use of solitary confinement and straitjackets and allowing long-term patients a greater degree of freedom, including tending gardens on the *hospício* grounds.[8] Pernambucano's suggestions fell on deaf ears, however, and administrators responded to his campaign to improve patient care by punishing him for insubordination. Despite ongoing conflict with administrators, Pernambucano's competency and advocacy were never seriously called into question, and he was eventually appointed director of the *hospício* in 1922. His administrative skills and willingness to implement needed reforms later resulted in his appointment as director of the Escola Normal in 1924 and the Ginásio Pernambucano in 1927, the state's two public secondary schools. It was not uncommon for officials to occupy several government positions, and while this usually reflected the distribution of political patronage, it was clear in Pernambucano's case that he continued to be devoted to both his medical and administrative careers. This put him in a unique position to oversee reforms of both education and mental health care.

In 1925, shortly after the state government's takeover of the *hospício*, the Department of Health and Assistance created the Instituto de Psicologia (Institute of Psychology, or IP) which was also placed under Ulysses Pernambucano's direction. The IP was created in order to "produce studies intended [to create] a perfect knowledge of the mentality of our people." The institute was charged with the task of developing psychological and intelligence tests that would be used as aids in "educating and diagnosing abnormal and supernormal infants," "examin[ing] candidates for professions whose conduct is of particular interest to public power," and "organiz[ing] work in industrial establishments."[9] IP research was designed to complement research on Pernambucans' physical characteristics that was being carried out by the Inspectorate of Social Hygiene. IP staff conducted psychological and intelligence tests of mental patients, criminals, students, soldiers, and workers, initially using tests developed in the United States and Europe by Alfred Binet, Théodore Simon, and Lewis Terman, all pioneers of intelligence testing. Within a year of the IP's founding, Pernambucano had produced a study of three hundred candidates for the Escola Normal using a modified version of Lewis Terman's IQ test.[10]

In 1929, the IP was renamed the Institute of Professional Selection and Orientation (Instituto de Selecção e Orientação Profissional, or ISOP), and newly developed psychological tests were utilized in factories, businesses, and government offices. The ISOP was charged with developing comprehensive "physio-psychological exams" for candidates interested in public employment as police officers, members of the civil guard, drivers, signalmen, and guards as well as placement exams for teachers and Department of Education technical staff.[11] In 1930, the ISOP began publishing the results of the research it had conducted in the state's public elementary schools, the Escola Normal, the Ginásio Pernambucano, and technical schools. What is most striking about early psychological research in Pernambuco is the degree to which it rejected eugenic ideals, which were typically embraced by the advocates of intelligence testing in the United States, most of whom were devoted eugenicists. Pernambucan intelligence testing was developed primarily for the purpose of assisting educators in evaluating students, not as a means for weeding out the feebleminded.[12] Pernambucan researchers could not entirely escape the influence of eugenics, however. In one study of the relationship between intelligence and physical development among Pernambucan public school students, José Lucena and Lourdes Paes Barreto, a research assistant for the Serviço de Assistencia a Psicopatas (Assistance for Psychopaths Service) and a primary school teacher, respectively, found a correlation between intelligence and physical development suggesting that students who were less robust physically were less intelligent. They nevertheless concluded that their results should not be generalized and quoted Rio de Janeiro educator Leoni Kaseff, who argued that "neither the dimensions of the physical body nor health provide a sufficient indication of mental normality, superiority, or inferiority."[13] Despite the fact that Pernambucans and *nordestinos* were believed to be less developed physically and less healthy than their southern counterparts, researchers concluded that there was no evidence that they were less intelligent. For Pernambucan educators and psychologists, intelligence testing was a tool to be used primarily in the evaluation of students. Test results were used to place students of equal abilities in the same classroom and to assess individual strengths and weaknesses, not to exclude them from access to education.

The revolution that brought Getúlio Vargas to power in 1930 led the federal government to assume greater control over state government finances and services. Coimbra's government continued to favor many of the progressive reforms that were initiated under his predecessor, however.[14] Federal financial and political support for public health reforms increased, and in 1931 the state legislature created the Serviço de Assistencia a Psicopatas or SAP.[15] The SAP administered state psychiatric hospitals and asylums, the Institute of Psychology/Institute of Professional Selection and Orientation, an asylum for the criminally insane (Manicômio Judiciário), an agricultural colony on Itamaracá for institutionalized patients, and a newly created preventive Mental Hygiene Service, the first such service in Brazil.[16] Ulysses Pernambucano, who served as the director of SAP from 1931 to 1935, lauded the government's efforts, writing that it had, "in organizing the first official Mental Hygiene Service in Brazil, endeavored, as much as possible, to give it a scientific direction that takes regional problems into consideration."[17] From its inception, the service was charged with discovering "the most frequent causes of mental illness in our midst," in addition to caring for the mentally ill.[18] In a long publication describing the service's activities, Pernambucano emphasized that the Mental Hygiene Service would address "regional problems" in its work by collecting data on mental diseases in other northeastern states and by sponsoring lectures and conferences in which mental health experts from the entire region would discuss their work.[19]

The most significant reform in the treatment of the mentally ill after the creation of the SAP was the implementation of "open services," which allowed institutionalized patients to return to their homes on a part- or full-time basis. Pernambucano was also concerned with relieving overcrowding at the Hospital of Nervous and Mental Diseases.[20] Citing North American and European psychiatrists and psychologists, Pernambucano argued that many patients would recover more quickly if they were not subjected to continuous internment. He modeled his "open door policy" on one developed in the United States by Clifford Beers and created an outpatient service that included four specialized health centers in Recife along with visiting nurses who attended to patients in their homes.[21] Pernambucano also emphasized the importance of manual labor as treatment for certain patients, arguing that "work is a curative means." Initially, patients tended gardens on the grounds of the Hospital of Nervous and Mental Diseases, and later the program expanded to include agricultural colonies in suburban areas, with patients producing crops to be sold at local markets. Pernambucano also intended to create programs that utilized craftwork and light industrial production to treat patients, but he came to believe that agricultural work was the most appropriate and effective therapy because the majority of the patients at the Hospital of Nervous and Mental Diseases were from the interior of the state and thus were accustomed to agricultural work.[22] While Pernambucano's immediate goal was to treat Pernambucans' mental illnesses, he also saw the SAP as an institution that would serve to transform Pernambucan society: "We intend to obtain for these poor people—created by economic, social, and even in certain cases, biological contingencies from this point of view inferior to that of the slaves . . . more interest in the entirety of work that will be pursued positively in a utopia. We seek to reinstate the individual to society not only cured of his psychosis but only when he is relieved of his primitive mentality."[23] Pernambucano continued to believe, as did most physicians and intellectuals of his generation, that Pernambucans' supposedly inferior racial background produced a "primitive mentality." He believed, however, that this obstacle could be overcome.

The prevention of mental illnesses became an important activity of the SAP in the 1930s, and the Mental Hygiene Service, under the direction of psychiatrist José Lucena, was to administer preventive measures, which included the dissemination of educational information to the public via public demonstrations, lectures, pamphlets, magazine and newspaper articles, and weekly radio lectures, which reformers hoped would instill "precepts of neuro-psychiatric hygiene" in the general public.[24] The service was charged with the task of "combating the most accessible causes of mental illness," including alcohol abuse, sexually transmitted diseases, and "vulgar or low spiritism" (a term employed to describe Afro-Brazilian religions, including Candomblé).[25]

At the same time, the Mental Hygiene Service initiated several clinical studies of mental diseases in the state.[26] Finally, the Pernambucan legislature ordered that the Mental Hygiene Service should be used in the management of labor and factories by monitoring workers who were "predisposed to abnormalities in the industrial workplace" and by "seeking to promote, by way of applicable psychotechnical methods, the selection of workers in accordance with their mental aptitudes."[27] The service's various clinical, research, and educational activities were chronicled in the *Archivos da Assistencia de Psicopatas de Pernambuco*, a professional journal published biannually from 1931 to 1936.

In 1933, Ulysses Pernambucano founded and served as president of the state's League of Mental Hygiene, a privately funded organization that was not part of the state government, because he was concerned that the state's mentally ill would not receive adequate attention without the support and participation of the wider community.[28] Due to Pernambucano's efforts, economic and civic leaders increasingly viewed mental hygiene as an effective instrument of social reform. João Aureliano, an appellate court judge (*desembargador*) and, beginning in 1934, president of the League of Mental Hygiene, wrote that mental hygiene was indispensable to "the millenarian battle that man has maintained against the elements that are adverse to him." Aureliano believed that "as a branch of social hygiene, mental hygiene aims to prevent the growth of psychoses and, at the same time, to protect the civil collective against the pernicious influences of psycho-pathological manifestations, avoiding the dangers that could affect mad individuals." The most serious threats to Pernambucans' mental health, he continued, were "illnesses and intoxicants that, as a cause of degeneration, were transmitted from the ascendants to the descendants," including syphilis, tuberculosis, and alcoholism.[29] Aureliano believed that the state should make every effort to control these threats, and he suggested that the best method would be the use of "psychic education, principally in infancy, [which] has the power to create habits and tendencies that have the capacity to modify cerebral structure, in an attempt to give a new outline to human conduct." Aureliano contemplated stronger measures to ensure Pernambucans' mental health, including eugenics. Although he acknowledged the concerns of critics who argued that eugenic measures would result in a population decline, he recommended "the heroic prophylaxis of sterilization for degenerates, abnormals, criminals, the insane, amoral perverts, recidivists, and in general all individuals whose reproduction would be prejudicial to the interests and defense of society."[30] He also rejected as "simple palliatives" attempts to legislate prenuptial medical examinations because such exams were not obligatory.[31] Aureliano served as president of the League of

Mental Hygiene for only one year, but his position as state supreme court justice led him to pen an article endorsing the notion that mental illness constituted legal grounds for marital separation (*desquite*) and divorce, although the latter remained illegal in Brazil.[32] Aureliano's support for eugenics was unusual among psychiatrists and proponents of mental hygiene in Pernambuco, however. Ulysses Pernambucano believed that the mentally ill could be treated, cured, and returned to society. Indeed, the activities of the League of Mental Hygiene reflected this position; it concentrated on raising money to support the treatment, education, and rehabilitation of the state's mentally ill. By 1935, the league had succeeded in raising sixty-nine *contos* in subscriptions (US$5,720 at 1935 conversion rates), which were used to support the construction of a school for "abnormal children" as well as the league's other education and propaganda efforts.[33]

By the mid-1930s, the SAP had become an indispensable part of government efforts to improve public health conditions in Pernambuco. Ulysses Pernambucano had overseen substantial changes in the treatment of patients at state psychiatric hospitals and asylums, established outpatient services, founded the Institute of Psychology, created the Mental Hygiene Service devoted to raising public awareness of mental disorders, founded the League of Mental Hygiene in order to raise financial and political support for mental hygiene among the political and economic elite, and had overseen a staff of psychiatrists, nurses, researchers, and assistants who worked toward understanding and treating Pernambucans' psychological disorders. In addition to its clinical work in hospitals and asylums, the SAP focused its attention on two areas: promoting the use of psychological and intelligence testing in education and investigating the relationship between race and mental disorders. These areas of research produced knowledge of Pernambucans' psychological characteristics that became essential components of understandings of northeastern regional identity.

Education and Intelligence Testing

In the late 1920s and early 1930s, Pernambuco's Serviço de Assistencia a Psicopatas played an important role in public education by providing psychological and intelligence testing for elementary and secondary students as well as for students enrolled in the state's various technical and professional training programs. Education was deemed a crucial part of efforts to modernize the state and the region; reformers sought to prepare both agricultural and industrial workers for the challenges of the field and factory. Ulysses Pernambucano, while serving as director of the Escola Normal and then the Ginásio Pernambucano, utilized psychological and intelligence testing in both institutions. The founding of the Instituto de Psicologia in 1925 facilitated the use of testing in a variety of settings. IP employees utilized intelligence testing and psychological profiling in schools and technical training programs in order to establish baselines against which individual student progress could be compared and to place students in appropriate classrooms and programs. Educator Antônio Carneiro Leão's wide-ranging reform of the Pernambucan public education system in 1929 provided an opportunity to introduce intelligence testing and psychological profiling throughout the system. He argued that psychological testing was an essential tool of modern education: "the science of psychology is becoming, in all places, a fundamental preoccupation of governments, of industrial organizations, of the educational apparatus. No modern educational organization can ignore it."[34] Pernambucan political leaders quickly appreciated the promised benefits of psychological testing, and in his 1929 annual report to the state legislature, Governor Estácio de Albuquerque Coimbra wrote that "aiming to scientifically determine the individual inclinations, so that all can realize their tendencies and possibilities by means of tests of intelligence and aptitude, the Institute [of Psychology] will victoriously guide all individuals who are put in its trust, not only turning them away from unadvisable professions but correcting defects, indicating professions more in accord with their physical, mental, and moral disposition, benefiting equally the collectivity."[35]

Intelligence and psychological testing of students began in earnest in 1925 with a ten-year project to develop a "Pernambucan revision" of the Stanford-Binet IQ test. Developed originally by French psychologist Alfred Binet and adapted in 1916 by Stanford University psychologist Lewis Terman, the Stanford-Binet IQ test was used widely in educational testing in the United States.[36] The IP employed roving "assistants" and "monitors," usually women who had been teachers themselves, to administer tests and collect data. For each student, monitors compiled a detailed *ficha* (data card) that included biographical information, a psychological profile, and test results.[37] The *fichas* were gathered into a central archive to facilitate data retrieval and ongoing analysis of test data. IP researchers and Department of Education officials debated how students should be classified, with IP researchers arguing that "mental age," determined by comparing individual test results against aggregate data, should be used to place students of similar abilities in the same classroom.[38] This approach was later abandoned, however, with Department of Education officials preferring to categorize students according to age or physical aptitude. Another important issue that arose in the analysis of test results was the existence of "abnormal" and "supernormal" students in the public school system. Students determined to be "abnormal" were referred to the IP, where they were subjected to a thorough battery of tests from which a "psycho-pedagogic profile" was created. Students with similar disabilities were placed together in classrooms and schools that could better address their needs.[39] Ulysses Pernambucano and IP researchers paid considerable attention to students who fell outside their definition of "normal," and they urged the state government to address the problem of the education of "abnormal" students before their deficiencies became, as one researcher put it, "onerous to the collectivity."[40]

IP researchers utilized a wide variety of psychological and intelligence tests, and Pernambucan researchers spent considerable time translating tests from the United States and Europe into Portuguese and developing verbal tests for illiterates, which was essential in a society with low literacy rates. The IP's "Pernambucan revision" of the Stanford-Binet IQ was adopted as the standard and administered to all Pernambucan students between the ages of three and eighteen.[41] In 1932, IP researchers gave more than two thousand students a timed exam covering vocabulary, writing, drawing, mathematics, and reasoning. Three-year-old children were to point to the parts of their body, name familiar objects, state their gender, and repeat verbal phrases of six to seven syllables. Among other tasks, fourteen-year-olds were to complete a sixty-word vocabulary test, tell time, repeat verbal phrases of twenty-eight syllables, and name the president and king of Brazil (apparently student responses to trick questions like this one were deemed an acceptable measure of intelligence).[42] After the test was standardized and used for several years in the public school system, it was also used to test the intelligence of soldiers, criminals, and prisoners and patients in the state's psychiatric hospitals and asylums. Anita Paes Barreto, who served as the director of IP assistants and monitors and who was involved in the development of the test from its inception, argued that the test was an essential diagnostic tool in the evaluation of the mentally ill and mentally deficient. Barreto suggested that the "Pernambucan revision" should be utilized in other northeastern states; the similar social and cultural characteristics of neighboring states, she reasoned, would give "very useful results."[43] IP researchers also utilized a number of other psychological and intelligence tests, one of which involved asking subjects to draw a human figure that was then checked against a list of the elements that a drawing should contain according to the subject's age.[44] A puzzle test, designed to assess general intelligence and spatial cognition—qualities deemed essential to success in specific occupations—was administered to more than eight hundred students in Recife's technical-professional schools.[45] IP monitors and psychiatrists chose from among these and other tests based on their initial diagnosis of a patient, and, in almost all cases, initial evaluations of subjects were confirmed by test results.[46]

Beginning in 1925 and continuing through the mid-1930s, intelligence and psychological testing was utilized to evaluate candidates for high school placement and government civil service jobs, as well as patients in public hospitals, soldiers, and prisoners.[47] Candidates for admission to the Escola Normal were routinely subjected to IQ tests. Primary school students were tested in order to determine "mental age" and for placement in appropriate grade levels. Intelligence testing was used to determine the fitness of workers in different professions, including the state government's attempted regulation of domestic workers.[48] IP monitors tested the leaders of Candomblé temples in greater Recife in order to determine whether they were mentally "fit" to practice religion.[49] In 1932 alone, the IP conducted a total of seventy-four hundred intelligence and psychological tests. After 1935, however, the state government's interest in psychological and intelligence testing began to decline; in 1936, the IP administered only nineteen hundred tests.[50] The reasons for this decline were primarily political. As discussed in the previous chapter, by the mid-1930s the Department of Education had begun to place greater emphasis on students' physical development, a shift that reflected the political ethos of the Vargas era, which emphasized action rather than intellectual deliberation.[51] The decline of intelligence and psychological testing was hastened by the dismissal of Ulysses Pernambucano from his government posts in 1935. Leftist political sympathies, like those of Pernambucano, became a politically liability for state and federal political leaders as the government turned in an increasingly reactionary direction after the failed communist insurrection in 1935.

Understanding Mental Disorders

A significant area of activity for Ulysses Pernambucano and the SAP was research into the origins and causes of mental disorders, particularly the ways in which mental illnesses reflected regional social and cultural conditions. Most early-twentieth-century Brazilian understandings of mental disorders depended heavily on the ideas and scholarship of Raymundo Nina Rodrigues, who, in addition to his anthropological studies on Afro-Brazilians, wrote extensively on mental disorders and was a leading figure in the development and acceptance of legal medicine in Brazil.[52] His interpretations of collective behavior strongly influenced subsequent research on and interpretations of social movements in which religion played a significant role, and they formed the basis for SAP approaches to popular religion through the 1940s.[53] Aside from theories of collective behavior, early-twentieth-century alienists and psychiatrists developed working theories of the etiology of mental disorders and their effects on individuals. These early understandings of mental disorders were primarily somatic, that is, psychiatrists believed that mental disorders had physical causes. These causes included heredity, race, intoxicants such as alcohol and marijuana, communicable diseases that affected the nervous system, and social and environmental factors. By the late 1920s, Pernambucan psychiatrists and the SAP had adopted the Brazilian Society of Psychiatry, Neurology, and Legal Medicine's standardized categorization of mental disorders, which included "psychopathic" diseases (which produced anatomical lesions), "constitutional" diseases (which did not produce anatomical lesions), and "toxic and infectious psychoses."[54] Although this classification scheme worked well in theory, most Pernambucan psychiatrists and SAP researchers were less discriminating in their evaluations and diagnoses of patients. While the training of psychiatrists and SAP employees improved in the 1930s and 1940s under Pernambucano's tutelage, there was still considerable confusion with regard to the clinical diagnosis and treatment of mental disorders. The increasing influence of psychoanalysis and the work of Sigmund Freud in the late 1930s and early 1940s further complicated diagnosis and treatment, and SAP psychiatrists and researchers often cited Freud, along with psychiatrist Alfred Adler, neurologist Jean-Martin Charcot, and racial theorists Cesare Lombroso, Ludwig Gumplowicz, and Gustave Le Bon in discussing the etiologies of mental disorders. These theoretical and methodological inconsistencies were reflected in SAP psychiatrists' clinical work and publications. For example, although SAP psychiatrists frequently cited, and challenged, Freudian psychoanalytic theories based on clinical observations, Pernambucano unequivocally stated in a 1932 annual report that the SAP was not able to use psychoanalysis to treat patients due to a lack of resources, especially trained personnel.[55] By the late 1930s, however, researchers were publishing an increasing number of articles predicated on Freudian interpretations of mental disorders, the most striking of these articles being a study of street children.[56] Gonçalves Fernandes, who conducted psychological examinations of criminals for Recife's Office of Criminal Anthropology (Gabinete de Antropologia Criminal), diagnosed mental disorders according to Freudian theories, although he did not use psychoanalysis as a method of treatment.[57] SAP psychiatrists and monitors used Freudian terminology most frequently in analyses of childhood and young adulthood, including citing the Oedipus complex as an explanation for childhood disorders and socially unacceptable behavior.[58] Psychodynamic interpretations of mental disorders were generally incompatible with somatic interpretations. The former identified psychological factors, which were less obvious and more difficult to diagnose, as the causes of mental disorders, while the latter identified physical causes, which could include somatic diseases that affected the nervous system, drug and alcohol abuse, and physical and racial characteristics. Combining psychodynamic and somatic approaches to mental disorders did not prove especially troubling for SAP psychiatrists, however. Despite his reservations about using psychoanalysis to treat patients, Pernambucano did not favor one school over the other, and as with racial theories and theories of disease transmission, new theories and practices from Europe and the United States were applied whenever they seemed appropriate.

Under Pernambucano's direction, SAP researchers focused on studies that addressed the relationship between race and mental disorders. Political interest in northeastern regional identity and intellectual interest in race, deriving especially from the influence of Gilberto Freyre's writings of the 1920s and early 1930s, provided SAP researchers with a justification for their inquiries. SAP researchers approached race in three ways. First, researchers investigated whether *negros, mulatos,* and *brancos* suffered from the same mental illnesses and whether mental disorders affected racial groups differently. Second, building on Raymundo Nina Rodrigues's research at the turn of the century, SAP researchers undertook the study of the psychological aspects, both individual and social, of Afro-Brazilian religions, including Candomblé. SAP researchers and state public health authorities understood the spiritual leaders of Afro-Brazilian Candomblé *seitas* (meeting places, or, literally, sects) to be mentally unstable and a potential threat to the mental health of "normal" (i.e., Catholic) Pernambucans. Finally, SAP researchers undertook the study of *sertanejos'* psychological characteristics, concentrating on "fanatical" social and religious groups such as the devotees of Padre Cícero Romão Batista (*romeiros*) and the rural bandits of the northeastern interior (*cangaceiros*). The populations of the interior, who were constructed as the descendants of Europeans and Indians, were viewed as racially distinct from the Afro-Brazilian populations of coastal areas. SAP research on the relationship between race and mental disorders not only provided valuable information about the etiology of mental disorders, which was used to reform mental health services, but also provided politicians and reformers with information about Pernambucans' collective psychology, which was used in the design of social reform programs and to control the practice of Afro-Brazilian religion and millenarian Catholicism in the interior. SAP research was thus profoundly political, addressing not only current problems in psychiatry and psychology but also political elites' concerns about the social management of Pernambucan populations.

Race and Mental Hygiene

Ulysses Pernambucano had initiated the study of the racial aspects of mental disorders in 1930 by collecting data on the frequency of specific mental disorders according to race among the patients of the Hospital of Nervous and Mental Diseases. Pernambucano wanted to discover, as he put it, "if mental illnesses among the individuals of the black race [raça negra] are as frequent as in the other races." He argued for the necessity of investigating all possible causes of mental diseases, including "biological factors such as heredity, toxins, and infections (the predisposing role of alcoholism and of syphilis in certain psychoses), [and] social factors (living conditions, housing, influence of religions, fetishisms, etc.)"[59] There were, however, two problems that Pernambucano faced in conducting research on race and mental disorders in Pernambuco. First, despite the SAP's adoption of the Brazilian Society of Psychiatry, Neurology, and Legal Medicine's standardized categorization of mental disorders, Brazilian psychiatrists and psychologists did not agree on the classification of many mental disorders. It was difficult, if not impossible, for clinicians and researchers to provide consistent diagnoses of mental disorders that could be relied on for statistical purposes. Second, Pernambucano and fellow researchers had difficulty in classifying their patients according to race, which was, as they quickly recognized, an inherently subjective undertaking. Complicating matters further was the fact that there were few credible studies of the racial composition of the general population of Brazil and even fewer for Pernambuco. Pernambucano and Helena Campos, a Mental Hygiene Service monitor, used Arthur Lobo da Silva's 1928 study of the racial composition of the Brazilian military as a baseline for the study they planned. Lobo da Silva and his researchers had collected racial data for 966 Pernambucan praças, and those data indicated that 58 percent of the Pernambucan population was branco, 35 percent mestiço, 6 percent preto, and 1 percent caboclo (mixed Indian and European), which, even according to the most recent national census, underestimated the state's nonwhite population.[60]

Table 6.1
Racial composition of Pernambuco (percentage)

Race	1872 census	1890 census	1940 census	1928 Lobo survey	1935 Pernambucano survey
Branco	34.6	41.2	54.5	58	19.44
Pardo	50.5	47.3	29.9	35 (mestiço)	55.13 (mestiço)
Preto	14.9	11.5	15.5	6	25.42

Sources: Levine, Pernambuco, 12; Silva, "A anthropologia no exercito brasileiro," quarto I; and Pernambucano et al., "Alguns dados antropologicos da população do Recife," 42.

Initially, Pernambucano and Campos accepted these figures, noting that army conscripts were a representative cross-section of Pernambuco's general population. Comparing Lobo da Silva's data with their own, Pernambucano and Campos observed that there was a higher percentage of *pretos* (approximately 10 percent) in the Hospital of Nervous and Mental Diseases than in the Pernambucan general population (6 percent), which led Pernambucano and Campos to conclude that *pretos* were more likely than *mestiços* and *brancos* to suffer from mental disorders.[61]

Pernambucano and Campos noted that "the social situation of *negros* in Pernambuco is perfectly comparable to the great mass of our poor population of the other races" (among the general patient population), which they argued ruled out "social factors" as a cause of the differing rates of mental disorders among *brancos*, *mestiços*, and *pretos*. Thus, in this preliminary study of the relationship between race and mental disorders, Pernambucano and Campus concluded that race was a determining factor in susceptibility to mental illness. The researchers went further, however, addressing the issue of whether *negros* were more likely to suffer from certain disorders. Pernambucano and Campos divided their data according to whether patients suffered from "constitutional diseases," "psychopathic disorders," or "toxic and infectious psychoses." While they found that "constitutional diseases" were equally common among the three racial groups, their data indicated that *negros* were more likely than *mestiços* and *brancos* to suffer from "psychopathic disorders" and "toxic and infectious psychoses."[62] Pernambucano and Campos argued that *negros* were more likely than *mestiços* and *brancos* to suffer from the psychological effects of syphilis, alcoholism, and morphine addiction and from "debility," "imbecilism," "idiocy," and "general paresis" (paralysis). *Brancos*, on the other hand, were more likely to be schizophrenic and neurotic, which Pernambucano and Campos noted was "most interesting," without offering further explanation.[63] While their results were suggestive, they concluded that further research, including collecting data about patients' sex, age, marital status, and "social situation," would be necessary in order to determine definitively whether race was a predisposing factor in mental disorders.

There were, of course, problems with Pernambucano and Campos's study. Their racial categorizations relied on researchers' subjective definitions of race, based almost entirely on physical appearance, and assessments of social and economic status. One researcher might classify an individual as *branco*, while another might classify the same individual as *mestiço*. While SAP researchers may have held similar understandings of what constituted different racial groups, Pernambucano and Campos did not outline the standards that they used in their research. Another problem stemmed from Arthur Lobo da Silva's study, which contradicted the 1890 federal census data.[64] His sample size— 966 *praças*—was small, and it may not have accurately reflected Pernambuco's population as a whole, given that the racial composition of Pernambucan conscripts likely differed significantly from that of the general population (nonwhites were more likely to be conscripted).[65] While Pernambucano and Campos raised the issue of sample size, they did not complicate the issue of racial identification. Like the majority of intellectuals and scientists working in this era, they viewed race as an objective, scientifically measurable characteristic.

Pernambucano continued his research on mental disorders and race, collecting additional data in 1933 and 1934, and he presented his findings at the First Afro-Brazilian Congress, held in Recife in 1934.[66] This new research confirmed his earlier findings. Although he used the Brazilian Society of Psychiatry, Neurology, and Legal Medicine's updated classification of mental disorders in his research, he concluded that *brancos* and *mestiços* were more likely to suffer from "constitutional psychoses," which now included manic depressive psychosis, degeneration, psychotic degeneration, schizophrenia, paranoid dementia, paraphrenia, neurotic psychoses, and paranoia. Conversely, he concluded that *negros* were more likely to suffer from "organic psychoses," which now included epilepsy, cerebral lesions caused by syphilis, terminal dementias caused by arteriosclerosis, "oligophrenia," general paresis, and toxic and infectious psychoses.[67] Among *brancos* and *mulatos*, Pernambucano argued, the most important cause of mental disorders was the inability to cope with the stresses of modern life. Among *negros*, by contrast, the causes of disease were heredity and "toxic and infectious" psychoses. Pernambucano also pointed out that there were proportionally greater numbers of *negros* among the patients of the Hospital of Nervous and Mental Diseases than among the general population, which led him to conclude that there was "a manifest fragility of *negros* in our midst in relation to mental illness."[68] Pernambucano was careful to point out that social and economic factors were not significant variables in his study because, he argued, the majority of patients in Pernambucan state mental institutions were impoverished or of the working class. The majority of Pernambucans with the economic means to do so sought treatment with private physicians. Thus, he reasoned, race was the only possible cause of the differing rates of diseases. Gilberto Freyre strongly disagreed with his cousin's views on the role of race in mental disorders, and he argued in *Sobrados e mucambos* (1936), referring directly to Pernambucano's 1934 article, that differences among racial groups should be attributed to social factors rather than heredity: "it would seem to us that even among the poor classes there are at times influences operating that are unfavorable to *negros*—unfavorable to their success or triumphs in society or sentiments of love, for example— influences that may well interfere in their mental health and in the social normality of their life."[69] Freyre's social and cultural approach to race was not yet widely accepted by the Brazilian medical and scientific community, which had largely trained in a tradition that viewed race as an inherent, immutable characteristic to be treated as a pathology. Pernambucano left no evidence of a public response to his cousin's objections, but his research on race would soon begin to more closely reflect Freyre's approach to race.

Pernambucano and SAP researchers also sought to understand the role race played, if any, in the etiology and pathology of specific mental disorders. One study conducted toward that end was of general paresis, the protracted mental deterioration and paralysis caused by cerebral syphilis.[70] Pernambucano did not accept the commonly held belief that general paresis reflected "the new conditions of civilized life" and was thus more common among *brancos* than among *mulatos* and *negros*. Pernambucano divided patients with general paresis into racial groups, and comparing the racial distribution with that of the general population (again using Lobo da Silva's figures), he found that proportionally fewer *brancos* and more *negros* suffered from the condition.[71] While Pernambuco did not offer an explanation for these results, presumably because his data flatly contradicted then-current understandings of the disease, he nevertheless concluded that race was a causal factor.

Other SAP researchers expanded the scope of Pernambucano's research on race. In 1932, Maria da Graça Araujo published a study of "episodic deliriums" among the patients of the Hospital de Alienados, formerly known as the Hospício de Alienados.[72] Araujo categorized patients suffering from deliriums according to race and occupation, and while she did not find a direct correlation between race and the disorder, she found fewer cases among the "superior professions" and more among "manual laborers," who, she noted, were usually illiterate. She added that most patients suffering from deliriums showed signs of "intellectual weakness." Araujo attributed the higher number of cases among the illiterate manual laborers to the influence of "*baixo espiritismo*," a reference to Afro-Brazilian religion. She also noted that inhabitants of Pernambuco's interior displayed similar symptoms, which, she concluded, suggested that Afro-Brazilian religions were widely practiced in the interior.[73] In 1936, João Marque de Sá, a psychiatrist who began working for the SAP in the mid-1930s, conducted research on the intelligence of patients suffering from epilepsy. He found that among epileptics registered with the SAP's Open Service from 1931 to 1936, a high percentage of *pretos* tested at the "imbecile level," an IQ range from 26 to 50.[74] According to Sá, fewer *pardos* and *brancos* tested at this level. Conversely, more *brancos* tested at the "normal level," with an IQ between 91 and 110. Sá also noted that *pretos* were more likely than *pardos* and *brancos* to suffer from epilepsy.[75] His research led him to conclude that *branco* epileptics were more intelligent than *preto* epileptics and that *pardo* epileptics were somewhere in between *brancos* and *pretos*. In addition to affirming the notion that race was a factor in mental disorders, SAP research supported the notion of a racial hierarchy and *branqueamento*, which placed *brancos* at the top of Brazil's racial hierarchy and *pretos* at the bottom. In their studies of specific mental disorders, SAP researchers also emphasized the supposed causal connections between class, race, and religion. Pernambuco's largely nonwhite working classes, many of whom practiced syncretic Afro-Brazilian religions rather than traditional Catholicism, were believed to be more prone to contracting certain mental disorders. In addition, because the specific causes of many mental disorders were unknown, Pernambucan psychiatrists and SAP researchers often identified race as a cause of mental disorders.

By 1935, Ulysses Pernambucano and SAP researchers believed they had made significant progress in investigating the relationship between race and mental disorders—they had completed detailed studies of a number of specific disorders, including episodic deliriums, general paresis, schizophrenia, and epilepsy.[76] In the same year, Pernambucano initiated a more comprehensive study of the racial composition of the general population to serve as a baseline for continuing and future research. Pernambucano, Arnaldo Di Lascio, Almir Guimarães, and Jarbas Pernambucano (Ulysses' son) collected racial and biometric data from thirteen hundred volunteer subjects, including students from Recife's Faculdade de Medicina and Escola de Aperfeiçoamento (School of Improvement), "inhabitants of poor and middle-class neighborhoods," factory workers, soldiers from the Brigada Militar and the Batalhão da Caçadores (Light Infantry Division), as well as prisoners from the state penitentiary in Recife.[77] They utilized several anthropometric measures to analyze their data and classify their subjects, including skin color, hair color, and eye color plus measurements of subjects' noses and craniums, which were used to calculate a "cephalic index." Pernambucano and his colleagues determined that 19.44 percent of their subjects were *branco*, 55.13 percent *mulato*, and 25.42 percent *negro*.[78] These figures represented a radical departure from previous estimates of the racial composition of the state, especially compared to Lobo da Silva's 1928 study of the military. Pernambucano and his colleagues found that 80 percent of Recife's population was nonwhite, whereas Lobo da Silva had estimated that only 41 percent was nonwhite. Pernambucano and his colleagues' sample size was larger than Lobo da Silva 's (1,306 to 966), and, in spite of the fact that their data were gathered almost entirely at state-run institutions, they argued that their data were representative of the entire state's population because a significant percentage of Recife's inhabitants had migrated from the interior of the state.[79]

This study had a profound impact on research carried out by the SAP and, as it turned out, a profoundly negative impact on Pernambucano's public career and state political leaders' willingness to continue supporting the SAP. The new estimates of the racial composition of Recife's population suggested that all previous research on the relationship between race and mental disorders was erroneous. The new estimates implied that *negros* were actually less prone than *brancos* and *mulatos* to contracting certain diseases. More importantly, Pernambucano's estimates of the state's nonwhite population were flatly rejected by Pernambuco's political leaders, who by 1935 were becoming increasingly uncomfortable with reformers, intellectuals, and "political extremists" who questioned the social and political status quo.

As a result of his political activities and willingness to take on controversial social and political issues while serving as director of the SAP, Ulysses Pernambucano was fired from his position as director of the SAP in November 1935, immediately prior to the Intentona Comunista. Pernambucano was singled out for both his professional and intellectual interests and his political activities—he had played an instrumental role in organizing a regional congress of the Juventude Proletaria, Estudantil e Popular, a youth organization with ties to the Communist Party, and his support of a union confederation, the Frente Unica Syndical, the formation of which was deemed to be in violation of the recently promulgated Law of National Security.[80] After the uprising, Pernambucano was imprisoned for five weeks and unjustly accused of participating in the revolt.[81] At the same time, the state government moved quickly to distance itself from the political Left, and numerous progressive reformers were dismissed from their civil service positions in the repression that took place after the uprising. After the premature end of his public career, Pernambucano never had the opportunity to revise the SAP's official position on race and mental disorders.[82] In 1936, however, he founded the Sanatório Recife, the state's first private sanitarium devoted to the care of the mentally ill, where he continued tending to patients and conducting research. Excluded from publishing in the *AAPP* after his dismissal, he founded a new journal in 1938 entitled *Neurobiologia,* which published the results of his and others' research.[83]

Continuing the research he had started while serving as director of the SAP, Pernambucano began to ascribe causality to social and economic factors rather than to race. While aggregate statistics collected at the Sanatório Recife and state-run institutions indicated that *negros* were still more likely than *brancos* and *mestiços* to suffer from certain classes of disorders, Pernambucano argued that these differences were attributable to a "lack of hygienic education and [*negros'*] own inferior economic situation."[84] Gilberto Freyre would have approved of his cousin's new position on the role of race in mental disorders, but state political leaders did not. To argue that the deplorable social and economic conditions in which the majority of the state's Afro-Brazilian populations lived contributed to disease rates was politically unacceptable. During the remainder of the Estado Novo, Pernambucano's continuing efforts to advance understanding of the public health and racial aspects of mental disorders went largely unrecognized by Pernambucan authorities.

After Pernambucano's death in 1943, several colleagues continued research on race and mental disorders in other northeastern states. Although Luiz Cerqueira's 1944 study of patients' mental disorders in public hospitals and asylums in the states of Bahia and Sergipe indicated that *negros* suffered from higher rates of disease than *brancos* and *mestiços,* Cerqueira argued that "lighter-skinned" patients possessed sufficient financial resources to seek care at private hospitals. Thus, Cerqueira reasoned that *negros, mestiços,* and *brancos* in Bahia and Sergipe suffered from the same mental diseases as their counterparts in Pernambuco. He asked whether "it can be concluded that *negros* would be more afflicted by mental diseases simply because of a racial factor" and answered that "it seems to us that they are not."[85] Like Pernambucano, he believed that social and economic factors rather than race constituted predisposing factors in the propagation of mental disorders.

Leading Pernambucan intellectual Gilberto Freyre supported his cousin Pernambucano's investigations of race while the latter served as director of the SAP. Freyre viewed psychiatry and mental hygiene as crucial aspects of the state's efforts to address social problems and to rehabilitate the *mulato*. In *Nordeste* (1937), Freyre wrote that Pernambucano's research constituted an attempt to "escape the preconception of the biological inferiority of the *negro* and the *mulato* that dominated Nina Rodrigues and his school, [by] beginning to observe the social aspects and the stimulus or the influence of surroundings and of conditions, or we should say pathology, of the region in the problems of mental and nervous illnesses." For Freyre, Pernambucano's SAP research scientifically confirmed "that we do not encounter in the *mestiço* or the *negro* of the Northeast that absolute inferiority of race or of sub-races in which Nina Rodrigues believed."[86] In *Sobrados e mucambos*, Freyre cited research conducted by two Rio-based psychiatrists who, in a paper presented at the First Afro-Brazilian Congress, suggested that the differential frequency of mental disorders among racial groups should be interpreted as evidence of *branqueamento* in *mulatos*. Freyre opined that this research showed that "from the point of view of psychopathology, the Brazilian *mestiço* or *mulato* is steadily assimilating the qualities of *brancos*."[87] Freyre believed that SAP research would reveal key details about *nordestinos'* collective psychology, which would contribute to a scientific understanding of northeastern regional identity. He argued that "this group of Recife researchers is today one of the most insistent in the social aspects and in what could be called regional aspects—that is, of social milieu, including the economic—of psychiatry: the regional conditions of life, the predisposing role of alcoholism and of syphilis in certain psychoses, the action of fetishism, of 'low spiritism,' of marijuana and other factors."[88] While Freyre, unsurprisingly, interpreted SAP research in light of his own views on race and society, it is clear that he regarded the work being done by Ulysses Pernambucano and others as a significant step toward discrediting outdated approaches to race and in establishing a scientific understanding of northeastern regional identity.

Beyond Freyre's unbridled enthusiasm, understandings of the relationship between race and mental disorders had changed significantly since the late nineteenth century and Raymundo Nina Rodrigues's pioneering research. By the mid-1930s, Brazilian physicians and scientists had largely abandoned the essentialist theories of race that had dominated medical and scientific research and had instead adopted the position that social and economic factors played a role in the etiology of disease. There remained one area of inquiry, however, which continued to be influenced by outdated racial theories: the study of Afro-Brazilian religion.

Candomblé as a Threat to Mental Health

Soon after the creation of the SAP in 1931, researchers began to consider the psychological aspects of the practice of Afro-Brazilian religion, which, according to psychiatrists and mental hygienicists, posed a significant threat to Pernambucans' mental health.[89] SAP researchers focused on the practice of Candomblé, an African-derived syncretic religion that they called "low spiritism" (*baixo espiritismo*) or simply "spiritism" (*spiritismo*). Researchers considered Candomblé to be a manifestation of its predominantly nonwhite practitioners' supposed "primitive mentality," and they focused their research on spirit possession, an essential aspect of the religion, which they classified as a mental disorder and described as "episodic delirium." Candomblé received considerable attention from Pernambuco's political leaders in the 1930s and 1940s, including federal *interventors* Carlos de Lima Cavalcanti and Agamemnon Magalhães.[90] After the failed communist uprising in 1935, Cavalcanti, the police, and public health authorities approached heterodox cultural, religious, and political beliefs as a potential threat to social and political stability. The SAP was given the task of both studying Candomblé and controlling and restricting its practice. This was accomplished by conducting psychological examinations of the spiritual leader (*pai* or *mãe de santo*) of each Candomblé congregation (*seita*), investigating the psychological effects of spirit possession, controlling the illegal practice of medicine and use of marijuana that were often associated with the practice of Candomblé, and licensing all Candomblé *seitas* operating in Recife and its suburbs.

In the first published study of Afro-Brazilian religious practices in Pernambuco, J. C. Cavalcante Borges and Dinice Lima, an intern at the Hospital de Alienados and SAP mental hygiene service assistant, respectively, argued that *baixo espiritismo* constituted "a police and sanitary problem that is difficult to resolve." Based on observations of "*irmãos*" (meaning brothers or, less literally, followers) and "mediums" interned at the Hospital de Alienados, they argued that the devotees of Candomblé were susceptible to a wide variety of mental disorders and that spirit possession constituted an abnormal mental state and a manifestation of underlying mental illness. While Borges and Lima noted that Candomblé *seitas* were "refuges of poor, ignorant people who are looking for the alleviation of their ills," thus recognizing the marginal social and economic status of many Candomblé practitioners, they concluded that Candomblé *seitas* were "small gathering places where insignificant psychopaths encounter surroundings propitious for their morbid tendencies."

They believed, however, that, as with other mental illnesses, Candomblé could be "cured" and suggested that "prophylactic" measures be employed in order to "spare those predisposed to the systematic culture of imagination and the exaggeration of 'subliminal automatism.'"[91] The police and public health officials approached Afro-Brazilian religion as if it were an epidemic disease—SAP personnel were to control the propagation of the "disease" while attempting to identify and eliminate its causes.

Aside from profiles of hospitalized spiritual leaders, Pernambucan mental hygienicists possessed little concrete information about Recife's numerous *seitas* because police repression had forced many Candomblé *seitas* underground. Ulysses Pernambucano, in his capacity as SAP director, had commissioned a study of Recife *seitas*, and in 1934 Pedro Cavalcanti completed a survey of thirteen *seitas* that had registered with the Mental Hygiene Service in order to obtain a license to practice. Cavalcanti started from the position that the Mental Hygiene Service should endeavor to protect *seitas* from police interference, and as part of the licensing process, he carefully compiled information about beliefs and practices that would be used as evidence to allow *seitas* to continue functioning.[92] Although this strategy afforded the *seitas* some initial protection, as more information was collected by the Mental Hygiene Service in the registration and licensing process, researchers and officials began to rethink their position on the *seitas*.[93]

In research published in 1934 in the *AAPP*, Pedro Cavalcanti expanded his earlier survey of *seitas* and investigated the "mental capacity" of *seita* spiritual leaders.[94] He created a psychological profile for each medium, who was then subjected to the Pernambucan revision of the Stanford-Binet IQ test. Cavalcanti found that twelve of thirteen subjects tested "below the lower limit of normality," according to the original standards devised by Lewis Terman. Twelve mediums had an IQ between 50 and 70, and one subject tested at an IQ of 26. Only one tested "above the limits of mental debility," but even this individual was not, according to Cavalcanti, "an individual of normal intelligence."[95] Cavalcanti concluded, based on the test results, that the majority of mediums were "feebleminded." According to then-current understandings of crowd theory and mass hysteria, Cavalcanti and SAP researchers believed that Candomblé mediums posed a threat to "the masses" because they could cause "episodic deliriums" among their followers. He argued that the "mystical manifestations" and "antisocial reactions" incited by Antônio Conselheiro during the Canudos rebellion and by Padre Cícero among his followers at Juazeiro do Norte, Ceará, were analogous to the effects that Candomblé mediums had on their followers. In evoking Canudos and Juazeiro, Cavalcanti underscored the potential danger of the Afro-Brazilian religion in Pernambuco. He argued that Pernambuco's *seitas* demonstrated the "pressing need for mental hygiene to take action in the sense of avoiding these evils."[96] Cavalcanti warned against continued police repression, however, which he believed would only increase popular interest in Candomblé. He suggested instead controlling and limiting the popular appeal of Afro-Brazilian religion via regulation, licensure, and the use of propaganda.[97]

In 1935, Gonçalves Fernandes, a Mental Hygiene Service technical assistant who later took a position as a psychiatrist at a Paraíba asylum, visited sixteen Recife *seitas* in order to catalog religious practices, internal rules, and regulations and to document recent examples of police repression. Fernandes attended ceremonies, conducted interviews, and compiled vocabularies of African terms used in services. Although he approached spirit possession with an open mind, describing it in rich detail, in the end he concluded that it was a "pathological state, attached to pre-logical factors of a primitive mentality."[98] He observed, with derision, that the "*estado de santo*," or moment of spirit possession, was facilitated by the ingestion of "various drinks infused and decanted with herbs, among others the use of marijuana and hypnotic music."[99] In support of his interpretation of spirit possession, Fernandes cited nineteenth-century French neurologist Jean-Martin Charcot, who classified spirit possession as "hysteria," as well as Raymundo Nina Rodrigues, who argued that it was "nothing more than a state of sleepwalking provoked by the disintegration and substitution of personality," and contemporary Arthur Ramos, who wrote that it "is a very complicated phenomenon linked to various diseased states of mind."[100] To Fernandes, the practitioners of Candomblé were culturally, psychologically, and racially "primitive," and he cited Freud's concept of the "primitive man" from *Totem and Taboo* (1913) to support his point.[101] While Fernandes clearly believed that Candomblé deserved to be treated as a disease rather than viewed as a legitimate religion, he stressed that there were relatively few practitioners of Afro-Brazilian religion in Recife and that most were *mulatos* and "*crioulos*" from the "humble professions," including those employed as washerwomen, cooks, rural workers, and masons. "Nothing suggests that further development is likely," he concluded. Like Cavalcanti, Fernandes argued that regulation and education, rather than police repression, were the best methods of controlling Candomblé's influence, and he called for further study and "whatever prophylactic intervention is necessary."[102]

Such "prophylactic intervention" consisted primarily of anti-Candomblé propaganda disseminated by the SAP's Mental Hygiene Service. As a result of the 1931 reorganization of Pernambuco's mental health services, the Mental

Hygiene Service was responsible for "the diffusion of precepts of mental hygiene and eugenics not only to the public but also in medical and philanthropic circles."[103] By 1932, the Mental Hygiene Service had given "numerous instructive lectures in schools, barracks, theaters, etc.," and had handed out thousands of instructive pamphlets to workers and students.[104] An especially effective means of disseminating propaganda proved to be a series of weekly radio lectures broadcast by the Radio Clube de Pernambuco.[105] José Lucena, an SAP psychiatrist, outlined the Mental Hygiene Service's position on Candomblé in two radio broadcasts in January 1932. Lucena warned listeners of the supposed psychological dangers of "spiritualism," lecturing, in surprisingly technical language, that spirit possession was "a simple manifestation of [the medium's] subconscious mental activity." He suggested that individuals who were possessed by spirits could "present violent reactions, and in very rare cases, turn into criminals." Lucena further cautioned that Recife's "spiritual centers" were responsible for 10 percent of all the cases in state psychiatric hospitals and institutions.[106] In his second lecture, Lucena outlined the process by which spirit possession allegedly debased the practitioners of Candomblé and led to, as he put it, "a true annulment of the subconscious personality." He concluded that "spiritism is a dangerous mental habit; it can lead to insanity; it should be avoided."[107]

The radio lectures sparked considerable controversy. The Radio Clube's director, Oscar Moreira Pinto, wrote a letter to Ulysses Pernambucano complaining about the lectures, pointing out that many Radio Clube employees practiced Candomblé and demanding that the Clube not be used as a forum to attack religion.[108] Pernambucano took up the issue with the Pernambucan secretary of justice, education, and the interior, who responded by articulating a policy that prohibited Mental Hygiene Service representatives from criticizing Candomblé as a religion but that allowed them to criticize spirit possession.[109] The policy was, of course, absurd—spirit possession was an integral part of Candomblé religious practices—and it put the Mental Hygiene Service in the position of simultaneously acknowledging the legitimacy of Candomblé and criticizing its core practices. The episode also reflected the ambiguous and at times contradictory approach the SAP took toward Afro-Brazilian religion and racial issues. Although the relatively open political and intellectual atmosphere of the late 1920s and early 1930s encouraged progressive intellectuals and reformers to address social and racial issues, it became apparent that the state government and the medical community still considered Afro-Brazilian religion to be a social pathology that needed to be controlled and, ideally, eliminated rather than a legitimate religion practiced by a sizeable minority of the state's population. It is also clear that government authorities and the SAP would have gone further in their attempts to regulate Candomblé if there had not been popular resistance to their efforts.

The government's willingness to temper its anti-Candomblé message in the face of popular resistance would soon change, however. The post–Intentona Comunista backlash against the social and political Left in Pernambuco eventually contributed to the collapse of Carlos de Lima Cavalcanti's government in 1937.[110] After Ulysses Pernambucano was removed as director, the SAP took an increasingly confrontational stance toward the *seitas* under his replacement, Alcides Codeceira. It quickly became clear that the government intended to more closely monitor the practice of Candomblé and to close any problematic *seitas*, even those that had previously received a license from the SAP. Information that had been gathered under Ulysses Pernambucano's stewardship of the SAP was now used to openly repress the *seitas*. Continuing legal status required yet another "psychiatric health examination" of each *seita's* leader, including the completion of a psychological profile and determination of individual IQ. If a temple was allowed to remain open, the Mental Hygiene Service continued to monitor its activities as part of regular inspections. Any evidence of practices deemed to be "detrimental to mental health," including the use of narcotics or the practice of medicine without a license, provided, as Codeceira put it, "a political justification for the closing of the [temples], which are decidedly falling back into disrepute."[111] By the end of 1936, the Mental Hygiene Service had conducted psychological examinations of fifty-three "mediums," registered and licensed sixty-two "spiritual centers and African temples," and, more significantly, denied licenses to eighteen applicants.

Getúlio Vargas's appointment of Agamemnon Magalhães as Pernambucan *interventor* in 1937, after the establishment of the Estado Novo, hastened the crackdown against Recife's *seitas*. Magalhães had participated in drafting the 1934 constitution and served as Vargas's minister of labor from 1934 to 1937, prior to being appointed as federal *interventor* of Pernambuco, a post he held from 1937 to 1945.[112] Upon assuming power in Pernambuco, Magalhães dismantled many of the socially progressive reforms introduced by his predecessors Carlos de Lima Cavalcanti and Estácio Coimbra. While this process reflected the increasing federalization and centralization of social services under Vargas, Magalhães also pursued a political and social agenda that emphasized conservative and Catholic social and cultural values and attempted to eliminate potential social, cultural, and political challenges to those values. Two key aspects of Magalhães's conservative agenda shaped the state government's approach to Afro-Brazilian religion. First, Magalhães held a profoundly prejudicial attitude toward Afro-Brazilians. Prior to serving as minister of justice and minister of labor, Magalhães taught geography at Recife's Ginásio Pernambucano. In his 1921 thesis on northeastern physical and human geography, Magalhães wrote that "the *mestiço* is really an unstable type whose original racial hereditary influences have yet to be defined."[113] He argued that the mixed racial types of northeastern Brazil tended to "regress, by cross-breeding, to the type of origin whose characters are predominant in it." He believed that *matutos*, the mixed-race descendants of Africans and Europeans who resided in the Atlantic forest apart from sugar mills, were an "unstable type," while *sertanejos*, the descendants of Indians and Europeans, were, citing Euclydes da Cunha, the "core of Brazilian nationality."[114] Magalhães concluded that Africans and Indians were "rudimentary races, still in the primary stages of their development" while the Portuguese were superior, "originating from an elevated civilization."[115] Although he did not use such overtly racist language in public political discourse, it was clear that Magalhães had little tolerance for Afro-Brazilian culture.

During his interventorship, Magalhães emphasized Catholicism in both political discourse and in public policy. He cultivated close ties with the Church and lay Catholic organizations, and Catholic rituals became an integral aspect of public political events. The federal constitution of 1937 mandated the reintroduction of Catholic religious education in public schools, which was put into place in Pernambuco in a 1938 reform of the state public education system.[116] These reforms also mandated the introduction of physical education in primary, secondary, and normal schools, which led to a deemphasis on psychological approaches to student assessment and curriculum design, thus diminishing the influence of the SAP and the IP/ISOP, which Magalhães accused of promoting Candomblé.[117] By 1938, under Magalhães's orders, the Pernambucan police had initiated a campaign of "moral and social prophylaxis" that targeted gambling, brothels, and non-Catholic religions.[118] In a 1940 annual report to Getúlio Vargas, Magalhães singled out Candomblé as one of the greatest threats to public order, contending that Candomblé temples "have recently become well developed in Recife due to the acquiescence of authority and the influence of the propaganda of certain intellectual circles. The subtle nature of [the intellectuals'] interference and the conversion of individuals of color of the popular classes, [has resulted in] a proselytizing inimical to our culture and, hence, has given rise to ideas that corrupt our civilization."[119]

Magalhães accused his political opponents and the intellectuals who participated in the Afro-Brazilian Congress in 1934, including Gilberto Freyre, Jorge

Amado, Ulysses Pernambucano, and Mário de Andrade, of deliberately promoting public interest in Candomblé, and he suggested that they were actively recruiting for their alleged communist political agenda.[120] In Magalhães's reductionist and oppositional view of society and politics, Afro-Brazilian religion fell into the same category as communism, drug use, charlatanism, and prostitution. He ordered Pernambuco's secretary of security to take action against all "immediate and remote ills, which in the end, are connected and prejudicial to the security of the State."[121] These measures included renewed "licensing and permanent inspection by the police" and heightened "vigilance appropriate for pernicious activities" in order to check the temples' "pernicious activities."[122] The control of Candomblé became a symbol of the government's ability to maintain social and political order during the Estado Novo. In the political bravado he typically employed while serving as Pernambucan *interventor*, Magalhães claimed in 1942 that as a result of the campaign, all that remained of Candomblé were "cult objects" and "religious artifacts," which had been collected by the Mental Hygiene Service and placed in a special exhibition at the 1939–1940 National Exposition in Recife and later put on permanent display in the Institute of Psychology's Museum of Mental Hygiene. In a report entitled "The Accomplishments of the Estado Novo in Pernambuco," he concluded that "the African temples, low spiritism, unregulated gaming, offenses to public decorum, and other corrupting practices were problems that we confronted, [and we] defeated the resistance that their development offered to sanitary measures."[123] There is no evidence, however, that the Pernambucan government was as successful in repressing Afro-Brazil religion as Magalhães claimed. As had been the case during previous periods of government repression, Pernambucan Afro-Brazilians responded by taking the practice of Candomblé underground. The Pernambucan government's treatment of Candomblé reflected emerging understandings of Brazilian national identity in the 1930s, which simultaneously embraced cultural and racial hybridity and rejected blackness.[124] Thus, Candomblé, as a representation of black culture, was deemed dangerous. At the same time, the cultural and political status and treatment of Candomblé in Pernambuco presents an interesting contrast with Bahia. Kim Butler argues that Bahian middle- and upper-class participation in Candomblé, as well as the support of intellectuals such as Arthur Ramos, Edison Carneiro, and Jorge Amado, afforded Bahian Candomblé temples a degree of protection from government interference during the 1930s.[125] Although several Pernambucan intellectuals and professionals, including Ulysses Pernambucano and Gilberto Freyre, supported Afro-Brazilian culture and Pernambucan Candomblé temples, the political upheavals of the mid-1930s led the Pernambucan state government under Agamemnon Magalhães to actively repress Afro-Brazilian culture and deemphasize the role of Afro-Brazilians in constructions of northeastern regional identity.

Toward a Psychology of Region

The Pernambucan SAP took an active interest in assessing the psychology of not only Afro-Brazilian religion but also folk Catholicism and millenarianism.[126] Intellectual and political interest in "popular religion" had been instigated by the Canudos rebellion of 1893–1897 and Padre Cícero Romão Batista's popular following after 1889, when the communion host he distributed to a female parishioner in Juazeiro do Norte supposedly turned to blood in her mouth.[127] Raymundo Nina Rodrigues's portrayals of Antônio Conselheiro and the Canudos rebellion had suggested that the uprising was a collective manifestation of its participants' "primitive mentality," which Conselheiro exploited to serve his own psychopathic purposes.[128] In the 1920s and 1930s, his interpretations of Canudos shaped elite perceptions of *romeiros,* the followers of Padre Cícero who made an annual pilgrimage to Juazeiro do Norte to commemorate the miracles of 1889. Psychological explanations of folk Catholicism and millenarianism that downplayed the legitimate economic and political grievances of the rural working classes and instead emphasized *sertanejos'* supposedly primitive cultural and religious practices found a ready audience among Pernambucan politicians and ruling elites. Canudos and Juazeiro proved that popular religious movements could grow into rebellions and political movements that challenged the established social, economic, and political order in the region. In order to better understand millenarianism and thus avoid another Canudos or Juazeiro, SAP researchers began to investigate popular religious movements in Recife. SAP researchers understood the problem of "popular religion" to be distinct from that of Afro-Brazilian religion. The state's concern with "popular religion" reflected ruling class anxiety about labor and the mobilization of *sertanejos* in rural areas, which represented a potentially greater threat to social and economic stability than Afro-Brazilian religion. The latter, while at odds with nativist constructions of Brazilian national identity that emphasized orthodox and conservative social and cultural values, was threatening primarily on a symbolic and cultural level.

In 1933, Pedro Cavalcanti, a Mental Hygiene Service technical assistant, initiated the SAP's first study of popular religion. In it he described the Circulo Deus e Verdade, a "pantheistic *seita*" that followed the teachings of Bento Milagroso, a popular "prophet" who preached, engaged in faith healing, and, in 1915, revealed several prophecies. Milagroso had achieved, Cavalcanti wrote, "absolute prestige among the majority of the population of the city and the interior."[129] Cavalcanti pointed out that Milagroso's followers, who numbered in the hundreds, hailed almost entirely from the "most humble professions" and that they displayed "a notable tendency toward mysticism." In the services he personally observed, Cavalcanti noted some similarities with Candomblé, but he concluded that the Circulo Deus e Verdade had more in common with the "mysticism" of Antônio Conselheiro and Padre Cícero.[130] Citing French clinical psychologist Pierre Marie Félix Janet, he argued that "inferior religions" encouraged the "abnormal development of the culture of the subconscious," which resulted in "morbid manifestations." These "manifestations" were potentially dangerous, especially in social groups with charismatic leaders where "the masses [become] a servile reflection of the 'conductor' or of the prophet, and are therefore able to approximate the great manifestations of mysticism (Juazeiro, of Padre Cícero) or antisocial reactions (Canudos, Antônio Conselheiro)." "In either case," Cavalcanti cautioned, "the Mental Hygiene [Service] must be on alert. These deliriums, not always inoffensive to the collective in which they arise, have to be prevented. Repression, after the unleashing of the phenomenon, is 'police business,' but in our country it is oftentimes 'political business.'" He concluded that it was essential for political authorities to "understand the religions that are developing in large cities," especially among the "uncultured population," in order to avoid the "'epidemics' that populate [religious] sanctuaries and, at times, run in the blood."[131] Although Candomblé, which was more common in Recife than millenarian Catholicism, received more attention from the Mental Hygiene Service and the police, government officials researchers still wary of the specter of Canudos and Juazeiro paid close attention to "popular religion."

SAP researchers soon had the opportunity to study a popular religious uprising. In May 1936, in the *agreste município* of Panelas, a small town approximately 140 kilometers (87 miles) southwest of Recife, an agricultural worker named João Cícero (who was not related to Padre Cícero) exhibited abnormal behavior, including shouting fits and extended periods of silence after experiencing chest pains, according to a local police report.[132] Cícero stated that he had been possessed by a spirit, although he would not, or could not, say by whose spirit. The man then began to behave as if he were a priest, and soon his family "recognized" that he was possessed by the spirit of Padre Cícero, who had died two years previously. As news of Cícero's possession spread, locals flocked to see him, and he rapidly gained a following of close to seventy "believers." Taken aback by his popularity and fearing an uprising, local authorities ordered his arrest. Cícero and his followers armed themselves and attacked the local police inspector's house. A gunfight with the police ensued, and the inspector was killed. Cícero and his band then proceeded to another village, looting businesses and finally engaging the local police in a forty-minute confrontation that left five of Cícero's followers dead, three of them wounded, and three police officers wounded. Cícero and several members of his group escaped (Cícero was never found), and the police took eight of his followers into custody. After their arrest, the eight were transferred to the custody of the Mental Hygiene Service and subjected to IQ testing and psychological profiling. Officials concluded that all eight prisoners possessed an IQ far below that of "normal" individuals and that each showed signs of mental illness, although they could not provide specific diagnoses.[133]

José Lucena, a professor of psychiatry at the Faculdade de Medicina do Recife, wrote about the Panelas incident in the journal *Neurobiologia*. Lucena interpreted the incident as a collective "paranoid delirium" and cited Raymundo Nina Rodrigues's and Euclydes da Cunha's interpretations of the Canudos rebellion, Sigmund Freud's discussion of the psychology of "primitive man" in *Totem and Taboo*, and Arthur Ramos's notion that "the leaders of the *sertanejan* mystic masses are mentally deficient and are subject to paranoid outbreaks" to support his interpretation.[134] Although Lucena never personally examined João Cícero or any of his followers, he diagnosed Cícero as "paranoid" and "feebleminded."[135] Lucena also argued that the Panelas incident was not simply a manifestation of Cícero's madness, suggesting that social, racial, and environmental factors played a role in the revolt and that it was a "current tendency in psychiatry to consider the social background of these disorders . . . which compels us to relate the disturbance of these fanatics to the cultural group to which they belong." He believed that the geographic and cultural isolation and the backwardness of the northeastern interior regularly gave rise to revolts of this kind. He also argued that *sertanejos'* Indian ancestry, which he believed could be traced to "occidental" China, explained the rebels' propensity to blindly follow mentally disturbed leaders. Although Lucena noted similarities between the Panelas revolt and the Canudos rebellion, he concluded that the participants in religious revolts were, "in many cases, outside the nosological maps of psychiatry, and their frequently antisocial and disharmonious conduct escapes characterization of any clinical type."[136] And here lay the fundamental difficulty for SAP researchers: although they could explain away rebellions as the manifestation of individual and collective mental illness, they nonetheless struggled to come to terms with evidence that *sertanejos* possessed a supposedly "primitive mentality."

SAP researchers began to catalog numerous "mental disturbances" among the populations of the northeastern interior. They were especially concerned with particular "superstitions" and "taboos," which were interpreted as evidence of *sertanejos'* "primitive mentality."[137] Gonçalves Fernandes, a clinical psychiatrist at the Escola de Medicina e Cirurgia (School of Medicine and Surgery) in Rio de Janeiro, documented male *sertanejos'* "fundamental fear" of women, which he argued constituted a "primitive taboo."[138] Fernandes drew comparisons between the social and cultural practices of *sertanejos*, "indigenous tribes of northeastern Brazil," and "primitives" from Timor. As an example, Fernandes discussed the Northeast's most infamous *cangaceiro*, Lampião, whose followers attributed their defeat to the presence of women in their band.[139] Fernandes interpreted *sertanejos'* proscriptions regarding contact with women as a form of narcissism and a psychological manifestation of sexual impotence. Citing Freud, he argued that this psychosexual drama was an important part of *sertanejos'* daily lives and that "magic cults," hunting, and fighting constituted a substitute for sex.[140] In another article, Fernandes cited *sertanejos'* custom of looking at their own reflection in a basin of water during São João, the annual harvest festival held in June throughout the Northeast, as an example of narcissism and the influence of "archaic cultures."[141] Although many of Fernandes's colleagues would have likely questioned his Freudian approach to northeastern folk culture, what is crucial about his and others' analyses is the degree to which *sertanejos* were still regarded, some forty years after Canudos, as fundamentally different from the populations of civilized, coastal Brazil.[142] The language through which these differences were expressed had changed significantly, from discussions of geographic and racial determinism to psychology and psychoanalysis, but the conclusion was still the same.

The growing intellectual and political interest in the psychological dimensions of northeastern regional identity was reflected in the establishment of the Sociedade de Psiquiatria, Neurologia e Higiene Mental do Nordeste Brasileiro (Society of Psychiatry, Neurology, and Mental Hygiene of the Brazilian Northeast) in 1938 by Ulysses Pernambuco.[143] Although the society's members hailed from several states, including Paraíba, Sergipe, and Bahia, Pernambuco's psychiatric community played a leading role in the organization. Members who were public health officials and psychiatrists from neighboring states praised the successes of Pernambuco's Serviço de Assistencia a Psicopatas and hoped to create similar programs in their own states, and society members pushed for public funding for mental hygiene services in Sergipe and Rio Grande do Norte, which were to be modeled on existing services in Pernambuco.[144] J. da Costa Machado, director of the Hospital de Alienados in Natal, argued that "no nation can hope for future superiority if it is not zealous in improving the mental level of its people. The care of the mentally ill, both minor and major psychopaths, like the most perfect observance of established principles of mental hygiene, is a condition imposed by civilization."[145] Few northeastern intellectuals and reformers disagreed with his position. Gilberto Freyre, who supported the development of mental hygiene services in Pernambuco, addressed the society's second congress in 1940 and expressed belief that its work would produce a scientific understanding of the psychology of the region and its peoples.[146] Freyre argued that psychiatry, psychology, and sociology offered solutions to "the disharmony between human personality and the environment" and would thus "reduce the importance, which is actually enormous, of the social causes of disadjustment of personalities with environment, augmenting the number of individuals of a healthy, harmonious, and equilibrious nature."[147] Mental hygiene, Freyre concluded, should address the psychological consequences of a social and economic system that was at odds with basic human needs.

In his opening address to the society's third congress, in 1943, Ulysses Pernambucano called for members to work together to treat mental disorders common to the region. In adopting this approach, Pernambucano argued that the society should "disregard the political divisions that separate *nordestinos* into *cearenses, rio-grandenses do norte, paraibanos, pernambucanos, alagoanos, sergipanos*, and to a certain degree, *baianos*" and instead "unite in our common landscape, identical activities in the struggle for life, and populations of similar ethnic and cultural development, until we have dealt with our deficiencies, our sufferings, and even our calamities."[148] Unfortunately, Pernambucano's call for psychiatrists and public health officials to take a regional approach to mental hygiene was never realized. His premature death in late 1943 at the age of fifty-one marked the end of a period of increased advocacy on behalf of the mentally ill in Pernambuco. After his death, colleagues reflected on Pernambucano's impact on psychiatry in Pernambuco and the Northeast.[149] José Lucena suggested that Pernambucano was the central figure of a "true school of psychiatry" in Recife and argued that Recife's mental hygiene movement was more than "a simple grouping" of clinical psychiatrists. The SAP addressed not only "wide-ranging and socially repercussive" themes using a "sociological methodology" but also social issues of a "local, regional and national character."[150] Lucena acknowledged that Recife's "School of Psychiatry" was not as well "equipped and organized" as those of Paris or Berlin, which would have allowed researchers to take a more theoretical and reflective approach in their work, but he concluded that there was "a spirit of continuity in our work" that "gave us solutions to our problems."[151] Gilberto Freyre praised his cousin's efforts to improve social and economic conditions in the Northeast, pointing out that he was "most concerned with the problems of surroundings and environment that are, at the same time, of interest to sociologists and social anthropologists."[152] Freyre believed that Pernambucano would become an inspiration to all physicians, who, he argued, "should take part—and a salient part—in all that is social reform in our lives" and "[defend] general against private interests."[153]

Panegyrics to Pernambucano were possible only after his death, however. While he was alive, the Pernambucan government considered him a radical leftist because of his advocacy on behalf of the mentally ill as well as his interest in race and social problems. His founding of the Sociedade de Psiquiatria, Neurologia e Higiene Mental do Nordeste Brasileiro, whose members boldly addressed issues of regional identity during a time of political emphasis on national unity, was interpreted by Pernambucan leaders as a deliberate attempt to undermine political stability and challenge corporatist ideals.

In the late 1930s and early 1940s, Vargas's political appointees viewed the progressive reforms of the previous decade to have been an attempt by radicals to undermine the traditional foundations of Brazilian society. Although the politicization of public health had provided Ulysses Pernambucano with the opportunity to implement progressive reforms and to broach taboo subjects such as the status and treatment of Pernambuco's Afro-Brazilians, it also provided Agamemnon Magalhães with the opportunity to use government social services to repress and institutionalize Afro-Brazilians, whom he believed posed a threat to social and political stability.[154]

Mental hygienicists' concern with race was, as Mariza Corrêa has pointed out regarding Raymundo Nina Rodrigues's research, a paradoxical aspect of Brazilian science.[155] Despite the fact that by the late 1930s the majority of Brazilian intellectuals studying the racial question had agreed that inherent racial difference did not exist, it was indisputable that there were significant material, social, and cultural differences among racial groups in Brazilian society. Race thus remained a pressing question for reformers, intellectuals, scientists, and politicians. For Pernambucan researchers, the key problem—given decades of European immigration to southern Brazil that had produced the perception that the populations of the North and South were racially and culturally distinct—was to determine the racial, physiological, and psychological qualities of the peoples of northeastern Brazil. Pernambucan psychiatrists and psychologists provided information about *nordestinos'* psychological characteristics, which government authorities then used to determine how students, workers, soldiers, prisoners, Afro-Brazilians, and *sertanejos* were to become subjects of a modernizing state. Ultimately, however, this information was both less precise and less politically useful than researchers' understanding of *nordestinos'* physiological qualities. Political leaders cared less about what *nordestinos* thought, knew, or could learn than whether or not they were compliant citizens and workers.

7

Inventing the *Homem do Nordeste*

Race, Region, and the State, 1925–1940

IN A 1941 newspaper article, Agamemnon Magalhães, the federal *interventor* of Pernambuco, wrote that "southerners who do not know the Northeast are surprised with the ambience of combat and work that they observe when coming to the region. Here man is better than geography. Better than the natural factors that he has to defeat with his mind and with his arms. Man, in the Northeast, is in an agitated state when working. He is always moving. He is always doing something. He has initiative, or is seeking to possess it."[1] This characterization of *nordestinos* contrasted sharply with assessments of the region and its peoples that had dominated intellectual and political discourse since the late nineteenth century. The 1930s and 1940s were a period of considerable political and intellectual conflict over both regional and national identity. Magalhães used his vision of *nordestinos* as a socially, racially, and religiously homogenous people united in labor and in support of the state to justify new interventionist social and economic policies during the Estado Novo. His definition of northeastern regional identity also constituted a response to intellectuals and reformers who, since the 1920s, had questioned the social and racial status quo. Gilberto Freyre and Ulysses Pernambucano had offered an alternative view of race that challenged many of the underlying assumptions about *nordestinos* that political and economic elites used to justify their dominance of the working classes and the poor. Magalhães and his conservative allies in Pernambuco viewed northeastern intellectuals' interest in race with suspicion, attempted to suppress it, and responded by formulating their own vision of northeastern regional identity that excluded Afro-Brazilians.

The studies of *nordestinos'* physical and psychological characteristics that came about as a result of the expansion of government social and public health services produced a renewed interest in scientific and medical aspects of race. Concerns about *nordestinos'* health, education, and employability led researchers to challenge prevailing racial theories suggesting that *nordestinos* were racially inferior. At the same time, emerging notions of Brazilian national identity in an era of declining foreign immigration and new national labor policies emphasized native-born Brazilians and "*brasilidade*" over European social and cultural values. In the 1930s, it became acceptable for Brazilians to embrace their mixed racial heritage. The *mulato* became, if not the model Brazilian citizen, the subject of intense social, cultural, intellectual, and political interest. By the 1930s, most Brazilian intellectuals rejected the notions of strict racial hierarchy and inferior and superior races, but they continued to believe that racial groups possessed innate qualities that could be quantified and cataloged. A few Brazilian intellectuals, including Gilberto Freyre, adopted a cultural approach to race and rejected biological and racial determinism, but many Brazilian intellectuals did not, which resulted in intense debates about race that continued to the end of the Estado Novo. Finally, corporatist notions of citizenship and debates about the relationship between the state, society, and the individual that emerged during the Estado Novo shaped debates about northeastern regional identity. By the mid-1930s, *nordestinos* attracted a level of public, intellectual, and political interest unprecedented since the Great Drought and the Canudos rebellion.

Since the 1990s, Brazilianists have produced wide-ranging studies that have transformed the way in which race is understood both historically and in contemporary Brazilian society.[2] The most significant contribution of this scholarship is the idea that race is a foundational aspect of individual, social, regional, and national identities. Much recent scholarship on race, especially that produced by political scientists, anthropologists, and sociologists, examines contemporary racial issues in Brazil's postdictatorship era by focusing on prejudice, discrimination, and racial politics. Generally speaking, less attention has been paid to the origins of racial identities, the ways in which race became an essential component of Brazilian national identity in the post-abolition era. At the same time, the majority of scholarship on race has focused on Rio de Janeiro and São Paulo while the Northeast, with the significant exception of Salvador and the state of Bahia, has received less attention.[3] Scholars have concluded that regional and national identities develop in tandem; thus, by paying closer attention to regional identities, researchers can gain a better understanding of national identities.[4] Through the first half of the nineteenth century, northeastern regional identity reflected republican separatist movements, but by the twentieth century, northeastern regional identity was underscoring the nation's universal social and racial origins by highlighting the ways in which *nordestinos,* while unique culturally, were nonetheless quintessentially Brazilian. This transformation became possible only after Brazilian intellectuals and politicians had reinterpreted racial theories and repositioned the Northeast and *nordestinos* in relation to Brazilian national identity.

Racial Thought in Pernambuco, 1920–1930

Despite increased interest in the "racial question" that arose with the abolition of slavery, northeastern intellectuals and politicians paid surprisingly little attention to it until the 1920s. During the First Republic, northeastern ruling elites and intellectuals seldom discussed the racial question openly and government reports made few references to race. The need to ensure a docile work force dictated that potentially disruptive social and political issues, such as race, not be discussed publicly. This did not mean, however, that northeastern elites did not endorse a particular view of race. Government officials and intellectuals generally accepted without question the idea of *branqueamento,* and economic elites and politicians thus attempted to promote white European immigration to the region as a means of improving the labor force and the regional economy. In short, northeastern ruling elites desired a whiter, more European work force.

Although the Northeast and South shared a common history in which economic production had once depended heavily on slave labor, the failure of federal and state efforts to encourage European immigration to the Northeast produced the perception that northeastern populations had not "progressed" socially or racially since the abolition of slavery and were thus significantly less white than southern populations.[5]

Although there was little European immigration to the Northeast, census results from 1872 and 1890 indicated that region's population was becoming whiter.[6] The problem with relying on census figures to estimate the racial composition of Brazil, however, is that racial categories are subjective, dependent on individual and institutional considerations of social and economic status.

Furthermore, as Thomas Skidmore has pointed out, understandings of racial categories in Brazil varied widely between 1870 and 1945.[7] Census takers and scientific researchers categorized individuals according to subjective conceptions of race and pseudoscientific measurements and of physical and racial characteristics, which were shaped as much by data collectors' personal racial biases as by any supposedly objective definition of race. Brazilian intellectuals nonetheless fully embraced the notion that the nation was becoming whiter, an idea that was perhaps best articulated by João Batista de Lacerda in a 1911 paper that projected that Brazil would, through the dual processes of European immigration and racial miscegenation, become an almost entirely white nation by the year 2010.[8] Researchers nevertheless attempted to provide racial data about the region, but their conflicting results suggested that their understandings of race varied so widely that even the leading experts of the period could not agree on the exact definition of *branco*, *negro*, and *mulato* or on the relative proportion of each in Brazilian society.[9]

The constructed nature of Brazilian racial categories also became apparent in the various racial classificatory schemes that researchers utilized in their research and writing. Brazilian racial theorists generally made use of two different, but related, sets of racial categories. The first comprised the three "original races" that populated Brazil: Europeans, Indians, and Africans. Most racial commentators agreed that centuries of intense racial miscegenation had produced few "pure" Africans and Indians, but a concomitant belief in *branqueamento* paradoxically led them also to argue that there were many pure Europeans.[10] The second set of racial categories consisted of the primary terms *branco*, *mulato*, and *negro*, each of which represented points on a black-white racial continuum. The terms *mestiço* (mixed), *pardo* (brown), and *mulato* were used to describe and classify mixed-race Brazilians. These two sets of racial categories were often used interchangeably to describe Brazilian racial types. All possible racial mixtures could not be described with these terms alone, however, and the terms *cafuso*, *caboclo*, *mameluco*, and *cariboca* were used to describe and classify the various racial mixtures of Indians with Africans and Europeans.[11] By the early 1930s, leading Brazilian anthropologist Edgar Roquette-Pinto had devised a racial classification scheme that included the categories of *mulato*, *branco*, *caboclo*, and *negro*, which many Brazilian racial theorists subsequently adopted.[12]

Within the Northeast, racial theorists made further distinctions based on geography and social class. The most common distinction was between the populations of the arid interior (*sertanejos*) and the populations of the coastal sugar-growing region, for which there was no specific racial term.[13] While this distinction was primarily geographic, it was also racial, as prior to abolition, African slave labor was more common in coastal areas and less common in the interior where the Indian influence was stronger. Some racial theorists made a further distinction between the inhabitants of the *sertão* and the *agreste* region (the semiarid highlands between the coast and the interior) or between the inhabitants of sugar-growing regions and coastal fishing towns. Others argued that there were significant racial differences among the populations of Ceará, Pernambuco, and Bahia. Intellectuals and politicians alike regularly used terms such as *vaqueiro* (cowboy), *romeiro* (follower of Padre Cícero), *jagunço* (follower of Antônio Conselheiro), and *cangaceiro* (social bandit) to make further distinctions among the populations of the region. While the majority of these terms were geographic or historical in origin, by the 1920s they had taken on racial and, in some cases, scientific attributes. Individual commentators on the northeastern racial problem possessed unique understandings of these terms and used them interchangeably, which often led to contradictions and ambiguities in the use of racial terminology.

During the First Republic, politicians and civil servants made few direct references to race, which was one indicator of the widespread acceptance of *branqueamento.* Another indicator was continued interest in promoting European immigration to the region. The Pernambucan and federal governments actively sought to bring European immigrants to the state as late as 1925.[14] In a report on continuing government efforts to mitigate effects of the 1923 drought, one federal official argued that foreign immigration was essential to efforts to develop the region:

> As an indispensable complementary measure, we urge the consideration of the formation of centers of foreign colonization, preferably of Latin origins, that would, indeed must, be able to be taught immediately in the fresh and healthy lands of the hills and, later, in the same healthy areas of the plains. These centers in the *sertão* will be the most fecund and efficient schools for the rural population, by virtue of example and contiguity, and this is the only way that we can seem to profit from the populations of the *sertão* in light of the state of peculiar indifference of their depressed spirits that are caused by misery.[15]

While this official made no overt references to race, he clearly believed that native *nordestinos* were incapable of improving the region and that the best prospects for the future lay in settling the region with racially superior European immigrants.

Although notions of *branqueamento* dominated Brazilian racial thought during the First Republic, there were important shifts in racial theory during this period. The science of race was more developed and more complex in the 1920s than it had been in the 1890s. Prominent Brazilian intellectuals, including Oliveira Viana, Edgar Roquette-Pinto, and Afranio Peixoto, continued to debate the racial question, but allegedly scientific racism continued to appear in the writings of several key figures.[16] As discussed in a previous chapter, new scientific approaches to human development, including eugenics and biotypology, gave new life to older racial theories. New "scientific" racial theories and terminology obfuscated overt racism, made published studies of race inaccessible to all but the specialist, and allowed intellectuals and government officials to discuss race without resorting to the use of overtly racial language.[17]

In the 1920s, growing social and economic disparities between North and South precipitated a reconsideration of northeastern identity. After the turn of the century, northeastern planters and political elites had had to adjust to lower profits and government revenues from sugar production, and they understood that the region was rapidly becoming an economic backwater within the nation, despite their attempts to modernize production and promote industrialization.[18] Coffee plantations and the burgeoning industrial sector of the South rapidly eclipsed the economic production of the Northeast, and the region's political fortunes declined as its economy stagnated. The reordering of the Brazilian political system that had taken place with the establishment of the republic favored the economically powerful states of the South, and the Northeast, which had enjoyed considerable political influence during the empire period, became less powerful during the First Republic. In these rapidly changing political and economic contexts, the racial differences between the Northeast and the South became even more apparent and were used to explain, in part, the region's economic and political decline. If race was accepted as a cause of Brazil's inferiority vis-à-vis the United States and Europe, then race could also be used to explain the vast social, economic, and political divide between the Northeast and the South. By the late 1920s, the social, economic, and political changes that had accompanied the relative decline of the Northeast prompted a fundamental reconsideration of Brazilian national identity and the place of the Northeast and *nordestinos* within the nation.

Gilberto Freyre: Nordeste e Raça

It was in this context of the Northeast's decline that Gilberto Freyre (1900–1987) began to exert a profound impact on Brazilians' understandings of their society, history, and regional and national identity. Academic approaches to

Freyre have focused on examining his impact on understandings of race in the 1930s, which saw the publication of his two best-known and widely read works, *Casa-grande & senzala* (1933) and *Sobrados e mucambos* (1936), and on critically examining his later works, in which he was concerned with developing and disseminating the concepts of racial democracy and Luso-tropicalism.[19] While recent approaches to Freyre's work have emphasized the intellectual, historical and political contexts that shaped his thought in the 1920s and 1930s, less attention has been paid to Freyre's profound impact on understandings of race in northeastern Brazil and the development of northeastern regional identity.[20] Freyre, descended from a wealthy planter family in the sugar-growing region of Pernambuco, often found himself an outsider in established intellectual and political circles in Recife. Educated at a school run by Baptist missionaries from the United States, Freyre went on to receive his undergraduate degree from Baylor University in Waco, Texas, in 1921 and a master's degree in sociology from Columbia University in 1922, studying with, among others, anthropologist Franz Boas.[21] Even in his academic work, Freyre showed an interest in northeastern regional identity, addressing the relationship between the Northeast and southern Brazil in his master's thesis, "Social Life in Brazil in the Middle of the Nineteenth Century," which was published in the *Hispanic American Historical Review* in 1922. In this work, Freyre explained that he intended to "make clear to myself what the Brazil of the middle of the nineteenth century was like" by outlining the social, cultural, and economic history of Rio de Janeiro, São Paulo, Minas Gerais, Pernambuco, Bahia, and the *sertão*. However, the majority of Freyre's characterizations of Brazilian society were based on Pernambuco and, more specifically, on Recife, and the private, public, and political lives of Pernambucan elite planter families became the standard by which he measured the historical development of the nation. Pernambucan sugar society was, for Freyre, the foundation of Brazil, and he displayed an unrestrained romanticism about Pernambuco in his early writing. Pernambucan planters, he argued, were "descended from some of the best blood of Portugal, and it was through their ancestors that the vague thing we call culture first reached Portuguese America."[22] For Freyre, this culture, forged in the colonial period, partially influenced by native Brazilians and African slaves, served as the mythical foundation of Brazilian society. Writing during the final years of the First Republic, when the political and economic decline of Pernambuco and other northeastern states had become only too apparent, Freyre emphasized Pernambuco's supposed social, cultural, and, surprisingly, economic superiority over southern states, especially São Paulo. Although Freyre's thesis concentrated on the middle of the nineteenth century, when

São Paulo had not yet risen to the position of economic and political dominance it would achieve by the end of the century, he presented Pernambuco's
sugar economy as if it were Brazil's most important economic resource. He
discounted the importance of coffee cultivation, noting that it accounted for
the prosperity only of São Paulo, not of the entire nation. While admitting
São Paulo's prosperity, Freyre argued that it was socially and intellectually inferior to Pernambuco, citing the intellectual innovations of Recife's Faculdade
do Direito and the Escola do Recife as examples of Pernambucan intellectual
and cultural superiority.[23] Freyre's conception of regional identity was predicated on differences and conflict that reflected both the ongoing political strug-
gles of the First Republic and the increasing economic disparities between
the Northeast and the South.

Freyre's imagined Northeast was not entirely idyllic, however. He was critical of certain aspects of traditional patriarchal society, including the treatment
of women.[24] He also noted the miserable plight of *sertanejos* who migrated
from the *sertão* to escape the Great Drought, if only in noting that they were
a curiosity and "colorful memories" for his grandmother.[25] Freyre did not, however, condemn slavery, a position that was characteristic of the majority of his
writings through the 1930s. He instead presented slavery as an economic necessity and an integral aspect of the colonization and development of Brazil.
Because he idealized planter society, he was unwilling to acknowledge any collective social harm arising out of slavery. "As a rule," he asserted, "the slaves
were not overworked in the households either in the plantations or in the
city." He suggested that nineteenth-century reports of the "cruel treatment of
slaves in Brazil" were deliberately circulated by British antislavery propagan-
dists and were not accurate portrayals of the treatment of slaves. Freyre concluded that, "as a matter of fact, slavery in Brazil was anything but cruel. The
Brazilian slave lived the life of a cherub if we contrast his lot with that of the
English and other European factory-workers in the middle of the last century."[26] To support this contention, Freyre provided numerous favorable accounts of slavery from nineteenth-century travelers' accounts. Freyre was, in
short, both an apologist for slavery and a propagandist for the landed elite
who dominated northeastern society and politics. Perhaps to a North American audience, his thesis would have been revealing, but to Brazilians, especially those with a political and intellectual interest in Afro-Brazilians, race,
and the history of slavery, it would have been perceived as naive at best and
irresponsible at worst.

Freyre's portrayal of the Northeast evolved significantly over the course of
the late 1920s and early 1930s. After completing his master's degree in sociology

and traveling in the United States and Europe, Freyre returned to Recife in 1923 and worked as a journalist, penning some 160 articles for the Recife newspaper *Diário de Pernambuco* between 1923 and 1926. He also served as the newspaper's editor and later as the editor of a rival newspaper, *A Província*.[27] In one piece written for the 1925 centenary edition of the *Diário*, Freyre quoted Manuel de Oliveira Lima (1866–1928), the former Brazilian ambassador to the United States and Freyre's mentor during his years in the United States, who wrote that the Northeast was the "refuge of the soul of Brazil" where "*a brasilidade* [Brazilianess], the spirit that will one day animate a courageously Brazilian culture, is longed for and strengthened more than in the South."[28] In his articles for the *Diário*, as in his master's thesis, Freyre universalized the history of the northeastern Brazil, especially the sugar-growing region, as *the* history of Brazil.

Through family connections and his writing, Freyre befriended several prominent northeastern writers, intellectuals, and artists, including *paraibano* novelists José Lins do Rego (1901–1957) and José Américo de Almeida (1887–1980).[29] By the late 1920s, Freyre had emerged as the intellectual leader of a nascent northeastern regionalist movement in Recife. His interest in regionalism grew out of the Pernambucan modernist movement, which originated in 1922 as a response to São Paulo modernism and Modern Art Week, an exhibition of modernist art and literature by visual artists Graça Aranha and Anita Malfatti, poet and folklorist Mário de Andrade, and poet Oswald de Andrade. Pernambucan modernism centered on the Recife literary journal *Revista do Norte* and in the work of poets Bendito Monteiro and Joaquim Cardozo and was actively championed by Pernambucan-born lawyer and journalist Joaquim Inojosa.[30] Both *paulista* and *pernambucano* modernism combined European aesthetics, including international modernism and futurism, with indigenous Brazilian and Afro-Brazilian culture while challenging romanticist- and impressionist-based establishment high culture and conventional social and cultural sensibilities.[31] Freyre, who did not return to Brazil from Europe until 1923, was neither artist, poet, nor novelist; he nonetheless rejected *paulista* modernism on nativist grounds as European rather than authentically Brazilian and began to organize a regionalist movement that instead emphasized traditional northeastern social and cultural values.[32] The original Pernambucan modernists came to view Freyre's brand of regionalism as reactionary, and Joaquim Inojosa later described Freyre a "traditionalist."[33]

Freyre's regionalism found an audience in the First Regionalist Congress of the Northeast, which met in Recife over the course of four days in February 1926. The congress proved instrumental in shaping and clarifying Freyre's conception of the Northeast and northeastern regional identity. Congress attendees included powerful Pernambucan political figures such as Amaury de Medeiros, the director of the Department of Health and Assistance, Secretary of Agriculture Samuel Harman, Secretary of Justice Aníbal Fernandes, and Eurico Souza Leão, Recife's police chief.[34] Also attending were prominent northeastern intellectuals, artists, and writers, including Inojosa, who became increasingly critical of Freyre's attempts to commandeer the Pernambucan modernist movement to serve his own intellectual and political ends.[35] Freyre did serve as the congress secretary, however, and he presented a paper, "The Esthetics of Regional Cuisine."[36] According to the official program, the purpose of the congress was "to develop a sentiment of the unity in the Northeast, already very clearly characterized in its geographic condition and historical evolution, and at the same time to work on behalf of regional interests in the diverse areas of society, economics, and culture." At the congress's closing session, Amaury de Medeiros opined that the purpose of the "regionalist movement" was to "conserve and cultivate the just roots of pride in a common nation, giving to our things a Brazilian character."[37] Medeiros carefully added that northeastern regionalism served to bolster rather than to undermine national unity and that the congress "did not have a political point of view." After the conclusion of the congress, Freyre responded to critics who suggested that the regionalist movement was politically divisive and constituted an attempt to promote political separatism by writing in an article for the *Diário de Pernambuco* that "a regionalist Brazil would be a Brazil not divided, but united in its diversity."[38] In a second article, Freyre argued that northeastern regionalism was an attempt substitute an "artificial" political regionalism with one based on common traditions, sentiments, and economic interests. This regionalism, he asserted, "could not be more Brazilian. Nor less separatist."[39] Freyre had clearly become more cognizant of the political dimensions of his traditionalist northeastern regionalism and was sensitive to those critics who suggested that the congress constituted an attempt to divide the nation. Several northeastern intellectuals who did not participate in the congress offered further criticisms. Despite their friendship, José Américo de Almeida suggested that Freyre's regionalism was a "caricature" of Pernambucan modernism.[40] These criticisms aside, northeastern regionalism, as imagined by Pernambucan political and intellectual elites who lamented the region's cultural and political passage from center to periphery, became a powerful expression of regional pride and regional cultural identity. As the South gradually assumed the political and economic leadership of the nation, Freyre's regionalism seemed anachronistic to southern intellectuals.[41] Northeastern regionalism was significant, however, not only because it represented a rejection of *paulista* modernism but also because it became a point of departure for further debates about the content and political significance of northeastern regional identity.

Soon after the First Regionalist Congress, Freyre formally entered the world of Pernambucan politics, and, as a result, his social and political understanding of the Northeast changed significantly. From 1926 to 1930, he served as a personal secretary, or as he would later put it "chief of staff," to Pernambucan governor Estácio de Albuquerque Coimbra, who assumed office in late 1926.[42] Although Coimbra represented entrenched *usineiro* (sugar refinery owner) interests, he undertook numerous social and economic reforms designed to stimulate the Pernambucan economy and to improve social conditions.[43] Coimbra consulted Freyre on a wide variety of policy matters, especially, as Freyre put it, "difficult and delicate affairs."[44] Freyre took a special interest in cultural matters, most notably education. Although Freyre benefited personally from education reforms implemented by the Coimbra administration (receiving an appointment to a newly created chair in anthropology at Recife's Escola Normal) and generally supported the administration's attempt to modernize public education, he nonetheless criticized certain aspects of the reforms. He argued that they promoted "modernist" elements, and he considered the architect of the reforms, Antônio Carneiro Leão and José Ribeiro Escobar, the new secretary of education and public health hired to implement the reforms, to be outsiders unfamiliar with Pernambuco.[45] Although Freyre allowed that the two men were "good technicians," he also described them as "country bumpkins" (*matutões*) from the interior of São Paulo who were unfamiliar with the problems of urban society.[46]

Carneiro Leão's reforms met widespread resistance, especially from the Jesuits, which Freyre and other critics attributed to the Catholic Church's unwillingness to cede control of education to the government and to the order's condemnation of supposedly immoral education reforms, especially sex education classes.[47] The public furor over the reforms led to a personal crisis for Freyre. His father, Alfredo Freyre, who served as the director of the Escola Normal during the Coimbra administration, publicly opposed the Carneiro Leão reforms, and he was fired in 1930 as a result of his opposition. Freyre faced a difficult choice—support his father or remain loyal to Coimbra, to whom he owed his cabinet position, his position as editor of *A Província*, and his chair in anthropology at the Escola Normal.[48] Freyre chose the latter, recognizing that he would be accused of being a bad son.[49] The dismissal of the

Freyre patriarch did little to quell the controversy. Coimbra was eventually forced to abandon the educational reforms, which, rather than ending the controversy, only further energized his opponents.

The contested presidential election of 1930 would prove decisive for the Coimbra administration and Freyre's political career. After the Liberal Alliance military commander Juarez Távora took control of Recife in November 1930, Coimbra went into exile and Freyre followed. Freyre's biographers present his exile as a decisive moment in his intellectual development. It was during these two years (1930–1932) that he began working on *Casa-grande & senzala*. While several scholars have pointed out that the end of Freyre's political career afforded him time to work on *Casa-grande & senzala*, in fact the end of his political career and his exile marked a more significant shift in his writing, especially that which dealt expressly with northeastern Brazil. After his stint as Coimbra's chief of staff, Freyre became more attuned to social and economic problems and the complexities in addressing those problems politically. In short, his writing became more expressly concerned with the political. In his own recollections of this period, Freyre wrote that Coimbra's opponents had labeled him a "communist" and an "agitator" because he proved willing to intervene in political matters on behalf of the disenfranchised.[50] He also recalled Coimbra occasionally referring to him as "his socialist."[51] To call either Coimbra or Freyre, both men of privilege, a socialist or communist was absurd, but both proved willing to question and, in Freyre's case at least, challenge the political status quo. In a 1928 meeting at the governor's palace in Recife, Gonçalves Ferreira, a local *coronel* (rural political boss) and son of a close family friend, accused Freyre of being a communist because he had written letters recommending for minor civil service positions "humble men" who had been excluded from established patronage channels.[52] Freyre also directed his students in anthropology at the Escola Normal to work on themes that dealt expressly with social, economic, and public health issues.[53] It was clear that Freyre was becoming more cognizant of the concerns of Pernambuco's poor and working classes.

Freyre examined social, cultural, and racial aspects of northeastern regional identity in *Casa-grande & senzala* (1933), *Sobrados e mucambos* (1936), and *Nordeste* (1937).[54] In these works, Freyre introduced several ideas about race and identity, which by the late 1930s would become widely accepted in Brazilian and northeastern intellectual and political circles. The most important of these was the notion that *nordestinos*, especially populations from the interior, constituted a racial group that could be distinguished from other Brazilian racial groups. In *Casa-grande & senzala*, Freyre described *nordestinos* and *sertanejos* as if they possessed inherent racial characteristics with both biological and sociological origins. In describing the differences between Africans and Indians, he wrote that the latter "are gloomy, silent and reserved, sly, and even surly, without the infectious cheerfulness of the Bahians and without their at times irritating petulance, without their grace, their spontaneity, their courtesy, their hearty and contagious laughter."[55] Among the populations of the northeastern interior, he noted, "certain tendencies in the character of the *sertanejo*, or backlander, that incline him to asceticism; a certain suspiciousness in his habits and attitudes; that air of a seminary student that he preserves all his life long; his extraordinary physical endurance; his angular Quixote-like frame, contrasting with the more rounded and sleeker figures of the marshland-dwellers [*brejeiros*]."[56] In *Nordeste*, Freyre argued that although the most recent research on race constituted a "signal that we do not see in the *mestiço* or *negro* of the Northeast that absolute racial or sub-racial inferiority in which Nina Rodrigues believed," he nonetheless endorsed the racial ideal of *branqueamento* by arguing that Pernambucans' supposedly progressive racial characteristics derived from their European ancestors.[57] "What we are able to confirm still today," he wrote, "is that the population of the Northeast is infused with, in its anthropology, the persistence of Nordic features." He pointed to the presence of "blond individuals with blue eyes, [and] pink cheeks" among coastal populations and families "dislocated from the slaveholding and sedentary coast . . . [who were] almost all blond with a more lively racial consciousness and stronger adventurous spirit" as evidence of the positive influence of European blood.[58] Like many contemporaries, Freyre believed that this marked European ancestry did not result from Portuguese colonists but rather from the Dutch colonists who occupied Pernambuco from 1630 to 1654.

Freyre also argued that the supposedly progressive and desirable characteristics of the region's *mulatos* derived from the "better quality" of African slaves imported to the region, writing that "the predominant type of *negro* in the extreme Northeast seems to have been of a regular or average height, strong body, powerful trunk, *not very black*, pretty figure, beautiful teeth, and small ears."[59] Although he wrote that Pernambucan slaves were not as culturally, morally, or materially "refined" as their Bahian counterparts, he believed that Pernambucan slaves were "dominated by a plastic and strong type of *negro*" that was "genetically good and technologically already in the agricultural phase: apt for laboring in the cane fields that were the surroundings selected for *negros* in the agrarian Northeast." Freyre reasoned, in fact, that northeastern slaves were perfectly suited to the cultivation of sugar. This "black element of good origins" combined with the Portuguese, who were "in great part also of good genetic composition and superior social situation," to produce *mulatos,* who were "the most capable of our mixed population."[60] In *Sobrados e mucambos,* Freyre concluded that *mulatos,* rather than Africans, represented the racial future of the nation: "possibilities are to be found today in Brazil in the *mulato* rather than in the pure *negro,* who for almost half a century—the period of the steadiest rise of our colored population—has become rare among us."[61] As further evidence that *nordestinos* were not racially inferior, Freyre included in *Nordeste* a photograph of a Pernambucan "*mestiço*" taken as part of a state government research biotypology project that collected biometric data on Pernambucan soldiers. The choice is notable because of the distinctly European features of the subject. Freyre added the caption "Eugenic Mixed Type of the Northeast" to the photograph, thus endorsing the notion that northeastern populations were racially progressive and almost white.[62]

While delineating the racial characteristics of northeastern populations, Freyre was paradoxically arguing that the causes of apparent racial differences were social and cultural rather than biological, psychological, and climatic. There was nothing new in arguing, as had Euclydes da Cunha and Raymundo Nina Rodrigues, that inherent biological racial characteristics were not the only factors that determined individual and collective identity and social and economic status. However, Freyre attempted to distance himself from the previous generation of scholars, writing in *Casa-grande & senzala* that "an attempt is being made to rectify the anthropo-geography of those who, oblivious of diet, would attribute everything to the factors of *race* and *climate.*"[63] For Freyre, social and historical factors were of crucial importance. He argued that Brazilian *negros'* physical and psychological degradation resulted from "slavery and the one-crop system" rather than inherent racial or biological inferiority.[64] In *Sobrados e mucambos,* Freyre expanded this concept, explaining how individual and social factors produced apparent racial differences: "Many of the qualities associated with race have developed as the result of historical, or, rather, dynamic forces of culture exerted on the group and the individual. Conditioned by race and, certainly, by environment, but not created by the one nor determined by the other. Race gives predispositions, conditions the special forms of human culture. But such specializations are developed by the totality of the environment—the social more than the merely physical—peculiar to the region or the class to which the individual belongs."[65]

This complex interaction between biology, psychology, society, and culture gave rise to unique regional identities, Freyre argued. In *Sobrados e mucambos,* he wrote that "we must not lose sight of the force with which the regional situation of the individual or family, independently of color, race, class, and the condition of being naturalized or native-born, led to his integration with cultures, or regional expressions of culture." Freyre emphasized cultural and social factors in his discussions of northeastern regional identity, arguing that in the Northeast, "the racial factor pales under the more powerful effects of similarities in social formation."[66] Throughout his discussions of Brazilian history, Freyre extolled Brazilians' ability to adapt to their environment, a theme he also emphasized in his portrayals of northeastern Brazil.[67] He argued that this process had taken place in northeastern Brazil since the founding of the original captaincies in the early colonial period. In *Nordeste*, Freyre wrote that "the truth is that it was in the extreme Northeast and Bahian *recôncavo* . . . that Brazilian physiognomy was first established and took root—the features, the values, the Portuguese together with the African and indigenous traditions, constitute this profound Brazil that today is felt to be the most Brazilian."[68] The populations of northeastern Brazil—Portuguese, African, and Indian—had adapted perfectly to regional social and environmental conditions, despite the degradations of centuries of slavery. This process, Freyre concluded, produced the quintessential Brazilian, the *nordestino*.

As with the heated discussions of northeastern regional identity that arose during and immediately following the First Regionalist Congress in 1926, Freyre consistently emphasized that regional identities, while occasionally becoming the basis of political conflict, should not constitute the basis for regional political separatism. In *Sobrados e mucambos*, he wrote that "the shocks of antagonisms in the social or cultural life of Brazil are still frequent; they are reflected in politics, stimulated by difficulties and rivalries between groups and regions. Rivalries between '*gauchos*' and '*bahianos*'; between *paulistas* and '*cabeças chatas*.' But this interpretation cannot be made by the simplistic criteria of conflicts between races that make them biologically or psychologically incapable of understanding and accommodating one another."[69] Freyre rejected the notion that regional identities were based on racial differences and were thus insuperable. At the same time, he struggled to reconcile his affection for Pernambuco and the Northeast with strong intellectual and political support for Brazilian national identity. Although he could have subsumed northeastern regional identity to Brazilian national identity, he instead argued that northeastern identity actually constituted the basis of Brazilian national identity.

The culmination of Freyre's thought on northeastern regional identity came with the publication of *Nordeste*, his least-known and least-read work of the 1930s. Freyre conceived of *Nordeste* as "an ecological study of northeastern Brazil" in which he would examine the relationship between humans, animals, plants, and environment from the perspective of culture, science, and "social philosophy." What immediately strikes the reader of *Nordeste*, especially given Freyre's almost apologetic approach to the Northeast in *Casa-grande & senzala* and *Sobrados e mucambos*, is the degree to which he is critical of the sugar-based northeastern economy and openly discusses social and economic problems. Especially problematic for Freyre was the emphasis planters placed on the cultivation of sugar to the exclusion of other crops. Freyre discussed monoculture as a "social pathology" that "has opened the deepest wounds in life, in the landscape and in the character of the people."[70] Although he argued that Pernambucan sugar planters had created a superior civilization, one that gave rise to the best Brazilian political, esthetic, and intellectual values, he wrote that those values were created in "social and economic conditions that deformed them, or at least affected them, in a morbid and unique way." In short, the Northeast was a region in which economic inequality had given rise to severe social and economic problems. In the conclusion of *Nordeste*, Freyre wrote that southern Brazil, including Minas Gerais and São Paulo, were "civilizations that were more healthy, more democratic, and more equal in the distribution of wealth and goods" than the "old sugar civilization of the northeast."[71] Freyre offered few solutions to the social and economic problems that he so readily identified, however. In 1935, he, Ulysses Pernambucano, Sylvio Rabello, and Olivio Montenegro began a study of labor in sugar factories that they hoped would be used to improve conditions for the working classes. He noted, however, that they were "repelled" and "denounced as agitators" by the Pernambucan establishment, which suggests that his social and economic criticisms of sugar cultivation were not welcome.[72]

In his writing on the Northeast, Freyre both questioned widely accepted conventions about race and regional identity and presented new ideas that became the basis for further discussions. While he worked to overturn outdated understandings of race, rejecting racial determinism and the idea that *mulatos* were inherently inferior, his work also served to underscore differences between the Northeast and the South. With the publication of *Casagrande & senzala*, Freyre almost single-handedly revived national interest in the racial question.[73] Although Freyre presented his ideas as a radical break from the work of Euclydes da Cunha and Raymundo Nina Rodrigues, it is more useful to see his contributions as a continuation and extension of their work. Each author sought to reinterpret Brazil's "racial problem" in light of contemporary social, economic, and political changes that were transforming the nation. Freyre's contributions to the study of race also stand out in that he took both a cultural and a scientific approach. Although he believed that social and cultural factors were more important than biological and racial factors in determining individual and collective identities, he nonetheless continued to argue for the validity of scientific approaches to studying Brazil's social and economic problems.[74] He believed that his contributions to discussions of race and regional identity represented progress toward a better understanding of race in Brazil. Freyre's ideas proved to be controversial and formed the basis of further discussions of race and regional identity by Brazilian intellectuals and political elites in the 1930s and 1940s.

Estudos Afro-Brasileiros

In the aftermath of the publication of *Casa-grande & senzala* in 1933, intellectual and political interest in Afro-Brazilians and race increased to the point that Freyre organized Brazil's First Afro-Brazilian Congress, which was held in Recife in November 1934.[75] The main focus of the congress was the presentation of academic papers on Afro-Brazilian culture, religion, and history as well as recent anthropological, scientific, and medical research on race. Presenters included prominent Brazilian and foreign intellectuals and professionals such as Mario de Andrade, Jorge Amado, Arthur Ramos, Edison Carneiro, Luiz da Camara Cascudo, and University of Chicago anthropologist Melville Herskovits. The papers presented at the congress were published in two volumes, *Estudos afro-brasileiros* (1935) and *Novos estudos afro-brasileiros* (1937). An examination of these papers provides an opportunity to analyze the ways in which Brazilian and northeastern intellectuals and professionals understood race and the social and economic status of Afro-Brazilians in the mid-1930s.

Approximately half of the papers took a social and cultural approach to race, focusing on Afro-Brazilians and Afro-Brazilian culture as integral aspects of the social and historical development of Brazil. Several papers took a special interest in Afro-Brazilian religion, including Arthur Ramos and Edison Carneiro's examination of the importance of the orisha Xangô in Brazilian Candomblé, and Luiz da Camara Cascudo's discussion of Candomblé, *catimbó*, and *macumba*, three Afro-Brazilian religions widely practiced in northeastern Brazil.[76] Compared to the intellectual approaches toward Afro-Brazilian religion and culture adopted in the immediate post-emancipation period (best exemplified in the work of Raymundo Nina Rodrigues), what is most striking about these authors' approaches is the degree to which they had dispensed with the notions that Afro-Brazilian religion was inferior to Catholicism and that it was a manifestation of its practitioners' supposed primitive mentality. They argued instead that Afro-Brazilian religions were legitimate and deserved respectful attention from Brazilian scholars. A similar approach was adopted by authors who presented papers on Afro-Brazilian folklore, music, and dance, including Mário de Andrade, a principal organizer of Modern Art Week in São Paulo, and Jorge Amado, the Bahian novelist.[77] Several papers treated Brazilian slavery, including the origins of the slave trade, the importance of slavery to sugar cultivation, the treatment of slaves, slave rebellions, and abolition. These authors attempted to correct popular and academic portrayals of slavery that had deemphasized the historical significance of slavery as well as its brutal nature.[78] While a few of the papers took an apologetic approach to slavery, which was consistent with Freyre's writings of the early 1930s, the majority of the presenters concluded that Brazilian slavery was an unjust, cruel institution that produced severe social and economic inequalities. Overall, the authors who focused on social and cultural aspects of race took the position that Afro-Brazilians and Afro-Brazilian culture were integral aspects of Brazilian society that deserved additional attention from Brazilian scholars in order to better understand Brazil's "racial question."

The second broad approach adopted at the congress was scientific. Approximately half the papers examined race from the perspective of psychology, psychiatry, medicine, physical anthropology, biotypology, and eugenics. What is most striking about these papers is the continuing legitimacy of scientific approaches to race despite Freyre's oft-stated position that Brazilian intellectuals no longer believed in the validity of racial science.[79] The authors of the scientific papers presented at the congress generally sought first to disprove the notion that Brazilian *mulatos* and *negros* were inherently inferior to *brancos* and second, contradictorily, to prove that *branqueamento* was improving Brazil's populations. Although researchers possessed widely varying positions on the individual and social effects of racial mixing, they generally agreed that physiological and psychological racial characteristics existed and could be studied objectively. Researchers universally classified their human subjects into the *branco*, *mulato*, and *negro* racial groups. Several biotypological studies concluded that racial differences were discernible in the study of body size and shape.[80] Physicians from Rio de Janeiro and Recife presented research that they argued proved that racial groups possessed distinct blood types and, as a result, differing levels of immunity to diseases.[81] Most researchers argued that *brancos, mulatos,* and *negros* possessed distinct but not necessarily superior or inferior psychological and physiological qualities, but a few argued that *mulatos* and *negros* were inherently inferior to *brancos*. One paper discussed criminal "delinquents," including a *mulato* subject whom researchers described as "the most terrible and celebrated delinquent known in our midst."[82] In a paper on race and mental disorders, Ulysses Pernambucano concluded that a higher incidence of specific mental disorders among black Pernambucans "seems to indicate a manifest fragility of *negros* . . . in relation to mental diseases."[83] In a paper that examined the relationship between mental disorders and race, two Rio-based researchers argued that although *negros* suffered from a higher incidence of mental diseases than *mulatos* and *brancos,* "everything seems to favor [*negros'*] rapid assimilation . . . where Aryanizing factors are introduced in a satisfactory manner."[84] Antônio Austregesilo Lima, a *carioca* psychiatrist and educator, argued that Brazilian *mestiços* were "fragile elements that will be progressively reduced by the mysterious and protective life force of the species."[85] Geraldo de Andrade argued that Pernambucan *mulatos* were "becoming more like the white man [*homem branco*]."[86] Several papers presented racial mixing more optimistically, however, endorsing the view that *mulatos* were not inherently degenerate, with one researcher concluding that "white-black *mestiçagem* produces offspring that, at birth, can be considered as physically apt as the pure [races]."[87] The scientific research presented at the congress concluded that Brazil's nonwhite populations continued to suffer the legacies of qualities inherited from their African ancestors while simultaneously benefiting from the progressive social and biological effects of *branqueamento.*

None of the papers presented at the congress attempted to present a wholly new understanding or definition of race. However, researchers' tentative rejection of racial determinism required another explanation of the origins and causes of the apparent social and biological differences among racial groups. Although new cultural and scientific approaches to race questioned the notion that there were inferior and superior races, few Brazilian reformers, intellectuals, or politicians would have argued that significant social and economic differences among racial groups did not exist. They instead argued that climate, diseases, and social and economic factors produced differences among individuals and racial groups. This idea was, of course, not new; Brazilian reformers and intellectuals had taken this position in the 1910s and 1920s.[88] What is significant is that this point still needed to be made in 1934. In his discussion of the eugenic implications of racial mixing, Antônio Austregesilo Lima argued that "the Brazilian type of today is not inferior or degenerate: it is 'wanting.'" The Brazilian, he concluded, "does not know how to read, does not know how to eat, and does not know how to work, that is, he is wanting in culture. In addition, endemic diseases destroy the coasts and the interior of the nation and here are the reasons for our apparent inferiority."[89] Brazilian *mulatos* were inferior, he reasoned, but not because of race. Freyre weighed in on the subject, presenting a paper on "deformities in the bodies of runaway slaves," based on analysis of physical descriptions of slaves in nineteenth-century newspaper advertisements. Freyre concluded that slaves were not "a dysgenic element or carrier of African illnesses and diseases" but rather that they were disfigured and demeaned by "too much agricultural labor, labor in bourgeois houses, sleeping and eating poorly, living conditions in the *senzalas*, punishments, vices, work accidents, and work at a young age using brute force."[90] Although Freyre and his colleagues rejected racial determinism, they could not ignore social and economic realities. As any observer could plainly see, Brazil was a highly hierarchical society in which *mulatos* and *negros* were clearly disadvantaged.

Collectively, the papers presented at the congress were concerned primarily with questioning long-held notions of racial hierarchy and inherent racial differences by examining the social, cultural, and biological implications of racial mixing and the origins of racial inequality. Thus, the congress was simultaneously a cultural *and* a scientific endeavor.[91] Although the social and political dimensions of racial inequality constituted the topics of only a small number of the papers presented at the congress, this did not mean that the congress was apolitical, as Freyre and some historians have argued. Jovelino M. Camargo Júnior wrote that "racial prejudice existed in the past and continues to exist today" and that in Brazil "everything was reserved for whites," while Edison Carneiro, employing Marxist terminology, discussed Afro-Brazilians' "deplorable situation," the need for improved educational opportunities and working conditions, and Afro-Brazilians' support for the Brazilian Communist Party.[92]

Although few papers directly addressed contemporary social, economic, and political issues, the congress nevertheless constituted a challenge to the Pernambucan ruling elite in that it raised broad questions about race and social justice, issues that they felt uncomfortable acknowledging, much less addressing.[93] Contrary to Freyre's assertion that "the congress of Recife was, still, the most independent of congresses" and that "it did not receive any support from the government, it was not associated with any political movement, nor any religious doctrine, nor any party," the congress nonetheless became a point of contention in the acrimonious political debates of the mid-1930s.[94] As Robert Levine has shown, the Pernambucan ruling classes responded to the congress by accusing Freyre and his collaborators of being subversives, making common cause with communists, and undermining the authority of the Catholic Church, while simultaneously rejecting the notion that Afro-Brazilians were worthy of scholarly, much less political, attention.[95] The effect of the congress was ultimately twofold. First, it served to legitimize the intellectual study of race in Pernambuco, and second, the issues Freyre and his colleagues raised at the congress would become points of contention during the political crisis that would unfold in Pernambuco between 1935 and 1937.

Conservative Responses

Intellectual and political conservatives reacted immediately and strongly to the challenges posed by Freyre's scholarship and the First Afro-Brazilian Congress. Conservatives' understanding of race and northeastern regional identity is not easily characterized, but in general they continued to emphasize the supposedly inherent biological characteristics of Brazil's populations, harking back to older theories of race, and employed the notion of a strict racial hierarchy that served to reinforce the economic and political status quo. In other words, conservatives' vision of race reflected their desire to maintain their position of power and dominance over largely nonwhite, working-class populations. Conservatives' understanding of race was not merely reactionary, however. Several intellectual and political figures, most notably Agamemnon Magalhães, sought to update existing theories of race in the context of new social and political ideals. An examination of conservative conceptions of race and regional identity is crucial for understanding the ways in which northeastern regional identity was articulated during the Estado Novo.

Agamemnon Magalhães (1893–1952) was a crucial figure in the development of northeastern regional identity during the 1930s and 1940s. He was born in Vila Bela (now Serra Talhada) in the Pernambucan *sertão* some 380 kilometers (230 miles) west of Recife, graduated from the Faculdade de Direito do Recife in 1916, and began a career as a public prosecutor (*promotor público*). At the same time, he joined the Partido Republicano Democrata and was elected a state deputy in 1918 and a federal deputy in 1923. His ardent opposition to the Estacío Coimbra administration led him to support Getúlio Vargas in the 1930 election, support for which he was rewarded with a series of federal government appointments. He served as a Pernambucan representative to the 1934 Constituent Assembly, and he was appointed by Vargas to direct the Ministério do Trabalho, Indústria e Comércio (MTIC) from 1934 to 1937 and the Ministério da Justiça e Negócios Interiores in 1937 before assuming the position of federal *interventor* of Pernambuco from 1937 to 1945. In addition to pursuing his political career, Magalhães occupied a chair in geography at the Ginásio Pernambucano from 1922 to 1933 and was appointed to a chair in public and constitutional law at Recife's Faculdade de Direito in 1933, although he never occupied the position because he was appointed to the MTIC the following year.[96]

Magalhães's academic and political careers put him in a unique position; he wrote about the Northeast and northeastern regional identity as both a geographer and the most powerful politician in Pernambuco. In his 1921 *concurso* thesis, "The Brazilian Northeast," Magalhães argued that Brazilians possessed inherent physical and psychological characteristics and that *mestiços* were, quoting Louis Agassiz, "an indescribable type, whose physical and mental energy are known to be weakened."[97] As a geographer, Magalhães argued that physical environment and climate exerted a profound influence on human populations, and he believed that conditions in coastal and interior regions gave rise to "ethnic types that are being defined and perfected, adapted to the necessities of Brazilian labor and industries." The results of this process were varied, however. Racial types of the northeastern interior, he concluded, were a "defined ethnic type" while coastal *mestiços*, whom he argued were predominantly of African rather than indigenous descent, were in a state of "disequilibrium."[98] Magalhães presented the *sertanejo* as the quintessential Brazilian, whom he described as a "heroic man, chastised by climatic and social fatalities" who served to "strengthen the energies of our historic race." He also invoked Euclydes da Cunha's celebrated *Os sertões* description of the *sertanejo* as the "core of Brazilian nationality." The northeastern "hinterland," he reasoned, was "a new world, the Brazil of the future."[99] Magalhães concluded his thesis by arguing that the social, racial, and economic transformation of the region was of national importance: "In the Northeast we are at the resolution of the most vital national problems. Without its development, the *sertão* will be uninhabited, weakening the most vigorous energies of the race, reducing nationality, submerging our political unity in the conflict of opposing tendencies that result from the diversity of populations, without ethnic homogeneity."[100] For Magalhães it was the *sertanejo*, not the coastal *mestiço*, who represented the ideal Brazilian racial type. He believed that the racial and social ascendance of the *sertanejo* would eliminate racial conflict and result in racial homogeneity. While it is easy to dismiss Magalhães's racial geography as second-rate scholarship written to gain a chair in geography at the high-school level, the thesis is significant in that Magalhães's political career put him in a position to put these ideas into practice. More than fifteen years later, while serving as the minister of labor, Magalhães ordered the republication of his thesis in the official journal of the ministry, thus giving his ideas a wider audience among government and labor officials.

In 1933, Magalhães wrote a second thesis, "The State and Contemporary Reality," for which he was awarded the chair in public and constitutional law at the Faculdade do Direito.[101] This piece is striking in that he had moved beyond his 1921 thesis to imagine a Brazil in which race did not matter, and the work was ostensibly an attempt to define the role of the state in modern society. Borrowing from Italian fascism, he conceived of the state as "a force of social integration, an orienting power with organs and functions that achieve an equilibrium of tendencies and dominant facts in certain periods in the evolution of peoples, that is discipline and coordination." Magalhães denounced liberalism as "indifferent to social inequalities and injustices, originating in class antagonism and problems of the masses."[102] Contemporary society, he reasoned, did not originate with a Lockeian or Rousseauian social contract but rather as a result of a Durkheimian "social solidarity" that arose from "the interdependence of all social values." Social solidarity, he concluded, would ensure "the unity of social ends—justice and universal peace."[103] This model did not allow for individualism, which, Magalhães argued, was "going to disappear," replaced by the principle of "cooperation." To Magalhães, the ideal society was corporatist, overseen by an interventionist state that "exercised thus the specific function of discipline and integration of social forces by the means of law."[104] Beyond the state, Magalhães endorsed an "organic nationalism" that, unlike in Nazi Germany, included all Brazilians, regardless of race, and reflected, in noted Brazilian conservative Alberto Torres's words, "the spontaneous activity of society, in the defense of its character and of its economy, in the organic preparation of its material development, and in the education of its spirit."[105] Magalhães emphasized what united rather than what divided Brazilians. Race thus constituted an impediment to social and political unity—it served only to protect individual and group interests and thus did not advance the common social good in a period in which the state was gradually assuming greater control over the individual and society. In contrast, Gilberto Freyre valued racial differences as the foundation of both individual and collective Brazilian identities.

In the 1920s and 1930s, the racial, psychological, and moral characteristics of the populations of the northeastern interior became the subject of extensive commentary and analysis by regional and national intellectual and political conservatives. Collectively, their depictions of the region, especially the interior, relied heavily on Euclydes da Cunha's and Raymundo Nina Rodrigues's interpretations of the Canudos rebellion and thus focused on the racial background and psychology of rural populations.[106] *Cangaceiros, jagunços,* and *fa-naticos* (religious fanatics) were singled out as threats to social and political stability and were systematically excluded from their discussions of north-eastern regional identity. Gustavo Barroso (1888–1959), who also wrote under the pen name João do Norte, was instrumental in shaping public and political perceptions of northeastern regional identity beginning in the 1910s. Barroso was born in Fortaleza, Ceará, and received a law degree from the Faculdade de Direito de Rio de Janeiro in 1911 before pursuing careers in journalism, teaching, and politics. In the 1930s, he became the intellectual leader of the fascist Brazilian Integralist movement, three-time president of the Brazilian Academy of Letters, and director of the Museu Histórico Nacional.[107] Much of his early writing focused on northeastern folklore, but he also wrote about northeastern regional identity and the populations of the arid interior in works such as *Terra de sol* (1912), *Heróes e bandidos* (1917), and *Alma sertaneja* (1923). Barroso characterized *sertanejos* as the descendants of Portuguese set-tlers and Indians and argued that there were few *mestiços* of African descent in the northeastern interior.[108] He further divided the populations of the *sertão* into "normal" and "abnormal" types, the former consisting of *sertanejos*, farmers, ranchers, and cowboys and the latter, of *cangaceiros* and *curandeiros* (charlatans). In a race-based diatribe, Barroso described *cangaceiros* as

profoundly odious and infinitesimally miserable, complete degenerates, ignoble neuropaths, having the audacity of all turpitudes and an inclination for all crimes, muddled souls that never demonstrate a compassionate gesture and never possess the smallest human sentiments; perverse, cowards, born with all defects, prone to all psychoses, rarely white, always *mestiços* of dubious origins, brachycephalic, prognathic, asymmetrical, deformed, horrible faces. . . . Mental disturbances run riot and wild in their brains, inciting them to crime. They are true monsters, at times epileptic, with vile faces, deformed craniums, accumu-lating disturbing hereditary factors, related to the most vile inherited defects. Their names produce horror in the minds of pacific populations, who are ter-rified. Each one of them is a rosary of tortures, ill-treated, displaying Daho-mean barbarities, repugnant scenes of abject sensualism, the stigma of the most base and depraved inclinations.[109]

Barroso's characterizations went far beyond Euclydes da Cunha's and Raymundo Nina Rodrigues's racialized portrayals of the populations of the northeastern interior. For Barroso, *cangaceiros* possessed the worst human quali-ties. In *Heróes e bandidos,* he described Antônio Silvino (1875–1944), a notori-ous bandit who operated in Pernambuco and Paraíba, as "socially backward, a man of another era" who was predisposed to crime by race, education, and social surroundings that "made him a criminal."[110] The society of the interior was "the result of the ruin of three races," which "collapse[d] in a melting pot of confused *mestiçagem*."[111] Barroso reasoned that scientific laws "rule and produce criminality in the interior" and resulted in a society that "has not evolved." Little could be done to improve the populations of the northeastern interior, he reasoned, because "the legacy of crime and rebelliousness . . . is passed from generation to generation."[112] Barroso's characterizations of the *sertão* and *sertanejos* found a new audience in the 1930s because of the rising intellectual and political influence of the extreme Right. Conservative intellectuals and politicians concerned with the "northeastern problem" cited his work extensively and accepted the notion that the populations of the rural interior were essentially different from the populations of the coast.

Throughout the 1930s, intellectuals and politicians' assessments of the populations of the northeastern interior emphasized these same themes. While commentators updated the racial theories they employed to describe the populations, they still focused on *sertanejos'* supposedly essential, unchanging qualities. In *O outro nordeste* (1937), Djacir Menezes cited John Dewey, Franz Boas, Oliveira Viana, and Gilberto Freyre in describing interior populations as "a race of strong men, not sick, as has been held true by the pessimistic writings of pseudo-science." To those who insisted that *sertanejos* were racially inferior, Menezes responded that the cause of apparent racial inferiority was "the disadjustment between man and his social surroundings, [and] the lack of education . . . produces these apparently unemployed, vagrant, or sick individuals, colored by theorists of superior and inferior races."[113] While he rejected racial essentialism, Menezes nonetheless presented a reductionist view of *sertanejos*, who, he wrote, possessed both unfathomable "physical resistance and moral energy" as well as "depressive tendencies attributable to the predominance of the psychic characters of the Indian." He concluded that "the *caboclo* of the Northeast already is a clearly individualized ethnographic type, a type ethnically representative of Brazil."[114]

Conservative intellectual approaches to northeastern identity were adopted by political leaders at both the state and national level. After seizing power in 1930, Getúlio Vargas focused on consolidating political power and put in place a number of political reforms that transformed the relationship between state and federal governments. As a result, the Vargas government showed more interest in Pernambucan and northeastern politics and governance than had been the case during the First Republic. The severe drought of 1930–1932 prompted the federal government to refocus attention on social and economic conditions in the region.[115] In a series of speeches delivered in northeastern state capitals in 1933, Vargas highlighted the federal government's efforts to provide relief for those affected by the drought and its funding of water reclamation projects, irrigation projects, and economic development projects tailored to each state's situation and economic strengths. He emphasized the social and economic hardships endured by populations who lived in the drought zone and referred to *sertanejos*, in yet another invocation of Euclydes da Cunha, as the "core of nationality."[116] In one speech, he suggested that the populations of Ceará, Bahia, and Paraíba possessed common social and cultural characteristics. At the same time, he downplayed race as a factor that differentiated the populations of the Northeast and the South, stating that "the conditions of the physical environment, more than ethnic factors, complicate the peculiar problem of the progress of social groups." Despite what he admitted were considerable economic and cultural differences, Vargas believed that "antagonisms did not exist between North and South, as apparently some superficial and hurried observers would note."[117] He consistently emphasized nation over region, stating that "it was impossible to have preferences between the Brazilian North and South." At the same time, he concluded that the nation "ought to pay attention, out of preference, to those of her children that most need support."[118] The solution was to create social and economic development programs that addressed "the northern secular problem of the conciliation of man with the land."[119] These included government subsidies and loans to modernize the sugar industry, as well as increased funding for drought relief, water reclamation projects, and the construction of roads and rail lines. While *nordestinos* were clearly disadvantaged, Vargas conceived of them as a national resource to be developed.

The exodus of *nordestinos* from the drought-stricken interior in the early 1930s prompted a more thoroughgoing examination of the social, economic, and political problems of the region.[120] Federal agencies took an active interest in northeastern regional identity. Several studies of *nordestinos* were published in the *Boletim da Inspectoria Federal de Obras Contra as Secas* (*BIFOCS*), the official journal of the inspectorate, which primarily examined drought relief efforts, public health programs, public works projects, and agricultural development programs. Thomaz Pompeu Sobrinho (1880–1967), a native of Ceará, engineer, agronomist, and anthropologist, authored two articles on *nordestinos* that appeared in *BIFOCS* in 1934.[121] Pompeu's intent was to "try to give an outline of the establishment of the civilized man of the Brazilian Northeast, attempting to discern the principal connections with nature."[122] Like da Cunha, Freyre, and Magalhães, Pompeu argued that *nordestinos* constituted a distinct racial group: "The Northeast constitutes a well-defined natural, physical, and social zone" in which "climatic, architectural, ethnographic, and social conditions present a homogeneity that is consequently able to perfectly characterize and differentiate it from other regions of America."[123] He concluded that "these factors sufficiently explain the anthropo-social specialization that individualizes our people and makes them recognizable wherever they appear outside their *habitat*." In writing for *BIFOCS*, however, Pompeu's primary concern was to determine how *nordestinos* would respond to federal social and economic development projects. To this end, the careful delineation of *nordestinos'* racial characteristics was essential. He argued that in order to "arrive at an extremely precise definition of the *homem nordestino*," it was necessary to "analyze, with prudent attention . . . historical geography according to established ethnographic zones."[124] Although he recognized that a significant number of the northeastern interior's inhabitants were *mulato*, he concluded that "the contribution of African blood in the northeastern populations is small and is diminishing."[125] Pompeu also argued that the populations of the *sertão* were whiter, and thus more progressive, than those of the littoral. Race was significant in that it lent certain qualities to *nordestinos* as workers. He argued that *nordestinos* possessed tremendous energy, good eyesight, could walk long distances, were adept at laboring in a stooped position, resistant to disease, and "extraordinarily fecund."[126] Pompeu believed that *nordestinos*, although prone to fatalism, suffering from diseases, and largely uneducated, could nonetheless become productive workers and thus, according to Vargas-era understandings of national identity, citizens of the nation.

Agamemnon Magalhães's stewardship of the Ministério do Trabalho, Indústria e Comércio from 1934 to 1937 provided an opportunity for the Vargas administration to further explore and refine its position on northeastern Brazil. Between 1935 and 1945, the ministry's journal published more than a dozen articles that examined race and regional identity in the Northeast, six of them by Ovidio da Cunha (1912–1997). Born in Recife and lettered in law by the Faculdade Nacional de Direito in Rio de Janeiro, da Cunha was in his early twenties when he wrote these articles and seemed unconcerned with or unaware of contemporary debates about race and identity. He did, however, accept the notion that social and cultural factors were more important than inherent biological characteristics in the formation of racial identities. He also took the position that racial differences were expressed primarily in terms of culture and collective psychology.[127] Da Cunha made a fundamental distinction between populations of the coast, which he argued bore the legacy of their African ancestry, and the populations of the interior, which he claimed were free of African influence, ultimately concluding that *sertanejos* were racially superior to coastal populations. While the majority of contemporary scholars took the position that the populations of the northeastern interior were racially mixed, da Cunha asserted that *sertanejos* were predominantly white and traced their ancestry to Portuguese settlers, whom he described, using the language of biotypology, as "long-headed blondes" (*dólico-louros*). Da Cunha acknowledged the presence of *mulatos* and *mestiços* in the interior, but he argued that "the *sertão*, as we know, is a region of *brancos* where the poorly established *negro* remains completely inassimilable in small settlements such as Padre Cícero's Juazeiro."[128] Thus, da Cunha constructed local populations that were difficult to control, such as the followers of Padre Cícero, as black, despite the fact that *romeiros* were no different racially than the population of the *sertão* as a whole.[129] Da Cunha concluded that nonwhite populations would eventually be assimilated or eliminated through the "progressive Aryanization of the populations of the *sertão*."[130] He did not believe that coastal populations would completely disappear but rather that a "symbiosis" would develop between the two groups and would "permit the future affirmation of a strong nationality."[131] Echoing Magalhães, da Cunha portrayed the supposedly white *sertanejo* as the personification of northeastern regional identity, in sharp contrast to Freyre's championing of the coastal *mulato* as the quintessential working-class *nordestino*. Conservative intellectuals and politicians claimed, like Euclydes da Cunha, that *sertanejos* constituted the core of nationality but that they needed to be stripped of their less desirable characteristics. The careful and deliberate delineation of exactly which populations of the Northeast were to be considered proper *nordestinos* constitutes the construction of a northeastern regional identity by the process of elimination, which Roberto Schwarz has identified in the work of Brazilian literary critics and philosophers who contemplated Brazilian national identity beginning in the 1870s.[132] It was political and intellectual conservatives' characterizations of the region that would form the basis of discussions of northeastern regional identity in the late 1930s and early 1940s as Agamemnon Magalhães assumed power in Pernambuco.

The Homem do Nordeste

The coup d'état of September 1937 and the imposition of the Estado Novo provided the opportunity to put this conservative vision of northeastern regional identity into practice. In November 1937, Getúlio Vargas replaced Pernambucan *interventor* Carlos de Lima Cavalcanti with Agamemnon Magalhães. As discussed in previous chapters, the Cavalcanti administration's progressive social and political reforms proved difficult to implement and controversial for the state's conservative elements. Lima Cavalcanti's alleged support for the communist-led Aliança Nacional Libertadora (ANL, or National Liberating Alliance) and the 1935 Intentona Comunista as well as his opposition to Vargas in the campaigning for the scheduled 1938 presidential elections prompted his removal from power.[133] With Lima Cavalcanti's departure and Magalhães's appointment in his place, the more open social and political atmosphere that had produced the First Afro-Brazilian Congress of 1934 no longer existed, and any open discussion of racial issues came to an end. This shift resulted in the ascendance of conservative theories of race and regional identity and their application in governing Pernambuco. The Magalhães administration narrowed its focus from investigating the broader "race question" as defined by Gilberto Freyre and his collaborators to focusing on *nordestinos'* physiological and psychological capabilities as workers. Afro-Brazilian culture and religion, as well as the economic and political aspects of race, were no longer considered legitimate areas of inquiry. The new direction reflected not only Agamemnon Magalhães's personal views on race, outlined in his 1921 and 1933 theses, but also the changing political climate, in which the Estado Novo regime sought to eliminate all forms of social, cultural, and political dissent.

The Magalhães administration did continue to study race and northeastern regional identity, however, and did so using biotypology. Although several Pernambucans, including Geraldo de Andrade, had been conducting biotypological research since the late 1920s, the changing political climate after 1935 generated renewed interest in biotypological research. Whereas the research of the late 1920s and early 1930s had been used primarily as a diagnostic tool to measure Pernambucans' physical development and to design physical education programs, by the mid-1930s, biotypology was being used as part of social engineering efforts in institutions over which the state had direct control, such as schools, prisons, and the military. During the Estado Novo, biotypology was also used to articulate a formal, supposedly scientific definition of northeastern regional identity based on *nordestinos'* physical and racial characteristics. Three researchers employed by the state government, Luiz Ignacio, Miguel Ignacio de Andrade Lima Júnior, and Alvaro Ferraz, conducted physical examinations of thousands of Pernambucan students, soldiers, and prisoners from 1936 through 1946. They argued, based on the collection and analysis of biometric data, that *nordestinos* possessed common physical features and thus constituted a distinct racial sub-type, whereas earlier biotypological research had suggested that *nordestinos* merely possessed distinct regional characteristics. The notion that *nordestinos* were physically underdeveloped persisted, and such negative assessments of *nordestinos,* the result of statistical comparisons with supposedly "normal" and "well-developed" Brazilians and North Americans, could not be used to construct a positive northeastern regional identity. During the Estado Novo, Pernambucan biotypologists instead concluded that *nordestinos* compared favorably with other Brazilians and even to Europeans and North Americans.[134] Biotypological research proved that *nordestinos* were robust, capable workers and citizens who would contribute to the social and economic development of the nation. This reversal reflected the ways in which the supposedly objective "science" of biotypology, which traced its origins to eugenics, in fact reflected the social and political concerns of researchers and ruling elites. During the Estado Novo, new understandings of Brazilian national identity made *nordestinos* full members of the body politic, and thus state-sponsored research, including biotypology, anthropology, and geography, supported prevailing political agendas.

Biotypological researchers further argued that *pernambucanos, paraibanos,* and *alagoanos* shared common physical and psychological characteristics. At the same time, the researchers claimed that *pernambucanos* were, more so than the populations of any other state, typical *nordestinos.*[135] Biotypological research thus confirmed what Euclydes da Cunha had argued in *Os sertões* some forty years earlier—that *nordestinos* constituted a distinct regional type, physically and psychologically adapted to life in the region.[136] Researchers and politicians began to employ the formal term *homem do Nordeste* (man of the Northeast) in their descriptions of the populations of the region. The authors of one biotypological study argued that 98 percent of children born and raised in Pernambuco were endowed with "an immensely regional stamp, which is the result of everything that is syntonized to our climate, diet, and individuality."[137] Biotypological researchers stopped short of arguing that *nordestinos* constituted a unique racial type, however. Given that scientists and intellectuals almost universally utilized the racial categories of *branco, mulato,* and *negro,* it would have been intellectually difficult to argue that *nordestinos* constituted a separate race. Researchers instead classified *nordestinos* as a "sub-race," as had Euclydes da Cunha in *Os sertões.*

The publication of Alvaro Ferraz and Andrade Lima Júnior's *A morfologia do homem do Nordeste* in 1939 represented the height of the influence of biotypological research in Pernambuco. The researchers collected biometric data on fifteen hundred Pernambucan enlisted men and classified their subjects both according to race, using the terms *leucodermo, faiodermo,* and *melanodermo* for *branco, mulato,* and *negro,* respectively, and biotype, using the terms *normolineo, longilineo,* and *brevilineo.* Ferraz and Lima Júnior argued that there was an "average man" for each racial and biotypological group against which individuals could be compared.[138] These statistical avatars compared favorably, they argued, to classical Greek statues of Apollo and Antaeus, sketches of which they included alongside photographs of carefully chosen individual subjects. The comparisons with Greek statuary must have seemed fantastic to contemporary readers, as they do today, but the essential point they were making was clear: while Pernambucans and, by extension, all *nordestinos* possessed uniquely regional physical characteristics, they were, in fact, entirely normal. Any apparent physiological and psychological differences between Pernambucans and *nordestinos* and the Brazilian population as a whole were explained as historical and geographic accident, as the natural result of the complex interaction between individuals and their environment, not as the result of inherent racial or biological inferiority.

Most importantly, Ferraz and Lima Júnior discussed the *homem do Nordeste* as it if were a discernible type, bearing the distinct marks of the influence of ancestry, geography, and history. The *homem do Nordeste* constituted a category outside conventional definitions of race. Their use of the terms *leucodermo, faiodermo,* and *melanodermo* for *branco, mulato,* and *negro* permitted the discussion of supposedly innate racial characteristics without making reference to specific racial groups. Although they acknowledged that *nordestinos* were nonwhite, they insisted that the *homem do Nordeste* did not possess the negative characteristics usually associated with *negros* and *mulatos.* In a 1941 biotypological study of Pernambucan police officers, Alvaro Ferraz recognized the racial anxiety that arose in intellectual and political discussions of *nordestinos'* racial ancestry: "who has not thought that we are irremediably burdened with the physical stigmas of degeneracy, attributed by some anthropologists to *mestiços*[?]"[139] He assuaged his readers by asserting that "there is no reason to worry." Instead of engaging in a discussion of race, Ferraz and his fellow researchers discussed biotypes. Thus, the biotype "*longilineo*" corresponded to *sertanejos,* whom they argued were essentially *branco,* and the biotype "*brevilineo*" corresponded to coastal *mulatos.* Although they focused on the *longilineo* as the ideal, in their 1939 study Ferraz and Lima emphasized that they did not consider *brevilineos* to be "ethnically inferior." In a 1945 study, Ferraz went so far as to argue that *brevilineos* were better suited to heavy agricultural labor because they were appropriately proportioned for hoeing fields, a conclusion he had reached by studying prisoners under "scientifically controlled circumstances" at the Pernambucan government's agricultural prison colony at

Itamaracá.[140] The implication was that northeastern *mulatos* were perfectly suited for agricultural labor on plantations while *sertanejos,* "adventurous and idealistic," were highly adaptable and held greater potential as workers and citizens in the Brazil of the future.[141] Thus, both *sertanejos* and *mulatos,* the two types that collectively constituted the *homem do Nordeste,* exhibited redeeming characteristics. At its core, Pernambucan biotypological research presented an essentialist view of *nordestinos.* The *homem do Nordeste* possessed specific, quantifiable physical, psychological, and moral qualities that would become the focus of social and economic development programs during the Magalhães administration.

Ideas in Practice

The biotypological research carried out in Pernambucan schools, prisons, and military barracks was part of a larger effort to promote a new vision of Pernambucan and northeastern regional identity that was compatible with Estado Novo notions of citizenship and national identity.[142] Social policies and programs developed by Magalhães's administration from 1937 to 1945 had profound impact not only on the way in which the region and its peoples were understood but also on Pernambucans' daily lives.[143] The most important consequence of the Magalhães administration's deployment of new understandings of northeastern regional identity was the social, political, and symbolic marginalization of Afro-Brazilians. The Magalhães administration constructed Afro-Brazilian culture and religion as a profound threat to the maintenance of social and political order in Pernambuco. As outlined in the previous chapter, social and political conservatives viewed the research conducted by Ulysses Pernambucano and the SAP on the relationship between race and mental diseases as socially and politically subversive. The persecution of Afro-Brazilians increased substantially after the failed Intentona Comunista of 1935. Although there were few politically active Afro-Brazilians who openly expressed their support for the Aliança Nacional Libertadora or the Communist Party, after 1935 all Afro-Brazilian organizations, political or religious, were viewed with suspicion by the Pernambucan government. After Magalhães assumed power in 1937, Recife's vibrant Afro-Brazilian community was actively repressed. Magalhães blamed Gilberto Freyre and those who participated in the First Afro-Brazilian Congress for inciting popular unrest among Afro-Brazilians and for generating interest in Afro-Brazilian culture and religion among the general population. Magalhães asserted that "the subtle nature of [Freyre and his collaborators'] interference and the conversion of individuals of color of the popular classes [has resulted in] a proselytizing inimical to our culture and, hence, has given rise to ideas that corrupt our civilization."[144] He further described Afro-Brazilian religions as "offensive to our culture" and "propitious to the ideas that destroy our civilization" and called for the immediate "repression of these pernicious activities with all the necessary rigor."[145] In early 1938, the Magalhães administration did begin a campaign to repress Afro-Brazilian culture and religion, including supposedly related threats to the "social collective" such as gambling, prostitution, and witchcraft.[146]

Magalhães and his conservative political allies claimed that all Pernambucans, including Afro-Brazilians, were Catholic. At a 1938 commemoration of the fiftieth anniversary of abolition held in Recife, Augusto Alvaro da Silva, the archbishop of Bahia and primate of Brazil, suggested that Catholicism was "a religion because of its excellence of universal fraternity; it does not recognize the inferiority of race or of color."[147] Thus, all Brazilians, regardless of race, were united in Christian community. In 1942, Magalhães claimed that the ongoing campaign against Afro-Brazilian culture and religion had been successful: "The African *seitas*, low spiritism, uncurbed gambling, offenses to public decorum, and other corrupting practices are problems that we have confronted, defeating the resistance they put forth to sanitary measures." Magalhães also claimed, with typical bravado, that all remaining material evidence of the practice of Afro-Brazilian religion had been collected by public health officials and put on display at the 1942 Exposição Nacional de Pernambuco and the Museu do Estado.[148] The Magalhães administration's persecution of Afro-Brazilians in Pernambuco stood in stark contrast to the Vargas administration's celebration of Afro-Brazilian culture through Carnival and radio and reflected the more politically conservative bent of Pernambucan politics.[149]

Afro-Brazilians were not the only group to be excluded from the Magalhães administration's understanding of regional identity and citizenship. Both the federal and Pernambucan governments identified northeastern bandits as a threat to social and political order. In the 1920s, Pernambucan officials argued that banditry could be reduced and ultimately eliminated through efforts to improve economic and social conditions in the interior. In 1925, Pernambucan governor Sergío Loreto announced a series of reforms that focused on "educating and civilizing" the populations of the interior.[150] At the same time, government officials endorsed the use of the military and the police to combat banditry, which they hoped would produce "a noticeable attenuation of all disturbances against order that have ruined the *sertão* zone."[151] In the mid-1930s, official discussions of banditry focused increasingly on its supposedly deleterious effect on the "moral fabric" of the region. In 1936, the Pernambucan government had a force of two hundred soldiers assigned exclusively to the "systematic combat against banditry."[152] Lampião (Virgulino Ferreira da Silva, 1898–1938), the most powerful and notorious northeastern bandit in the 1920s and 1930s, proved especially worrisome. The Pernambucan government referred to his band as a "sinister group" that caused "terror and panic in the hearts of *sertão* populations."[153] In 1936, Pernambucan troops battled a group of thirty Lampião-affiliated fanatics, a group they described as "a dangerous organization that made use of the activities of the young and the so-called Communist Youth Party."[154] As with Afro-Brazilians, Pernambucan government officials attempted to link bandits with communism and the 1935 uprising, effectively marginalizing them within constructions of northeastern regional identity.

The symbolic end of banditry in the northeastern interior came with coordinated police and military efforts to eliminate Lampião, who was ambushed and summarily executed by federal forces in Alagoas in 1938. In a political stunt reminiscent of the treatment of Antônio Conselheiro's remains, Lampião's decapitated head was subjected to an autopsy in Maceió, Alagoas, by physician and medical examiner José Lages Filho, who concluded that Lampião exhibited "physical indicators of degeneracy" and was a "born criminal" according to the standards of Italian criminal anthropology widely used in legal medicine.[155] Following Lampião's execution, Magalhães wrote in a Recife newspaper that "a special law in order to combat banditry is . . . necessary. I condone the summary execution, without recourse to appeal or pardon, of all those who, because of cowardliness or interest, lend help to, for however long, the most terrible and cruel of bandits." Magalhães also indicated that he accepted Lages Filho's postmortem diagnosis of Lampião as scientific proof of northeastern bandits' supposed degeneracy.[156] Although bandits remained a potent symbol of social disorder into the 1940s, Magalhães promoted Lampião's execution as an example of the government's ability to eliminate undesirable and potentially dangerous elements from the social body. In a 1940 report, Magalhães identified the most dangerous threats to the "social collective" as banditry, Candomblé, communism, and "sensationalist journalism." While banditry was "a problem that challenged the most energetic precautions of public power," Magalhães claimed that Pernambucan government had successfully freed the *sertão* from "the nefarious actions of the *bandoleiros*."[157] Magalhães had thus eliminated another group that did not conform to his idealized conception of northeastern regional identity.

While repressing Afro-Brazilians and eliminating bandits, the Magalhães administration also emphasized the positive qualities that all *nordestinos* supposedly possessed. In a 1940 report, Magalhães wrote that "following the political ideals of the moment, all citizens are on the same plan, one with moral, social, and economic value."[158] This crucial idea informed the administration's social policies and programs. Bureaucrats and politicians emphasized the social, cultural, and moral qualities that Pernambucans supposedly held in common while recognizing that rural and urban populations presented different challenges. This corporatist approach to citizenship was implemented in several areas of government activity after Magalhães assumed power in 1937. One area of concern was public education. Shortly after coming to power, Magalhães fired administrators and teachers who had shown support for the ANL and the political opposition as well as those who had supported education reforms implemented during the Coimbra administration in 1928 and the Lima Cavalcanti administration in 1931. According to Magalhães and his political allies, the Department of Education was a hotbed of radicalism and a potential breeding ground for communism. In 1939, the Magalhães administration ordered a change in school curriculum, one that would emphasize the teaching of social and cultural traditions—Christianity and patriotism.[159] This new focus was also mandated by the federal Ministério da Educação e Saúde.[160] Magalhães criticized what he characterized as "liberal" and "communist" approaches to education and instead promoted the supposed "genius" of Italian fascism for its authoritarian, militaristic, and religious approach. Magalhães wrote that "the existence of God—the basis of all ethical norms, the spiritualist meaning of life, the sentiment of obligation, respect for the family, the love of the Fatherland, work, and our Christian and Iberian traditions— ought to shape pedagogy in Brazilian schools."[161] These universal values would be inculcated in optional religion classes in all Pernambucan public schools. In 1940, Magalhães reported that twenty-nine thousand Pernambucan public school students, representing some 90 percent of all enrolled students, had opted to participate in religion classes.[162] The Magalhães administration further encouraged conformity, corporatism, and militarism among students by promoting scouting, which, according to Magalhães, would "cultivate discipline and patriotic passion and in turn create excitement for proper militarism."[163] By 1942, there were sixty troops of some thirty-two hundred scouts in Pernambuco. Thus, although physical education and patriotism were important aspects of public education prior to the Estado Novo, the Magalhães administration emphasized morality and patriotism in public education and attempted to reorganize students according to the precepts of a corporatist society.

Another area of government activity that advanced the Magalhães administration's corporatist notions of identity and citizenship was its campaign against *mocambos*, the self-help housing of Recife's poor and working classes.[164] In 1939, the administration created the Liga Social Contra o Mocambo (Social League against the Mocambo), which was charged with addressing the problem of housing in Recife. A comprehensive survey completed in the same year found that 164,837 individuals lived in *mocambos,* or approximately one-third of the population of greater Recife.[165] The survey was significant not only in that it was the first government report to recognize the full extent of urban poverty but also in the way in which it portrayed *mocambo* dwellers, who were categorized according to occupation, income, age, marital status, and education but not by race.[166] The most significant identifier for the administration was occupation, which reflected Magalhães's view that work rather than social class or race formed the basis of citizenship. Significantly, of the 164,837 *mocambo* dwellers, only 5,544 were categorized as unemployed, an unrealistic figure for that time.[167] To address the housing problem, the Magalhães administration oversaw the construction of ten thousand new homes in suburban workers' villages and demolished nine thousand *mocambos*.[168] Although these numbers were impressive (administrators noted with some dismay that *mocambos* were rebuilt almost as quickly as they were torn down), what was most significant with regard to identity and citizenship was that new housing was rented or sold according to occupation. There were separate workers' villages for laundresses, cooks, seamstresses, unionized workers, sailors, street cleaners, industrial workers, and railway and tramway workers as well as dock and port workers.[169] A 1943 report noted enthusiastically that several factory owners were constructing company housing for their workers.[170] These efforts to address the problem of urban housing and poverty reveal not only how the Magalhães administration conceived of citizenship—Pernambucans were first and foremost workers —but also the ways in which the state was attempting to remake society according to corporatist ideals that emphasized what united citizens rather than what differentiated them.

The Magalhães administration's social policies and programs represented a clear rejection of Gilberto Freyre's views, which celebrated Afro-Brazilians' substantial social, cultural, and economic contributions to the formation of Brazilian society. Magalhães and his interlocutors instead focused on what they believed united all Brazilians: labor, Christianity, Portuguese heritage, and specific social and cultural traditions. In embracing a corporatist understanding of identity and citizenship, Pernambucan political leaders rejected the notion that social, cultural, and racial differences should play a role in the social and political life of the nation. There was simply no place for Afro-Brazilians, religious fanatics, bandits, communists, liberals, Jews, or any other heterodox group in constructions of northeastern regional identity. Discussions of social and economic problems, which prior to the Estado Novo included a discussion of race and class, were reframed in terms of work and housing in order to circumvent discussion and criticism of the established social and political order. During the Estado Novo, Pernambucan government officials succeeded in creating and disseminating a new understanding of northeastern regional identity that emphasized *nordestinos'* nonblack cultural and racial attributes. The *homem do Nordeste* was a strong, capable, educable, and cooperative white, worker and citizen who did not question or challenge the economic and political status quo.

The *homem do Nordeste* provided a convenient exit from the labyrinth of racial theory dictating that *nordestinos* were racially inferior. If *nordestinos* could be depicted as essentially white, then the region's leaders would no longer have to acknowledge the existence of social and racial problems. Northeastern intellectuals and politicians were not only aware of the latest intellectual understandings of race, which they readily adapted to fit their needs, but they also placed the *homem do Nordeste* at the center of academic and political debates about race and national identity in the 1930s and 1940s.[171] These debates reflected an inherent tension between racial homogeneity and heterogeneity in understandings of national identity.[172] While *nordestinos* possessed distinct physiological and psychological characteristics, they were presented as appropriate and useful adaptations to the region's unique geography and climate. The *homem do Nordeste* thus represented the potential of the Northeast within new understandings of Brazilian national identity that demanded contributions from all citizens in realizing the nation's future. In contrast to the supposedly whiter, more progressive and economically productive populations of southern Brazil, the *nordestino* symbolized a backward and racialized "other." In this sense, the *nordestino* symbolically replaced *mulatos* and *negros* in discourses of national social and economic development. Ultimately, the *homem do Nordeste* served both to naturalize regional social and racial differences and to consecrate differences between the Northeast and the South.

ALTHOUGH THIS work has focused on the intellectual and political origins of northeastern regional identity, the Northeast and *nordestinos* have long been understood as natural and self-evident concepts that directly reflect the geographic, climatic, racial, social, and cultural characteristics of the region and its peoples. Intellectual approaches to identity formation have convincingly shown the ways in which racial, regional, and national identities reflect individual and collective social identities, as well as economic and political status.[173] The question is not whether regional and national identities are constructed but how they are constructed and for what purposes.

On one level, northeastern regional identity was consistently predicated on the notion that there were real and significant geographic, climatic, racial, and cultural characteristics that differentiated the Northeast from the rest of the nation. These characteristics, usually understood to be innate and immutable, included a formidable geography and difficult climatic conditions, including the arid, drought-prone *sertão* and the humid, tropical *litoral*, the social and cultural legacies of three and a half centuries of African slavery, especially in the sugar-growing zone, and a society and culture based on Portuguese traditions, including millenarian Catholicism. These characteristics would be used as starting points for those who, over the course of the nineteenth and twentieth centuries, would insist on the region's distinctiveness.

At the same time, northeastern regional identity reflected the interests of northeastern planters, especially sugar producers, who understood *nordestinos* according to their need for labor and their preference for certain physical and psychological characteristics among workers. This idealized *nordestino* was both hard working and accepting of paternalistic labor practices. Because local and state governments represented planters' economic and political interests, northeastern politicians and civil servants also conceived of *nordestinos* as idealized agricultural workers and pursued labor policies and social services that advanced planters' objectives with regard to labor management, including the establishment of labor camps, state-subsidized immigration, vagrancy laws, vocational education, and public health campaigns that were designed to improve workers' productivity.

The *nordestino* provided urban professionals, social reformers, and civil servants with both justification and material for social reform programs. From the late nineteenth century through the Estado Novo, progressive and conservative reformers alike argued that *nordestinos* needed to be improved. In Pernambuco, the social and economic development of the *nordestino* and the region occupied the attention of myriad charitable organizations and government agencies, including the Santa Casa de Misericórdia, sugar planters' associations, drought relief agencies, and federal and state agencies of commerce, labor, and education and health. The *nordestino* and the Northeast came to represent "problems" to be addressed by reformers, technocrats, and politicians who endeavored to construct a modern state with the capacity to identify and solve the most pressing social and political problems of the day. These efforts to improve *nordestinos* reflected new political ideas that reconceptualized the relationship between the individual, civil society, and the state. By the 1930s, *nordestinos,* as citizens of the nation, could expect to benefit from the same social programs that were extended, in theory, to all Brazilians. While reformers and politicians were often frustrated in their efforts to improve social and economic conditions in the region, their efforts nevertheless constituted an example of what Fernando Coronil has termed "subaltern modernity."[174] In this version of modernity, the *nordestino* represented the backward past, the problematic present, and the developed future. Thus, northeastern regional identity was more than a social and cultural idea; the *nordestino* served to further the development of the modern bureaucratic state.

Northeastern regional identity also reflected a century of political conflict. The Pernambucan Revolution (1817) and the Confederation of the Equator (1824), in which Pernambuco and adjacent provinces attempted to establish an independent republic, underscored the political and economic divide between the region and the nation as a whole. While republican and separatist sentiments shaped elite politics throughout the nineteenth century, the northeastern *povo* were generally understood to be apolitical. Revolts and rebellions with popular components did not lead planters and politicians to acknowledge the legitimacy of popular and working-class political and economic protests. Regional elites proved adept at controlling the poor and working classes and channeling popular sentiments to support their own causes. Thus, the idealized *nordestino* was understood not as an active political citizen but a passive client, supportive of paternalistic politics and, most importantly, incapable of challenging the political status quo. Rebels, outlaws, and bandits were common and celebrated regional types, especially in the rural interior, but were excluded from formal definitions of northeastern regional identity.

In the 1920s and 1930s, understandings of citizenship and political identity began to change with the rise of labor unions, political parties, and urban populism. While the Northeast has usually been portrayed as lacking a strong labor movement and significant social and political movements, in reality, continuing labor and political conflicts in the 1920s and 1930s forced Pernambucan ruling elites to address social and economic issues. At the same time, Pernambucan intellectuals and politicians, including Gilberto Freyre, sought to remake northeastern regional identity in order to rehabilitate the Northeast and *nordestinos* in the face of what was perceived as the increasing economic and political dominance of the South. Freyre and his allies advanced new perspectives on race and citizenship that embraced Afro-Brazilian culture and acknowledged new political movements, including the short-lived Frente Negra Brasileira.[175] While Freyre focused on social and cultural traditions in his portrayals of the region, he conceived of *nordestinos* as active political citizens, thus legitimizing *nordestinos'* claims to citizenship within the nation. While Freyre's perspectives were gaining legitimacy nationally, reactionary social and political conservatives in Pernambuco, led by Agamemnon Magalhães, were advancing their own conception of northeastern regional identity, which rejected Freyre's focus on *nordestinos'* African heritage. Adhering to fascist and corporatist ideals, Magalhães argued that Brazilians should be organized in corporate bodies according to occupation. According to Magalhães, race was socially and politically divisive and had no place in a nation that, during the Estado Novo, rejected individualism, liberalism, communism, and any form of social or political dissent. Although Magalhães recognized that there were social and economic problems, he believed that they should be addressed directly by the state rather than through the political process. Thus, during the Estado Novo, *nordestinos* remained inactive political citizens, the subjects of a paternalistic and corporatist state.

Northeastern regional identity also reflected changing conceptions of individual and collective identity. Diverse intellectual and scientific ideas, including positivism, social Darwinism, criminal anthropology, social medicine, psychiatry, eugenics, and biotypology, guided elites' attempts to understand and govern the region and its peoples. Brazilians did not, however, uncritically apply social and scientific ideas originating in Europe and North America but rather reformulated them to fit regional and national contexts.[176] While the creators of northeastern regional identity were influenced by broader trends in racial theory, within the region, race was both imagined and practiced differently than in the rest of the nation. Differing racial demographics between the Northeast and South led northeastern intellectuals and ruling elites to adopt a more pragmatic approach to race than that of their southern counterparts. This is not to say that racial prejudice and racial discrimination did not exist in the Northeast—they most certainly did. Both northeastern and southern planters and politicians touted the supposed advantages of white European laborers over native Brazilians. Northeastern intellectuals likewise utilized hierarchical and prejudicial racial theories in their analyses of the region. However, given that a high percentage of *nordestinos* were of African ancestry, race did not become a marker of social and economic status in the same way as in southern Brazil, especially with regard to the structuring of labor markets.[177] These social and demographic differences became intellectually significant by the end of the nineteenth century. Planters, politicians, and intellectuals tried to reconcile racial science and racialized narratives of social and political progress with social reality, which resulted in the tentative rejection of racial theories predicated on strict notions of racial hierarchy and, in public and government discourse, the almost complete absence of overt references to race. By the same token, social and labor management strategies employed in the region seldom focused on race. If the majority of *nordestinos*, especially the working classes and the poor, were Afro-Brazilian, then there was little to be gained, either economically or politically, in making race an issue.

At the same time, understandings of northeastern regional identity were thoroughly racialized, as has been noted in other regions of Brazil and Latin America.[178] In the 1920s, this racialized understanding of northeastern regional identity became an essential aspect of new conceptions of Brazilian national identity. On one level, northeastern regional identity functioned as an expression of regional distinctiveness. The *nordestino* represented what was to be celebrated in the region's social and cultural traditions as well as the strength and determination of the region's agricultural workers, who, according to nationalist development plans, would continue to cultivate the region's fertile agricultural lands. On another level, the *nordestino*, in conjunction with the *paulista*, personified Brazil's transformation from a traditional rural agricultural society dependent on slave labor to a modern urban industrialized society dependent on white European immigrant labor. The *nordestino* was thus positioned in contrast to the *paulista* within constructions of Brazilian national identity.[179]

The relationship between northeastern regional identity and other regional identities reflected continuing conflict over the content and meaning of Brazilian national identity. During the First Republic, São Paulo embraced a regional identity based on the myth of the heroic *bandeirante*, which Barbara Weinstein argues was "explicitly racist, exclusionary, and heirarchical."[180] *Paulistas* promoted this identity as a model for the nation and used it to justify the 1932 São Paulo "Constitutionalist" separatist movement. After the Constitutionalists' defeat, this identity was subsumed to more inclusive conceptions of Brazilian national identity under Vargas. This new understanding of national identity reflected declining foreign immigration, nationalist labor policies, and Freyre's intellectual reassessment of native-born, mixed-race Brazilians. It was in this context that Freyre promoted the mixed-race *nordestino* as the embodiment of Brazilian national identity. Despite Magalhães's efforts in Pernambuco, Freyre's views on race became the dominant ideal of Brazilian race relations beginning in the 1930s. In studies of Colombia, Peter Wade and Nancy Appelbaum have argued that racial and regional identities reflect a fundamental tension between social and racial homogeneity and heterogeneity.[181] Racialized regional identities serve to mediate between an idealized homogenous national identity and the actual heterogeneity of the nation, while the consolidation of the nation-state reflects the reduction of regional complexities to "a comprehensible and governable order."[182] Likewise, Brazil is simultaneously understood to be both a nation comprising *cariocas, paulistas, gaúchos, mineiros,* and *nordestinos* and a nation of Brazilians. Thus, as Barbara Weinstein argues, regionalism and nationalism are not antithetical concepts.[183] Regional identities reflect multiple social and political constituencies within the nation while national identity reflects common notions of citizenship and identity that apply to the nation as a whole. In Brazil, as in other nations, the relationship between regional and national identities also reflects cycles of state centralization and decentralization. The federalist First Republic produced strong state and regional identities while, under Vargas, state and regional identities were subsumed to an idealized, homogenous national identity that reflected the consolidation and centralization of federal political and economic power.

The question remains, however, whether *nordestinos* were or were not the archetype of Brazilian national identity, and neither Freyre nor his contemporary critics provided a definitive answer. The notion advanced in this study is that in the 1930s the *nordestino* came to constitute a racial category in and of itself. Upon first consideration, this notion seems counterintuitive—the *nordestino* is first and foremost the personification of a regional identity defined primarily in terms of political geography. In this sense, it is a category that, at least on the surface, is largely free of racial connotations, which was largely due to ruling elites' understanding of *nordestinos* as workers rather than as members of racial groups or social and political movements. At the level of national identity, however, *nordestinos* remained essentially different, marked as such by history, race, and culture, which allowed Brazilian politicians, intellectuals, and social reformers to discuss national social and economic development without making explicit reference to race. The *nordestino* replaced the *mulato* and *negro* in discussions of race and national identity while continuing to embody the contradictory racial ideals of *mestiçagem* and *branqueamento*.[184] Historians and sociologists have determined that Brazilian conceptions of race included categories that lay outside the black-white racial continuum.[185] The *nordestino* became, and remains, such a category—a powerful racialized symbol of the region's ambiguous and changing status within the nation. Northeastern regional identity at once served to underscore regional differences and to locate the region within a social, economic, and political hierarchy that was predicated on the dichotomy between white and black, modern and traditional, and developed and underdeveloped, constituting a form of neo-orientalism within the nation.[186] Thus, as scholarship on the modern nation-state in Brazil, Latin America, and elsewhere has confirmed, the formation and articulation of regional identities has been, and will continue to be, an integral aspect of nation building, state building, and the formation of national identities.

The question of whether *nordestinos* are or are not Brazilian continues to be asked. In modern nation-states, regional identities reflect fundamental and persistent social, economic, and political differences that must be recognized as significant. There is, however, a danger in this, which is the erosion of a sense of common national identity and the recognition of that which unites all citizens of a nation.[187]

NOTES

Acronyms

AAPP	*Arquivos da Assistencia a Psicopatas de Pernambuco (Psicologia-psiquiatria-hygiene mental)*
ADOPS	Arquivo de Departamento de Ordem Política e Social
APEP	Arquivo Público Estadual de Pernambuco
BIFOCS	*Boletim da Inspectoria Federal de Obras Contra as Secas*
BMTIC	*Boletim do Ministério do Trabalho, Industria e Commercio*
BPEP	Biblioteca Pública Estadual de Pernambuco
DOPS	Departamento de Ordem Política e Social (Department of Political and Social Order)
GEP	Governo do Estado de Pernambuco
HAHR	*Hispanic American Historical Review*
JLAS	*Journal of Latin American Studies*
JMP	*Jornal de Medicina de Pernambuco*
LARR	*Latin American Research Review*
LBR	*Luso-Brazilian Review*
PPRA	Provincial Presidential Reports (1830–1930), Alagoas
PPRP	Provincial Presidential Reports (1830–1930), Pernambuco
RAFDR	*Revista Academica da Faculdade de Direito do Recife*
RFA	Rockefeller Foundation Archives
RIAHGP	*Revista do Instituto Arqueológico Histórico e Geográfico Pernambucano*
RMP	*Revista Medica de Pernambuco*
SAP	Serviço de Assistencia a Psicopatas (Assistance for Psychopaths Service)

Chapter 1. Introduction

Unless otherwise noted, all translations from Portuguese are my own.

1. Agamemnon Magalhães, *O nordeste brasileiro* (Recife: Governo de Pernambuco, Secretaria de Educação e Cultura, Departamento de Cultura, 1970 [1922]), 77, Biblioteca da Faculdade de Direito do Recife.

2. See *Annaes do 4.o Congresso brazileiro de geographia, reunido na cidade de Recife de 7 a 17 de Setembro de 1915,* 3 vols. (Pernambuco: Imprensa Official, 1916).

3. Magalhães, *O nordeste brasileiro,* 60.

4. Other Brazilian communities, including *paulistas* (natives of São Paulo) as well as Syrian, Lebanese, and Japanese immigrants, have made similar claims. See Barbara Weinstein, "Racializing Regional Difference: São Paulo versus Brazil, 1932," in *Race and Nation in Modern Latin America,* ed. Nancy P. Appelbaum, Anne S. Macpherson, and Karin Alejandra Rosemblatt (Chapel Hill: University of North Carolina Press, 2003), 237–62; and Jeffrey Lesser, *Negotiating National Identity: Immigrants, Minorities, and the Struggle for Ethnicity in Brazil* (Durham: Duke University Press, 1999), 41–44, 158.

5. Gilberto Freyre, "Vida social no Nordeste: aspectos de um seculo de transição," in *Livro do Nordeste: commemorativo do primeiro centenario do Diario de Pernambuco, 1825–1925* (Recife: Officinas do Diario de Pernambuco, 1925), 75–90.

6. Gilberto Freyre, "A cultura da canna no nordeste: aspectos do seu desenvolvimento historico" in *Livro do Nordeste,* 155–59.

7. Freyre, "Vida social no Nordeste," 90.

8. These works by Gilberto Freyre include *Casa-grande & senzala,* 2 vols., 4th ed. (Rio de Janeiro: Livraria José Olympio, 1943); *The Masters and the Slaves (Casa-grande & senzala): A Study in the Development of Brazilian Civilization* (Berkeley: University of California Press, 1986); *Sobrados e mucambos: decadencia do patriarchado rural no Brasil* (São Paulo: Companhia Editora Nacional, 1936); *The Mansions and the Shanties (Sobrados e mucambos): The Making of Modern Brazil* (Berkeley: University of California Press, 1986); and *Nordeste: aspectos da influencia da canna sobre a vida e a paizagem do nordeste do Brasil* (Rio de Janeiro: Livraria José Olympio Editora, 1937).

9. Freyre, *Nordeste,* 188 (first quote), 122 (second quote).

10. Weinstein, "Racializing Regional Difference."

11. Evaldo Cabral de Mello, *O norte agrário e o Império, 1871–1889,* 2nd ed. (Rio de Janeiro: Topbooks, 1999).

12. Weinstein, "Racializing Regional Difference," 237–40.

13. See Sociedade Auxiliadora da Agricultura de Pernambuco, *Trabalhos do Congresso Agricola do Recife, outubro de 1878* (Recife: Typ. Manoel Figueiroa Faria & Filhos, 1879), 31; and Mello, *O norte agrário e o Império.*

14. Lilia Moritz Schwarcz, *O espetáculo das raças: cientistas, instituições e questão racial no Brasil, 1870–1930* (São Paul: Companhia das Letras, 1993), 99–140.

15. Gerald Greenfield, *The Realities of Images: Imperial Brazil and the Great Drought* (Philadelphia: American Philosophical Society, 2001), xii.

16. Durval Muniz de Albuquerque Jr., *A invenção do nordeste e outras artes* (Recife: Fundação Joaquim Nabuco/Editora Massangana, 1999), 68–74; Freyre, *Nordeste,* 20.

17. The *polígono* was revised several times in the 1940s and 1950s. Albert O. Hirschman, *Journeys toward Progress: Studies of Economic Policy-Making in Latin America* (New York: Twentieth Century Fund, 1963), 12.

18. Fábio de Macedo Soares Guimarães, "Divisão regional do Brasil," *Revista Brasileira de Geografia* 3:2 (April–June 1941): 318–73; "Divisão Regional," Instituto Brasileiro de Geografia e Estatística Ministério do Planejamento, Orçamento e Gestão, http://www.ibge.gov.br/home/geociencias/geografia/default_div_int.shtm (accessed October 20, 2008).

19. José de Alencar, *O Guaraní* (São Paulo: Editora Ática S.A., 1992 [1857]); José de Alencar, *Iracema* (São Paulo: Editora Ática, 1992 [1865]); Dorris Sommer, *Foundational Fictions: The National Romances of Latin America* (Berkeley: University of California Press, 1991); and David T. Haberly, *Three Sad Races: Racial Identity and National Consciousness in Brazilian Literature* (Cambridge: Cambridge University Press, 1983).

20. *Sertão* is a general term meaning interior, back country, or wilderness and has been used to describe interior regions in the South as well as the Northeast. In the Northeast, the term specifically refers to the arid interior of the region. On the southern *sertão* and its populations see, for example, Alfredo d'Escragnolle Taunay, *A retirada da Laguna: episodio da Guerra do Paraguay*, 10th ed. (São Paulo: Companhia Melhoramentos de São Paulo, 1935 [1871]); Bernardo Guimarães, *O garimpeiro* (Rio de Janeiro: H. Garnier, 1921 [1872]); and Nísia Trindade Lima, *Um sertão chamado Brasil: intelectuais e representação geográfica da identidade nacional* (Rio de Janeiro: Editora Revan/IUPERJ, 1999). A later fictional depiction of the *paulista sertanejo* was Monteiro Lobato's Jéca Tatú; see José Bento Renato Monteiro Lobato, "Urupês," in *Contos pesados: Urupês, Negrinha e o Macaco que se fez homem* (São Paulo: Companhia Editora Nacional, 1940), 21–35; and Thomas E. Skidmore, *Black into White: Race and Nationality in Brazilian Thought* (Durham: Duke University Press, 1993 [1974]), 179–84.

21. See Albuquerque Jr., *A invenção do nordeste*, 137–41; José Américo de Almeida, *A bagaceira*, 21st ed. (Rio de Janeiro: Livraria José Olympio Editora, 1980 [1928]); and José Américo de Almeida, *Trash* (London: Peter Owen, 1978).

22. See Peter L. Eisenberg, *The Sugar Industry in Pernambuco, 1840–1910: Modernization without Change* (Berkeley: University of California Press, 1974); Mello, *O norte agrário e o Império*; Dain Borges, *The Family in Bahia, Brazil, 1870–1945* (Stanford: Stanford University Press, 1992); Linda Lewin, *Politics and Parentela in Paraíba: A Case Study of Family-Based Oligarchy in Brazil* (Princeton: Princeton University Press, 1987); Robert M. Levine, *Pernambuco in the Brazilian Federation, 1887–1937* (Stanford: Stanford University Press, 1978); Ralph della Cava, *Miracle at Joaseiro* (New York: Columbia University Press, 1970); Robert M. Levine, *Vale of Tears: Revisiting the Canudos Massacre in Northeastern Brazil, 1893–1897* (Berkeley: University of California Press, 1992); and Greenfield, *Realities of Images*.

23. Lima, *Um sertão chamado Brasil*; Albuquerque Jr., *A invenção do nordeste*; and Durval Muniz de Albuquerque Jr., "Weaving Tradition: The Invention of the Brazilian Northeast," *Latin American Perspectives* 31:2 (2004): 42–61.

24. Albuquerque Jr., *A invenção do nordeste*, 35–36.

25. Ibid., 194.

26. Greenfield, *Realities of Images*, 104–10; Hirschman, *Journeys toward Progress*, 13–91.

27. Gilbert M. Joseph and Daniel Nugent, eds., *Everyday Forms of State Formation: Revolution and the Negotiation of Rule in Modern Mexico* (Durham: Duke University Press, 1994).

28. On regionalism in Brazil see Levine, *Pernambuco;* Joseph L. Love, *Rio Grande do Sul and Brazilian Regionalism* (Stanford: Stanford University Press, 1971); Joseph L. Love, *São Paulo in the Brazilian Federation, 1889–1937* (Stanford: Stanford University Press, 1980); John D. Wirth, *Minas Gerais in the Brazilian Federation, 1889–1937* (Stanford: Stanford University Press, 1977); Barbara Weinstein, "Brazilian Regionalism," *LARR* 17:2 (1982): 262–76; and Weinstein, "Racializing Regional Difference."

29. Michael O'Brien, "On Observing the Quicksand," *American Historical Review* 104: 4 (1999): 1202–7.

30. Love, *Rio Grande do Sul;* Wirth, *Minas Gerais;* Levine, *Pernambuco;* and Love, *São Paulo.*

31. Weinstein, "Brazilian Regionalism," 272; Barbara Weinstein, *The Amazon Rubber Boom, 1850–1920* (Stanford: Stanford University Press, 1983), 198–99. Levine defines Pernambuco's "satellite bloc," over which it exercised economic and political influence, as the states of Alagoas, Paraíba, Rio Grande do Norte, and Ceará. Levine, *Pernambuco,* 1. The tax structure of the First Republic (1889–1930), which pitted state against state in the pursuit of revenue, was a crucial factor that inhibited the formation of regional alliances.

32. Love, *Rio Grande do Sul,* 109.

33. Love, *São Paulo,* xvii, 274; Wirth, *Minas Gerais,* 29; Love, *Rio Grande do Sul,* 245.

34. Weinstein, *Amazon Rubber Boom,* 322.

35. James P. Woodard, *A Place in Politics: São Paulo, Brazil, from Seigneurial Republicanism to Regionalist Revolt* (Durham: Duke University Press, 2009); James P. Woodard, "Regionalismo paulista e política partidiária nos anos vinte," *Revista de História* 150:1 (2004): 41–56; Weinstein, "Racializing Regional Difference."

36. Celia Applegate, "A Europe of Regions: Reflections on the Historiography of Sub-National Places in Modern Times," *American Historical Review* 104:4 (1999): 1179.

37. See Skidmore, *Black into White;* and Stuart B. Schwartz, *Slaves, Peasants, and Rebels: Reconsidering Brazilian Slavery* (Urbana: University of Illinois Press, 1996).

38. Thomas E. Skidmore, "Raízes de Gilberto Freyre," in *Gilberto Freyre em quatro tempos,* ed. Ethel Volfzon Kosminsky, Claude Lépine, and Fernanda Arêas Peixoto (Bauru, São Paulo: EDUSC, 2003), 41–64; Levy Cruz, "Democracia racial: uma hipótese," in *Evocações e interpretações de Gilberto Freyre,* ed. Fátima Quintas (Recife: Fundação Joaquim Nabuco/Editora Massangana, 2003), 349–67; and Edward E. Telles, *Race in Another America: The Significance of Skin Color in Brazil* (Princeton: Princeton University Press, 2004), 33–46.

39. Skidmore, *Black into White;* Skidmore, "Raízes de Gilberto Freyre."

40. An exception is Schwarcz, *O espetáculo das raças.*

41. See John D. French, "The Missteps of Anti-Imperialist Reason: Bourdieu, Wacquant and Hanchard's *Orpheus and Power,*" *Theory, Culture & Society* 17:1 (2000): 107–28; John D. French, "Translation, Diasporic Dialogue, and the Errors of Pierre Bourdieu and Loïc Wacquant," *Nepantla: Views from South* 4:2 (2003): 375–89; Michael George Hanchard, *Orpheus and Power: The Movimento Negro of Rio de Janeiro and São Paulo, Brazil, 1945–1988* (Princeton: Princeton University Press, 1994); and Carl N. Degler, *Neither Black nor White: Slavery and Race Relations in Brazil and the United States* (Madison: University of Wisconsin Press, 1971).

42. See Skidmore, *Black into White;* Degler, *Neither Black nor White;* and Haberly, *Three Sad Races.*

43. See Barbara Weinstein, "Slavery, Citizenship, and National Identity in Brazil and the United States South," in *Nationalism in the New World,* ed. Don Doyle and Marco Antonio Pamplona (Athens: University of Georgia Press, 2006), 248–71; Maria Helena Pereira Toledo Machado, "From Slave Rebels to Strikebreakers: The Quilombo of Jabaquara and the Problems of Citizenship in Late-Nineteenth Century Brazil," *HAHR* 86:2 (2006): 247–74; Herbert S. Klein and Francisco Vidal Luna, "Free Colored in a

Slave Society: São Paulo and Minas Gerais in the Early Nineteenth Century," *HAHR* 80:4 (2000): 913–41; Hebe Maria Mattos, *Escravidão e cidadania no Brasil monárquico* (Rio de Janeiro: Jorge Zahar Editor, 2000); and Keila Grinberg, *O fiador dos brasileiros: cidadania, escravidão e direito civil no tempo de Antonio Pereira Rebouças* (Rio de Janeiro: Civilização Brasileira, 2002).

44. On understandings of race that fell outside the black-white racial continuum, see Lesser, *Negotiating National Identity;* Jeffrey Lesser, *Welcoming the Undesirables: Brazil and the Jewish Question* (Berkeley: University of California Press, 1995); and Seth Garfield, *Indigenous Struggle at the Heart of Brazil: State Policy, Frontier Expansion, and the Xavante Indians, 1937–1988* (Durham: Duke University Press, 2001).

45. On the importance of race in constructions of national identity in the national period in Latin America, see Appelbaum, Macpherson, and Rosemblatt, eds., *Race and Nation in Modern Latin America*, 1–31.

46. Michel Foucault, *Discipline and Punish: The Birth of the Prison* (New York: Vintage, 1979); Michel Foucault, *Madness and Civilization: A History of Insanity in the Age of Reason* (New York: Vintage, 1988); Ann Laura Stoler, *Race and the Education of Desire: Foucault's History of Sexuality and the Colonial Order of Things* (Durham: Duke University Press, 1995); Antonio Gramsci, *Selections from the Prison Notebooks* (New York: International Publishers, 2008). Scholars have questioned whether a Foucaultian approach to Latin America is useful, arguing that, while appropriate to the study of prisons, asylums, and hospitals, it does not adequately account for dictatorships, slavery, and other less subtle impositions of elite power common in nineteenth- and twentieth-century Latin America. See Laura Engelstein, "Combined Underdevelopment: Discipline and the Law in Imperial and Soviet Russia," *American Historical Review* 98:2 (1993): 338–53; Rudy Koshar, "Foucault and Social History: Comments on 'Combined Underdevelopment,'" *American Historical Review* 98:2 (1993): 354–63; and Jan Goldstein, "Framing Discipline with Law: Problems and Promises of the Liberal State," *American Historical Review* 98:2 (1993): 364–75.

47. See Joseph and Nugent, eds., *Everyday Forms of State Formation;* Ana del Sarto, Alicio Ríos, and Abril Trigo, *The Latin American Cultural Studies Reader* (Durham: Duke University Press, 2004); Claudio Lomnitz-Adler, *Exits from the Labyrinth: Culture and Ideology in the Mexican National Space* (Berkeley: University of California Press, 1992); Claudio Lomnitz-Adler, *Deep Mexico, Silent Mexico: An Anthropology of Nationalism* (Minneapolis: University of Minnesota Press, 2001); and Néstor García Canclini, *Hybrid Cultures: Strategies for Entering and Leaving Modernity* (Minneapolis: University of Minnesota Press, 1995).

48. See Nancy Leys Stepan, *"The Hour of Eugenics": Race, Gender, and Nation in Latin America* (Ithaca, NY: Cornell University Press, 1991); Marcos Cueto, ed., *Missionaries of Science: The Rockefeller Foundation and Latin America* (Bloomington: Indiana University Press, 1994); Marcos Cueto, ed., *Salud, cultura y sociedad en América Latina* (Lima: IEP/ Organización Panamericana de la Salud, 1996); José Leopoldo Ferreira Antunes, *Medicina, leis e moral: pensamento médico e comportamento no Brasil (1870–1930)* (São Paulo: Editora UNESP, 1998); and Gilberto Hochman, *A era do saneamento: as bases da política de saúde pública no Brasil* (São Paulo: Editora Hucitec/Anpocs, 1998);

49. See, for example, Sander L. Gilman, *Disease and Representation: Images of Illness from Madness to AIDS* (Ithaca, NY: Cornell University Press, 1988); Sander L. Gilman, *Difference and Pathology: Stereotypes of Sexuality, Race, and Madness* (Ithaca, NY: Cornell

University Press, 1985); Katherine Bliss, "The Science of Redemption: Syphilis, Sexual Promiscuity, and Reformism in Revolutionary Mexico City," *HAHR* 79:1 (1999): 1–40; and Alexandra Minna Stern, "Buildings, Boundaries, and Blood: Medicalization and Nation-Building on the U.S.-Mexico Border, 1910–1930," *HAHR* 79:1 (1999): 41–81.

50. See Fredric Jameson, *Postmodernism, or, The Cultural Logic of Late Capitalism* (Durham: Duke University Press, 1991); Canclini, *Hybrid Cultures;* Néstor García Canclini, "Contradictory Modernities and Globalisation in Latin America," in *Through the Kaleidoscope: The Experience of Modernity in Latin America,* ed. Vivian Schelling (London: Verso, 2000), 37–52; James C. Scott, *Seeing Like a State: How Certain Schemes to Improve the Human Condition Have Failed* (New Haven: Yale University Press, 1998); and John Beverley, José Oviedo, and Michael Aronna, eds. *The Postmodernism Debate in Latin America* (Durham: Duke University Press, 1995).

51. Stuart Hall et al., eds. *Modernity: An Introduction to Modern Societies* (Oxford: Blackwell, 1996), 8; Anthony Giddens, *The Consequences of Modernity* (Stanford: Stanford University Press, 1990), 16–17; Canclini, "Contradictory Modernities," 40; Jameson, *Postmodernism,* 310.

52. See Canclini, *Hybrid Cultures,* 41–65; Canclini, "Contradictory Modernities"; Fernando Coronil, *The Magical State: Nature, Money and Modernity in Venezuela* (Chicago: University of Chicago Press, 1997), 7–8; William Rowe and Vivian Schelling, *Memory and Modernity: Popular Culture in Latin America* (London: Verso, 1991); and Roberto Schwarz, *Misplaced Ideas: Essays on Brazilian Culture* (London: Verso, 1992).

53. Micael M. Herschmann and Carlos Alberto Messeder Pereira, "O imaginário moderno no Brasil," in *A invenção do Brasil moderno: medicina, educação e engenharia nos anos 20–30,* ed. Micael M. Herschmann and Carlos Alberto Messeder Pereira (Rio de Janeiro: Rocco, 1994), 11.

54. Levine, *Pernambuco,* 52, 130–31.

55. Ibid., 61; Eul-Soo Pang and Ron L. Seckinger, "The Mandarins of Imperial Brazil," *Comparative Studies in Society and History* 14:2 (1972): 215–44; Howard Craig Hendricks and Robert M. Levine, "Pernambuco's Political Elite and the Recife Law School," *The Americas* 37:3 (1981): 291–313; Howard Craig Hendricks, "Education and Maintenance of the Social Structure: The Faculdade de Direito do Recife and the Brazilian Northeast, 1870–1939" (PhD diss., State University of New York at Stony Brook, 1977).

56. Levine, *Pernambuco,* 20.

57. Weinstein, "Brazilian Regionalism," 272; Weinstein, *Amazon Rubber Boom,* 198–99.

58. Lewin, *Politics and Parentela,* 56–57, 95; Levine, *Pernambuco,* 161.

59. These intellectuals and politicians included Rodolfo Theophilo (1853–1932), Gustavo Barroso (1888–1959), and Rachel de Queiroz (1910–2003) from Ceará; José Américo de Almeida (1887–1980) and José Lins do Rego (1901–1957) from Paraíba; Graciliano Ramos (1892–1953) and Arthur Ramos (1903–1949) from Alagoas; Luís da Câmara Cascudo (1898–1986) from Rio Grande do Norte; and Raymundo Nina Rodrigues (1862–1906), Jorge Amado (1912–2001), and Edison Carneiro (1912–1972) from Bahia.

60. Kim D. Butler, *Freedoms Given, Freedoms Won: Afro-Brazilians in Post-Abolition São Paulo and Salvador* (New Brunswick, NJ: Rutgers University Press, 1998), 204, 207–9; Borges, *Family in Bahia,* 272, 248; Eul-Soo Pang, *Bahia in the First Brazilian Republic: Coronelismo and Oligarchies, 1889–1934* (Gainesville: University Presses of Florida, 1979), 197, 202–6.

Chapter 2. The Nineteenth-Century Origins of the Nordestino, 1850–1870

1. On the congress in Recife, see Gadiel Perruci, "Introdução," in *Trabalhos do Congresso*, i–xlii; and Mello, *O norte agrário e o Império*.

2. See Manuel Correia de Andrade, "Introdução," in *Os quebra-kilos e a crise da lavoura*, by Henrique Augusto Milet, 2nd ed. (São Paulo: Global, 1987 [1876]), 7–25.

3. Milet's speech quoted in Sociedade Auxiliadora da Agricultura de Pernambuco, *Trabalhos do Congresso*, 146. On that organization's responses to the questions presented by the imperial government to the congress held in Rio that year, see *Annexos ao relatorio da presidencia apresentado á assemblea provincial a 19 de dezembro de 1878* (Recife: Tip. de Manoel Figueiroa de Faria & Filhos [1879]), 1–2, Provincial Presidential Reports (1830–1930), Pernambuco, Brazilian Government Document Digitization Project, Center for Research Libraries, Chicago, Illinois, http://ecollections.crl.edu (hereafter, PPRP).

4. Sociedade Auxiliadora da Agricultura de Pernambuco, *Trabalhos do Congresso*, 315.

5. Congresso Agricola do Recife, *Reposta aos quesitos apresentados pelo governo imperial ao congresso do Rio de Janeiro* (Pernambuco: Typ. de Manoel Figueiroa de Faria & Filhos, 1879) in *Annexos ao relatório 19 de dezembro de 1878*, 1.

6. Stanley J. Stein, *Brazilian Cotton Manufacture: Textile Enterprise in an Underdeveloped Area, 1850–1950* (Cambridge, MA: Harvard University Press, 1957), 51.

7. Peter L. Eisenberg, "Abolishing Slavery: The Process on Pernambuco's Sugar Plantations," *HAHR* 52:4 (1972): 593; "Mappa statistico da populaçam da provincia de Pernambuco no anno de 1838," in Pernambuco, *Relatorio que a assemblea legislativa de Pernambuco apresentou na sessão ordinaria de 1839 o exm.o presidente da mesma provincia Francisco do Rego Barras* (Pernambuco: Typographia de Santos & C.a., 1839), PPRP; Pernambuco, *Relatorio do presidente Pedro Vicente de Azevedo ao vis-presidente Ignacio Joaquim de Souza Leão 27 outubro 1887* (Pernambuco: n.p., n.d.), 30, PPRP; Pernambuco, *Relatorio com que o exm. i.o vice-presidente dr. Ignacio Joaquim de Souza Leão passou a administração da provincia em 16 de abril de 1888 ao exm. presidente desembargador Joaquim José de Oliveira Andrade* (Recife: Typ. de Manoel Figueiroa de Faria e Filhos 1888), 19, PPRP.

8. Weinstein, "Slavery, Citizenship, and National Identity." On nineteenth-century Brazilian slavery, see Celia Maria Marinha Azevedo, *Onda negra, medo branco: o negro no imaginário das elites, século XIX* (Rio de Janeiro: Paz e Terra, 1987); Stuart B. Schwartz, *Slaves, Peasants, and Rebels: Reconsidering Brazilian Slavery* (Urbana: University of Illinois Press, 1996); Stuart B. Schwartz, *Sugar Plantations in the Formation of Brazilian Society: Bahia, 1550–1835* (Cambridge: Cambridge University Press, 1985); Rebecca J. Scott et al., *The Abolition of Slavery and the Aftermath of Emancipation in Brazil* (Durham: Duke University Press, 1988); Stanley J. Stein, *Vassouras: A Brazilian Coffee County, 1850–1900; The Roles of Planter and Slave in a Plantation Society* (Princeton: Princeton University Press, 1985); and Sidney Chalhoub, *Visões da liberdade: uma história das últimas décadas da escravidão na Corte* (São Paulo: Companhia das Letras, 1990). On slavery in Pernambuco, see Stein, *Brazilian Cotton Manufacture*, 50–65; Eisenberg, "Abolishing Slavery"; J. H. Galloway, "The Last Years of Slavery on the Sugar Plantations of Northeastern Brazil," *HAHR* 51:4 (1971): 586–605; Eisenberg, *Sugar Industry;* Jaime Reis, "The Abolition of Slavery and Its Aftermath in Pernambuco (1880–1920)" (PhD diss., University of Oxford, 1975); and Martha Knisely Huggins, *From Slavery to Vagrancy in Bra-*

zil: Crime and Social Control in the Third World (New Brunswick, NJ: Rutgers University Press, 1985).

9. Pernambuco, Commissão de Hygiene Publica, *Relatorio do estado sanitario da provincia de Pernambuco durante o anno de 1854 apresentado ao exm. presidente da mesma provincia* (Recife: Typographia de M.F. de Faria, 1855) in Pernambuco, *Relatorio que a assemblea provincia de Pernambuco apresentou no dia da abertura da sessão ordinaria de 1855 o exm. sr. conselheiro Dr. José Bento da Cunha Figueiredo presidente da mesma provincia* (Recife: Typographia de M.F. de Faria 1855), 14, PPRP.

10. Dr. Joaquim d'Aquino Fonseca, Presidente da Commissão de Hygiene Publica, *Relatorio 1856,* in Pernambuco, *Relatorio que a assemblea legislativa provincial de Pernambuco apresentou no dia da abertura da sessão ordinaria de 1856 o exm. sr. conselheiro dr. José Bento da Cunha e Figueiredo presidente da mesma provincia* (Recife: Typographia de M.F. de Faria, 1856), 28–29, PPRP.

11. Planters' and employers' belief that slaves were incapable of working for wages was instrumental in the structuring of free labor markets in the post-emancipation period. See George Reid Andrews, *Blacks and Whites in São Paulo, Brazil, 1888–1988* (Madison: University of Wisconsin Press, 1991).

12. On the importance of the Land Law of 1850 and its effects on the availability of labor, see Emilia Viotti da Costa, *The Brazilian Empire: Myths and Histories* (Chicago: Dorsey Press, 1985), 78–93.

13. Pernambuco, *Relatorio que á assemblea legislativa provincial de Pernambuco apresentou no dia da abertura da sessão ordinaria de 1857 o exm. sr. conselheiro Sergio Teixeira de Macedo presidente da mesma provincia* (Recife: Typographia de M.F. de Faria, 1857), 78–79, PPRP.

14. Pernambuco, *Relatorio apresentado á assembléa legislativa provincial em o 1.o de março de 1866 pelo exm. snr. conselheiro João Lustosa da Cunha Paranaguá presidente de Pernambuco* (Recife: Typographia do Jornal do Recife, 1866), 61, PPRP.

15. Pernambuco, *Falla com que o excellentissimo senhor desembargador Henrique Pereira de Lucena abrio a assembléa legislativa provincial de Pernambuco em o 1.o de março de 1875* (Pernambuco: Typographia de M. Figueiroa de F. & Filhos, 1875), 138, PPRP.

16. João José Reis, *Slave Rebellion in Brazil: The Muslim Uprising of 1835 in Bahia* (Baltimore: Johns Hopkins University Press, 1993); Guillermo de Jesus Palacios y Olivares, "Revoltas camponesas no Brasil escravista: a 'Guerra dos Marimbondos' (Pernambuco, 1851–1852)," *Almanack Braziliense* 3 (May 2006): 9–39; Hebe Maria Mattos, "Identidade camponesa, racialização e cidadania no Brasil monárquico: o caso da 'Guerra dos Marimbondos' em Pernambuco a partir da leitura de Guillermo Palacios," *Almanack Braziliense* 3 (May 2006): 40–46; Mattos, *Escravidão e cidadania;* Grinberg, *O fiador dos brasileiros;* José Murilo de Carvalho, *Cidadania no Brasil: o longo caminho,* 2nd ed. (Rio de Janeiro: Civilização Brasileira, 2002), 17–83; Judy Bieber, "When Liberalism Goes Local: Nativism and Partisan Identity in the Sertão Mineiro, Brazil 1831–1850," *LBR* 37:2 (2000): 75–93.

17. These revolts are examined in Palacios y Olivares, "Revoltas camponesas"; Armando Souto Maior, *Quebra-quilos: lutas sociais no outono do império* (São Paulo: Companhia Editora Nacional, 1978); Roderick J. Barman, "The Brazilian Peasantry Reexamined: The Implications of the Quebra-Quilo Revolt, 1874–1975," *HAHR* 57:3 (1977): 401–24; and Joan E. Meznar, "The Ranks of the Poor: Military Service and Social Differentiation in Northeast Brazil, 1830–1875," *HAHR* 72:3 (1992): 335–51.

18. Palacios y Olivares, "Revoltas camponesas," 12.

19. Ibid.; Mattos, *Escravidão e cidadania,* 23. Capuchin missionaries were called on to allay protestors' fears; see Pernambuco, *Relatorio 1 de março 1852* (Pernambuco: N.p., [1852]), 3–4, PPRP.

20. Palacios y Olivares, "Revoltas camponesas," 13.

21. Ibid., 32–39. On the distinction between military impressment and conscription, see Peter M. Beattie, *The Tribute of Blood: Army, Honor, Race, and Nation in Brazil, 1864–1945* (Durham: Duke University Press, 2001), xx–xxi.

22. Pernambuco, *Relatorio que á assemblea legislativa provincial de Pernambuco, appresentou no dia da abertura da sessão ordinaria de 1854 o exm. sr. conselheiro dr. José Bento da Cunha e Figueiredo presidente da mesma provincia* (Pernambuco: Typographia de M. F. de Faria, 1854), 3–4, PPRP.

23. Ibid., 4–5.

24. Pernambuco, *Relatorio 1854,* 4; Eisenberg, *Sugar Industry,* 166. On the 1835 Nagô slave rebellion, see Reis, *Slave Rebellion.*

25. *Relatorio 1857,* 21–22; Pernambuco, *Relatorio de presidente Joaquim Pires Machado Portella 14 outubro 1857* (Pernambuco: Typ. de M. F. de Faria, 1858), 3, PPRP; Pernambuco, *Relatorio com que o excellentissimo senhor conselheiro José Antonio Saraiva abrio a sessão ordinaria da assemblea legislativa desta provincia no primeiro de março de 1859* (Pernambuco: Typographia de M. F. de Faria, 1859), 14–15, PPRP; Pernambuco, *Relatorio com que o excellentissimo senhor Barão de Camaragibe apresentou ao excellentissimo senhor doutor Luiz Barbalho Muniz Fiuza por occasião de passar-lhe a administração desta provincia* (Pernambuco: Na Typografia de M. F. de Faria, 1860), 4, PPRP.

26. See Robert Conrad, *The Destruction of Brazilian Slavery, 1850–1888* (Berkeley: University of California Press, 1972); Costa, *Brazilian Empire,* 125–71; and Andrews, *Blacks and Whites,* 25–53.

27. There is a considerable literature on the transition from slavery to wage labor in Pernambuco. See Eisenberg, *Sugar Industry,* 180–214; Eisenberg, "Abolishing Slavery," 580–97; Marc J. Hoffnagel, "From Monarchy to Republic in Northeast Brazil: The Case of Pernambuco, 1868–1895" (PhD diss., Indiana University, 1975), 71–127; Galloway, "Last Years of Slavery"; and Leonardo Dantas Silva, ed., *A abolição em Pernambuco* (Recife: Fundação Joaquim Nabuco/Editora Massangana, 1988).

28. Eisenberg, *Sugar Industry,* 180–214.

29. Pernambuco, *Relatorio que á assemblea legislativa provincial de Pernambuco appresentou na abertura da sessão ordinaria em o 1.o de março de 1853 o exm. presidente da mesma provincia Francisco Antonio Ribeiro* (Recife: Na Typographia de M. F. de Faria, 1853), 4, PPRP.

30. Eisenberg, *Sugar Industry,* 166–79.

31. Carefully analyzing census and manumission records, Peter Eisenberg determined that the Pernambucan slave population declined by approximately two thousand per year between 1871 and 1887. Eisenberg, "Abolishing Slavery," 586. On slaves donated or purchased during the Paraguayan War, see Beattie, *Tribute of Blood,* 38–63.

32. Pernambuco, *Falla com que o exm. sr. commendador Henrique Pereira de Lucena abrio a sessão da assembléa legislativa provincial de Pernambuco em 1 de março de 1874* (Pernambuco: Typ de M. Figueiroa de F. & Filhos, 1874), 64, PPRP.

33. *Relatorio 27 outubro 1887,* 30; *Relatorio 16 abril 1888,* 19; and Levine, *Pernambuco,* 19. In 1888, the provincial government registered 36,807 *ingênuos,* of which 8,545 died, re-

sulting in a mortality rate of 23.2 percent for children of slave mothers. *Relatorio 16 abril 1888,* 19.

34. Eisenberg, *Sugar Industry,* 179 (quote); Eisenberg, "Abolishing Slavery," 592.

35. Eisenberg, *Sugar Industry,* 163–66.

36. "Circular 5.a Secção—Palacio da Presidencia de Pernambuco, em 16 de maio de 1888," in Pernambuco, *Falla que á assemblea legislativa provincial de Pernambuco no dia de sua installação a 15 de setembro de 1888 dirigio o exm. sr. presidente da provincia desembargador Joaquim José de Oliveira Andrade* (Recife: Typ. de Manoel Figueiroa de Faria & Filhos, 1888), 3, PPRP (emphasis added).

37. On seignorial ideology, see Reis, *Slave Rebellion;* Azevedo, *Onda negra;* and Huggins, *From Slavery to Vagrancy.*

38. "Circular 5.a Secção," 3 (emphasis added).

39. Pernambuco, *Relatorio que o illustrissimo e excellentissimo senhor dr. Antonio Borges Leal Castello Branco apresentou ao illm. e exm. sr. conselheiro João Lustosa da Cunha Paranaguá tendo entregado a administração da provincia ao illm. e exm. sr. Barão do Rio Formoso* (Recife: Typ. do Jornal do Recife, 1865), 20, PPRP.

40. On charity and mutual aid societies in Brazil, see A. J. R. Russell-Wood, *Fidalgos and Philanthropists: The Santa Casa da Misericórdia of Bahia, 1550–1755* (Berkeley: University of California Press, 1968); and João José Reis, *Death Is a Festival: Funeral Rites and Rebellion in Nineteenth-Century Brazil* (Chapel Hill: University of North Carolina Press, 2003).

41. *Relatorio Castello Branco* (1865), 32.

42. Commissão de Hygiene Publica, *Relatorio do estado sanitario 1854,* 9.

43. In Paraíba, however, it was common practice in the nineteenth century to the use orphans to replace slave labor. See Joan E. Meznar, "Orphans and the Transition from Slave to Free Labor in Northeast Brazil: The Case of Campina Grande, 1850–1888," *Journal of Social History* 27:3 (1994): 499–515.

44. *Relatorio Castello Branco* (1865), 32–33. Provincial officials implemented a complete reform of the *colegios* after the Colegio de Orphãos's director was accused of "deplorable" scandals.

45. *Relatorio 1857,* 50.

46. Presidente da Província, "Regulamento geral para a instrucção publica da provincia," in *Relatorio 1855,* 10.

47. *Relatorio 1857,* 17–18.

48. Ibid., 18.

49. *Falla 1874,* 27.

50. Pernambuco, *Falla com que o exm. sr. dr. Antonio Epaminondas de Barros Correia 1.o vice-presidente da provincia abrio a sessão da assemblea legislativa de Pernambuco em o 1.o de março de 1882 e officio com que a 11 o mesmo doutor entregou a administração da provincia ao exm. sr. conselheiro José Liberato Barroso* (Pernambuco: Typographia de M. Figueiroa de Faria & Filhos, 1882), 16, PPRP.

51. *Relatorio 1.o de março de 1866,* 30 (first quote), 31 (remaining quotes).

52. Pernambuco, *Relatorio com o qual s. exc. o sr. senador Frederico de Almeida e Albuquerque abrio a primeira sessão da assemblea legislativa provincial no 1.o de abril de 1870* (Pernambuco: Tipographia de M. Figuerôa de Faria & Filhos, 1870), 15, PPRP.

53. Pernambuco, *Falla com que o exm. sr. commendador João Pedro Carvalho de Moraes abrio a sessão da assembléa legislativa provincial em o 1.o de março de 1876* (Pernambuco: Typ. de M. Figueiroa de Faria & Filhos, 1876), 46, PPRP.

54. Pernambuco, *Falla com que o exm. sr. conselheiro Francisco Maria Sodré Pereira abrio no 1.o de março de 1883 a assembléa legislativa provincial de Pernambuco* (Pernambuco: Typographia de Manoel Figueiroa de Faria & Filhos, 1883), 33, PPRP.

55. *Índios* comprised less than 1 percent of the total population whether counted as a separate racial or separate social grouping. See "Mappas," in *Relatorio 14 outubro 1857*, n.p.

56. Pernambuco, *Relatorio apresentado a assembléa legislativo provincial de Pernambuco pelo exm. sr. Conde de Baependy presidente da provincia na sessão de insallacão em 10 de abril de 1869* (Pernambuco: Typographia de M. Figueiroa de F. & Filhos, 1869), 36, PPRP; and Schwartz, *Sugar Plantations,* 35–43.

57. Pernambuco, *Relatorio que á assembléa de Pernambuco apresentou na sessão ordinaria de 1844 o excellentissimo Barão da Boa Vista, presidente da mesma provincia* (Recife: Typographia de M. F. de Faria, 1844), 5 (first quote), 6 (second quote), PPRP.

58. Ibid., 5–6.

59. *Relatorio 1 de março de 1852,* 35.

60. *Relatorio 1853,* 11.

61. *Relatorio 1857,* 92.

62. *Relatorio 10 abril 1869,* 36.

63. *Falla 1875,* 146.

64. Pernambuco, *Falla com que o exm. sr. doutor Manoel Clementino Carneiro da Cunha abrio a sessão da assembléa legislativa provincial de Pernambuco em 2 de março de 1877* (Pernambuco: Typ. de Figueirôa de Faria & Filhos, 1877), 79, PPRP; Pernambuco, *Relatorio com que o exm. sr. dr. Adelino Antonio de Luna Freire 1.o vice-presidente passou ao exm. sr. dr. Adolpho de Barros Cavalcante de Lacerda presidente effectivo a administração desta provincia a 20 de maio de 1878* (Pernambuco: Typ. de M. Figueiroa de Faria & Filhos, 1878), 49, PPRP. At the time that the last two *aldeias* were disbanded, there were 329 settlers at Ipanema de Aguas Bellas and 363 at Brejo dos Padres in Tacaratú.

65. On the War of the Cabanos, see Jeffrey C. Mosher, "Challenging Authority: Political Violence and the Regency in Pernambuco, Brazil, 1831–1835," *LBR* 37:2 (2000): 45–47; Levine, *Vale of Tears;* and Manuel Correia de Andrade, *A guerra dos cabanos* (Rio de Janeiro: Conquista, 1965).

66. Pernambuco, *Relatorio que o exm. sr. 1.o vice-presidente dr. Manoel Clementino Carneiro da Cunha apresentou ao excellentissimo senhor conselheiro dr. Francisco de Paula Silveira Lobo, por occasião de entreger-lhe em novembro de 1866, a administração da provincia de Pernambuco* (Pernambuco: Typographia de Manoel de Figueiroa de Faria & Filhos, 1867), 36, PPRP.

67. *Relatorio 1854,* 39; *Relatorio 1857,* 91. In 1860, the Colonia Militar Leopoldina had 1,916 colonists. Alagoas, *Relatorio com que o exm. snr. dr. Manoel Pinto de Souza Dantas, presidente da provincia de Alagoas, entregou a administração da mesma provincia no dia 24 de abril de 1860, ao primeiro vice-presidente dr. Roberto Calheiros de Mello* (Maceió: Typ. Commercial de A. J. da Costa, 1860), 25, Provincial Presidential Reports, Alagoas, Brazilian Government Document Digitization Project, Center for Research Libraries, Chicago, Illinois, http://ecollections.crl.edu (hereafter, PPRA).

68. *Relatorio 1857,* 88–89; *Relatorio novembro 1866,* 47.

69. *Relatorio novembro 1866,* 36; Pernambuco, *Relatorio apresentado á assemblea legislativo provincial em 15 de abril de 1867 pelo exm. sr. conselheiro Francisco de Paula da Silveira Lobo presidente de Pernambuco* (Recife: Typographia do Jornal do Recife, 1867), 45, PPRP.

70. See Alagoas, *Relatorio com que o exm. snr. dr. João Marcellino de Souza Gonzaga entregou no dia 16 de março ao 1.o vice presidente exm. dr. Roberto Calheiros de Mello a presidente desta provincia* (Maceió: Typographia Progressista, 1864), 10, PPRA. The Colonia Militar Leopoldina eventually received status as a *vila* (town); see Alagoas, *Relatorio de José Martins Pereira de Alencastre, 10 julho 1867 annexos a relatorio apresentado à assembléa provincial das Alagoas na 2.a sessão da 17.a legislatura pelo presidente dr. Antonio Moreira de Barros* (Maceió: Typografia do Jornal O Progressista, 1867), 15–16, PPRA. On the emperor's visit to the northern provinces, see Roderick J. Barman, *Citizen Emperor: Pedro II and the Making of Brazil, 1825–91* (Stanford: Stanford University Press, 1999), 188.

71. Eisenberg, *Sugar Industry,* 200; and *Falla 1874,* 63.

72. *Falla 1875,* 116.

73. Fr. Fidelis Maria de Fognano, *Relatorio apresentado a s. exc. o sr. presidente da provincia pelo director de Colonia Isabel* (Pernambuco: Typ. de M. Figueiroa de Faria & Filhos, 1877), 3, in *Falla 2 março 1877.* On Capuchins in northern Brazil, see Barman, "Brazilian Peasantry Reexamined," 407.

74. Fognano, *Relatorio 1877,* 11.

75. The Colonia Isabel was not intended to provide an education or job training for *ingênuos,* the children born to slave mothers who were technically free but required to remain in their master's service until the age of twenty-one. An 1882 report noted that among 132 *colonos* there was only one *ingênuo.* See Fr. Fidelis Maria de Fognano, *Relatorio da Colonia Orphanologica Isabel,* in Antonio Epaminondas de Barros Corrêa, 1.o vice-presidente, *Relatorio 11 de março 1882* (Pernambuco: N.p., n.d.), 7, PPRP; and *Falla 1883,* 41–42. Martha Huggins suggests that Colonia Isabel was created in order to educate *ingênuos;* see Huggins, *From Slavery to Vagrancy,* 62–63. An 1869 provincial law designed to "liberate the greatest number of children of the female sex as possible" (superseded by the 1871 Rio Branco Law) stipulated that "all of the liberated are to remain being raised and maintained in the houses of their own liberators or in the houses of their tutors or a trustworthy person" rather than in the Santa Casa de Misericórdia's *colegio* for orphans; see Pernambuco, *Relatorio com que o excellentissimo senhor dr. M. de. N. Machado Portella passou a administração desta provincia ao excellentissimo senhor senador F. de Almeida e Albuquerque em 5 de novembro de 1869* (Pernambuco: Typographia de M. Figueiroa de F. & Filhos, 1870), 9, PPRP.

76. "Relatório do Barão de Jundia, Antonio Serrulo Pessoa de Lacerda, Claudino Correia de Mello e Gerrano Rodrigues Campelo ao illm. e exm. sr. dr. Franklin Americo de Menezes Doria, presidente da provincia," January 21, 1881, in Pernambuco, *Falla com que o exm. sr. dr. Franklin Americo de Menezes Doria abriu a sessão da assemblea legislativa provincial de Pernambuco em 1 de março de 1881* (Recife: Typ. de Manoel Figueiroa de Faria & Filhos, 1881), 1, PPRP. The new equipment allowed the processing of five thousand kilograms of cane per day. Pernambuco, *Falla que á assemblea legislativa provincial de Pernambuco no dia de sua installação a 2 de março de 1887 dirigio o exm. sr. presidente da provincia dr. Pedro Vicente de Azevedo* (Recife: Typ. de Manoel Figueiroa de Faria & Filhos, 1887), 50, PPRP.

77. Pernambuco, *Mensagem apresentado ao congresso legislativo do estado em 6 de março de 1898 pelo governador dr. Joaquim Corrêa de Araujo* (Pernambuco: Typ. de Manoel Figueirôa de Faria & Filhos, 1898), 33–34, cx. 1, Mensagens, Governo do Estado de Pernambuco (hereafter, GEP), APEP; Pernambuco, *Mensagem apresentada ao congresso legislativo do estado em 6 de março de 1900 pelo exm. sr. desembargador Sigismundo Antonio Gonçalves vice-presidente do senado no exercicio do cargo de governador do estado* (Pernambuco: Typ. de Manoel Figueroa de Faria & Filhos, 1900), 29–30, 43–45, cx. 1, Mensagens, GEP, APEP.

78. Pernambuco, *Relatorio da Colonia Agricola Orphanologica e Industrial Isabel* (Recife: Typ. de M. Figueiroa de F. & Filhos, 1883) in *Falla 1883*, 12–13.

79. Fognano, *Relatorio 1882*, 8.

80. Levine, *Pernambuco*, 19; *Falla 1883*, 43.

81. Pernambuco, *Mensagem apresentada ao congresso legislativo do estado em 6 de março de 1897 pelo governador dr. Joaquim Corrêa de Araujo* (Pernambuco: Typ. de Manoel Figueiroa de Faria & Filhos, 1897), 45, cx. 1, Mensagens, GEP, APEP.

82. Pernambuco, *Mensagem do exm. sr. desembargador Sigismundo Antonio Gonçalves, governador do estado, lida por occasião da insallação da segunda sessão ordinaria da 5.a legislatura do congresso legislativo do estado aos 6 de março de 1905* (Recife: Typ. do Diario de Pernambuco, 1905), 5, cx. 3, Mensagens, GEP, APEP.

83. Pernambuco, *Mensagem apresentada ao congresso legislativo na abertura da 1.a sessão da 13.a legislatura pelo governador do estado dr. Estacio de Albuquerque Coimbra* (Recife: N.p., 1928), 89–90, cx. 8, Mensagens, GEP, APEP.

84. Both penal colonies were still operating in the 1940s and still employing a work regimen that recalled a bygone era of forced labor.

85. *Relatorio 1857*, 84. European immigrants were especially valued in the textile industry. See Stein, *Brazilian Cotton Manufacture*, 50–53.

86. On the land law see Costa, *Brazilian Empire*, 78–93.

87. *Relatorio 1857*, 86.

88. Pernambuco, *Relatorio de Benvenuto Augusto de Magalhães Taques a assemblea legislativa 12 abril 1858* (Pernambuco: Typ. de M. F. de Faria, 1858), 9, PPRP; Eisenberg, *Sugar Industry*, 198–214.

89. *Relatorio 1859*, 14.

90. *Relatorio 1.o março de 1866*, 24, 58–59.

91. *Relatorio 10 abril 1869*, 20.

92. *Relatorio 1.o março de 1866*, 60 (both quotes).

93. Pernambuco, *Relatorio 1867*, 40; Pernambuco, *Relatorio apresentado à assemblea legislativa provincial de Pernambuco pelo exm. sr. Barão de Villa-Bella na sessão do 1.o de março de 1868* (Recife: Typographia do Jornal do Recife, 1868), 33, PPRP.

94. *Relatorio 10 abril 1869*, 20. The provincial government spent nearly 6 *contos* (5 *contos*, 914 *mil-réis*, 220 reis) in 1868 supporting the colonists. Peter Eisenberg indicates that the colonists planted only one crop of cotton. Eisenberg, *Sugar Industry*, 199.

95. Pernambuco, *Falla recitada na abertura da assemblêa legislativa provincial de Pernambuco pelo excellentissimo presidente da provincia conselheiro Diogo Velho Cavalcanti de Albuquerque no dia 1.o de março de 1871* (Recife: Typographia de M. F. de F. & Filhos, 1871), 35–36, PPRP.

96. Ibid., 35.

97. In 1874, 756 immigrants arrived, and of the 272 who left the province, the majority were Portuguese; see *Falla 1874*, 63. On plans to use land at Pimenteiras for immigrants, see Pernambuco, *Falla com que o exm. sr. commendador Henrique Pereira de Lucena abrio a sessão da assemblêa provincial no 10 de março de 1873* (Pernambuco: Typ. de M. Figueiroa de F. & Filhos, 1873), 47, PPRP; and Eisenberg, *Sugar Industry*, 200.

98. *Falla 1876*, 82.

99. *Annexos ao relatorio 1878*, 1; Sociedade Auxiliadora da Agricultura de Pernambuco, *Trabalhos do Congresso*, 413.

100. Sociedade Auxiliadora da Agricultura de Pernambuco, *Trabalhos do Congresso*, 413.

101. Pernambuco, *Relatorio com que o exm. sr. dr. Sancho de Barros Pimentel entregou ao exm. terceiro vice-presidente dr. Augusto de Souza Leão a administração da provincia de Pernambuco no dia 26 de janeiro de 1885* (Recife: Typ. de Manoel Figueiroa de Faria & Filhos, 1885), 38, PPRP.

102. Pernambuco, *Falla 1887*, 55.

103. Ibid., 56; *Falla 15 setembro 1888*, 61.

104. Sociedade Promotora da Immigração e Colonisação de Pernambuco, "Annexo I: Relatorio," in Pernambuco, *Annexos á falla que á assemblea legislativa provincial de Pernambuco no dia de sua installação a 15 de setembro de 1888 dirigio o exm. sr. presidente da provincia desembargador Joaquim José da Oliveira Andrade* (Recife: Typ. de Manoel de Figueiroa Faria & Filhos, 1888), 1 (first quote), 2 (remaining quotes), PPRP.

105. Inspectoria Especial de Terras e Colonisação de Pernambuco, "Annexo J: Relatorio 30 novembro de 1887," in *Annexos á falla 1888*, 1, 4.

106. *Falla 15 setembro 1888*, 61–64.

107. Pernambuco, *Relatorio com que o exm. sr. desembargador Joaquim José de Oliveira Andrade entregou a administração da provincia ao exm. sr. dr. Innocencio Marques de Araujo Góes em 3 de janeiro de 1889* (Recife: Typ. de Manoel Figueiroa de Faria & Filhos, 1889), 42, PPRP.

108. Pernambuco, *Falla que á assemblêa legislativa provincial no dia de sua installação a 1 de março de 1889 dirigio o exm. sr. presidente da provincia dr. Innocencio Marques de Araujo Góes* (Recife: Typ. de Manoel Figueiroa de Faria & Filhos, 1889), 36, PPRP.

109. Eisenberg, *Sugar Industry*, 202–3.

110. Eisenberg, "Abolishing Slavery," 590, 597.

111. Pernambuco, *Mensagem dirigida pelo governador dr. Alexandre José Barbosa Lima ao congresso do estado de Pernambuco em 6 de março de 1893* (Recife: Typ. de Manoel Figueirôa de Faria & Filhos, 1893), 83, est. 4, prat. b, num. 85, Mensagens do Governo de Pernambuco, APEP.

112. Ibid., 58.

113. Ibid., 59.

114. See Barman, "Brazilian Peasantry"; Souto Maior, *Quebra-quilos;* Beattie, *Tribute of Blood*, 88–91; Meznar, "Ranks of the Poor"; Lewin, *Politics and Parentela*, 75.

115. Souto Maior, *Quebra-quilos*, 169.

116. *Falla 1875*, 5. On liberal and conservative politics in Pernambuco during the second half of the nineteenth century, see Hoffnagel, "From Monarchy to Republic."

117. *Falla 1875*, 4.

118. Souto Maior, *Quebra-quilos*, 55–61.

119. Costa, *Brazilian Empire*, 208–12; Souto Maior, *Quebra-quilos*, 97–98; Boris Fausto, *A Concise History of Brazil* (Cambridge: Cambridge University Press, 1999), 135.

120. Souto Maior, *Quebra-quilos*, 91.

121. *Falla 1875*, 5–12.

122. Milet's series of articles for the *Jornal do Recife* were later published as Henrique Augusto Milet, *Os quebra-kilos e a crise da lavoura* (Recife: Typographia do Jornal do Recife, 1876). For his arguments, see Milet, *Os quebra-kilos*, 29–30. On the recruitment law, see Beattie, *Tribute of Blood;* and Meznar, "Ranks of the Poor."

123. *Falla 1875*, 5, 6–7. In the circular Lucena acknowledged the role of popular resistance to the recruitment law in the revolt. Several historians have also emphasized attempts to implement a draft lottery or a system of conscription as a cause of the revolt. See Meznar, "Ranks of the Poor"; and Beattie, *Tribute of Blood,* 84–85, 88–91.

124. *Falla 1875*, 6.

125. *Falla 1881*, 95.

126. On the drought, see Greenfield, *Realities of Images;* Hirschman, *Journeys toward Progress,* 11–91; Manuel Correia de Andrade, *The Land and People of Northeast Brazil* (Albuquerque: University of New Mexico Press, 1980); Gerald Michael Greenfield, "Migrant Behavior and Elite Attitudes: Brazil's Great Drought, 1877–1879," *The Americas* 43:1 (1986): 69–85; Gerald Michael Greenfield, "The Great Drought and Elite Discourse in Imperial Brazil," *HAHR* 72:3 (1992): 375–400; Martha Sofia Santos, "'Sertões Temerosos' (Menacing Backlands): Honor, Gender, and Violence in a Changing World, Ceará, Brazil, 1845–1889" (PhD diss, University of Arizona, 2004); Anthony L. Hall, *Drought and Irrigation in North-East Brazil* (Cambridge: Cambridge University Press, 1978); and Mello, *O norte agrário e o Império.*

127. Pernambuco, *Falla com que o exm. sr. dr. Adolpho de Barros Cavalcante de Lacerda presidente da provincia abrio a sessão da assembléa legislativa em 19 de dezembro de 1878* (Recife: Typ. de Manoel Figueiroa de Faria & Filhos, 1879), 4, PPRP.

128. Greenfield, *Realities of Images,* xxiii, 3–5.

129. Pernambuco, *Relatorio com que o exm. sr. dr. Manoel Clementino Carneiro da Cunha passou a administração desta provincia ao exm. sr. desembargador Francisco de Assis Oliveira Maciel a 15 de novembro de 1877* (Pernambuco: Typ. de Manoel Figueirôa de Faria & Filhos, 1878), 3–4, PPRP.

130. Greenfield, *Realities of Images,* 8–10; *Relatorio 15 novembro 1877,* 4.

131. *Relatorio 15 novembro 1877,* 4.

132. Recife shelters were located at the Arsenal de Marinha, in Coelhos, and in Santo Amaro, and rural shelters were located at Agua Preta, Boa Viagem, Giquiá, Itapissuma, Logoa do Carro, Olinda, Palmares, Páo Secco, Ilha do Pina, Prazeres, Preguiça, Tamarineira, and Victoria. *Falla 19 dezembro 1878,* 52.

133. Colonia Orphanologica Isabel, *Relatorio apresentado ao presidente da provincia pelo director frei Fidelis Maria de Fognano missionario apostolistico capuchinho em 31 de outubro de 1878* (Pernambuco: Typographia de Manoel Figueiroa de Faria & Filhos, 1879) in Pernambuco, *Annexos ao relatorio da presidencia apresentado á assemblea provincial a 10 de dezembro de 1879* (Recife: Tip. de Manoel Figueiroa de Faria & Filhos [1880]), 21, PPRP.

134. Adolpho de Barros Cavalcante de Lacerda to v. exc. illm. e exm. sr. conselheiro João Lins Vieira Consansão de Sinimbú, muito digno presidente do conselho de ministros, in Pernambuco, *Relatorio com que o exm. sr. dr. Adolpho de Barros Cavalcante de Lacerda passou ao exm. sr. dr. Adelino Antonio de Luna Freire primeiro vice-presidente a administração desta provincia em 18 de setembro de 1879* (Recife: Typ. de M. Figueiroa de F. & Filhos, 1879), 9, PPRP.

135. *Relatorio 20 maio 1878*, 7.

136. Adophio de Barros to Affonso Celso de Assis Figueiredo, ministro e secretario de estado dos negocios da fazenda, "N. 64 bis.—Secção 3.a palacio da presidente de Pernambuco, em 21 de junho de 1879. illm. e exm. sr. dando cumprimento ao que v. exc. me ordenou por telegramma de 3 do corrente, . . ." in *Relatorio 18 setembro 1879*, 7.

137. *Relatorio 20 maio 1878*, 7, 12. Relief officials also placed an additional 725 refugees at the nearby Colonia Isabel; see Colonia Orphanologica Isabel, *Relatorio 1878*, 21.

138. *Falla 19 dezembro 1878*, 9; Pernambuco, *Falla com que o exm. sr. dr. Lourenço Cavalcanti de Albuquerque abrio a sessão da assembléa provincial de Pernambuco, no dia 1 de março de 1880* (Pernambuco: Typ. de Manoel Figueiroa de Faria & Filhos, 1880), 35–36, PPRP.

139. *Relatorio 20 maio 1878*, 11.

140. *Falla 19 dezembro 1878*, 52.

141. Pernambuco, *Relatorio da commissão central de soccorros aos indigentes victimas da secca Pernambuco* (Typ. de Manoel Figueiroa de Faria & Filhos, 1878), in *Annexos ao relatório 19 de dezembro de 1878*, 3–4, PPRP.

142. Ibid., 4.

143. Adolpho de Barros Cavalcante de Lacerda to João Lins Vieira Consansão de Sinimbú, presidente do conselho de ministros, in *Relatorio 18 setembro 1879*, 10.

144. Pernambuco, Saúde Pública, *Relatorio que apresentou ao exm. sr. presidente da provincia em 27 de novembro de 1878 o inspector de saude publica dr. Pedro de Attahyde Lobo Moscoso* (Pernambuco: Typographia de Manoel Figueiroa de Faria & Filhos, 1979), in *Annexos ao relatorio 1879*, 10.

145. Ibid., 10–11.

146. Ibid., 11. *Sertanejo* is a racial term used to denote individuals from the arid northeastern *sertão*.

147. Greenfield, *Realities of Images*, 15–18. Peter Beattie argues that military impressment for the Paraguayan War was instrumental in raising national awareness of the Northeast as a distinct geographical space, as many recruits were from northeastern states. Greenfield argues that national political and popular perceptions of the Great Drought were instrumental in this process. See Beattie, *Tribute of Blood*, 132; and Greenfield, *Realities of Images*, 1–21.

148. Lacerda to Sinimbú, in *Relatorio 18 de setembro de 1879*, 10.

149. Pernambuco, *Relatorio com que o exm. sr. dr. Adelino Antonio de Luna Freire 1.o vice-presidente passou a administração ao exm. sr. dr. Franklin Americo de Menezes Doria em 28 de junho de 1880* (Pernambuco: Typ. de M. Figueiroa de Faria & Filhos, 1880), 13, PPRP; *Falla 1 de março de 1881*, 50.

150. On the disjunctive between liberal ideals and Brazilian social and political reality, see Schwarz, *Misplaced Ideas*, 19–32. On nineteenth-century Brazilian liberalism, see José Murilo de Carvalho, *A construção da ordem: a elite política imperial— Teatro de sombras: a política imperial* (Rio de Janeiro: Civilização Brasileira, 2003); José Murilo de Carvalho, *Os bestializados: o Rio de Janeiro e a república que não foi*, 3rd ed. (São Paulo: Companhia das Letras, 1991); Carvalho, *Cidadania no Brasil*, 15–83; and Richard Graham, *Patronage and Politics in Nineteenth-Century Brazil* (Stanford: Stanford University Press, 1990).

Chapter 3. Racial Science in Pernambuco, 1870–1910

1. E. Bradford Burns, *A History of Brazil*, 3rd ed. (New York: Columbia University Press, 1993), 223–24; Azevedo, *Onda negra*.

2. Constituicão da República dos Estados Unidos do Brazil (de 24 de fevereiro de 1891), http://www.presidencia.gov.br (accessed July 6, 2006).

3. See Levine, *Pernambuco*, 73–84; and Hoffnagel, "From Monarchy to Republic," 208–51.

4. Levine, *Pernambuco*; Love, *Rio Grande do Sul*; Wirth, *Minas Gerais*; Love, *São Paulo*; Weinstein, "Brazilian Regionalism"; Pang, *Bahia*; and Lewin, *Politics and Parentela*.

5. On elite concerns about labor after the abolition of slavery, see Andrews, *Blacks and Whites*; and Azevedo, *Onda negra*.

6. Andrews, *Blacks and Whites*, 54–89.

7. On understandings of race during the First Republic, see esp. Andrews, *Blacks and Whites*; Skidmore, *Black into White*; Azevedo, *Onda negra*; Schwarcz, *O espetáculo das raças*; and Lesser, *Welcoming the Undesirables*.

8. On northeastern constructions of race, see esp. Robert M. Levine, "The First Afro-Brazilian Congress: Opportunities for the Study of Race in the Brazilian Northeast," *Race* 15:2 (1973): 185–93; Schwarcz, *O espetáculo das raças*, 141–72; and Huggins, *From Slavery to Vagrancy*.

9. See Clóvis Beviláqua, *Historia da Faculdade de Direito do Recife: 11 de agosto de 1827, 11 de agosto de 1927*, 2 vols. (Rio de Janeiro: Livraria Francisco Alves, 1927).

10. Lilia Moritz Schwarcz, *The Spectacle of the Races: Scientists, Institutions, and the Race Question in Brazil, 1870–1930* (New York: Hill and Wang, 1999), 175–76.

11. See Schwarcz, *O espetáculo das raças*, 143–72; João Cruz Costa, *A History of Ideas in Brazil: The Development of Philosophy in Brazil and the Evolution of National History* (Berkeley: University of California Press), 76–81, 186–87; Skidmore, *Black into White*, 32–37, 55–56; and Marshall C. Eakin, "Race and Identity: Sílvio Romero, Science, and Social Thought in Late 19th Century Brazil," *LBR* 22:2 (1985): 151–74.

12. Eakin, "Race and Identity," 155–56; Skidmore, *Black into White*, 32–37; Hendricks, "Education and Maintenance," 73–88.

13. Sílvio Romero, *Estudos sôbre a poesia popular do Brasil* (Rio de Janeiro, 1888), 10; quoted in Raymundo Nina Rodrigues, *Os africanos no Brasil*, 3rd ed. (São Paulo: Companhia Editora Nacional, 1945), 15.

14. Eakin, "Race and Identity," 169.

15. Schwarcz, *Spectacle of the Races*, 175–86.

16. On Brazilian positivism, see Robert G. Nachman, "Positivism, Modernization and the Middle Class in Brazil," *HAHR* 57:1 (1977): 1–23; and Robert G. Nachman, "Positivism and Revolution in Brazil's First Republic: The 1904 Revolt," *The Americas* 84:1 (1977): 20–39.

17. Charles A. Hale, "Political Ideas and Ideologies in Latin America, 1870–1930," in *Ideas and Ideologies in Twentieth Century Latin America*, ed. Leslie Bethell (Cambridge: Cambridge University Press, 1996), 148.

18. "Palavras iniciaes," *RAFDR* 1:1 (1891): 6.

19. Schwarcz, *O espetáculo das raças*, 30.

20. Schwarcz, *Spectacle of the Races*, 186.

21. "Palavras iniciaes," 5.

22. Clóvis Beviláqua, *Esboços e fragmentos* (Rio de Janeiro: Laemmert e Cia., 1899), 114.

23. "Palavras iniciaes," 6.

24. Laurindo Leão, "Analogias sociaes," *RAFDR* 7 (1897): 105.

25. Clóvis Beviláqua, "Applicações do darwinismo ao direito," *RAFDR* 7 (1897): 120.

26. Ibid., 124.

27. Beviláqua, *Esboços*, 89.

28. Schwarcz, *Spectacle of the Races*, 184–86.

29. Beviláqua, *Esboços*, 89, 121.

30. T. A. Araripe Júnior, "Introducção," in Beviláqua, *Esboços*, li.

31. Beviláqua, *Esboços*, 271.

32. Beviláqua's position was the same as that of Romero and Barreto, which was reiterated in work of Gilberto Freyre and others writing in the 1920s and 1930s.

33. Beviláqua, *Esboços*, 273–74.

34. Ibid., 274, 278.

35. See Skidmore, *Black into White*, 54–56; and Euclydes da Cunha, *Rebellion in the Backlands (Os Sertões)* (Chicago: University of Chicago Press, 1944), 108–9.

36. See Stephen Jay Gould, *The Mismeasure of Man* (New York: Norton, 1996), 152–75; and Stepan, *"Hour of Eugenics,"* 51, 114–15.

37. Clóvis Beviláqua, "Notas sobre a criminalidade no estado do Ceará (ao desembargador Pedro de Queiróz)," *RAFDR* 1:2 (1891): 157 (first quote), 176 (second and third quotes).

38. Laurindo Leão, "A questão do criminoso nato, do seu typo e da sua interpretação," *RAFDR* 21 (1913): 76, 80, 134.

39. Ibid., 134.

40. Augusto Lins e Silva, "Influencia de clima e de molestia no typo anthropologico brasileiro (Excerto da memoria apresentada ao 4.o Congresso Brasileiro de Geographia reunido em Pernambuco, em setembro de 1915)," *RAFDR* 29 (1921): 209–10.

41. Ibid., 209.

42. Carvalho, *A construção da ordem*, 82; Woodard, *Place in Politics*, 130; Pang and Seckinger, "Mandarins of Imperial Brazil," 243–44.

43. Julyan G. Peard, *Race, Place, and Medicine: The Idea of the Tropics in Nineteenth-Century Brazilian Medicine* (Durham: Duke University Press, 1999), 101–6.

44. Ibid., 101.

45. Mariza Corrêa has suggested that Nina Rodrigues's legacy should be interpreted in light of the social and political upheavals of the early republic and that he, like his contemporaries, including Euclydes da Cunha, was concerned most with the question of Brazilian national identity. Mariza Corrêa, "As ilusões da liberdade: a escola Nina Rodrigues e a antropologia no Brasil" (PhD diss., Universidade de São Paulo, 1982), 3. She also suggests that, while he was proclaimed a racist by later scholars, including Gilberto Freyre and Arthur Ramos, he was in fact merely utilizing the racial theory available to him at the time. Ibid., 243. She concludes that Nina Rodrigues's views on race were no more racist or exclusionary than those of anthropologists and social theorists working in the 1930s. Ibid., 249–50. Thomas Skidmore argues that Nina Rodrigues

was "the most prestigious doctrinaire Brazilian racist of his era." Skidmore, *Black into White*, 58.

46. Nina Rodrigues, *Os africanos no Brasil*, 28.

47. Raymundo Nina Rodrigues, "Os mestiços brazileiros," *Gazeta Medica da Bahia* 21:9 (1890): 402, reprinted in *As collectividades anormaes* (Rio de Janeiro: Civilização Brasileira, 1939).

48. Raymundo Nina Rodrigues, "Valor social das raças e povos negros que colonizaram o Brasil, e dos seus descendentes," in *Os africanos no Brasil*, 418.

49. Nina Rodrigues, "Os mestiços brazileiros," 206–10 (quote, 210).

50. Raymundo Nina Rodrigues, *O animismo fetichista dos negros bahianos* (Rio de Janeiro: Civilização Brasileira, 1935), 126–27, 193, originally published in *Revista Brasileira* (1896).

51. Julyan Peard argues that the *tropicalistas* worked to show that race and climate did not adversely affect Brazilians but that they nevertheless remained "largely silent on the racial question." Julyan Peard, "Tropical Disorders and the Forging of a Brazilian Medical Identity, 1860–1890," *HAHR* 77:1 (1997): 36.

52. Corrêa, "As ilusões da liberdade," 107–8.

53. Nina Rodrigues, *O animismo*, 126–27.

54. Ibid., 45.

55. Raymundo Nina Rodrigues, "A abasia choreiforme epidemica no norte do Brasil," in *As collectividades anormaes*, 49, originally published in *Brazil Medico* (1890).

56. Arthur Ramos, *O negro brasileiro: ethnographia religiosa e psychanalyse* (Rio de Janeiro: Civilização Brasileira 1934), 198.

57. On later interpretations of Afro-Brazilian religion see Arthur Ramos, *O folk-lore negro no Brazil: demopsychologia e psychanalyse* (Rio de Janeiro: Civilização Brasileira, 1935); Arthur Ramos, *As culturas negras no novo mundo*, 2nd ed. (São Paulo: Companhia Editora Nacional, 1946); and René Ribeiro, "Messianic Movements in Brazil," *LBR* 29:1 (1992): 71–81.

58. Nina Rodrigues, *Os africanos*, 29–30.

59. Ibid., 29–30n4.

60. Raymundo Nina Rodrigues, "A loucura epidemica de Canudos: Antonio Conselheiro e os Jagunços," in *As collectividades anormaes*, 52, originally published in *Revista Brazileira* (1897).

61. Ibid., 77.

62. Ibid., 64.

63. Ibid., 64–65.

64. Ibid., 65.

65. Ibid., 65–66.

66. Raymundo Nina Rodrigues, "A loucura das multidões: nova contribuição ao estudo das loucuras epidemicas no Brasil," in *As collectividades anormaes*, 86–91. On the influence of Le Bon, Lombroso, and Gumplowicz in interpretations of the Canudos rebellion, see Dain Borges, "'Puffy, Ugly, Slothful, and Inert': Degeneration in Brazilian Social Thought, 1880–1940," *JLAS* 25:2 (1993): 235–56; and Levine, *Vale of Tears*, 1–2. On Nina Rodrigues's shift from physiological to psychological approaches to race, see Corrêa, "As ilusões da liberdade," 108.

67. Nina Rodrigues, "A loucura das multidões," 87, 126, 129.

68. Ibid., 129. Nina Rodrigues uses the word *seita* generally to refer to any religious group.

69. Nina Rodrigues, "A loucura das multidões," 131, 133.

70. It was, of course, impossible to provide a psychiatric evaluation of a decapitated head. Their diagnosis reveals the degree to which nineteenth-century physicians had moved away from racial degeneracy as an explanation of human behavior. See Borges, "'Puffy.'"

71. Nina Rodrigues, "A loucura das multidões," 141. See also Levine, *Vale of Tears*, 218–19.

72. Nina Rodrigues, "A locura das multidões," 151.

73. Peard, "Tropical Disorders," 43.

74. Corrêa, "As ilusões da liberdade," 3.

75. Ibid., 244. Nina Rodrigues questioned jurists' competency to address scientific issues, including the legal definition of mental incapacity. See Raymundo Nina Rodrigues, *O alienado no direito civil Brasileiro*, 3rd ed. (São Paulo, Companhia Editora Nacional, 1939 [1901]), 15–18.

76. Carvalho, *Os bestializados*, 66–139.

77. Da Cunha used the racial term *sertanejo* generally for inhabitants of the northeastern *sertão* and *jagunço* for *sertanejos* who participated in the rebellion. Samuel Putnam, in his translation of *Os sertões*, renders *sertão* with the more general English term "backlands." Here I use the Portuguese term.

78. Levine, *Vale of Tears*, 16; Robert M. Levine, "'Mud-Hut Jerusalem': Canudos Revisited," in *The Abolition of Slavery and the Aftermath of Emancipation in Brazil*, ed. Rebecca J. Scott et al. (Durham: Duke University Press, 1988), 119–66.

79. See Euclydes da Cunha, *Os sertões*, 38th ed. (Rio de Janeiro: Francisco Alves, 1997); and Cunha, *Rebellion*. I quote Putnam's translation of *Os sertões* unless otherwise noted; however, I use the original Portuguese racial terms.

80. Skidmore, *Black into White*, 105–6; Levine, *Vale of Tears*, 20.

81. Euclydes da Cunha, *Canudos: diario de uma expedicão* (Rio de Janeiro: Livraria José Olympio Editora, 1939); the original articles were republished in 2002 by *Estado de São Paulo* at http://www.estadão.com.br/sertões.

82. Throughout *Os sertões* da Cunha used the term "*Norte*" (North) rather than "*Nordeste*" (Northeast) to refer to the region as a whole, and I retain this distinction.

83. Sommer, *Foundational Fictions*.

84. See Eric Hobsbawm, *Bandits*, rev. ed. (New York: Pantheon Books, 1969); Eric Hobsbawm, *Primitive Rebels: Studies in Archaic Forms of Social Movement in the 19th and 20th Centuries* (New York: Norton, 1965); and Rui Facó, *Cangaceiros e fanáticos: gênese e lutas* (Rio de Janeiro: Editôra Civilização Brasileira, 1963), 6. See also Levine, *Vale of Tears*, 217–45.

85. See della Cava, *Miracle at Joaseiro;* and Todd Diacon, *Millenarian Vision, Capitalist Reality: Brazil's Contestado Rebellion, 1912–1916* (Durham: Duke University Press, 1991).

86. Translator Samuel Putnam renders da Cunha's original "*sertanejan* sub-races" as "subraces." See da Cunha, *Rebellion*, xxix; and da Cunha, *Os sertões*, 7.

87. Da Cunha, *Rebellion*, xxix.

88. Ibid., xxix, 51.

89. Ibid., 67.
90. Da Cunha, *Rebellion*, 84–89; da Cunha, *Os sertões*, 122–27.
91. Da Cunha, *Rebellion*, 85.
92. Ibid., 86, 89.
93. Ibid., 88.
94. Ibid., 87.
95. Ibid., 134, 444.
96. This belief in environmental determinism was typical of nineteenth-century scientific and medical approaches to race. Nicolau Sevcenko, *Literatura como missão: tensões sociais e criação cultural na primeira república* (São Paulo: Brasiliense, 1983), 136–40.
97. Da Cunha, *Rebellion*, 61.
98. Ibid., 88, 195.
99. Ibid., 89, 90, 378.
100. Ibid., 93.
101. Ibid., 386.
102. Ibid., 471.
103. Ibid., 441.
104. Ibid.
105. Ibid., 470.
106. Ibid., 438.
107. Da Cunha, *Os sertões*, 597. Samuel Putnam translates the phrase as "originally white." Da Cunha, *Rebellion*, 438.
108. Da Cunha, *Rebellion*, 407. The Dutch, unlike the Portuguese, allowed the practice of Judaism during their occupation of Pernambuco. See José Antônio Gonsalves de Mello, *Gente da nação: cristãos-novos e judeus em Pernambuco, 1542–1654* (Recife: Fundação Joaquim Nabuco, Editora Massangana, 1989); and José Antônio Gonsalves de Mello, *Tempo dos flamengos: influência da ocupação holandesa na vida e na cultura do Norte do Brasil* (Rio de Janeiro: José Olympio, 1947).
109. Da Cunha, *Rebellion*, 407.
110. Ibid., 84.
111. Da Cunha, *Rebellion*, 112.
112. Borges, "'Puffy,'" 247–48.
113. Da Cunha, *Rebellion*, 120–21.
114. Ibid., 155, 476.
115. Ibid., 476. Da Cunha did not acknowledge that Nina Rodrigues found nothing physically or medically wrong with Conselheiro's head, despite the fact that Nina Rodrigues published his conclusions in 1898, four years before *Os sertões* appeared.
116. Da Cunha, *Rebellion*, 197 (first quote), 408 (remaining quotes).
117. Pernambuco, *Relatorio apresentado ao sr. dr. governador do estado de Pernambuco pelo questor dr. Antonio Pedro da Silva Marques em 31 de janeiro de 1898*, in *Mensagem apresentada ao congresso legislativo do estado em 6 de março 1898 pelo governador dr. Joaquim Corrêa de Araujo* (Pernambuco: Typographia de Manoel Figueiroa de Faria e Filhos, 1898), 2, cx. 1, Mensagens, GEP, APEP.
118. Antonio Pedro da Silva Marques, *Relatorio sobre a administração do serviço policial do estado no decurso do anno de 1898*, in Pernambuco, *Mensagem apresentada ao congresso*

legislativo do estado em 6 de março de 1899 pelo governador dr. Joaquim Corrêa de Araujo (Pernambuco: Typ. de Manoel Figueirôa de Faria & Filhos, 1899), 2, cx. 1, Mensagens, GEP, APEP.

119. *Relatorio apresentado ao governador pelo questor 1898*, 2.

120. Ibid., 5.

121. Ibid., 6.

122. Marques, *Relatorio sobre a administração do serviço policial 1898*, 24.

123. Ibid., 4.

124. Senado do Estado de Pernambuco, "Sessão ordinaria em 1 de junho de 1898," *Annaes do senado do estado de Pernambuco, sessão ordinaria de 1898 (1.a da 3.a legislatura)* (Recife: Typ. de Manoel Figueiroa de Faria & Filhos, 1898), 137, est. 27, p. 2, cx. 2, Senado do Estado de Pernambuco, APEP.

125. Marques, *Relatorio sobre a administração do serviço policial 1898*, 60–62.

126. Ibid., 60–61.

127. *Mensagem 6 março 1898*, 11.

128. *Mensagem 1900*, 16.

129. Huggins, *From Slavery to Vagrancy*, 73. See also Pernambuco, *Relatorio com que o exm. sr. conselheiro Manoel Alves de Araujo entregou a administração da província ao exm. sr. dr. Sigismundo Antonio Gonçalves em 14 de novembro de 1889* (Recife: Typ. de Manoel Figueiroa de Faria & Filhos, 1890), 35.

130. Pernambuco, *Relatorio apresentado ao dr. governador do estado, em 19 de fevereiro de 1900 pelo dr. Leopoldo Marinho de Paula Lins, chefe de policia*, in *Mensagem 1900*, 4.

131. Pernambuco, *Mensagem apresentada ao congresso legislativo do estado em 6 de março de 1901 pelo ex.ma. sr. dr. Antonio Gonçalves Ferreira governador do estado* (Pernambuco: Typ. de Manoel Figueiroa de Faria & Filhos, 1901), 9, cx. 1, Mensagens, GEP, APEP; Pernambuco, *Mensagem apresentada ao congresso estadual na abertura da segunda sessão da quarta legislatura pelo governador do estado Antonio Gonçalves Ferreira* (Pernambuco: Typ. do Diario de Pernambuco, 1902), 16, cx. 1, Mensagens, GEP, APEP.

132. *Relatorio apresentado ao governador pelo questor 1898*, 2. Anthropometry, or *bertillonage*, was based on the use of eleven physical measurements of the human body as a means of identifying criminals. The use of anthropometry in police work was augmented and later superseded by fingerprinting.

133. *Mensagem 6 março 1897*, 10.

134. *Relatorio apresentado ao governador pelo chefe de policia 1900*, 5.

135. Corrheiro da Cunha, "Hygiene: o ensino da hygiene na Europa," *RAFDR* 3 (1893): 122.

136. See, e.g., *Mensagem 1898*; *Mensagem 1899*; and *Mensagem 1900*.

137. *Relatorio apresentado ao governador pelo questor 1898*, 9.

138. See especially Huggins, *From Slavery to Vagrancy*; J. H. Galloway, "The Sugar Industry of Pernambuco during the Nineteenth Century," *Annals of the Association of American Geographers* 58:2 (1968): 285–303; and Galloway, "Last Years of Slavery."

139. On this transition, see Galloway, "Last Years of Slavery"; and Eisenberg, "Abolishing Slavery."

140. Levine, *Pernambuco*, 23–24.

141. See Huggins, *From Slavery to Vagrancy*, chaps. 3 and 4.

Chapter 4. The Medicalization of Nordestinos, *1910–1925*

1. Pernambuco, *Mensagem apresentada ao congresso legislativo na abertura da 4.a sessão da 12.a legislatura pelo governador do estado dr. Estacio de Albuquerque Coimbra* (Recife: [n.p.], 1927), 23–24, cx. 8, Mensagens, GEP, APEP.

2. Hochman, *A era do saneamento;* Emerson Elias Merhy, *A saúde pública como política: um estudo de formuladores de políticas* (São Paulo: Editora Hucitec, 1992); and Luiz Antonio de Castro Santos and Lina Rodrigues de Faria, *A reforma sanitária no Brasil: ecos da primeira república* (Bragança Paulista: EDUSF, 2003).

3. See Skidmore, *Black into White,* 174–75; and Luiz A. de Castro Santos, "Power, Ideology, and Public Health in Brazil, 1889–1930" (PhD diss., Harvard University, 1986), 121–31.

4. See Steven C. Williams, "Nationalism and Public Health: The Convergence of Rockefeller Foundation Technique and Brazilian Federal Authority during the Time of Yellow Fever, 1925–1930," in *Missionaries of Science: The Rockefeller Foundation and Latin America,* ed. Marcos Cueto (Bloomington: Indiana University Press, 1994), 23–51.

5. In the 1910s and 1920s, assessments of *nordestinos'* moral and racial qualities derived largely from Euclydes da Cunha and the Recife law school faculty; see Schwarcz, *O espetáculo das raças,* 143–72.

6. General histories of Brazilian public health in the late nineteenth and early twentieth centuries include Sidney Chalhoub, *Cidade febril: cortiços e epidemias na Corte imperial* (São Paulo: Companhia das Letras, 1996); Hochman, *A era do saneamento;* Madel T. Luz, *Medicina e ordem política brasileira: políticas e instituições de saúde (1850–1930)* (Rio de Janeiro: Edições Graal, 1982); Merhy, *A saúde pública como política;* Gilberto Hochman and Diego Armus, eds. *Cuidar, controlar, curar: ensaios históricos sobre saúde e doença na América Latina e Caribe* (Rio de Janeiro: Editora Fiocruz, 2004); de Castro Santos and Faria, *A reforma sanitária no Brasil.*

7. Comparisons of public health in São Paulo and the Northeast include de Castro Santos and Faria, *A reforma sanitária no Brasil;* Luiz Antonio de Castro Santos, "Poder, ideologias e saúde no Brasil da primeira república: ensaio de sociologia história" in Hochman and Armus, eds., *Cuidar, controlar, curar,* 249–93; Hochman, *A era do saneamento;* and José Policarpo de Araújo Barbosa, *História da saúde pública do Ceará: da colônia a Vargas* (Fortaleza: Edições UFC, 1994).

8. De Castro Santos, "Poder, ideologias e saúde," 283.

9. Hochman, *A era do saneamento,* 168–69.

10. On public health in northeastern Brazil, see de Castro Santos, "Power, Ideology, and Public Health"; Peard, *Race, Place, and Medicine;* Peard, "Tropical Disorders"; and Veloso Costa, *Medicina, Pernambuco e tempo* (Recife: Universidade Federal de Pernambuco, 1978).

11. Public health officials were aware that outbreaks of yellow fever were less common in years of below-average rainfall; identification of mosquitoes as the carriers of the disease would come later.

12. *Mensagem 6 março 1897,* 44.

13. Emilio Béringer, *Estudos sobre o clima e a mortalidade da capital de Pernambuco (Brazil)* (Pernambuco: Typographia Commercial, 1891), 69.

14. Ibid., *77, 78.*

15. José Octávio de Freitas, *O clima e a mortalidade da cidade do Recife* (Recife: Imprensa Industrial, 1905), 3.

16. On concerns about the redundancy of federal, state, and municipal public health services, see Pernambuco, *Relatorio apresentado á s. exc. o sr. governador do estado conselheiro Joaquim Correia de Araujo pelo dr. Rodolpho Galvão inspector geral de hygiene de Pernambuco* (Recife: Typographia de Manoel Figueiroa de Faria e Filhos, 1898), 4, Relatórios Diversos, 1856–1910, APEP.

17. Freitas, *O clima;* Béringer, *Estudos sobre o clima e a mortalidade.*

18. *Relatorio pelo inspector geral de hygiene 1898,* 37.

19. Ibid., 3.

20. In ibid., 72.

21. Pernambuco, *Mensagem do exm. sr. dr. Manoel Antonio Pereira Borba governador do estado, lida por occasião da installação da 1.a sessão da 9. legislatura do congresso legislativo do estado aos 6 de março de 1916* (Recife: Imprensa Official Recife, 1916), 5–6, cx. 2, Mensagens, GEP, APEP.

22. Pernambuco, *Mensagem do exm. sr. dr. Manoel Antonio Pereira Borba governador do estado, lida por occasião da installação da 2.a sessão da 9.a legislatura do congresso legislativo do estado aos 6 de março de 1917* (Pernambuco: Typ. da "Imprensa Official" 1917), 21, cx. 2, Mensagens, GEP, APEP.

23. On understandings of the relationship between climate and disease, see Peard, *Race, Place, and Medicine,* 81–108.

24. Pernambuco, *Mensagem do exm. sr. desembargador Sigismundo Antonio Gonçalves governador do estado lida por occasião da installação da terceira sessão ordinaria da 5.a legislatura do congresso legislativo do estado aos 6 de março de 1906* (Recife: Typographia do Diario de Pernambuco, 1906), 5, cx. 2, Mensagens, GEP, APEP.

25. Pernambuco, *Mensagem do exm. sr. dr. Herculano Bandeira de Mello governador do estado lida por occasião da installação da sessão ordinaria da 6.a legislatura do congresso legislativo do estado aos 6 de março de 1909* (Recife: Typographia do Diario de Pernambuco, 1909), 5, cx. 2, Mensagens, GEP, APEP.

26. Pernambuco, *Relatorio apresentado ao exm. sr. dr. Herculano Bandeira de Mello governador do estado pelo secretario geral do estado bacharel José Osorio de Cerqueira em 31 de janeiro de 1910* (Recife: Typographia do Diario de Pernambuco, 1910), 90, cx. 2, Mensagens, GEP, APEP.

27. *Mensagem 1916,* 5.

28. Pernambuco, *Mensagem do exm. sr. general Emygdio Dantas Barreto governador do estado lida por occasião da installação de 3.a sessão ordinaria da 7.a legislatura do congresso legislativo do estado aos 6 de março de 1912* (Recife: Typographia do Jornal do Recife, 1912), 7, cx. 2, Mensagens, GEP, APEP.

29. Pernambuco, *Regulamento para o serviço de hygiene publica do estado de Pernambuco* (Recife: Imprensa Industrial, 1905), Exposição, GEP, APEP; Pernambuco, *Regulamento do serviço sanitario do estado de Pernambuco a que se refere o decreto legislativo n. 1201 de 12 de junho de 1913* (Recife: Emp. d'O Tempo, 1913), Exposição, GEP, APEP.

30. De Castro Santos and Faria argue that "economic, cultural and above all political-ideological" factors shaped public health reforms. De Castro Santos and Faria, *A reforma sanitária no Brasil,* 42.

31. *Mensagem 1917*, 24. One *conto* was worth approximately US$331 in 1912 and US$225 in 1920. On exchange rates, see Love, *São Paulo*, 302–3; and Borges, *Family in Bahia*, ix.

32. Freitas, *O clima*, 56.

33. Ibid., 86–87; *Mensagem 1897*, 42.

34. On the *revolta da vacina*, see Teresa Meade, "'Civilizing Rio de Janeiro': The Public Health Campaign and the Riot of 1904," *Journal of Social History* 20:2 (1986): 301–22; Carvalho, *Os bestializados*, 91–139; and Nicolau Sevcenko, *A revolta da vacina: mentes insanas em corpos rebeldes* (São Paulo: Editora Scipione, 1993). On a planned mandatory smallpox vaccination campaign, see Pernambuco, *Mensagem apresentada ao congresso estadual na abertura da primeira sessão da quinta legislatura pelo governador do estado Antonio Gonçalves Ferreira* (Recife: Typ. do Diario de Pernambuco, 1904), 13, cx. 1, Mensagens, GEP, APEP.

35. José Octávio de Freitas, *Os trabalhos de hygiene em Pernambuco: relatório apresentado ao secretario geral do estado* (Recife: Officinas Graphicas da Imprensa Official, 1919), 83.

36. On the history of inoculation and vaccination in Brazil, see Chalhoub, *Cidade febril*, 97–185.

37. On disinfection in the United States, see Nancy Tomes, *The Gospel of Germs: Men, Women, and the Microbe in American Life* (Cambridge, MA: Harvard University Press, 1998); and Alan M. Kraut, *Silent Travelers: Germs, Genes, and the "Immigrant Menace"* (New York: Basic Books, 1994).

38. *Relatorio pelo inspector geral de hygiene 1898*, 22.

39. *Relatorio 1910*, 89.

40. In 1917, the Disinfection Service incinerated ninety-nine houses in six rural *municípios*. Freitas, *Os trabalhos*, 29–35.

41. Freitas, *Os trabalhos*, 22.

42. Williams, "Nationalism," 25.

43. *Regulamento para o serviço de hygiene publica*, 13.

44. Freitas, *Os trabalhos*, 23.

45. Ibid., 26–29.

46. Pernambuco, *Mensagem do exm. sr. general Emygdio Dantas Barreto governador do estado lida por occasião da installação da 2.a sessão da 8.a legislatura do congresso legislativo do estado aos 6 de março de 1914* (Recife: Typographia d'O Tempo, 1914), 12, cx. 4, Mensagens, GEP, APEP; Pernambuco, *Mensagem do exm. sr. general Emygdio Dantas Barreto, governador do estado, lida por occasião da installação da 3.a sessão da 8.a legislatura do congresso legislativo do estado aos 6 de março de 1915* (Recife: Typographia do "Jornal do Recife," 1915), 13–14, cx. 2, Mensagens, GEP, APEP.

47. *Mensagem 1916*, 29; Pernambuco, *Mensagem do exm. sr. dr. Manoel Antonio Pereira Borba governador do estado lida por occasião da installação da 1.a sessão da 10.a legislatura do congresso legislativo do estado aos 6 de março de 1919* (Pernambuco: Officinas Graphicas da "Imprensa Official," 1919), 45, cx. 5, Mensagens, GEP, APEP.

48. See Salomão Kelner et al., *História da Faculdade de Medicina do Recife 1915–1985* (Recife: Universidade Federal de Pernambuco, Centro de Ciências da Saúde, 1985); José Otávio de Freitas, *História da Faculdade de Medicina do Recife, 1895 a 1943* (Recife: Imprensa Oficial, 1944); and Costa, *Medicina, Pernambuco e tempo*.

49. Kelner et al., *História*, 28.

50. Edgar Altino, "Lição de abertura do curso de medicina publica pelo professor dr. Edgar Altino," *RAFDR* 26 (1918): 80.

51. "Faculdade de Medicina do Recife," Dicionário histórico-biográfico da ciências da saúde no Brazil (1832–1930), Casa de Oswaldo Cruz/Fiocruz, http://www.dichioriasaude.coc.fiocruz.br (accessed October 4, 2006).

52. Directoria de Hygiene de Pernambuco, "Editorial," *Archivos de Hygiene Publica e Medicina Tropical* 1:1 (June 1915): 2.

53. *Mensagem 1909*, 5.

54. Freitas, *O clima*, 52 (original emphasis); *Mensagem 1912*, 7.

55. *Mensagem 1914*, 3.

56. Only two of the expeditions' reports were published: Arthur Neiva and Belisário Penna, "Viagem cientifica pelo norte da Bahia, sudoeste de Pernambuco, sul do Piauhí e de norte a sul de Goiaz," *Memorias do Instituto Oswaldo Cruz* 8:3 (1916): 74–224; and Adolpho Lutz and Astrogildo Machado, "Viagem pelo rio S. Francisco e por alguns dos seus afluentes entre Pirapora e Joazeiro," *Memorias do Instituto Oswaldo Cruz* 7:1–2 (1915): 5–50.

57. See Nísia Trindade Lima and Gilberto Hochman, "'Pouca saúde e muita saúva': sanitarismo, interpretações do país e ciências socias," in Hochman and Armus, eds., *Cuidar, controlar, curar*, 500–501; Hochman, *A era do saneamento*, 62–79; Lima, *Um sertão chamado Brasil*, 84–89; de Castro Santos, "Power, Ideology, and Public Health," 125–29; and Skidmore, *Black into White*, 179–84.

58. These diseases included one known as *entalação* (literally, to be put in a difficult situation) and another as *vexame do coração* (vexation of the heart). Physicians theorized these were psychiatric disorders arising from drought-related stress. See Neiva and Penna, "Viagem cientifica," 132–42.

59. Neiva and Penna, "Viagem cientifica," 221–22.

60. Ibid., 180–81.

61. Ibid., 191 (original emphasis).

62. Lima and Hochman, "'Pouca saúde e muita saúva,'" 500–507; Lima, *Um sertão chamado Brasil*, 84, 116.

63. Neiva and Penna, "Viagem cientifica," 167.

64. Lutz and Machado, "Viagem pelo rio S. Francisco," 8–9.

65. Ibid., 172–73.

66. The Oswaldo Cruz Institute physicians argued that *sertanejos* descended from African slaves while most northeastern politicians and intellectuals argued that they descended from Indians and Portuguese settlers.

67. Neiva and Penna, "Viagem cientifica," 175, 181.

68. Skidmore, *Black into White*, 64–69.

69. Neiva and Penna, "Viagem cientifica," 221.

70. On Penna's later rejection of racial determinism, see Belisário Penna, *Saneamento do Brasil: sanear o Brasil é povoal-o; é enriquecel-o; é moralisal-o* (Rio de Janeiro: Typographia Revista dos Tribunaes, 1918), 14.

71. Penna, *Saneamento*, 159.

72. Lima and Hochman, "'Pouca saúde e muita saúva,'" 500.

73. Skidmore, *Black into White*, 183; de Castro Santos, "Power, Ideology, and Public Health," 126–49; Nísia Trindade Lima and Nara Britto, "Salud y nacíon: propusta para el saneamiento rural: un estudio de la revista Saúde (1918–1919)," in *Salud, cultura y socie-*

dad en América Latina, ed. Marcos Cueto (Lima: IEP/Organización Panamericana de la Salud, 1996), 147–56.

74. Freitas, *Os trabalhos*, 54.

75. Penna, *Saneamento*, 150, 152.

76. Lima and Hochman, "'Pouca saúde e muita saúva,'" 505–7; Lima, *Um sertão chamado Brasil*, 113–16; Hochman, *A era do saneamento*, 60–61.

77. De Castro Santos, "Power, Ideology, and Public Health," 58, 61–66; de Castro Santos and Faria, *A reforma sanitária no Brasil*, 141–42; Hochman, *A era do saneamento*, 183, 197; de Castro Santos, "Poder, ideologias e saúde no Brasil," 284.

78. Historians disagree about the Rockefeller Foundation's impact in northeastern Brazil. Luiz Antonio de Castro Santos argues that the foundation played an important role in "promoting rural sanitation programs in Brazil" but concludes that "the contribution of the Rockefeller Foundation—though having an early and direct impact on public health—should not be overestimated." De Castro Santos, "Power, Ideology, and Public Health," 135–36. See also Cueto, *Missionaries of Science*.

79. The foundation's campaign against malaria did not begin until the 1940s, however.

80. On nineteenth-century understandings and treatments of ancylostomiasis, see Peard, *Race, Place, and Medicine*, 64–78.

81. L. W. Hackett, "Report on Hookworm Infection Survey of the State of Rio de Janeiro, Brazil from November 22, 1916, to March 31, 1917," 31, f. 135, bx. 23, s. 2, r.g. 5, Rockefeller Foundation Archives (hereafter RFA), Rockefeller Archive Center, Tarrytown, NY.

82. See John Ettling, *The Germ of Laziness: Rockefeller Philanthropy and Public Health in the New South* (Cambridge, MA: Harvard University Press, 1981).

83. Pernambuco, *Mensagem do exm. sr. dr. Manoel Antonio Pereira Borba governador do estado lida por occasião da installação da 3.a sessão da 9.a legislatura do congresso legislativo do estado aos 6 de março de 1918* (Pernambuco: Officinas da "Imprensa Official," 1918), 20, cx. 2, Mensagens, GEP, APEP.

84. A census of the island in 1919 counted 2,134 inhabitants. *Mensagem 1919*, 46.

85. Fred L. Soper, "Hookworm Infection Survey of the State of Pernambuco, Brazil, May 17th, 1920 to August 31st, 1920," 28, f. 150, bx. 25, s. 2, r.g. 5, RFA.

86. Ibid., 14, 30.

87. Wickliffe Rose, "Public Health Situation and Work of the International Health Board in Brazil," 8, f. 153, bx. 25, s. 2, r.g. 5, RFA.

88. De Castro Santos, "Power, Ideology, and Public Health," 146–47; Pernambuco, *Mensagem do exmo. sr. dr. Sergio T. Lins de B. Loreto governador do estado lida ao installar se a 3.a sessão da 11.a legislatura do congresso legislativo de Pernambuco aos 6 de março de 1924* (Pernambuco: Officinas Graphicas da Penitenciaria do Recife, 1924), 14, cx. 5, Mensagens, GEP, APEP.

89. Pernambuco, *Mensagem do exm. sr. dr. José Rufino Bezerra Cavalcanti governador do estado lida ao installar-se a 2.a sessão da 10.a legislatura do congresso legislativo de Pernambuco aos 6 de março de 1920* (Pernambuco: Officinas Graphicas da "Imprensa Official," 1920), 12, cx. 5, Mensagens, GEP, APEP.

90. Pernambuco, *Mensagem do exm. sr. dr. José Rufino Bezerra Cavalcanti governador do estado lida ao installar-se a 3.a sessão da 10.a legislatura do congresso legislativa de Per-

nambuco aos 6 de março de 1921 (Pernambuco: Officinas Graphicas do "Jornal do Commercio," 1921), 5, cx. 5, Mensagens, GEP, APEP; Gouveia de Barros, *Programma sanitario em Pernambuco* (Recife: Imprensa Industrial, 1921), 20, Coleções Especiais, BPEP.

91. Joaquim Pimenta, "Saúde e riqueza (Conferencia que, por motivo de molestia, deixou de pronunciar o autor na sessão inaugural da Sociedade de Medicina e Hygiene Tropical, realizado no dia de julho de 1919)," *RAFDR* 27 (1919): 57, 60.

92. Rockefeller Foundation officials realized that ancylostomiasis could not be completely eradicated. See Ilana Löwy, "Representação e intervenção em saúde pública: vírus, mosquitos e especialistas da Fundação Rockefeller no Brasil," *História, Ciências, Saúde—Manguinhos* 5:3 (1998–1999): 5.

93. *Mensagem 1924,* 14. See also Löwy, "Representação e intervenção"; and Jaime Larry Benchimol, ed., *Febre amarela: a doença e a vacina, uma história inacabada* (Rio de Janeiro: Editora Fiocruz, 2001).

94. Williams, "Nationalism," 24–25.

95. By way of comparison, the commission employed 1,462 workers in Rio de Janeiro in the same year. See D. B. Wilson, "Annual Report Yellow Fever Service," Brazil 1932, 25, bx. 116, s. 3, r.g. 5, RFA.

96. Eleyson Cardoso, *Instrucções geraes para os guardas do serviço de febre amarella* (Rio de Janeiro: Typ. dos "Annaes," 1931), in Yellow Fever Service, Brazil, Annual Report 1930, bx. 115, s. 3, r.g. 5, RFA.

97. Quoted in Alexander W. Burke, "Bahia, Brazil Station Journal," June 11, 1928, Monthly Statistical Reports 1928, bx. 128, s. 3, r.g. 5, RFA. For other examples of violence, see Royal A. Henry, "Yellow Fever Brazil, Bahia, Monthly Reports," and "Cases of Yellow Fever from May to August 1926," October 1926, bx. 127, s. 3, r.g. 5, RFA; and Elsmere R. Rickard, "Diary of Elsmere R. Rickard," January 8, 1931, f. 265, box 50, s. 305, r.g. 1.1, RFA.

98. Lucian C. Smith, "Yellow Fever Annual and Monthly Reports," December 26, 1927, Pernambuco, 1927, bx. 131, s. 3, r.g. 5, RFA.

99. Porter J. Crawford, "Pernambuco Monthly Station Journals," August 6, 1928, bx. 131, s. 3, r.g. 5, RFA.

100. See, for example, M. E. Connor, "Diary of the Yellow Fever Commission of Brazil," November 8, 1927, in December 26, 1926, to December 31, 1927, bx. 40, s. 305, r.g. 1.1, RFA.

101. "Aggravando a penuria e triando o socego do povo. Legiões de 'mata-mosquitos' investam contras as jarras, destruindo-as furiosamente! As latas de kerosine ou gasolina são mais hygienicas, affirma o Departamento de Saúde!" unidentified clipping in Porter J. Crawford, "Yellow Fever Commission of Brazil, Annual Report 1928," Recife, Pernambuco Station, 89, bx. 100, s. 3, r.g. 5, RFA.

102. Porter J. Crawford, "Pernambuco Monthly Station Journals," October 11, 1928, bx. 131, s. 3, r.g. 5, RFA.

103. E. R. Rickard, "Recife Journal," October 6, October 13, 1930, in Fred Soper, "Yellow Fever Service Diary," v. 1, f. 207, bx. 27, s. 305, r.g. 1.1, RFA.

104. M. E. Connor, "Summary of Activities of the Commissão de Febre Amarella in Brazil in 1927," 11, bx. 114, s. 3, r.g. 5, RFA.

105. Porter J. Crawford, "Annual Report 1928 Recife—Pernambuco Station, Yellow Fever Commission of Brazil, The International Health Division, The Rockefeller Commission," bx. 100, s. 3, r.g. 5, RFA.

106. "Yellow Fever," *A noite,* cited in Alexander W. Burke, "Bahia, Brazil Station Journal, Monthly Statistical Reports 1928," August 30, 1928, bx. 128, s. 3, r.g. 5, RFA. Pernambucan public health officials recorded an average of 8.6 deaths per year from yellow fever between 1897 and 1918. See Freitas, *Os trabalhos,* 25, 28–29.

107. The standard greeting used by *guardas* upon entering a house can be found in Lucian C. Smith, "Yellow Fever, Brazil, Parahyba do Norte, Monthly Reports," Station Journal, April 19, 1928, bx. 130; and "Instrucções para os guardas," in Yellow Fever, Brazil, Pernambuco 1927 Annual and Monthly Reports, bx. 131, both in s. 3, r.g. 5, RFA.

108. Barros, *Programma sanitario,* 5.

109. Pimenta, "Saúde e riqueza," 44–61, 53–54.

110. In 1925, a total of 4,367 *contos* was spent on public health in Pernambuco, with the state government providing 2,566 *contos,* the federal government providing 620 *contos,* municipal governments providing 181 *contos,* and the Rockefeller Foundation providing 1,000 *contos.* Pernambuco, *Mensagem apresentada ao congresso legislativo, em 7 de setembro de 1926, 3.a sessão da 12.a legislatura, pelo dr. Sergio Loreto, governador do estado de Pernambuco* (Recife: n.p., [1926]), 65–67, cx. 6, Mensagens, GEP, APEP.

111. Amaury de Medeiros, *Saude e assistencia: doutrina, experiencias e realisações 1923–1926* (Recife: n.p., [1926]), 43, APEP.

112. Pernambuco, *Mensagem do exmo. sr. dr. Sergio T. Lins de B. Loreto governador do estado lida ao installar-se a 2.a sessão da 11.a legislatura do congresso legislativo de Pernambuco aos 6 de março de 1923* (Pernambuco Officinas Graphicas do Jornal do Commercio, 1923), 12, cx. 5, Mensagens, GEP, APEP.

113. *Mensagem 1926,* 46.

114. I used five-year averages rather than individual years in order to avoid comparing years with heightened death rates due to epidemics. De Castro Santos and Faria suggest that the improvements in public health in Pernambuco were due primarily to improvements in the city's water supply and sewerage systems, which were in full operation by 1915. However, there was not a significant decline in overall mortality rates in the city until the early 1920s, suggesting that the sewer system improvements were not the only cause of declining mortality rates. See Francisco Saturnino Rodrigues de Brito, *Saneamento de Recife: descrição e relatorios,* 2 vols. (Recife: Typ. da "Imprensa Official," 1917); de Castro Santos, "Poder, ideologias e saúde," 258–61; and de Castro Santos and Faria, *A reforma sanitária no Brasil,* 80.

115. Freitas, *Os trabalhos,* 6.

116. Hochman, *A era do saneamento,* 207; de Castro Santos and Faria, *A reforma sanitária no Brasil,* 141.

117. De Castro Santos and Faria, *A reforma sanitária no Brasil,* 15, 141.

Chapter 5. Social Hygiene

1. José Octávio de Freitas, "Saúde publica e providencias sanitarias: palestra lida no Rotary Club do Recife," *JMP* 31:11 (1935): 168.

2. See, e.g., Jerry Dávila, *Diploma of Whiteness: Race and Social Policy in Brazil, 1917–1945* (Durham: Duke University Press, 2003); Diego Armas, ed., *Disease in the History of Modern Latin America: From Malaria to AIDS* (Durham: Duke University Press, 2003);

and Jurandir Freire Costa, *Ordem médica e norma familiar*, 4th ed. (Rio de Janeiro: Edições Graal, 1999).

3. Skidmore, *Black into White*, chaps. 4 and 5; Herschmann and Pereira, eds., *A invenção do Brasil moderno*; Levine, *Pernambuco*; Meade, *"Civilizing" Rio*; Barbara Weinstein, *For Social Peace in Brazil: Industrialists and the Remaking of the Working Class in São Paulo, 1920–1964* (Chapel Hill: University of North Carolina Press, 1996); and Susan K. Besse, *Restructuring Patriarchy: The Modernization of Gender Inequality in Brazil, 1914–1940* (Chapel Hill: University of North Carolina Press, 1996).

4. Borges, "'Puffy'"; Stepan, *"Hour of Eugenics"*; Peard, *Race, Place, and Medicine*.

5. See, e.g., Hochman, *A era do saneamento*.

6. In other words, historians of medicine and science should be investigating local social, cultural, and political contexts rather than tracing the origins of new ideas about medicine. See Katherine Elaine Bliss, *Compromised Positions: Prostitution, Public Health, and Gender Politics in Revolutionary Mexico City* (University Park: Pennsylvania State University Press, 2001); Alexandra Minna Stern, *Eugenic Nation: Faults and Frontiers of Better Breeding in Modern America* (Berkeley: University of California Press, 2005); Ann Zulawski, "New Trends in Studies of Science and Medicine in Latin America," *LARR* 34:3 (1999): 241–51; Weinstein, *For Social Peace*; and Stepan, *"Hour of Eugenics."*

7. For the most relevant works on eugenics, see Daniel J. Kevles, *In the Name of Eugenics: Genetics and the Uses of Human Heredity* (Cambridge, MA: Harvard University Press, 1995); Desmond King, *In the Name of Liberalism: Illiberal Social Policy in the United States and Britain* (Oxford: Oxford University Press, 1999); Stepan, *"Hour of Eugenics"*; Nancy Leys Stepan, "Eugenics in Brazil, 1917–1940," in *The Wellborn Science: Eugenics in Germany, France, Brazil, and Russia*, ed. Mark B. Adams (New York: Oxford University Press, 1990), 110–52; and Dávila, *Diploma of Whiteness*.

8. *Mensagem 1927*, 23–24.

9. Ibid., 23, 26–27.

10. *Mensagem 1928*, 37.

11. Levine, *Pernambuco*, 66–72; Souza Barros, *A década 20 em Pernambuco (Uma interpretação)*, 2nd ed. (Recife: Fundação de Cultura, Cidade do Recife, 1985), 85–108.

12. *Mensagem 1920*, 12, 21.

13. Barros, *Programma sanitario*, 20.

14. Pernambuco, *Recenseamento do Recife 1923* (Recife: Secção Technica da Repartição de Publicações Officiaes, 1924), 3.

15. *Mensagem 1916*, 6.

16. Stepan, *"Hour of Eugenics,"* 46–54; Stepan, "Eugenics in Brazil," 110–52.

17. Stepan, *"Hour of Eugenics,"* 51–53.

18. Ibid., 46–54.

19. An example of the influence of eugenics in medicine and public health can be seen in the proceedings of the First Brazilian Eugenics Congress, held in Rio de Janeiro in 1929. See *1.o Congresso Brasileiro de eugenia: actas e trabalhos* (Rio de Janeiro: n.p., 1929).

20. Stepan, *"Hour of Eugenics,"* 126.

21. Ibid., 162–70; Lesser, *Welcoming the Undesirables*, 66–67; Constituição da República dos Estados Unidos do Brasil (de 16 de julho de 1934), article 121, section 6 (à garantia da integração étnica e capacidade física e civil do imigrante) and article 145 (apresenta-

ção pelos nubentes de prova de sanidade física e mental), http://www.planalto.gov.br/ ccivil_03/Constituicao (accessed November 8, 2006); Constituição dos Estados Unidos do Brasil (de 10 de novembro de 1937), article 127 (a infância e a juventude devem ser objeto de cuidados e garantias especiais por parte do Estado, que tomará todas as medidas destinadas a assegurar-lhes condições físicas e morais de vida sã e de harmonioso desenvolvimento das suas faculdades), http://www.planalto.gov.br/ccivil_03/Constituicao/ (accessed November 8, 2006).

22. Stepan, *"Hour of Eugenics,"* 90; Dávila, *Diploma of Whiteness,* 24–27.

23. Dávila, *Diploma of Whiteness,* 26–27.

24. Simon Schwartzman, Helena Maria Bousquet Bomeny, and Vanda Maria Ribeiro Costa, *Tempos de Capanema* (São Paulo: Editora Paz e Terra, 2000), 183.

25. Levine, *Pernambuco,* 81–89.

26. Ibid., 70–72.

27. See Barbara Weinstein, "Unskilled Worker, Skilled Housewife: Constructing the Working-Class Woman in São Paulo, Brazil," in *The Gendered Worlds of Latin American Women Workers: From Household and Factory to the Union Hall and Ballot Box,* ed. John D. French and Daniel James (Durham: Duke University Press, 1997), 72–99; Weinstein, *For Social Peace;* Besse, *Restructuring Patriarchy;* Susan K. Besse, "Crimes of Passion: The Campaign against Wife Killing in Brazil, 1910–1940," *Journal of Social History* 22: 4 (1989): 653–66; Sueann Caulfield, "Getting into Trouble: Dishonest Women, Modern Girls, and Women-Men in the Conceptual Language of *Vida policial,* 1925–1927," *Signs* 19:1 (1993): 146–76; Sueann Caulfield, *In Defense of Honor: Sexual Morality, Modernity, and Nation in Early-Twentieth-Century Brazil* (Durham: Duke University Press, 2000); and Borges, *Family in Bahia.*

28. See Besse, *Restructuring Patriarchy,* 5–7; Caulfield, *In Defense of Honor,* 48–55; Magareth Rago, *Do cabaré ao lar: a utopia da cidade disciplinar; Brasil 1890–1930* (Rio de Janeiro: Paz e Terra, 1985), 61–116; and Costa, *Ordem médica.*

29. Stepan, *"Hour of Eugenics,"* 103–4.

30. See Weinstein, "Unskilled Worker." Lower levels of industrialization led to fewer economic opportunities for women in Pernambuco compared to São Paulo.

31. See Besse, *Restructuring Patriarchy,* 89–109; Rago, *Do cabaré ao lar,* chap. 3; Borges, *Family in Bahia,* 46–84, 90–100; and Alcir Lenharo, *Sacralização da política* (Campinas: Papirus, 1986).

32. On the medicalization of childhood, see Rago, *Do cabaré ao lar,* 117–35.

33. Medeiros, *Saude e assistencia,* 155.

34. *Mensagem 1928,* 35.

35. Ibid., 36.

36. Pernambuco, *Mensagem apresentada ao congresso legislativo na abertura da 2.a sessão de 13.a legislatura pelo governador do estado dr. Estacio de Albuquerque Coimbra* (Recife: Imprensa Official, 1929), 39–40, cx. 9, Mensagens, GEP, APEP.

37. Pernambuco, *Mensagem apresentada ao congresso legislativo na abertura da 3.a sessão da 13.a legislatura pelo governador do estado dr. Estacio de Albuquerque Coimbra* (Recife: Imprensa Official, 1930), 40–41, cx. 10, Mensagens, GEP, APEP.

38. Ibid., 40.

39. *Mensagem 1929,* 41–42.

40. *Mensagem 1930*, 40.

41. Celso Caldas, "Aumento da mortalidade em Bom Jardim e causas determinantes," *RMP* 4:6 (1934): 212–13.

42. Pernambuco, *Realizações do estado novo em Pernambuco* (Recife: Oficinas Gráficas da Imprensa Oficial, 1942), Relatório 1942–1955, est. 51, pac. 1, GEP, APEP.

43. Geraldo de Andrade, "Primogeniture e mortalidade infantil em Recife," in *Annaes do quinto Congresso de Hygiene: Recife, 17 a 22 de outubro de 1929, volume II sessões plenarias* (Rio de Janeiro: Officinas Graphicas da Inspectoria de Demographia Sanitaria, 1930), 267–80; Meira Lins, "Nos horizontes da pediatria," *RMP* 2:3 (1932): 89–99; Matheus de Lima, "A hygiene do alietamento," *JMP* 24:7 (1928): 105–6.

44. Nancy Scheper-Hughes, *Death without Weeping: The Violence of Everyday Life in Brazil* (Berkeley: University of California Press, 1992), 316–26.

45. Caldas, "Aumento da mortalidade," 214.

46. *Mensagem 1927*, 24.

47. João Rodrigues, "Do Hospital Infantil Manoel S. Almeida e da sua actuação em 1933," in Pernambuco, *Anuário do Departamento de Saúde Publica: anno II, 1933* (Recife: Imprensa Industrial, 1934), 247, APEP.

48. *Mensagem 1927*, 24–25; and Pernambuco, *Programma da escola de educação sanitaria, anno de 1930* (Recife: Imprensa Official, 1930), Coleções Especiais, BPEP.

49. *Mensagem 1927*, 25.

50. Medeiros, *Saude e assistencia*, 198; Pernambuco, *Annuario do Departamento de Saúde Publica: anno I, 1932* (Recife: Imprensa Industrial, 1933), 24–25, APEP.

51. Pernambuco, *Relatorio apresentado ao exmo. snr. presidente da república em virtude do art. 46 do decreto-lei federal n.o 1202* (Recife: Imprensa Official, 1940), 102–3, Relatório, est. 51, pac. 1, GEP, APEP; and *Annuario do Departamento de Saúde Publica 1932*, 25.

52. *Annuario do Departamento de Saúde Publica 1932*, 24–26.

53. See Dávila, *Diploma of Whiteness*, 52–89; and Levine, *Pernambuco*, 61–65, 70–71.

54. Levine, *Pernambuco*, 62, 71.

55. *Mensagem 1921*, 26.

56. *Mensagem 1923*, 18.

57. On educational reforms under Getúlio Vargas, see Schwartzman, Bomeny, and Costa, *Tempos de Capanema*, 189–219.

58. Quoted in *Mensagem 1929*, 5.

59. Antônio Carneiro Leão, "Conferencia proferida pelo Sr. A. Carneiro Leão, na Associação Brasileira de Educação," in Pernambuco, *Organização da educação no estado de Pernambuco (justificação, lei organica, explicação e commentarios, opinião associações e da imprensa)* (Recife: Imprensa Official, 1929), 164, Coleções Especiais, Relatórios Diversos, nos. 104–7, APEP.

60. *Mensagem 1929*, 5–9; and *Organização da educação*.

61. "Vida educacional," *Boletim da Diretoria Technica de Educação* 1 (1931): 111, Coleções Especiais, BPEP.

62. Pernambuco, Departamento de Educação, *Programas de educação primaria* (Recife: Imprensa Official, 1937), 17, 21, Coleções Especiais, BPEP.

63. Ibid., 17–21.

64. *Organização da educação*, 76–77.

65. Ibid., 76.

66. Ibid., 76–77. There is no documentation that speaks to the popularity of these courses. However, it is likely that they were taken with few reservations, given the lack of other educational opportunities for women.

67. Auryno Maciel, "Da necessidade das escolas domesticas: a emancipação da mulher não se realiza apenas com a capacidade political, com a simples conquista do direito do voto; na Escola Domestica a menina aprende a derramar em torno de si os beneficios da collaboração e do altruismo," *Boletim da Diretoria Technica de Educação* 2:1–2 (1932): 161–66, Coleções Especiais, BPEP.

68. Publio Dias, "Escola, estudo de um edificio e inspeção medias dos escolares, visando principalmente a nutrição, dentes, opilação," *RMP* 3:3 (1933): 81.

69. Abreu e Lima, "Aspectos atuais da assistencia maternal," *RMP* 11:8 (1941): 207.

70. *Organização da educação*, 70.

71. *Mensagem 1930*, 30–32. In 1930, 209 students enrolled at the Escola Profissional Masculina and 390 enrolled at the Escola Profissional Feminina.

72. Pernambuco, *Exposição apresentada ao chefe do governo provisorio da republica exm.o sr. dr. Getulio Vargas pelo interventor federal em Pernambuco Carlos de Lima Cavalcanti, periodo administrativo de outubro de 1930 a junho de 1933* (Recife: Imprensa Oficial, 1933), 166, Exposição, est. 51, pac. 2, GEP, APEP.

73. Besse, *Restructuring Patriarchy*, 111–28. These reforms were similar to the educational reforms carried out under Gustavo Capanema in his capacity as minister of education and health. See the 1937 Plano Nacional de Educação in Schwartzman, Bomeny, and Costa, *Tempos de Capanema*, 123–24.

74. On Brazilian eugenics, see Stepan, *"Hour of Eugenics"*; Stepan, "Eugenics in Brazil"; and Dávila, *Diploma of Whiteness*, 21–51. On the medicalization of the family, marriage, and childrearing, see Antunes, *Medicina, leis e moral;* and Costa, *Ordem médica*.

75. Some historians argue that eugenics inspired the social, educational, and public health reforms of the 1920s and 1930s. However, it can be argued that government officials adopted eugenics because it provided a means of describing and addressing social problems. While several politicians and public health official did recommend controlling reproduction, few of their proposals were put into practice. See Stepan, *"Hour of Eugenics,"* 122–28, 153–69; and Dávila, *Diploma of Whiteness*.

76. On Medeiros's reforms, see Medeiros, *Saude e assistencia;* Amaury de Medeiros, *Actos de fé: discursos* (Rio de Janeiro: Imprensa Medica, 1928); and *Mensagem 1926*, 50–55.

77. Medeiros, *Saude e assistencia*, 163.

78. Teodolino Castiglione, *A eugenia no direito de família: o código civil brasileiro e a lei sôbre a organização e proteção da família perante a eugenia* (n.p.: Livraria Acadêmica Saraiva & Cia., 1942), 126–130. See also Stepan, *"Hour of Eugenics,"* 126.

79. Waldemar de Oliveira, "O exame medico pré-nupcial, Tese de Concurso á Livre Docencia de Hygiene da Faculdade de Medicina do Recife" (Recife: Officinas Graphicas da S.A. Revista da Cidade, 1928), 55, Coleções Especiais, BPEP.

80. Stepan, *"Hour of Eugenics,"* 126. On opposition to the bill, see Castiglione, *A eugenia no direito de família*, 127–29.

81. Kevles, *In the Name of Eugenics*, 85.

82. Oliveira, "O exame medico pré-nupcial," 13.

83. Ibid., 33.

84. Ibid., 99.

85. João Aureliano, "Do exame medico pre-nupcial," *AAPP* 4:2 (1934): 132.
86. Valdemir Miranda, "Exame pré-nupcial," *AAPP* 5:1–2 (1935): 208–11.
87. Celso Arcoverde de Freitas, "Matrimonio precoce e maternidade conciente," *JMP* 31:9 (1935): 144, 146.
88. Jorge Lôbo, "Eugenica (Conferencia realizada na sociedade de internos de Recife)," *JMP* 29:6 (1933): 114.
89. Ibid., 109–10.
90. Stepan, *"Hour of Eugenics,"* 201.
91. See the comments of Ulysses Pernambucano, Edgar Altino, Benjamin Vasconcellos, and Gildo Neto appended to Augusto Lins e Silva, "Eugenia e crime," *RMP* 1:12 (1931): 750–55.
92. Lins e Silva, "Eugenia e crime," 751.
93. Ibid., 754.
94. *Mensagem 1928*, 37.
95. See Pernambuco, *Contribuição ao estudo da anthropologia social em suas relações com a hygiene em Pernambuco (Trabalho da Inspectoria de Hygiene Social, dr. Geraldo de Andrade Inspector) fasiculo I* (Recife: Impresa Official, 1929), Coleções Especiais, BPEP.
96. Data cards were used extensively in eugenics, criminal anthropology, and biotypology. Researchers attempted to create a comprehensive database that would be used to classify individuals according to race, predisposition to certain crimes, and aptitude for certain professions. See Stepan, *"Hour of Eugenics,"* 119–21.
97. *Mensagem 1928*, 37.
98. Geraldo de Andrade, "Verificações biometricas em Pernambuco," *JMP* 24:9 (1928): 151–56.
99. Geraldo de Andrade, "Anthropometria das classes domesticas de Pernambuco (Memoria apresentada ao 4.o Congresso Brasileiro de Hygiene, reunida na Bahia em janeiro de 1928)," *JMP* 24:8 (1928): 131.
100. Ibid., 124–25.
101. Andrade, "Verificações biometricas," 155 (first two quotes), 156 (remaining quotes).
102. On the idea of social harmony in Brazilian politics during the Vargas era, see Weinstein, *For Social Peace in Brazil.*
103. See Weinstein, *For Social Peace in Brazil;* and Dulce Chaves Pandolfi, *Pernambuco de Agamenon Magalhães: consolidação e crise de uma elite política* (Recife: Fundação Joaquim Nabuco/Editora Massangana, 1984), 54–57.
104. Schwartzman, Bomeny, and Costa, *Tempos de Capanema*, 183.
105. Arthur Lobo da Silva, "A anthropologia no exercito brasileiro," *Archivos do Museu Nacional* 30 (1928): 16.
106. Oliveira Viana, "Introdução," in Geraldo de Andrade, *Contribuição ao estudo da antropologia social em suas relações com a hygiene em Pernambuco* (Recife: Imprensa Official, 1929), 1.
107. Andrade, *Contribuição*, 35; Geraldo de Andrade, "Hygiene do trabalho e registro de sanidade," *RMP* 1:6 (1931): 243.
108. Geraldo de Andrade, "Hygiene do trabalho em Pernambuco," *RMP* 1:7 (1931): 318–35.
109. Ibid., 326.

110. João Rufino, *Discurso proferido em memoriam do prof. Geraldo de Andrade, em sessão solene do Instituto Pernambucano de Historia da Medicina* (Recife: Divulgação do Laboratório Clímax, n.d.), Coleções Especiais, BPEP.

111. Jurandyr Mamede, "Esboçando um relatorio geral, já em principio de outubro deste anno havia a Secretaria da Justiça, Educação e Interior divulgado as seguintes considerações," *Boletim da Directoria Technica de Educação* 1 (1931): 9, Coleções Especiais, BPEP.

112. *Exposição 1933*, 161.

113. Mamede, "Esboçando um relatorio geral," 10.

114. Pernambuco, *Mensagem apresentada pelo governador Carlos de Lima Cavalcanti á assembléa legislativa de Pernambuco a 1.o de agosto de 1936* (Recife: Imprensa Oficial, 1936), 48, cx. 12, Mensagens, GEP, APEP; Pernambuco, *Mensagem apresentada pelo governador Carlos de Lima Cavalcanti á assembléa legislativa de Pernambuco a 1.o de agosto de 1937* (Recife: Imprensa Oficial, 1937), 78, cx. 13, Mensagens, GEP, APEP.

115. Waldemar de Oliveira, "A practica anthropometrica: como preencher, neste particular, a ficha de educação physica (para as monitoras de educação physical)," *Boletim da Diretoria Technica de Educação* 1 (1931): 27–41, Coleções Especiais, BPEP.

116. *Mensagem 1937*, 78.

117. *Exposição 1933*, 161.

118. Researchers considered physical underdevelopment a problem to be treated with physical exercise. Generally speaking, no mention was made of malnutrition or hunger.

119. *Mensagem 1936*, 49. See also *Escoteirismo: orgão dos escoteiros da Escola Técnico Profissional Masculina* 2:2 (1934), Coleções Especiais, BPEP.

120. Anibal Bruno, "Uma programma de politica educacional: exposição apresentada ao exmo. sr. Secretario do Interior de Pernambuco," *Boletim de Educação* 4 (1934): 11.

121. Gil de Campos and Armando Macedo, "Contribuição á antropometria do escola recifense," in *Annuario do Departamento de Saúde Publica: anno II, 1933*, Estado de Pernambuco, 135–42.

122. Luiz Ignacio and Andrade Lima Júnior, "O indice Ponderal," *RMP* 8:5 (1938): 111–16; Andrade Lima Júnior and Luiz Ignacio, "O biotipo do escolar em Pernambuco," *Boletim de Educação* 5:7 (1936): 83.

123. *Relatorio 1940*, 36.

124. *Mensagem 1936*, 125; *Relatorio 1940*, 157.

125. Stepan, *"Hour of Eugenics,"* 114–17.

126. Alvaro Ferraz and Andrade Lima Júnior, *A morfologia do homem do nordeste (estudo biotipologico)* (Rio de Janeiro: Livraria José Olympio Editora, 1939), 22–23.

127. *Relatorio 1940*, 169.

128. Alvaro Ferraz, "Educação fisica e reconstrução nacional," *Neurobiologia* 4:1 (1941): 50.

129. Ferraz and Lima Junior, *A morfologia do homem*, 309; Alvaro Ferraz, "Biotipos e trabalho agrário," *Neurobiologia* 8:2 (1945): 151.

130. See chaps. 6 and 7.

131. Scheper-Hughes, *Death without Weeping*, 129–30; Josué de Castro, *Geografia da fome: a fome no Brasil* (Rio de Janeiro: Emprêsa Gráfica "O Cruziero," 1946), 13.

132. *Mensagem 1927*, 26–27.

133. George Rosen, *A History of Public Health* (Baltimore: Johns Hopkins University Press, 1993), 380–95; Roy Porter, *The Greatest Benefit to Mankind: A Medical History of Humanity* (New York: Norton, 1997), 551–60.

134. Da Cunha, *Rebellion*, 108; da Cunha, *Os sertões*, 152.

135. See, e.g., Meira Lins, "Nos horizontes da pediatria"; Leduar de Assis Rocha, "Aumento da mortalidade em Bom Jardim e causas determinantes," *RMP* 4:6 (1934): 202–14; Orlando Parahym, *O problema alimentar no sertão* (Recife: Imprensa Industrial, 1940); and A. J. de Sampaio, *A alimentação sertaneja e do interior do Amazonia: onomastica da alimentação rural* (São Paulo: Companhia Editora Nacional, 1944).

136. Lins, "Nos horizontes da pediatria," 94; Paulino Barros, "O 'Facies' medico da mortalidade infantil no interior," *RMP* 9:8 (1939): 225; *Mensagem 1928*, 35–36.

137. In their biotypological research, Alvaro Ferraz and Andrade Lima Júnior did not raise the question of whether *nordestinos* were malnourished.

138. Medeiros, *Saude e assistencia*, 135.

139. Ibid., 134–35.

140. Ibid., 135.

141. On Josué de Castro's approaches to hunger, see Rosana Magalhães, *Fome: uma (re)leitura de Josué de Castro* (Rio de Janeiro: Editora Fiocruz, 1997); Eronides da Silva Lima, *Mal de fome e não de raça: génese, constituição e ação política da educação alimentar Brasil—1934–1946* (Rio de Janeiro: Editora Fiocruz, 2000), 45–148; and Francisco de Assis Guedes de Vasconcelos, "Fome, eugenia e constituição do campo de nutrição em Pernambuco: uma análise de Gilberto Freyre, Josué de Castro e Nelson Chaves," *História, Ciências, Saúde—Manguinhos* 8:2 (2001): 315–39.

142. Josué de Castro, "O problema fisiologico da alimentação no Brasil" (Tése de Concurso para a Faculdade de Medicina do Recife, 1932), 8, Coleções Especiais, BPEP.

143. Josué de Castro, *Alimentação e raça* (Rio de Janeiro: Civilização Brasileira, 1936), 91. See also Josué de Castro, *As condições de vida das classes operarias no Recife: estudo economico de sua alimentação* (Rio de Janeiro: Departamento de Estatistica e Publicidade, Ministerio do Trabalho, Industria e Commercio, 1935).

144. De Castro, *As condições de vida*, 17.

145. De Castro, *Alimentação e raça*, 102.

146. Antônio Carneiro Leão, *A sociedade rural: seus problemas e sua educação* (Rio de Janeiro: Editôra S.A. A Noite, [1937]), 55.

147. De Castro, *Alimentação e raça*, 104–7; de Castro, *As condições de vida*, 17–8; Raul Senna de Caldas, "Aspectos do problema da seccas: conferencia realisado no Instituto de Estudos Brasileiros, em 2 de junho de 1939," in Fundação Guimarães Duque, *Memorial da Seca*, org. Vingt-Un Rosado (Mossoró: Coleção Mossoroense, 1981), 123–50.

148. De Castro, *Alimentação e raça*, 38, 89–90.

149. De Castro, *As condições de vida*, 7.

150. Freyre, *Casa-grande*, 1:132.

151. On the differences between de Castro and Freyre's approaches to hunger, see Vasconcelos, "Fome, eugenia e constituição," 323.

152. Freyre took the position that de Castro and others exaggerated the influence of diet. Freyre, *Casa-grande*, 1:133–34.

153. De Castro, *Geografia da fome*, 217.

154. Ibid., 274. De Castro described the psychological effects of drought and chronic hunger in the *sertão* on *cangaceiros* and *romeiros,* implying that hunger was one cause of social upheaval and folk religious movements.

155. De Castro, *Alimentação e raça,* 18, 92.

156. Robert M. Levine, *The Vargas Regime: The Critical Years, 1934–1938* (New York: Columbia University Press, 1970), 74.

157. De Castro, *Alimentação e raça,* 174–75.

158. De Castro, *Geografia da fome,* 301–4.

159. Ibid., 305.

160. *Exposição 1933,* 210; Pernambuco, *Exposição apresentada pelo interventor federal dr. Carlos de Lima Cavalcanti á assembléa constituinte do estado* (Recife: Imprensa Oficial, 1935), 86, est. 51, pac. 2, Exposição, GEP, APEP. Officials estimated that 60 percent of infant deaths were due to what they termed "alimentary danger." Lessa de Andrade, "Relatório dos trabalhos realizados pelos postos de higiêne em 1940," *Arquivos da Diretoria de Higiene do Interior* 3:1 (1941): 1–7, Coleções Especiais, BPEP.

161. See Parahym, *O problema alimentar no sertão;* Sampaio, *A alimentação sertaneja;* Vasconcelos Torres, *Condições de vida do trabalhador na agro-indústria do açúcar* (Rio de Janeiro: Edição do Instituto do Açúcar e do Álcool, 1945); and Nelson Chaves, *O problema alimentar do nordeste brasileiro (introdução ao seu estudo econômico social)* (Recife: Livraria Editora Medico Cientifica, 1946), Coleções Especiais, BPEP.

162. Agamemnon Magalhães, "Um problema nacional," *Folha da Manha* and Rádio Clube de Pernambuco, June 26, 1941, Prontuário Historico Agamemnon Sergio de Godoy Magalhães, SSP 31602-a, Arquivo de Departamento de Ordem Política e Social (hereafter, DOPS), APEP.

163. *Mensagem 1927,* 26.

164. Comissão Censitaria dos Mucambos do Recife, *Observações estatisticas sobre os mucambos do Recife baseadas no censo efetuado pela comissão censitaria dos mucambos criado pelo dec. n.o 182, de 17 de setembro de 1938* (Recife: Imprensa Oficial, 1939), APEP.

165. *Mensagem 1917,* 21; Amaury de Medeiros, "O caminho da iqualidade, discurso pronunciado no momento da inauguração do primeiro grupo de casas da villa da fundação 'a casa operaria' em 1 de maio de 1925," in *Actos de fé,* 73–80.

166. Medeiros, "O caminho da iqualidade," 76.

167. *Realizações do estado novo;* and Pernambuco, Liga Social Contra o Mocambo, *Relatorio das atividades da Liga Social contra o Mocambo, lido na sessão extraordinária do dia 12 de julho de 1941, comemorativa do 2.o aniversário de sua fundação* (Recife: Oficinas da Imprensa Oficial Pernambuco, n.d.), Coleções Especiais, BPEP.

168. See Pernambuco, *Relatório da Liga Social Contra o Mocambo julho de 1939 a julho de 1941* (Pernambuco: Oficinas da Imprensa Oficial, 1941).

169. *Realizações do estado novo.*

170. Pernambuco, *Relatorio da liga social contra o mocambo julho de 1939 a julho de 1943* (Recife: Oficinas da Imprensa Oficial de Pernambuco, n.d.), 24, Coleções Especiais, BPEP.

171. Agamemnon Magalhães, "Estamos Certos," *Folha da Manha* and Rádio Clube de Pernambuco, June 3, 1941, Prontuário Serviço Social Contra Mocambo, doc. 359-D, fundo SSP no. 1015, DOPS, APEP.

172. Pernambuco, Secretaria da Segurança Pública Pernambuco, *Decreto no. 181,* July 15, 1939, Prontuário Serviço Social Contra o Mocambo, doc. 359-D, 1939–1972, SSP n. 1041, DOPS, APEP.

173. See Stepan, *"Hour of Eugenics";* Dávila, *Diploma of Whiteness;* Alexandra Minna Stern, "From Mestizophilia to Biotypology: Racialization and Science in Mexico, 1920–1960," in *Race and Nation in Modern Latin America,* ed. Appelbaum et al., 187–210; and Alexandra Minna Stern, "Responsible Mothers and Normal Children: Eugenics, Nationalism, and Welfare in Post-revolutionary Mexico, 1920–1940," *Journal of Social History* 12:4 (1999): 369–97.

174. See Dávila, *Diploma of Whiteness,* 24–27; and Kevles, *In the Name of Eugenics,* 74–76.

175. Stern, "Responsible Mothers," 375.

Chapter 6. Mental Hygiene

1. See Corrêa, "As ilusões da liberdade"; Jurandir Freire Costa, *História da psiquiatria,* 4th ed (Rio de Janeiro: Xenon, 1989); Galdino Loreto, "A psiquiatria de Pernambuco nos últimos cem anos," *Neurobiologia* 49:1 (1986): 17–36.

2. Corrêa, "As ilusões da liberdade," 243.

3. For historical analysis of how race became an object of inquiry in early-twentieth-century psychiatry, see Costa, *História da psiquiatria;* Corrêa, "As ilusões da liberdade"; Ricardo A. Sobral de Andrade, "Avatares da história da psicanálise: da medicina social no Brasil à medicina nazista e à medicina romântica alemã," in *A invenção do Brasil moderno,* ed. Herschmann and Pereira, 66–87; Warwick Anderson, "The Trespass Speaks: White Masculinity and Colonial Breakdown," *American Historical Review* 102:5 (1997): 1343–70; and Loreto, "A psiquiatria de Pernambuco."

4. On the history of the *hospício,* see Loreto, "A psiquiatria de Pernambuco," 17–36.

5. Pernambuco, *Relatorio apresentado á junta administrativa da Santa Casa de Misericórdia do Recife pelo provedor commendador José Maria de Andrade na sessão de posse da actual junta no dia 4 de julho de 1912* (Pernambuco: Escola Typographia do Collegio Orphanologico São Joaquim, 1913), 107, cx. 8, GEP, Mensagens, APEP; Pernambuco, *Relatorio apresentado á junta administrativa da Santa Casa de Misericordia do Recife pelo provedor commendador José Maria de Andrade na sessão de posse da actual junta no dia 1 de junho de 1906* (Recife: Typographia do *Diario de Pernambuco,* 1906), Relatórios Diversos, APEP.

6. Loreto, "A psiquiatria de Pernambuco," 22–23.

7. Medeiros, *Saude e assistencia,* 416; Loreto, "A psiquiatria de Pernambuco," 20–23.

8. Loreto, "A psiquiatria de Pernambuco," 21, 22.

9. Medeiros, *Saude e assistencia,* 315.

10. Ibid., 315–16.

11. Pernambuco, *Regulamento do Instituto de Selecção e Orientação Profissional* (Recife: Imprensa Oficial, 1929), 3, Relatórios Diversos, Coleção Especial Annos 1926 a 1930; 1928 a 1929 nos. 104–7, APEP.

12. On intelligence testing and eugenics, see Edwin Black, *War against the Weak: Eugenics and America's Campaign to Create a Master Race* (New York: Thunder's Mouth

Press, 2004), 76–85; Kevles, *In the Name of Eugenics,* 77–84; Gould, *Mismeasure of Man,* 176–263; and Leon J. Kamin, "The Pioneers of IQ Testing," in *The Bell Curve Debate: History, Documents, Opinions,* ed. Russell Jacoby and Naomi Glauberman (New York: Times Books, 1995), 476–509.

13. José Lucena and Lourdes Paes Barreto, "Nivel de inteligencia e desenvolvimento fisico (Estudo experimental)," *AAPP* 2:1 (1932): 128–32.

14. Levine, *Pernambuco,* 84–87.

15. Loreto, "A psiquiatria de Pernambuco," 24; Pernambuco, *Decreto n. 26 de 10 de janeiro de 1931—Reforma o serviço de assistencia a psychopathas, acto n. 583 de 4 de abril de 1931—Regulamento de assistencia a psychopathas, acto n. 645 de 5 de maio de 1931—Providencia o aproveitamento das rendas do Hospital de Alienados* (Recife: Imprensa Official, 1931), 1, Anos 1931, 1932, 1933, no. 124, est. 39, Coleção Especial, APEP.

16. Loreto, "A psiquiatria de Pernambuco," 24.

17. Ulysses Pernambucano, *A Assistencia a Psicopatas em Pernambuco: idéias e realizações* (Recife: Imprensa Industrial, 1932), Colecões Especiais, BPEP, 47.

18. *Decreto n. 26 1931,* 4.

19. Pernambucano, *A Assistencia,* 47.

20. Ibid., 4, 10.

21. Ibid., 8.

22. Ibid., 6 (quote), 7.

23. Ulysses Pernambucano, "O trabalho dos alienados na Assistencia a Psicopatas de Pernambuco," *AAPP* 4:1 (1934): 24.

24. Pernambucano, *A Assistencia,* 47.

25. *Exposição 1933,* 174; Pernambucano, *A Assistencia,* 47.

26. Pernambucano, *A Assistencia,* 47.

27. Pernambuco, Assistencia a Psychopathas, *Acto n.o 583 de 24 de abril de 1931, Regulamento da Assistencia a Psychopathas* (Recife: Imprensa Official, 1931), 20, Anos 1931, 1932, 1933, no. 124, est. 39, Coleção Especial, APEP.

28. Loreto, "A psiquiatria de Pernambuco," 25. Pernambucano's league was independent of the Liga de Higiene Mental founded by Gustavo Reidel in Rio de Janeiro in 1922.

29. João Aureliano, "As diretrizes da higiene mental," *AAPP* 4:1 (1934): 47 (first quote), 48 (second and third quotes).

30. Ibid., 49, 50.

31. João Aureliano, "Do exame medico pre-nupcial," *AAPP* 4:2 (1934): 130–34.

32. João Aureliano, "A alienação mental como causa de divorcio ou desquite," *AAPP* 5:1 (1935): 1–5.

33. Cirene Coutinho, "O problema dos deficientes em Recife," *AAPP* 5:1 (1935): 6–11, and 5:2 (1935): 8–9.

34. *Organização da educação,* 28; Leão, *A sociedade rural.*

35. *Mensagem 1929,* 8.

36. Anita Paes Barreto, "Revisão pernambucana da escala métrica de inteligencia Binet-Simon-Terman," *Neurobiologia* 6:4 (1943): 161–73; Alda Campos, "Revisão da escala Binet-Simon-Terman," *AAPP* 2:1 (1932): 84–87; Alda Campos, "Revisão da escala Binet-Simon-Terman: teste de vocabulario aplicado a crianças de 8 a 14 anos," *AAPP* 2:2 (1932): 163–68.

37. In 1932, more than one thousand students underwent psychological testing. *Exposição 1933*, 176.

38. See Estevão Pinto, "Como classificar os alunos?" *Boletim de Educação, Diretoria Técnica de Educação* 3:3 (1933): 47–50; and Anita Paes Barreto, "A organização de classes homogeneas nas escolas primarias," *Neurobiologia* 3:4 (1940): 275–94.

39. Pernambuco, *Acto n.o 583 1931*, 1.

40. Pedro Cavalcanti and Helena Campos, "Descoberta de crianças anormais do meio escolar do Recife," *AAPP* 2:2 (1932): 221.

41. Barreto, "Revisão pernambucana da escala métrica"; Campos, "Revisão da escala Binet-Simon-Terman"; Campos, "Revisão da escala Binet-Simon-Terman: Teste de vocabulario."

42. Barreto, "Revisão pernambucana da escala métrica," 162–63, 166.

43. Ibid., 171.

44. Maria Leopoldina de Oliveira, "Test de desenho de Miss Florence Goodenough (experimentação em Recife e Maceió)," *AAPP* 2:1 (1932): 70–78.

45. Monitors noted that male students often did better than female students on the same puzzle tests, although they did not offer an explanation of this difference and viewed results in terms of their own gendered and racialized expectations regarding intelligence. See Beatriz Cavalcanti, "A inteligencia espacial e o teste de 'puzzle,'" *AAPP* 2:2 (1932): 169–77.

46. See Cirene Coutinho, "Padronização do 'Northumberland mental test,'" *AAPP* 3:2 (1933): 101–10; René Ribeiro, "Alguns resultados do estudo de 100 'mediuns': trechos de um trabalho em preparo organisado nos moldes das precedentes contribuições ao estudo das religiões do Recife," in *Estudos pernambucanos dedicados a Ulysses Pernambucano* (n.p., [1944]), 73, Biblioteca Blanche Knopf; and *Exposição 1933*, 176. On intelligence testing in the Pernambucan military, see *Mensagem 1937*, 74.

47. João Marque de Sá, "A organização do serviço de neuro-psiquiatria da Brigada Militar de Pernambuco," *AAPP* 5:1 (1935): 82–86.

48. Andrade, "Anthropometria das classes domesticas," 121–33.

49. See Alcides Codeceira, "Relatorio da assistencia a psicopatas de Pernambuco, no periodo de 1935," *AAPP* 6 (1936): 80–81.

50. *Exposição 1933*, 176; *Mensagem 1937*, 74.

51. Waldemar de Oliveira, "A educação em primeiro lugar," *Boletim de Educação* 3:3–4 (1933): 119–39, Coleções Especiais, BPEP.

52. See Corrêa, "As ilusões da liberdade"; Peard, "Tropical Disorders"; and Nina Rodrigues, *O alienado*.

53. Borges, "'Puffy,'" 241.

54. In the terminology of the era, psychopathic diseases included epilepsy, involution psychosis, cerebral lesions due to syphilis and arteriosclerosis, debility, imbecility, idiocy, and general paresis; constitutional diseases included manic depressive psychosis, cyclothemia, atypical states of degeneration and degenerative psychosis, schizophrenia, paranoid dementia, paraphrenia, and neurotic psychoses. Toxic and infectious psychoses included alcoholism, morphine addiction, and other "infectious psychoses." Ulysses Pernambucano and Helena Campos, "As doenças mentais entre os negros de Pernambuco," *AAPP* 2:1 (1932): 126.

55. Pernambucano, *A Assistencia*, 42.

56. Nelson Pires, "Estudo de um tipo de cidade—o malandro," *Neurobiologia* 1:1 (1938): 47–59. Brazilian street children are usually referred to as *moleques*.

57. Gonçalves Fernandes, "Uma concepção individual-analitica-associativa sobre o sentimento-de-inferioridade, o 'Edipo' e a delinquência," *Neurobiologia* 4:4 (1941): 187.

58. Fernandes, "Uma concepção"; Arthur Ramos, "A dinamica afetiva do filho mimado," *Neurobiologia* 1:3 (1938): 265–86; Nelson Pires, "As manobras anti-conceptionais, as neuroses e o adulteiro," *Neurobiologia* 1:3 (1938): 287–311.

59. Pernambucano and Campos, "As doenças mentais," 120.

60. Silva, "A anthropologia no exercito," quadro I; Pernambucano and Campos, "As doenças mentais," 122–23.

61. Pernambucano and Campos, "As doenças mentais," 123.

62. Ibid., 125–27.

63. Ibid., 127. In early-twentieth-century understandings of mental diseases, whites were believed to suffer more often from neurotic disorders, including neurasthenia. Gilman, *Difference and Pathology*, 199–204.

64. See Levine, *Pernambuco*, 12.

65. On the racial composition of Brazil's general population, see Skidmore, *Black into White*, 38–48, 52. On the racial composition of the Brazilian military, see Beattie, *Tribute of Blood*, 155–56, 257–58.

66. Ulysses Pernambucano, "As doenças mentaes entre os negros de Pernambuco," in *Estudos afro-brasileiros: trabalhos apresentados ao 1.o congresso afro-brasileiro reunido no Recife em 1934*, ed. Gilberto Freyre et al. (Rio de Janeiro: Editora Ariel, 1935), 93–98.

67. Ibid., 97.

68. Ibid., 94.

69. Freyre, *Sobrados e mucambos*, 351; as well as Freyre, *Masters and the Slaves*, 408–9.

70. Ulysses Pernambucano, "Estudo estatistico da paralisa geral," *AAPP* 3:2 (1933): 155–64.

71. Ibid., 158 (quote), 162.

72. Maria da Graça Araujo, "Os delirios eposodicos no Hospital de Alienados (Estudo estatistico)," *AAPP* 2:1 (1932): 134–37.

73. Ibid., 137.

74. João Marque de Sá, *Contribuição ao estudo do quociente intelectual dos epiléticos, tese de concurso para o cargo de médico da assistência a psicopatas* (Recife: Typographia da Empresa Jornal do Commercio S.A., 1936), Coleções Especiais, BPEP.

75. Ibid., 43–46, 60–61.

76. SAP research on schizophrenia is summarized in René Ribeiro, *As esquizofrenias: estudo estatistico e sua aplicação á higiene mental; tese para livre docente de clinica psiquiatrica na Faculdade de Medicina do Recife* (Recife: n. p., 1937), 70–71, Coleções Especiais, BPEP.

77. Ulysses Pernambucano, Arnaldo Di Lascio, Jarbas Pernambucano, and Almir Guimarães, "Alguns dados antropologicos da população do Recife," *AAPP* 5:1–2 (1935): 40–45.

78. Ibid., 41, 42.

79. Ibid., 40–42.

80. See "1.o Congresso da Juventude Proletaria, Estudantil, e Popular," *Folha do Povo* 1:31 (August 14, 1935); and Etelvino Lins de Albuquerque, Secretaria de Segurança Publica to Secretario do Interior, April 24, 1939, 3–4, Ulysses Pernambucano de Melo, Prontuário Individual, fundo SSP n. 3459, arq. 2, prontuário 1734, DOPS, APEP.

81. Ulysses Pernambucano de Melo, Prontuário Individual, fundo SSP n. 3459, arq. 2, prontuário 1734, DOPS, APEP. On the Intentona Comunista, see Homero Costa, *A insurreição comunista de 1935: Natal—o primeiro ato da tragédia* (São Paulo: Ensaio; Rio Grande do Norte: Cooperativa Cultural Universitária do Rio Grande do Norte, 1995).

82. Alcides Codeceira was appointed as the second director of the mental hygiene service in 1936. Pernambucano was labeled a communist and hounded by the police and the right-wing press until his death in 1944. Levine, *Pernambuco,* 71–72.

83. The *AAPP,* the official publication of the Pernambucan government's Serviço da Assistencia a Psicopatas, ceased publication in 1936. *Neurobiologia,* although not subsidized by the Pernambucan government, published research and articles by SAP psychiatrists and researchers.

84. Ulysses Pernambucano and Arnaldo Di Lascio, "Estudo estatistico das doenças mentais encontradas em quatrocentos primeiros internados em casa de saúde particular," *Neurobiologia* 3:4 (1940): 503.

85. Luiz Cerqueira, "Incidencia das psicopatias nos leporrinos, mesorrinos e platirrinos da Bahia e Sergipe," *Neurobiologia* 7:1–2 (1944): 26.

86. Freyre, *Nordeste,* 189.

87. Cunha-Lopes and J. Candido de A. Reis, "Ensaio ethno-psychiatrico sobre negros e mestiços (nota prévia)," in *Estudos afro-brasileiros,* ed. Freyre et al., 17–20; Freyre, *Sobrados e mucambos,* 350; and Freyre, *Mansions and the Shanties,* 408.

88. Freyre, *Nordeste,* 189.

89. On Candomblé, see Dale T. Graden, "'So Much Superstition among These People!': Candomblé and the Dilemmas of Afro-Bahian Intellectuals, 1864–1871," 57–73; and Michel Agier, "Between Affliction and Politics: A Case Study of Bahian Candomblé," 134–57, both in *Afro-Brazilian Culture and Politics: Bahia, 1790s–1990s,* ed. Hendrik Kraay (Armonk, NY: M. E. Sharpe, 1998); and Leni Silverstein, "The Celebration of Our Lord of the Good End: Changing State, Church, and Afro-Brazilian Relations in Bahia," in *The Brazilian Puzzle: Culture on the Borderlands of the Western World,* ed. David J. Hess and Roberto A. DaMatta (New York: Columbia University Press, 1995), 134–51.

90. Aside from Raymundo Nina Rodrigues's work, Candomblé had received little attention from Pernambucan political elites and intellectuals until the 1920s.

91. J. C. Cavalcante Borges and Dinice C. Lima, "Investigações sobre as religiões no Recife: o espiritismo," *AAPP* 2:1 (1932), 138 (first quote), 145 (remaining quotes).

92. Pedro Cavalcanti, "As seitas africanas do Recife," in *Estudos afro-brasileiros,* ed. Freyre et al., 243–44.

93. Kim Butler discusses the ways in which Bahian artists, intellectuals, and researchers afforded Bahian *terreiros* a measure of protection from the police and government officials. Butler, *Freedoms Given,* 204–9.

94. Pedro Cavalcanti, "Contribuição ao estudos do estado mental dos mediums," *AAPP* 4:2 (1934): 135–45. Cavalcanti used the Pernambucan revision of the Binet-Simon-Terman test to determine IQ.

95. Cavalcanti, "Contribuição," 137–38.

96. Ibid., 143.

97. Ibid., 144.

98. Gonçalves Fernandes, "Investigações sobre os cultos negro-fetichistas do Recife," *AAPP* 5:1–2 (1935): 134.

99. Ibid., 132.

100. Quoted in ibid., 133; Ramos, *O negro brasileiro*, 198.

101. Fernandes, "Investigações," 133.

102. Ibid., 135.

103. Pernambuco, *Acto n.o 583 1931*, 21.

104. Pernambucano, *A Assistencia*, 48 (quote); Ulysses Pernambucano to Secretario de Justiça, Educação e Interior, November 11, 1931, Saúde Pública 1930 a 1932, n. 221, APEP.

105. Pernambucano, *A Assistencia*, 48.

106. José Lucena, "Espiritismo," filed with José Lucena to Director Geral da Assistencia Psychopathas (Ulysses Pernambucano), February 4, 1932, Saúde Pública, 1930 a 1932, n. 221, APEP.

107. José Lucena, "Meus caros ouvintes," filed with José Lucena to Director Geral da Assistencia Psychopathas (Ulysses Pernambucano), February 4, 1932, Saúde Pública, 1930 a 1932, n. 221, APEP.

108. Oscar Moreira Pinto to Ulysses Pernambucano, January 26, 1932, Saúde Pública, 1930 a 1932, n. 221, APEP.

109. Ulysses Pernambucano to Secretario de Justiça, Educação e Interior (Luis Delgado), February 5, 1932, Saúde Pública, 1930 a 1932, n. 221, APEP.

110. Costa, *A insurreição comunista;* Levine, *Vargas Regime*, 112–17, 138–58.

111. Alcides Codeceira, "Relatorio da assistencia a psicopatas de Pernambuco, no periodo de 1935," *AAPP* 6 (1936): 81.

112. On Magalhães's career and influence under Vargas see Levine, *Pernambuco*, 85–88; Levine, *Vargas Regime*, 150–52; Maria das Graças Andrade Ataíde de Almeida, *A construcção da verdade autoritária* (São Paulo: Humanitas/FFLCH/USP, 2001); and Pandolfi, *Pernambuco de Agamenon Magalhães*.

113. Agamemnon Magalhães, "O nordeste brasileiro," *BMTIC* 2:20 (1936): 251. Magalhães published the thesis in the federal labor ministry's journal in 1936.

114. Magalhães, "O nordeste brasileiro," 251 (first quote), 256 (second and third quotes).

115. Ibid., 248.

116. *Relatorio 1940*, 31; *Realizações do estado novo;* Levine, *Pernambuco*, 88. The federal constitution of 1937 required that religious instruction be offered in all primary, secondary, and normal schools. See Constituição do Estado Unidos do Brasil (de 10 de novembro de 1937), art. 133, www.planalto.gov.br/ccivil_03/Constituicao/ (accessed August 7, 2007).

117. *Relatorio 1940*, 31–32; Constituição 1937, art. 131. The Pernambucan government began to classify students according to physical development rather than IQ, mental age, or grades completed.

118. Also in 1938, the Mental Hygiene Service began to study the use of alcohol and marijuana among the practitioners of Candomblé as part of their efforts to understand altered mental states. See *Mensagem 1937*, 75–76; José Lucena, "Os fumadores de maconha em Pernambuco," *RMP* 5:9 (1935): 255–365, 5:10 (1935): 391–404, 5:11 (1935): 429–41, 5:12 (1935): 467–83; and Nestor Cesar, "Os males da maconha," *RMP* 15:10 (1945): 221–28.

119. *Relatorio 1940*, 151.

120. Freyre et al., *Estudos afro-brasileiros;* Gilberto Freyre et al., eds., *Novos estudos afro-brasileiros (segundo tomo): trabalhos apresentados ao 1.o congresso afro-brasileiro do Recife* (Rio de Janeiro: Civilização Brasileira, 1937).

121. *Relatorio 1940*, 150.

122. Ibid., 151.

123. *Realizações do estado novo.*

124. Hermano Vianna, *The Mystery of Samba: Popular Music and National Identity in Brazil* (Chapel Hill: University of North Carolina Press, 1999); Peter Wade, "Race and Nation in Latin America: An Anthropological View," in *Race and Nation in Modern Latin America*, ed. Appelbaum et al., 262–81.

125. Butler, *Freedoms Given*, 204.

126. On Brazilian millenarianism, see Diacon, *Millenarian Vision;* Levine, *Vale of Tears;* and Patricia R. Pessar, *From Fanatics to Folk: Brazilian Millenarianism and Popular Culture* (Durham: Duke University Press, 2004).

127. The popular response to Padre Cícero's death in 1934 heightened Pernambucan elites' anxiety about "popular religion." See Della Cava, *Miracle at Joaseiro.*

128. See Rodrigues, "A loucura epidemica," 50–77.

129. Pedro Cavalcanti, "Investigações sobre as religiões no Recife: uma seita panteista," *AAPP* 3:1 (1933): 58.

130. Ibid., 62–63.

131. Ibid., 63.

132. A similar event took place in 1897 in Bom Jardim, Pernambuco, led by José Guedes dos Santos Barbosa, who was committed to psychiatric care at the Asylo de Alienados in Pernambuco. See *Mensagem 1898,* 9.

133. José Lucena, "Uma pequena epidemia mental em Pernambuco: os fanaticos dos municípios de Panelas," *Neurobiologia* 3:1 (1940): 58.

134. Ibid., 61–73.

135. Ibid., 81, 82.

136. Ibid., 87.

137. Otavio de Freitas Júnior, "A noção de mana nas superstições do norte do Brasil," *Neurobiologia* 3:4 (1940): 505–7; Gonçalves Fernandes, "Ensaio analítico sôbre alguns tabus de conduta das populações do nordeste do Brasil," *Neurobiologia* 3:3 (1940): 257–61; Gonçalves Fernandes, "O temor fundamental á mulher e outros tabús de conduta nor-destinos," *Neurobiologia* 5:1 (1942): 20–24.

138. Fernandes, "O temor fundamental."

139. See Billy Jaynes Chandler, *The Bandit King: Lampião of Brazil* (College Station: Texas A&M University Press, 1978); Facó, *Cangaceiros e fanáticos.*

140. Fernandes, "O temor fundamental."

141. Fernandes, "Ensaio analítico," 260.

142. See Levine, *Vale of Tears,* 11–65; and Dain Borges, "A Mirror of Progress," in *The Brazil Reader: History, Culture, Politics,* ed. Robert M. Levine and John J. Crocitti (Durham: Duke University Press, 1999), 93–99.

143. Loreto, "A psiquiatria de Pernambuco," 26.

144. Levine, *Pernambuco,* 1–3; Luiz Cerqueira, "A ação social do serviço de assistencia a psicopatas de Sergipe," *Neurobiologia* 3:4 (1940): 437–44; J. da Costa Machado, "Con-tribuição ao estudo da assistencia ao doente mental no Rio Grande do Norte," *Neuro-biologia* 1:2 (1938): 204–11.

145. Costa Machado, "Contribuição ao estudo," 204.

146. Reported in Cerqueira, "A ação social," 438.

147. Gilberto Freyre, "Sociologia, psicologia e psiquiatria," *Neurobiologia* 4:1 (1941): 5, 16.

148. Ulysses Pernambucano, "A ação social do psiquiatria," *Neurobiologia* 6:4 (1943): 154.

149. *Estudos pernambucanos.* See also the issue of *Neurobiologia* dedicated to Pernambucano: *Neurobiologia* 8:4 (1945).

150. José Lucena, "Characteristicas da escola psiquiatrica orientada pelo prof. Ulysses Pernambucano," in *Estudos pernambucanos,* 21–25.

151. Ibid., 25.

152. Gilberto Freyre, "Os medicos e as reformas sociais em Pernambuco," in *Estudos pernambucanos,* 55.

153. Ibid., 57. Freyre ignored the contributions of other key figures in the Pernambucan public health movement, including José Octávio de Freitas and Amaury de Medeiros, because of their positions on race. Freyre chastised Freitas for propagating the idea that Africans brought deadly infectious diseases to Brazil during the slave trade and Medeiros, for advocating eugenics.

154. In her study of psychiatry in Porfirian Mexico, Cristina Rivera-Garza argues that "thus, by the early twentieth century, using the same body of European ideas, psychiatrists and social commentators alike referred to the mentally ill as dangerous individuals who imperiled the basis of modernity and the future of the nation at large." Cristina Rivera-Garza, "'She Neither Respected nor Obeyed Anyone': Inmates and Psychiatrists Debate Gender and Class at the General Insane Asylum La Castañeda, Mexico, 1910–1930," *HAHR* 81:3 (2001): 669.

155. Corrêa, "As ilusões da liberdade," 26.

Chapter 7. *Inventing the* Homem do Nordeste

1. Agamemnon Magalhães, "O Nordeste Brasileiro," *Folha da Manhã,* October 22, 1941, reprinted in Agamemnon Magalhães, *Idéias e lutas* (Recife: Editora Raiz, 1985), 287.

2. See Telles, *Race in Another America;* Livio Sansone, *Blackness without Ethnicity: Constructing Race in Brazil* (New York: Palgrave Macmillan, 2003); Hanchard, *Orpheus and Power;* French, "Missteps of Anti-Imperialist Reason"; and French, "Translation."

3. See Reis, *Slave Rebellion;* Reis, *Death Is a Festival;* and Butler, *Freedoms Given.*

4. See Nancy P. Appelbaum, "Post-Revisionist Scholarship on Race," *LARR* 40:3 (2005): 206–17; Nancy P. Appelbaum, "Whitening the Region: Caucano Mediation and Antioqueño Colonization in Nineteenth-Century Colombia," *HAHR* 79:4 (1999): 631–67; Appelbaum, *Muddied Waters: Race, Region, and Local History in Colombia, 1846–1948* (Durham: Duke University Press, 2003); Weinstein, "Racializing Regional Difference"; and Peter Wade, *Blackness and Race Mixture: The Dynamics of Racial Identity in Colombia* (Baltimore: Johns Hopkins University Press, 1993).

5. On elite justifications for preferring European rather than Brazilian workers, see Andrews, *Blacks and Whites,* 54–89; and Azevedo, *Onda negra.*

6. *Brancos* had increased from 34.6 to 41.2 percent of the population while *pardos* and *pretos* had decreased from 50.5 to 47.3 percent and from 14.9 to 11.5 percent of the population, respectively. Levine, *Pernambuco,* 12.

7. Skidmore, *Black into White,* 45.

8. Cited in ibid., 64–67.

9. Arthur Lobo da Silva quoted in Pernambucano and Campos, "As doenças mentais," 122–23; Pernambucano et al., "Alguns dados antropologicos."

10. This was, of course, impossible. If racial miscegenation was "improving" Africans and Indians, then surely it was having a detrimental effect on Europeans. This was but one of the many paradoxes of *branqueamento*.

11. *Caboclo* usually signified Indian and European ancestry, while *cafuso, mameluco,* and *cariboca* usually signified Indian and African ancestry.

12. The racial categories proposed by Roquette-Pinto included *phaiodermos* (*mulatos*), *leucodermos* (*brancos*), *xanthodermos* (*caboclos*), and *melanodermos* (*negros*). See Edgar Roquette-Pinto, "Prefacio," in *Estudos afro-brasileiros,* ed. Freyre et al., ii–iv. Although the federal government did not use official racial categories during the First Republic and the Vargas era, geographers employed by the federal government attempted to define and classify Brazilians according to their racial characteristics. See, e.g., Pierre Deffonaines, *Geografia humana do Brasil* (Rio de Janeiro: Instituto de Geografia e Estatística, Conselho Nacional de Geografia 1940); and Josué de Castro, *Geografia humana: estudo da paisagem cultural do mundo* (Pôrto Alegre: Edição da Livraria do Globo, 1939).

13. José Américo de Almeida employs the term *brejeiros* to describe coastal inhabitants. See Almeida, *A bagaceira.*

14. Pernambuco, *Mensagem apresentada ao congresso legislativo, em 7 de setembro de 1925, 2.a sessão da 12.a legislatura, pelo dr. Sergio Loreto, governador do estado de Pernambuco* (Recife: n.p., [1925]), 71–72, cx. 6, Mensagens,GEP, APEP.

15. Brazil, Inspectoria Federal de Obras Contras as Seccas, *Relatorio apresentado ao governo federal pela commissão imumbida de visitar as obras contra as seccas, que se estão executando no nordéste do Brasil* (Rio de Janeiro: Imprensa Nacional, 1923), in Fundação Guimarães Duque, *Memorial da seca,* 74.

16. See, e.g., Jeffrey Needell, "History, Race, and the State in the Thought of Oliveira Viana," *HAHR* 75:1 (1995): 1–30.

17. On the notion that elites' concerns with social and political stability often are expressed in racial language, see Eduardo A. Zimmermann, "Racial Ideas: and Social Reform: Argentina, 1890–1916," *HAHR* 72:1 (1992): 22–46.

18. See Eisenberg, *Sugar Industry.*

19. Freyre articulated the concept of racial democracy in 1963 in the English edition of *Sobrados e mucambos:* "For Brazil is becoming more and more a racial democracy, characterized by an almost unique combination of diversity and unity." Freyre, *Mansions and Shanties,* 431. This sentence did not appear in the original edition of *Sobrados e mucambos;* see Freyre, *Sobrados e mucambos,* 377; also Cruz, "Democracia racial." Beginning with UNESCO-sponsored studies of race carried out in the 1950s, the concept of racial democracy has been discredited as a sociologically valid interpretation of Brazilian race relations. See Fernando Henrique Cardoso and Octávio Ianni, *Côr e mobilidade social em Florianópolis* (São Paulo: Companhia Editora Nacional, 1960); Octávio Ianni, *Raças e classes sociais no Brasil,* 3rd ed. (São Paulo: Editora Brasiliense, 1987); Florestan Fernandes, *A integração do negro na sociedade de classes,* 2 vols., 3rd ed. (São Paulo: Editora Atica, 1978); Emília Viotti da Costa, *The Brazilian Empire: Myths and Histories* (Chicago: Dorsey Press, 1985), 234–46; and Andrews, *Blacks and Whites,* 6–10, 129–39.

20. Thomas Skidmore argues for the need to historicize Freyre's writing. Skidmore, "Raízes de Gilberto Freyre," 42–43.

21. See Jeffrey D. Needell, "Identity, Race, Gender, and Modernity in the Origins of Gilberto Freyre's *Oeuvre*," *American Historical Review* 100:1 (1995): 51–77; Vamireh Chacon, *Gilberto Freyre: uma biografia intelectual* (Recife: Fundação Joaquim Nabuco/ Editora Massangana; São Paulo: Companhia Editora Nacional, 1993); and Maria Lúcia Garcia Pallares-Burke, *Gilberto Freyre: um vitoriano dos trópicos* (São Paulo: Editora UNESP, 2005).

22. Gilberto Freyre, "Social Life in Brazil in the Middle of the Nineteenth Century," *HAHR* 5:4 (1922): 597, 602.

23. Ibid., 599, 601–2.

24. Ibid., 605.

25. Ibid., 603–4.

26. Ibid., 607.

27. Chacon, *Gilberto Freyre*, 199–200.

28. Oliveira Lima quoted in Freyre, "Vida social no Nordeste," 90.

29. Chacon, *Gilberto Freyre*, 174; Albuquerque Jr., *A invenção do nordeste*, 129–41. Américo's political career would lead him to support Getúlio Vargas and run as the official government candidate in the 1938 presidential elections, which were preempted by the coup d'état of 1937.

30. On São Paulo modernism, Mário de Andrade, Anita Malfatti, and Oswaldo de Andrade, see Daryle Williams, *Culture Wars in Brazil: The First Vargas Regime, 1930–1945* (Durham: Duke University Press, 2001), 39–42. On northeastern regionalism see Needell, "Identity," 59–61; and Barros, *A década 20*, 151–78.

31. See Williams, *Culture Wars in Brazil*, 26–48.

32. Barros, *A década 20*, 169; Needell, "Identity"; and Schwarz, *Misplaced Ideas*, 108–25.

33. Quoted in Joaquim Inojosa, *O movimento modernista em Pernambuco*, vol. 1 (Rio de Janeiro: Editôra Gráfica Tupy, 1968–1969), 183, 187.

34. Inojosa, *O movimento modernista*, 208–9.

35. Freyre exaggerated his role in organizing and leading the congress, later publishing a "Manifesto Regionalista" that was never, in fact, presented at the congress. Inojosa proves that Freyre's *manifesto* was in fact a paper delivered at the congress and later rewritten and retitled. See Inojosa, *O movimento modernista;* and Gilberto Freyre, *Manifesto regionalista de 1926* (Recife: Edições Região, 1952). Scholars generally agree with Inojosa's view, that Freyre exaggerated his role in the congress, but see Chacon, *Gilberto Freyre*, 183.

36. Inojosa, *O movimento modernista*, 257, 264.

37. Quoted in ibid., 231, 263.

38. Ibid., 263; Gilberto Freyre, "Ação regionalista no nordeste," *Diário de Pernambuco*, February 7, 1926, republished in Gilberto Freyre, *Tempo de aprendiz: artigos publicados em jornais na adolescência e na primeira mocidade do autor (1918–1926)*, vol. 2 (São Paulo: Instituto Brasileira de Difusão Cultural, 1979), 264–65.

39. Gilberto Freyre, "O nordeste separatista?" *Diário de Pernambuco*, March 26, 1926, republished in Freyre, *Tempo de aprendiz*, 277.

40. Inojosa, *O movimento modernista*, 260.

41. See Costa, *Brazilian Empire*, 234–48; Andrews, *Blacks and Whites*, 5–10; and Hanchard, *Orpheus and Power*, 43–44.

42. See Needell, "Identity," 62–63; Chacon, *Gilberto Freyre;* and Gilberto Freyre, *Tempo morto e outros tempos: trechos de um diário de adolescência e primeira mocidade, 1915–1930* (Rio de Janeiro: Livraria José Olympio Editora S.A., 1975), 236–37.

43. Needell, "Identity," 62; Gilberto Freyre, "Estácio Coimbra, governador de Pernambuco," in *Perfil de Euclides e outros perfis*, 2nd ed. (Rio de Janeiro: Record, 1987), 171–80.

44. Freyre, *Tempo morto,* 237.

45. Ibid., 213–14; and *Mensagem 1929,* 5–6.

46. Freyre, *Tempo morto,* 214.

47. Chacon, *Gilberto Freyre,* 201–20; Levine, *Pernambuco,* 71; Waldemar Valente, "Estácio Coimbra: a reforma Carneiro Leão e a sociologia na Escola Normal do Estado de Pernambuco," in *Estácio Coimbra: homem representativo do seu meio e do seu tempo,* ed. Gilberto Freyre et al. (Recife: Instituto Joaquim Nabuco de Pesquisas Sociais, 1973), 57–60.

48. In 1926, Freyre became the editor of the *Diário de Pernambuco,* a position he held until 1928, when he was appointed editor of *A Província* by Estácio Coimbra. Chacon, *Gilberto Freyre,* 200.

49. Freyre, *Tempo morto,* 241.

50. Ibid., 215.

51. Gilberto Freyre, "Estácio Coimbra: homem representativo," in *Estácio Coimbra,* ed. Freyre et al., 16.

52. Freyre, *Tempo morto,* 214–15.

53. Chacon, *Gilberto Freyre,* 201.

54. As Jeffrey Needell points out, Freyre frequently revised his main works, making it problematic to rely on later editions as representations of his earlier ideas. Needell, "Identity," 52. Wherever possible I have checked quotes from later English editions against the original Portuguese editions.

55. Freyre, *Masters and the Slaves,* 284–85.

56. Ibid., 399–400.

57. Freyre, *Nordeste,* 189.

58. Ibid., 165.

59. Ibid., 170 (emphasis added).

60. Ibid., 170–71, 174.

61. Freyre, *Mansions and the Shanties,* 407.

62. Freyre, *Nordeste,* 190. Freyre obtained the photograph from Ferraz and Lima Júnior, *A morfologia do homem.*

63. Freyre, *Masters and the Slaves,* 60; Freyre, *Casa-grande & senzala,* 152.

64. Freyre, *Masters and the Slaves,* 271.

65. Freyre, *Mansions and the Shanties,* 426.

66. Ibid., 245, 424.

67. Freyre believed that Brazilians and their racial progenitors were well suited to life in tropics, an idea he developed more fully in later writings. See Gilberto Freyre, *New World in the Tropics: The Culture of Modern Brazil* (New York: Vintage, 1959); Maria do Carmo Tavares de Miranda, *Homem, terra e região tropical: anais do v encontro regional de tropicologia* (Recife: Fundação Joaquim Nabuco, Editora Massangana, 1990); and Williams, *Culture Wars in Brazil,* 247–51.

68. Freyre, *Nordeste,* 29.

69. Freyre, *Sobrados e mucambos,* 373–74. *Cabeças chatas* (flat heads) is a pejorative term used to describe *nordestinos.*

70. Freyre, *Nordeste,* 9, 12.

71. Ibid., 200 (quote), 220.

72. Ibid., 191.

73. See Skidmore, *Black into White,* 190–92; Needell, "Identity"; Chacon, *Gilberto Freyre;* and Edson Nery da Fonseca, ed., *Casa-grande & senzala e a crítica brasileira de 1933 a 1944* (Recife: Companhia Editora de Pernambuco, 1985).

74. Prior to the development and institutionalization of the social sciences in Brazil, Freyre thought of himself as a scientist, and he believed himself competent to evaluate scientific research. He rejected Mendelian genetics and endorsed a neo-Lamarckian theory of the inheritance of acquired characteristics, a position adopted by many Brazilian intellectuals well into the 1940s. See Freyre, *Masters and the Slaves,* 287, 289–90; and Freyre, *Mansions and the Shanties,* 408–9, 416–17. On the popularity of neo-Lamarckianism in Latin America, see Stepan, *"Hour of Eugenics,"* 64–76.

75. The congress has received little attention from scholars, in part, because the Northeast is not generally regarded by scholars to have been at the center of debates about race, citizenship, and national identity in the twentieth century. Treatments of the congress include Levine, "First Afro-Brazilian Congress"; Levine, *Pernambuco,* 69–70; and Butler, *Freedoms Given,* 42–43.

76. Arthur Ramos, "Os mythos de Xangô e sua degradação no Brasil," in *Estudos afro-brasileiros,* ed. Freyre et al., 49–54; Edison Carneiro, "Xangô," 139–45; and Luiz da Camara Cascuso, "Notas sobre o catimbó," 75–129, both in *Novos estudos afro-brasileiros,* ed. Freyre et al.

77. Mário de Andrade, "A calunga dos maracatús," in *Estudos afro-brasileiros,* ed. Freyre et al., 39–47; and Jorge Amado, "'Bibliotheca do povo' e 'collecção moderna,'" in *Novos estudos afro-brasileiros,* ed. Freyre et al., 262–324.

78. Alfredo Brandão, "Os negros na historia de Alagôas," 55–91; Adhemar Vidal, "Tres seculos de escravidão na Parahyba," 105–52; Jovelino M. Camargo Júnior, "Abolição e suas causas," 153–70; Edison Carneiro, "Situação do negro no Brasil," 237–57, all in *Estudos afro-brasileiros,* ed. Freyre et al.; and Rodrigues de Carvalho, "Aspectos da influencia africana na formação social do Brasil," 15–74; Jovelino M. Camargo Júnior, "A Inglaterra e o trafico," 170–84, both in *Novos estudos afro-brasileiros,* ed. Freyre et al.

79. Gilberto Freyre, "O que foi o 1.o congreso afro-brasileiro do Recife," in *Novos estudos afro-brasileiros,* ed. Freyre et al., 348–52; and Freyre, *Masters and the Slaves,* 306–7.

80. Bastos de Avila, "Contribuição ao estudo do indice de Lapicque (nota prévia)," 29–38; and L. Robalinho Cavalcanti, "Longevidade (sua relação com os grupos ethnicos da população)," 99–103, both in in *Estudos afro-brasileiros,* ed. Freyre et al.; Bastos de Avila, "O negro em nosso meio escolar," in *Novos estudos afro-brasileiros,* ed. Freyre et al., 334–47.

81. Abelardo Duarte, "Grupos sanguineos da raça negra," 171–79; and Alvaro de Faria, "O problema da tuberculose no preto e no branco e relações de resistencia racial," 215–25, both in *Estudos afro-brasileiros,* ed. Freyre et al.

82. Leonidio Ribeiro, W. Berardinelli, and Isaac Brown, "Estudo biotypologico de negros e mulatos brasileiros normaes e delinquentes," in *Novos estudos afro-brasileiros,* ed. Freyre et al., 154–55.

83. Pernambucano, "As doenças mentaes," in *Estudos afro-brasileiros,* ed. Freyre et al, 97.
84. Cunha-Lopes and J. Candido de A. Reis, "Ensaio ethno-psychiatrico sobre *negros* e mestiços (nota prévia)," in *Estudos afro-brasileiros,* ed. Freyre et al., 18.
85. Antônio Austregesilo Lima, "A mestiçagem no Brasil como fator eugenico," in *Novos estudos afro-brasileiros,* ed. Freyre et al., 332.
86. Geraldo de Andrade, "Nota anthropologica sobre os mulatos pernambucanos," in *Estudos afro-brasileiros,* ed. Freyre et al., 261. Other researchers came to similar conclusions; see, e.g., Bastos de Avila, "O negro em nosso meio escolar," in *Novos estudos afro-brasileiros,* ed. Freyre et al., 334–47.
87. J. Robalinho Cavalcanti, "O recem-nascido branco, negro e mulato," in *Estudos afro-brasileiros,* ed. Freyre et al., 187–89.
88. Skidmore, *Black into White,* 179–84.
89. Lima, "A mestiçagem," 327.
90. Gilberto Freyre, "Deformações de corpo dos negros fugidos," in *Novos estudos afro-brasileiros,* ed. Freyre et al., 247–48.
91. Kim Butler argues that "the most popular topic of the papers was the effect of biological and physical characteristics on cultural behavior," while Robert Levine argues that the majority of the papers "focused on Afro-Brazilian folklore and culture." Butler, *Freedoms Given,* 42–43; Levine, "First Afro-Brazilian Congress," 188–89.
92. Camargo Júnior, "A Inglaterra e o trafico," 170–84; Carneiro, "Situação do negro no Brasil," 241.
93. Robert Levine argues that the congress did not touch in any substantive way on contemporary social and economic problems faced by Afro-Brazilians. Levine, "First Afro-Brazilian Congress," 189–90; Levine, *Pernambuco,* 69–70.
94. Freyre, "O que foi," 351.
95. Levine, "First Afro-Brazilian Congress," 187–88; Levine, *Pernambuco,* 70.
96. Pernambucano and Magalhães both occupied academic chairs at the Ginásio Pernambucano in the late 1920s, and the former served as director of the school beginning in 1928. Ulysses Pernambucano to exmo. sr. dr. secretario da justiça e negocios interiores, May 6, 1929, Secretária Geral, Inspectoria de Instrução Pública, Ginásio Pernambucano, pac. 232, APEP.
97. Magalhães, "O nordeste brasileiro," 2:20 (1936): 251.
98. Ibid., 256, 257.
99. Ibid.
100. Ibid., 277.
101. Agamemnon Magalhães, *O estado e a realidade contemporanea* ([Recife]: Officinas Graphicas do "Diario da Manhã," [1933]); Chacon, *Gilberto Freyre,* 266.
102. Magalhães, *O estado,* 7, 167–68.
103. Ibid., 177–78.
104. Ibid., 31, 59.
105. Alberto Torres, *O problema nacional brasileira: introducção a um programma de organização nacional,* 2nd ed. (São Paulo: Companhia Editora Nacional, Bibilotéca Pedagogica Brasileira, 1933), 61, quoted in ibid., 130–31. On Torres, see Skidmore, *Black into White,* 118–23.
106. See Edgar Teixeira Leite, "O problema do cangaço no nordeste," *RIAHGP* 83:155–58 (1933–1935): 27–41.

107. Lesser, *Welcoming the Undesirables;* Williams, *Culture Wars in Brazil,* 136–50, 232–37; Maria Luiza Tucci Carneiro, *O anti-semitismo na era Vargas: fantasmas de uma geração (1930–1945)* (São Paulo: Editora Perspectiva, 2001), 272–92; Gustavo Barroso, *Terra de sol (natureza e costumes do norte),* 3rd ed. (Rio de Janeiro: Livraria Francisco Alves, 1930 [1912]); Gustavo Barroso, *Heróes e bandidos (os cangaceiros de nordeste),* 2nd. ed. (Rio de Janeiro: Livraria Francisco Alves, 1931 [1917]); Gustavo Barroso, *Alma sertaneja (contos tragicos e sentimentaes do sertão)* (Rio de Janeiro: B. Costallat e Miccolis, 1923); and Gustavo Barroso, *O sertão e o mundo* (Rio de Janeiro: Livraria Leite Ribeiro, 1923).

108. Barroso, *Terra de sol,* 170.

109. Ibid., 122–23.

110. Barroso, *Heróes e bandidos,* 278. On Antônio Silvino, see Lewin, *Politics and Parentela,* 291–95.

111. Barroso, *Heróes e bandidos,* 18.

112. Ibid., 15, 35, 69.

113. Djacir Menezes, *O outro nordeste: formação social do nordeste* (Rio de Janeiro: Livraria José Olympio Editora, 1937), 177.

114. Ibid., 89, 176.

115. Hirschman, *Journeys toward Progress,* 37–50.

116. Getúlio Vargas, "O problema do nordeste e a ação do govêrno provisório (discurso pronunciado em Fortaleza, a 18 de setembro de 1933)," in *A nova política do Brasil,* vol. 2 (Rio de Janeiro: Livraria José Olympio Editora, 1938), 163–64.

117. Getúlio Vargas, "O açúcar e a industrialização do álcool (discurso pronunciado em Recife a 5 de setembro de 1933)," in *A nova política do Brasil,* 130.

118. Vargas, "O problema do nordeste," 163.

119. Getúlio Vargas, "A Paraíba na revolução e as obras contra as sêcas (discurso pronunciado em João Pessôa, a 8 de setembro de 1933)," in *A nova política do Brasil,* 152.

120. On migration from the Northeast to the South, see Thomas W. Merrick and Douglas H. Graham, *Population and Economic Development in Brazil, 1800 to the Present* (Baltimore: Johns Hopkins University Press, 1979), 118–45.

121. Thomaz Pompeu Sobrinho, "Terra das secas," *BIFOCS* 1:5 (1934): 210–19; Thomaz Pompeu Sobrinho, "O homem do nordeste," *BIFOCS* 1:6 (1934): 239–56; 2:1 (1934): 24–35; 2:2 (1934): 56–65.

122. Pompeu Sobrinho, "O homem do nordeste," 1:6 (1934): 242.

123. Pompeu Sobrinho, "Terra das secas," 211 (original emphasis).

124. Pompeu Sobrinho, "O homem do nordeste," 1:6 (1934): 241.

125. Ibid., 253.

126. Pompeu Sobrinho, "O homem do nordeste," 2:1 (1934): 32–35.

127. Ovidio da Cunha, "Introducção á africanologia brasileira," *BMTIC* 1:10 (1935): 253; Ovidio da Cunha, "Da individualidade da raça negra," *BMTIC* 4:38 (1937): 281–93; 4:39 (1937): 278–81.

128. Ovidio da Cunha, "Questões de sociologia regional," *BMTIC* 4:42 (1938): 273, 275.

129. della Cava, *Miracle at Joaseiro;* Ralph della Cava, "Brazilian Messianism and National Institutions: A Reappraisal of Canudos and Joaseiro," *HAHR* 48:3 (1968): 402–20; Gerald Michael Greenfield, "*Sertão* and *Sertanejo:* An Interpretive Context for Canudos," *LBR* 30:2 (1993): 35–45; Greenfield, "Great Drought"; and Greenfield, "Migrant Behavior."

130. Da Cunha, "Questões de sociologia regional," 275.

131. Da Cunha, "Introducção á africanologia brasileira," 291.

132. See Lesser, *Welcoming the Undesirables*, 10; and Schwarz, *Misplaced Ideas*.

133. Levine, *Pernambuco*, 85–87; and Levine, *Vargas Regime*, 139.

134. Compare, e.g., Campos and Macedo, "Contribuição á antropometria do escola recifense," 141, APEP; Andrade Lima Júnior, "O indice de Froes," *RMP* 8:3 (1938): 57–60; and Luiz Ignacio and Andrade Lima Júnior, "O indice ponderal," *RMP* 8:5 (1938): 111–16.

135. Andrade Lima Júnior and Luiz Ignacio, "O biotipo do escolar em Pernambuco," *Boletim de Educação* 5:7 (1936): 81.

136. Da Cunha, *Rebellion*, 84; da Cunha, *Os sertões*, 122.

137. Luiz Ignacio and Andrade Lima Júnior, "O indice torace-pelvico nos escolares do Recife," *RMP* 8:1 (1937): 25.

138. Alvaro Ferraz and Andrade Lima Júnior, *A morfologia do homem do nordeste (Estudo biotipologico)* (Rio de Janeiro: Livraria José Olympio Editora, 1939), 262–73.

139. Ferraz, "Educação fisica e reconstrução nacional," 50.

140. Ferraz and Lima Júnior, *A morfologia do homem*, 309; Ferraz, "Biotipos e trabalho agrário."

141. Ferraz and Lima Júnior, *A morfologia do homem*, 294–317.

142. Magalhães praised Ferraz and Lima's work as "laudable" and as "necessary for the improvement of soldiers' capacity and physical possibilities." *Relatorio 1940*, 169.

143. On Magalhães's administration of Pernambuco, see Maria Neto, "'O importante não é falar'"; Almeida, *A construção da verdade autoritária;* and Pandolfi, *Pernambuco de Agamenon Magalhães.*

144. Quoted in *Relatorio 1940*, 151. See also Levine, "First Afro-Brazilian Congress"; and Levine, *Pernambuco*, 190.

145. *Relatorio 1940*, 151; *Realizações do estado novo.*

146. *Relatorio 1940*, 149–50.

147. Pernambuco, "Conferencia do exmo. e revmo. dom Augusto Alvaro da Silva, arcebisbo da Baía e primaz do Brasil, no Teatro Santa Isabel," in Pernambuco, *Comemoração do cincoentenario da abolição: discursos oficiais* (Pernambuco: [Imprensa Oficial], 1938), 32.

148. *Realizações do estado novo.*

149. Vianna, *Mystery of Samba;* Bryan McCann, *Hello, Hello Brazil: Popular Music in the Making of Modern Brazil* (Durham: Duke University Press, 2004), 59–62.

150. *Mensagem 1925*, 45.

151. *Mensagem 1927*, 5.

152. *Mensagem 1936*, 131.

153. *Mensagem 1926*, 116, 119.

154. *Mensagem 1936*, 67–68.

155. Quoted in Melchiades da Rocha, *Bandoleiros das catingas* (Rio de Janeiro: Francisco Alves, 1988 [1942]), 47–49.

156. Agamemnon Magalhães, *Correio da Manhã*, July 31, 1938, quoted in Rocha, *Bandoleiros das catingas*, 118.

157. *Relatorio 1940*, 149.

158. Ibid., 148.

159. Ibid., 28.

160. Schwartzman, Bomeny, and Costa, *Tempos de Capanema,* 189–219.

161. *Relatorio 1940,* 28, 31.

162. *Realizações do estado novo.*

163. *Programas de educação primaria.*

164. Zélia de Oliveira Gominho, *Veneza americana x mucambópolis: o estado novo na cidade do Recife (décadas de 30 e 40)* (Recife: Companhia Editora de Pernambuco, 1998); Pandolfi, *Pernambuco de Agamenon Magalhães;* Almeida, *A construção da verdade autoritária.*

165. Comissão Censitaria dos Mucambos do Recife, "Os mucambos do Recife," *BMTIC* 5:60 (1939): 245.

166. Comissão Censitaria dos Mucambos do Recife, *Observações estatisticas sobre os mucambos do Recife, baseadas no censo efetuado pela comissão censitaria dos mucambos criada pelo dec. n.o 182 de 17 de setembro de 1938* (Recife: Imprensa Oficial, 1939), 7–22, APEP.

167. Comissão Censitaria dos Mucambos do Recife, "Os mucambos do Recife," 245.

168. *Realizações do estado novo.*

169. *Relatorio da Liga Social contra o Mocambo 1939 a 1943,* 8–12.

170. Ibid., 13.

171. Lilia Moritz Schwarcz argues that northeastern intellectuals and politicians had failed to keep up with recent developments in racial theory. Schwarcz, *O espetáculo das raças,* 183–88.

172. Wade, *Blackness and Race Mixture;* Vianna, *Mystery of Samba.*

173. Joseph and Nugent, eds., *Everyday Forms of State Formation;* Stepan, *"Hour of Eugenics";* Skidmore, *Black into White;* Telles, *Race in Another America;* Weinstein, "Racializing Regional Difference"; Lesser, *Welcoming the Undesirables;* Lesser, *Negotiating National Identity;* Appelbaum, *Muddied Waters;* and Wade, *Blackness and Race Mixture.*

174. Coronil, *Magical State,* 8.

175. On the Frente Negra, see Hanchard, *Orpheus and Power,* 104–9; and Butler, *Freedoms Given,* 113–28.

176. On Brazilians' adoption of European political and intellectual ideas, see Schwarz, *Misplaced Ideas,* 19–32.

177. See Andrews, *Blacks and Whites,* 90–121.

178. Wade, *Blackness and Race Mixture;* Appelbaum, *Muddied Waters;* Weinstein, "Racializing Regional Difference"; Woodard, "Regionalismo paulista."

179. See Weinstein, "Racializing Regional Difference," 245–26.

180. Ibid., 243, 256.

181. Wade, "Race and Nation"; Wade, *Blackness and Race Mixture,* 335–50; Peter Wade, *Music, Race, and Nation: Música Tropical in Colombia* (Chicago: University of Chicago Press, 2000), 3–7, 141; Appelbaum, *Muddied Waters,* 207–8. On homogeneity and heterogeneity in Brazilian culture and national identity in the 1930s, see Vianna, *Mystery of Samba.*

182. Appelbaum, *Muddied Waters,* 207–8.

183. Weinstein, "Racializing Regional Difference," 240.

184. As Peter Wade has argued in the case of Colombia, the idealization of the *mestizo* and rejection of "blackness" and "Indianness" are, in fact, complementary racial ideals. Wade, *Blackness and Race Mixture,* 19.

185. Lesser, *Welcoming the Undesirables;* Lesser, *Negotiating National Identity;* Garfield, *Indigenous Struggle.*

186. See Jane Schneider, ed., introduction to *Italy's Southern Question: Orientalism in One Country* (Oxford: Berg, 1998), 1–23; René Girard, *The Scapegoat* (Baltimore: Johns Hopkins University Press, 1986); and Edward W. Said, *Orientalism* (New York: Vintage, 1979).

187. On changing conceptions of Brazilian citizenship in the twentieth century, see Carvalho, *Cidadania no Brasil.*

GLOSSARY

agreste: Semiarid interior zone of the Northeast
alagoano: Native of Alagoas
aldeia: Indian village, or simply a village
amazonense: Native of Amazonas
bacharel: Graduate of a law or medical school
baiano: Native of Bahia
bandeirante: Colonial-era pioneer from São Paulo
barão: Baron; a title of nobility granted in nineteenth-century Brazil
braço: Worker
branco: White, or individual of white European racial ancestry
branqueamento: The concept of racial whitening
brejeiro: Native of coastal *brejos*, or marshlands
caboclo: Individual of mixed Indian and European ancestry
cabra: Individual of mixed African, European, and Indian ancestry
cafuso: Individual of mixed Indian and African ancestry
caipira: Native of southern rural interior
Candomblé: Afro-Brazilian religion based on African antecedents
cangaceiro: Rural bandit of the Northeast
carioca: Native of Rio de Janeiro
cearense: Native of Ceará
colono: Colonist
comarca: Juridical division of territory
conto: Brazilian currency in use to 1942; equivalent to one thousand *mil-réis*
coronel: Rural political boss; rank of colonel in the national guard
coronelismo: Exercise of political power by *coronéis*
desembargador: Appellate court judge
emancipado: Emancipated slave
engenho: Sugar mill
escravo: Slave
fazenda: Large estate, plantation, or ranch

flagelado: Afflicted one; drought victim
gaúcho: Native of Rio Grande do Sul; cowboy
homem do Nordeste: Man of the Northeast
índio: Indian
ingênuo: Child born to a slave mother
Intentona Comunista: 1935 Communist uprising in Natal, Recife, and Rio de Janeiro
interventor: Federally appointed state governor(s) who served from 1930 to 1945
irmãos: Brothers; followers or practitioners of spiritism
jagunço: Rural ruffian; a participant in the Canudos rebellion
Jéca Tatú: Fictional character in Monteiro Lobato's *Urupês* (1918); rural *paulista*
lavrador: Sharecropper; cane farmer
liberto: Freed or manumitted slave
litoral: Coastal region
mameluco: Individual of mixed Indian and European ancestry
maranhense: Native of Maranhão
mato: Woods or jungle
matuto: Backwoodsman who lives in *mato*
mestiço: Individual of mixed racial ancestry
mil-réis: Brazilian currency in use to 1942; equivalent to one thousand *reis*
mineiro: Native of Minas Gerais
mocambo: Runaway slave community; urban self-help housing in Recife
mulato: Mulatto, or an individual of black and white racial ancestry
município: County or municipality; capital of same
negro: Black; individual of black African racial ancestry
Nordeste: Northeast
nordestino: Native of northeastern Brazil
Norte: North
paraense: Native of Pará
paraibano: Native of Paraíba
pardo: Brown; individual of mixed black and white racial ancestry
paulista: Native of São Paulo
pernambucano: Native of Pernambuco
piauiense: Native of Piauí
povo: The people; the poor and working classes
prefeito: Mayor; political chief of *município*
quilombo: Settlement of runaway slaves
recôncavo: Coastal sugar-growing region
retirante: Quitter; drought refugee
romeiro: Follower of Padre Cícero Romão Batista
salvações: Federal military interventions to replace state political machines in Ceará, Alagoas, Pernambuco, and Sergipe in 1911–1912
seca: Drought
seita: Afro-Brazilian religious congregation
senzala: Slave quarters
sergipano: Native of Sergipe
sertanejo: Native of the *sertão*

sertão: Arid interior zone of the Northeast; backlands
Sul: South
tabaréu: Military recruit; rural northeasterner
tenente: Lieutenant
terras devolutas: Government-controlled public lands
terreiros: Physical spaces where religious rituals are performed
usina: Sugar refinery
vaqueiro: Northeastern cowboy
visitadora: Visiting nurse or public health worker
zona da mata: Coastal sugar-growing zone of the Northeast

BIBLIOGRAPHY

Archives and Libraries

Arquivo Departamento de Ordem Política e Social, Arquivo Público Estadual de Pernambuco. Recife.
Arquivo Público Estadual de Pernambuco. Recife.
Biblioteca Blanche Knopf, Fundação Joaquim Nabuco. Recife.
Biblioteca da Faculdade de Direito do Recife. Recife.
Biblioteca Pública Estadual de Pernambuco, Coleções Especiais. Recife.
Center for Research Libraries. Chicago.
Rockefeller Foundation Archives, Rockefeller Archive Center. North Tarrytown, NY.

Books, Articles, and Theses

Abreu e Lima. "Aspectos atuais da assistencia maternal." *RMP* 11:8 (1941): 204–9.
Agier, Michel. "Between Affliction and Politics: A Case Study of Bahian Candomblé." In *Afro-Brazilian Culture and Politics: Bahia, 1790s–1990s,* edited by Hendrik Kraay, 134–57. Armonk, NY: M. E. Sharpe, 1998.
Albuquerque Jr., Durval Muniz de. *A invenção do nordeste e outras artes.* Recife: Fundação Joaquim Nabuco/Editora Massangana, 1999.
———. "Weaving Tradition: The Invention of the Brazilian Northeast." *Latin American Perspectives* 31:2 (2004): 42–61.
Alencar, José de. *Iracema.* São Paulo: Editora Ática, 1992 [1865].
———. *O Guaraní.* São Paulo: Editora Ática S.A., 1992 [1857].
Almeida, José Américo de. *A bagaceira.* 21st ed. Rio de Janeiro: Livraria José Olympio Editora, 1980 [1928].
———. *Trash.* London: Peter Owen, 1978.
Almeida, Maria das Graças Andrade Ataíde de. *A construção da verdade autoritária.* São Paulo: Humanitas/FFLCH/USP, 2001.
Alonso, Ana María. *Thread of Blood: Colonialism, Revolution, and Gender on Mexico's Northern Frontier.* Tucson: University of Arizona Press, 1995.

Altino, Edgar. "Lição de abertura do curso de medicina publica pelo professor dr. Edgar Altino." *RAFDR* 26 (1918): 71–80.

Anderson, Warwick. *The Cultivation of Whiteness: Science, Health, and Racial Destiny in Australia.* New York: Basic Books, 2003.

———. "The Trespass Speaks: White Masculinity and Colonial Breakdown." *American Historical Review* 102:5 (1997): 1343–70.

———. "Where Is the Postcolonial History of Medicine?" *Bulletin of the History of Medicine* 72:3 (1998): 522–30.

Andrade, Geraldo de. "Anthropometria das classes domesticas de Pernambuco (Memoria apresentada ao 4.o Congresso Brasileiro de Hygiene, reunida na Bahia em janeiro de 1928)." *JMP* 24:8 (1928): 121–33.

———. *Contribuição ao estudo da antropologia social em suas relações com a hygiene em Pernambuco.* Recife: Imprensa Official, 1929.

———. "Hygiene do trabalho e registro de sanidade." *RMP* 1:6 (1931): 241–44.

———. "Hygiene do trabalho em Pernambuco." *RMP* 1:7 (1931): 318–35.

———. "Primogeniture e mortalidade infantil em Recife." In *Annaes do quinto congresso de hygiene Recife, 17 a 22 de outubro de 1929, volume II sessões plenarias,* 267–80. Rio de Janeiro: Officinas Graphicas da Inspectoria de Demographia Sanitaria, 1930.

———. "Em torno do indice cephalico horizontal." *RMP* 1:1 (1931): 81–97.

———. "Verificações biometricas em Pernambuco." *JMP* 24:9 (1928): 151–56.

Andrade, Lessa de. "Relatório dos trabalhos realisados pelos postos de higiêne em 1940." *Arquivos da Diretoria de Higiene do Interior* 3:1 (1941): 1–7.

Andrade, Manuel Correia de. *A guerra dos cabanos.* Rio de Janeiro: Conquista, 1965.

———. "Introdução." In *Os quebra-kilos e a crise da lavoura,* by Henrique Augusto Milet, 7–25. 2nd ed. São Paulo: Global, 1987 [1876].

———. *The Land and People of Northeast Brazil.* Albuquerque: University of New Mexico Press, 1980.

Andrews, George Reid. *Blacks and Whites in São Paulo, Brazil, 1888–1988.* Madison: University of Wisconsin Press, 1991.

Annaes do 4.o Congresso brasileiro de geographia, reunido na cidade de Recife de 7 a 17 de Setembro de 1915. 3 vols. Pernambuco: Imprensa Official, 1916.

Antunes, José Leopoldo Ferreira. *Medicina, leis e moral: pensamento médico e comportamento no Brasil (1870–1930).* São Paulo: Fundação Editora da UNESP, 1999.

Appelbaum, Nancy P. *Muddied Waters: Race, Region, and Local History in Colombia, 1846–1948.* Durham: Duke University Press, 2003.

———. "Post-Revisionist Scholarship on Race." *LARR* 40:3 (2005): 206–17.

———. "Whitening the Region: Caucano Mediation and Antioqueño Colonization in Nineteenth-Century Colombia." *HAHR* 79:4 (1999): 631–67.

———, Anne S. Macpherson, and Karin Alejandra Rosemblatt, eds. *Race and Nation in Modern Latin America.* Chapel Hill: University of North Carolina Press, 2003.

Applegate, Celia. "A Europe of Regions: Reflections on the Historiography of Sub-National Places in Modern Times." *American Historical Review* 104:4 (1999): 1157–82.

Araujo, Maria da Graça. "Os delirios eposodicos no Hospital de Alienados (Estudo estatistico)." *AAPP* 2:1 (1932): 134–37.

Armas, Diego, ed. *Disease in the History of Modern Latin America: From Malaria to AIDS.* Durham: Duke University Press, 2003.

Aureliano, João. "A alienação mental como causa de divorcio ou desquite." *AAPP* 5:1 (1935): 1–5.

———. "As diretrizes da higiene mental." *AAPP* 4:1 (1934): 47–52.

———. "Do exame medico pre-nupcial." *AAPP* 4:2 (1934): 130–34.

Azevedo, Celia Maria Marinho de. *Onda negra, medo branco: o negro no imaginário das elites, seculo XIX.* Rio de Janeiro: Paz e Terra, 1987.

Barbosa, José Policarpo de Araújo. *História da saúde pública do Ceará: da colônia a Vargas.* Fortaleza: Edições UFC, 1994.

Barman, Roderick J. "The Brazilian Peasantry Reexamined: The Implications of the Quebra-Quilo Revolt, 1874–1975." *HAHR* 57:3 (1977): 401–24.

———. *Citizen Emperor: Pedro II and the Making of Brazil, 1825–91.* Stanford: Stanford University Press, 1999.

Barreto, Anita Paes. "Estudo psicotecnico de quatro supernormais." *AAPP* 2:1 (1932): 60–69.

———. "A organização de classes homogeneas nas escolas primarias." *Neurobiologia* 3:4 (1940): 275–94.

———. "Revisão pernambucana da escala métrica de inteligencia Binet-Simon-Terman." *Neurobiologia* 6:4 (1943): 161–73.

———. "Uma teste de inteligencia," *AAPP* 2:2 (1932): 151–62.

Barros, Gouveia de. *Programma sanitario em Pernambuco.* Recife: Imprensa Industrial, 1921.

Barros, Paulino. "O 'Facies' medico da mortalidade infantil no interior." *RMP* 9:8 (1939): 221–28.

Barros, Souza. *A década 20 em Pernambuco (uma interpretação).* 2nd ed. Recife: Fundação de Cultura, Cidade do Recife, 1985.

Barroso, Gustavo. *Alma sertaneja (contos tragicos e sentimentaes do sertão).* Rio de Janeiro: B. Costallat & Miccolis, 1923.

———. *Heróes e bandidos (os cangaceiros de nordeste).* 2nd ed. Rio de Janeiro: Livraria Francisco Alves, 1931 [1917].

———. *O sertão e o mundo.* Rio de Janeiro: Livraria Leite Ribeiro, 1923.

———. *Terra de sol (natureza e costumes do norte).* 3rd ed. Rio de Janeiro: Livraria Francisco Alves, 1930 [1912].

Beattie, Peter M. *The Tribute of Blood: Army Honor, Race, and Nation in Brazil, 1864–1945.* Durham: Duke University Press, 2001.

Benchimol, Jaime Larry, ed. *Febre amarela: a doença e a vacina, uma história inacabada.* Rio de Janeiro: Editora Fiocruz, 2001.

Béringer, Emilio. *Estudos sobre o clima e a mortalidade da capital de Pernambuco (Brazil).* Pernambuco: Typographia Commercial, 1891.

Besse, Susan K. "Crimes of Passion: The Campaign against Wife Killing in Brazil, 1910–1940." *Journal of Social History* 22:4 (1989): 653–66.

———. *Restructuring Patriarchy: The Modernization of Gender Inequality in Brazil, 1914–1940.* Chapel Hill: University of North Carolina Press, 1996.

Beverley, John, José Oviedo, and Michael Aronna, eds. *The Postmodernism Debate in Latin America.* Durham: Duke University Press, 1995.

Beviláqua, Clovis. "Applicações do darwinismo ao direito." *RAFDR* 7 (1897): 117–32.

———. *Esboços e fragmentos.* Rio de Janeiro: Laemmert e Cia., 1899.

————. *Historia da Faculdade de Direito do Recife: 11 de agosto de 1827, 11 de agosto de 1927.* 2 vols. Rio de Janeiro: Livraria Francisco Alves, 1927.

————. "Notas sobre a criminalidade no estado do Ceará (ao desembargador Pedro de Queiróz)." *RAFDR* 1:2 (1891): 157–77.

Bieber, Judy. *Power, Patronage, and Political Violence: State Building on a Brazilian Frontier, 1822–1889.* Lincoln: University of Nebraska Press, 1999.

————. "Race, Resistance, and Regionalism: Perspectives from Brazil and Spanish America." *LARR* 32:3 (1997): 152–68.

————. "When Liberalism Goes Local: Nativism and Partisan Identity in the Sertão Mineiro, Brazil, 1831–1850." *LBR* 37:2 (2000): 75–93.

Black, Edwin. *War against the Weak: Eugenics and America's Campaign to Create a Master Race.* New York: Thunder's Mouth Press, 2004.

Bliss, Katherine Elaine. *Compromised Positions: Prostitution, Public Health, and Gender Politics in Revolutionary Mexico City.* University Park: Pennsylvania State University Press, 2001.

————. "The Science of Redemption: Syphilis, Sexual Promiscuity, and Reformism in Revolutionary Mexico City." *HAHR* 79:1 (1999): 1–40.

Borges, Dain. *The Family in Bahia, Brazil, 1870–1945.* Stanford: Stanford University Press, 1992.

————. "A Mirror of Progress." In *The Brazil Reader: History, Culture, Politics,* edited by Robert M. Levine and John J. Crocitti, 93–99. Durham: Duke University Press, 1999.

————. "'Puffy, Ugly, Slothful, and Inert': Degeneration in Brazilian Social Thought, 1880–1940." *JLAS* 25:2 (1993): 235–56.

————. "The Recognition of Afro-Brazilian Symbols and Ideas, 1890–1940." *LBR* 32:2 (1995): 59–78.

————. "Salvador's 1890s: Paternalism and Its Discontents." *LBR* 30:2 (1993): 47–57.

Borges, J. C. Cavalcante, and Dinice C. Lima. "Investigações sobre as religiões no Recife: o espiritismo." *AAPP* 2:1 (1932): 138–45.

Bourdieu, Pierre, and Loïc Wacquant. "On the Cunning of Imperialist Reason." *Theory, Culture & Society* 16:1 (1999): 41–58.

Brito, Francisco Saturnino Rodrigues de. *Saneamento de Recife: descrição e relatorios.* 2 vols. Recife: Typ. da "Imprensa Official," 1917.

Bruno, Anibal. "Uma programma de politica educacional: exposição apresentada ao exmo. sr. Secretario do Interior de Pernambuco." *Boletim de Educação* 4 (1934): 5–75.

Burns, E. Bradford. *A History of Brazil.* 3rd ed. New York: Columbia University Press, 1993.

Butler, Kim D. *Freedoms Given, Freedoms Won: Afro-Brazilians in Post-Abolition São Paulo and Salvador.* New Brunswick, NJ: Rutgers University Press, 1998.

Caldas, Celso. "Aumento da mortalidade em Bom Jardim e causas determinantes." *RMP* 4:6 (1934): 202–14.

Campos, Alda. "Revisão da escala Binet-Simon-Terman." *AAPP* 2:1 (1932): 84–87.

————. "Revisão da escala Binet-Simon-Terman: teste de vocabulario aplicado a criança de 8 a 14 anos." *AAPP* 2:2 (1932): 163–68.

Campos, Gil de, and Armando Macedo. "Contribuição á antropometria do escola recifense." In *Anuário do Departamento de Saúde Publica: anno II, 1933,* Estado de Pernambuco, 135–42. Recife: Imprensa Industrial, 1934.

Canclini, Néstor García. "Contradictory Modernities and Globalisation in Latin America." In *Through the Kaleidoscope: The Experience of Modernity in Latin America*, edited by Vivian Schelling, 37–52. London: Verso, 2000.

———. *Hybrid Cultures: Strategies for Entering and Leaving Modernity*. Minneapolis: University of Minnesota Press, 1995.

Cardoso, Eleyson. *Instrucções geraes para os guardas do serviço de febre amarella*. Rio de Janeiro: Typ. dos "Annaes," 1931.

Cardoso, Fernando Henrique, and Octávio Ianni. *Côr e mobilidade social em Florianópolis*. São Paulo: Companhia Editora Nacional, 1960.

Carneiro, Maria Luiza Tucci. *O anti-semitismo na era Vargas: fantasmas de uma geração (1930–1945)*. São Paulo: Editora Perspectiva, 2001.

Carvalho, José Murilo de. *Os bestializados: o Rio de Janeiro e a república que não foi*. 3rd ed. São Paulo: Companhia das Letras, 1991.

———. *Cidadania no Brasil: o longo caminho*. 2nd ed. Rio de Janeiro: Civilização Brasileira, 2002.

———. *A construção da ordem: a elite política imperial—Teatro de sombras: a política imperial*. Rio de Janeiro: Civilização Brasileira, 2003.

Castiglione, Teodolino. *A eugenia no direito de família: o código civil brasileiro e a lei sôbre a organização e proteção da família perante a eugenia*. N.p.: Livraria Acadêmica Saraiva & Cia., 1942.

Castro, Josué de. *Alimentação e raça*. Rio de Janeiro: Civilização Brasileira, 1936.

———. *As condições de vida das classes operarias no Recife: estudo economico de sua alimentação*. Rio de Janeiro: Departamento de Estatistica e Publicidade, Ministerio do Trabalho, Industria e Commercio, 1935.

———. *Geografia da fome: a fome no Brasil*. Rio de Janeiro: Emprêsa Gráfica "O Cruziero," 1946.

———. *Geografia humana: estudo da paisagem cultural do mundo*. Pôrto Alegre: Edição da Livraria do Globo, 1939.

———. "O problema fisiologico da alimentação no Brasil." Tése de Concurso para a Faculdade de Medicina do Recife, 1932.

Castro Santos, Luiz Antonio de. "Power, Ideology, and Public Health in Brazil, 1889–1930." PhD dissertation, Harvard University, 1986.

———, and Lina Rodrigues de Faria. *A reforma sanitária no Brasil: ecos da primeira república*. Bragança Paulista: EDUSF, 2003.

Caulfield, Sueann. "Getting into Trouble: Dishonest Women, Modern Girls, and Women-Men in the Conceptual Language of *Vida policial*, 1925–1927." *Signs* 19:1 (1993): 146–76.

———. *In Defense of Honor: Sexual Morality, Modernity, and Nation in Early-Twentieth-Century Brazil*. Durham: Duke University Press, 2000.

Cavalcanti, Beatriz. "A inteligencia espacial e o teste de 'puzzle.'" *AAPP* 2:2 (1932): 169–77.

Cavalcanti, Pedro. "Contribuição ao estudos do estado mental dos mediums." *AAPP* 4:2 (1934): 135–45.

———. "Investigações sobre as religiões no Recife: uma seita panteista." *AAPP* 3:1 (1933): 58–63.

Cavalcanti, Pedro, and Helena Campos. "Descoberta de crianças anormais do meio escolar do Recife." *AAPP* 2:2 (1932): 211–21.

Cerqueira, Luiz. "A ação social do serviço de assistencia a psicopatas de Sergipe." *Neurobiologia* 3:4 (1940): 437–44.

———. "Incidencia das psicopatias nos leporrinos, mesorrinos e platirrinos da Bahia e Sergipe." *Neurobiologia* 7:1–2 (1944): 18–38.

Cesar, Nestor. "Os males da maconha." *RMP* 15:10 (1945): 221–28.

Chacon, Vamireh. *Gilberto Freyre: uma biografia intelectual.* Recife: Fundação Joaquim Nabuco/Editora Massangana; São Paulo: Companhia Editora Nacional, 1993.

Chalhoub, Sidney. *Cidade febril: cortiços e epidemias na corte imperial.* São Paulo: Companhia das Letras, 1996.

———. *Visões da liberdade: uma história das últimas décadas da escravidão na corte.* São Paulo: Companhia das Letras, 1990.

Chandler, Billy Jaynes. *The Bandit King: Lampião of Brazil.* College Station: Texas A&M University Press, 1978.

Chasteen, John Charles. "Fighting Words: The Discourse of Insurgency in Latin American History." *LARR* 28:3 (1993): 83–111.

Chaves, Nelson. *O problema alimentar do nordeste brasileiro (introdução ao seu estudo econômico social).* Recife: Livraria Editora Medico Cientifica, 1946.

Codeceira, Alcides. "Relatorio da assistencia a psicopatas de Pernambuco, no periodo de 1935." *AAPP* 6 (1936): 80–81.

Comissão Censitaria dos Mucambos do Recife. "Os mucambos do Recife." *BMTIC* 5:60 (1939): 224–51.

Conrad, Robert. *The Destruction of Brazilian Slavery, 1850–1888.* Berkeley: University of California Press, 1972.

Coronil, Fernando. *The Magical State: Nature, Money, and Modernity in Venezuela.* Chicago: University of Chicago Press, 1997.

Corrêa, Mariza. "As ilusões da liberdade: a escola Nina Rodrigues e a antropologia no Brasil." PhD dissertation, Universidade de São Paulo, 1982.

Costa, Emília Viotti da. *The Brazilian Empire: Myths and Histories.* Chicago: Dorsey Press, 1985.

Costa, Homero. *A insurreição comunista de 1935: Natal—o primeiro ato da tragédia.* São Paulo: Ensaio; Rio Grande do Norte: Cooperativa Cultural Universitária do Rio Grande do Norte, 1995.

Costa, Jurandir Freire. *História da psiquiatria.* 4th ed. Rio de Janeiro: Xenon, 1989.

———. *Ordem médica e norma familiar.* 4th ed. Rio de Janeiro: Edições Graal, 1999.

Costa, Veloso. *Medicina, Pernambuco e tempo.* Recife: Universidade Federal de Pernambuco, 1978.

Coutinho, Cirene. "Padronização do 'Northumberland mental test.'" *AAPP* 3:2 (1933): 101–10.

———. "O problema dos deficientes em Recife." *AAPP* 5:1 (1935): 6–11, and 5:2 (1935): 8–9.

Crandall, Roderic. *Geographia, geologia, supprimento d'agua, transportes e açudagem nos estados orientaes do norte do Brazil, Ceará, Rio Grande do Norte, Parahyba.* Rio de Janeiro: Inspectoria de Obras Contra as Seccas, 1910.

Cruz, Levy. "Democracia racial: uma hipótese." In *Evocações e interpretações de Gilberto Freyre,* edited by Fátima Quintas, 349–67. Recife: Fundação Joaquim Nabuco/Editora Massangana, 2003.

Cruz Costa, João. *A History of Ideas in Brazil: The Development of Philosophy in Brazil and the Evolution of National History.* Berkeley: University of California Press, 1964.

Cueto, Marcos, ed. *Missionaries of Science: The Rockefeller Foundation and Latin America.* Bloomington: Indiana University Press, 1994.

―――, ed. *Salud, cultura y sociedad en América Latina.* Lima: IEP/Organización Panamericana de la Salud, 1996.

Cunha, Corrheiro da. "Hygiene: o ensino da hygiene na Europa." *RAFDR* 4 (1894): 111–22.

Cunha, Euclydes da. *Canudos: diario de uma expedição.* Rio de Janeiro: Livraria José Olympio, 1939.

―――. *À margem da história.* 5th ed. Porto: Livraria Lello e Irmao, 1941.

―――. *Rebellion in the Backlands (Os Sertões).* Translated by Samuel Putnam. Chicago: University of Chicago Press, 1944.

―――. *Os sertões.* 38th ed. Rio de Janeiro: Francisco Alves, 1997.

Cunha, Ovidio da. "Da individualidade da raça negra." *BMTIC* 4:38 (1937): 281–93, 4:39 (1937): 278–81.

―――. "Geographia humana das seccas." *BMTIC* 3:28 (1937): 297–301

―――. "Introducção á africanologia brasileira." *BMTIC* 1:8 (1935): 361–75, 1:9 (1935): 286–64, 1:10 (1935): 253–64.

―――. "Introducção á anthropogeographia sertaneja." *BMTIC* 2:21 (1936): 278–85.

―――. "Questões de sociologia regional." *BMTIC* 4:42 (1938): 263–76.

―――. "Sistematica da geografia humana." *BMTIC* 6:72 (1940): 271–82.

Cury, Maria Zila Ferreira. "Os sertões, de Euclides da Cunha: espaços." *LBR* 41:1 (2004): 71–79.

Dávila, Jerry. *Diploma of Whiteness: Race and Social Policy in Brazil, 1917–1945.* Durham: Duke University Press, 2003.

Dean, Warren. *Rio Claro: A Brazilian Plantation System, 1820–1920.* Stanford: Stanford University Press, 1976.

Deffonaines, Pierre. *Geografia humana do Brasil.* Rio de Janeiro: Instituto de Geografia e Estatística, Conselho Nacional de Geografia, 1940.

Degler, Carl N. *Neither Black nor White: Slavery and Race Relations in Brazil and the United States.* Madison: University of Wisconsin Press, 1971.

della Cava, Ralph. "Brazilian Messianism and National Institutions: A Reappraisal of Canudos and Joaseiro." *HAHR* 48:3 (1968): 402–20.

―――. *Miracle at Joaseiro.* New York: Columbia University Press, 1970.

Diacon, Todd A. *Millenarian Vision, Capitalist Reality: Brazil's Contestado Rebellion, 1912–1916.* Durham: Duke University Press, 1991.

―――. *Stringing Together a Nation: Cândido Mariano da Silva Rondon and the Construction of a Modern Brazil, 1906–1930.* Durham: Duke University Press, 2004.

Dias, Publio. "Escola, estudo de um edificio e inspeção medias dos escolares, visando principalmente a nutrição, dentes, opilação." *RMP* 3:3 (1933): 67–83.

Dimas, Antonio, Jacques Leenhardt, and Sandra Jatahy Pesavento, eds. *Reinventar o Brasil: Gilberto Freyre entre história e ficção.* Porto Alegre: Editora da UFRGS, 2006.

Directoria de Hygiene de Pernambuco. "Editorial." *Archivos de Hygiene Publica e Medicina Tropical* 1:1 (1915): 2.

Domingues, Aurelio. "Memoria apresentada á Sociedade de Medicina de Pernambuco em conferencia realisada em 12 de julho de 1933." *JMP* 29:11 (1933): 192–202.

Eakin, Marshall C. "Race and Identity: Sílvio Romero, Science, and Social Thought in Late 19th Century Brazil." *LBR* 22:2 (1985): 151–74.

Eisenberg, Peter L. "Abolishing Slavery: The Process on Pernambuco's Sugar Plantations." *HAHR* 52:4 (1972): 580–97.

———. *The Sugar Industry in Pernambuco, 1840–1910: Modernization without Change.* Berkeley: University of California Press, 1974.

Ellis, Alfredo. *"Race de gigantes": a civilização no planalto paulista.* São Paulo: Editorial Helios, 1926.

Engelstein, Laura. "Combined Underdevelopment: Discipline and the Law in Imperial and Soviet Russia." *American Historical Review* 98:2 (1993): 338–53.

Estudos pernambucanos dedicados a Ulysses Pernambucano. N.p., [1944].

Ettling, John. *The Germ of Laziness: Rockefeller Philanthropy and Public Health in the New South.* Cambridge, MA: Harvard University Press, 1981.

Facó, Rui. *Canagceiros e fanáticos: gênese e lutas.* Rio de Janeiro: Editôra Civilização Brasileira, 1963.

Fausto, Boris. *A Concise History of Brazil.* Cambridge: Cambridge University Press, 1999.

Fernandes, Florestan. *A integração do negro na sociedade de classes.* 2 vols. 3rd ed. São Paulo: Editora Atica, 1978.

Fernandes, Gonçalves. "Uma concepção individual-analitica-associativa sobre o sentimento-de-inferioridade, o 'Edipo' e a delinquência." *Neurobiologia* 4:4 (1941): 180–88.

———. "Ensaio analítico sôbre alguns tabus de conduta das populações do nordeste do Brasil." *Neurobiologia* 3:3 (1940): 257–61.

———. "Investigações sobre os cultos negro-fetichistas do Recife." *AAPP* 5:1–2 (1935): 87–135.

———. "O temor fundamental á mulher e outros tabús de conduta nordestinos." *Neurobiologia* 5:1 (1942): 20–24.

Ferraz, Alvaro. "Biotipos e trabalho agrário." *Neurobiologia* 8:2 (1945): 146–52.

———. "Debilidade fisica e desnutrição dos colegiais." *Neurobiologia* 1:3 (1939): 317–26.

———. "Educação fisica e reconstrução nacional." *Neurobiologia* 4:1 (1941): 44–54.

———. "A idade na formação dos contingentes militares." *Neurobiologia* 2:3 (1939): 237–46.

Ferraz, Alvaro, and Gonçalves Fernandes. "Organização do serviço de antropologia nas penitenciarias do Estado de Pernambuco." *Neurobiologia* 3:4 (1940): 488–96.

Ferraz, Alvaro, and Andrade Lima Junior. *A morfologia do homem do nordeste (Estudo biotipologico).* Rio de Janeiro: Livraria José Olympio Editora, 1939.

———. "A morphologia do normotypo do nordeste." *BMTIC* 3:31 (1937): 280–302.

Ferrer, Ada. *Insurgent Cuba: Race, Nation, and Revolution, 1868–1898.* Chapel Hill: University of North Carolina Press, 1999.

Finchelstein, Federico. "The Anti-Freudian Politics of Argentine Fascism: Anti-Semitism, Catholicism, and the Internal Enemy, 1932–1945." *HAHR* 87:1 (2007): 77–110.

Fonseca, Edson Nery da, ed. Casa-grande & senzala *e a crítica brasileira de 1933 a 1944.* Recife: Companhia Editora de Pernambuco, 1985.

Foucault, Michel. *The Birth of the Clinic: An Archaeology of Medical Perception.* New York: Vintage, 1994.

———. *Discipline and Punish: The Birth of the Prison.* New York: Vintage, 1979.

———. *Madness and Civilization: A History of Insanity in the Age of Reason.* New York: Vintage, 1988.

Freitas, Celso Arcoverde de. "Matrimonio precoce e maternidade conciente." *JMP* 31:9 (1935): 138–46.

Freitas, José Octávio de. *O clima e a mortalidade da cidade do Recife.* Recife: Imprensa Industrial, 1905.

———. *Doenças africanas no Brasil.* São Paulo: Companhia Editora Nacional, 1935.

———. *História da Faculdade de Medicina do Recife, 1895 a 1943.* Recife: Imprensa Oficial, 1944.

———. "Saúde publica e providencias sanitarias: palestra lida no Rotary Club do Recife." *JMP* 31:11 (1935): 161–68.

———. *Os trabalhos de hygiene em Pernambuco: relatorio apresentado ao secretario geral do estado.* Recife: Officinas Graphicas da Imprensa Official, 1919.

Freitas Jr., Otavio de. "A noção de mana nas supertições do norte do Brasil." *Neurobiologia* 3:4 (1940): 505–7.

French, John D. *The Brazilian Workers' ABC: Class Conflict and Alliances in Modern São Paulo.* Chapel Hill: University of North Carolina Press, 1992.

———. "The Missteps of Anti-Imperialist Reason: Bourdieu, Wacquant and Hanchard's *Orpheus and Power.*" *Theory, Culture & Society* 17:1 (2000): 107–28.

———. "Translation, Diasporic Dialogue, and the Errors of Pierre Bourdieu and Loïc Wacquant." *Nepantla: Views from South* 4:2 (2003): 375–89.

Freyre, Gilberto. *Casa-grande & senzala.* 2 vols. 4th ed. Rio de Janeiro: Livraria José Olympio, 1943.

———. *Manifesto regionalista de 1926.* Recife: Edições Região, 1952.

———. *The Mansions and the Shanties (Sobrados e mucambos): The Making of Modern Brazil.* Berkeley: University of California Press, 1986.

———. *The Masters and the Slaves (Casa-grande & senzala): A Study in the Development of Brazilian Civilization.* Berkeley: University of California Press, 1986.

———. "Os medicos e as reformas sociais em Pernambuco." In *Estudos pernambucanos dedicados a Ulysses Pernambuco,* 55–57. N.p., [1944].

———. *New World in the Tropics: The Culture of Modern Brazil.* New York: Vintage, 1959.

———. *Nordeste: aspectos da influencia da canna sobre a vida e a paizagem do nordeste do Brasil.* Rio de Janeiro: Livraria José Olympio Editora, 1937.

———. *Perfil de Euclides e outros perfis.* 2nd ed. Rio de Janeiro: Record, 1987.

———. *Sobrados e mucambos: decadencia do patriarchado rural no Brasil.* São Paulo: Companhia Editora Nacional, 1936.

———. "Social Life in Brazil in the Middle of the Nineteenth Century." *HAHR* 5:4 (1922): 597–630.

———. "Sociologia, psicologia e psiquiatria." *Neurobiologia* 4:1 (1941): 3–16.

———. *Tempo de aprendiz: artigos publicados em jornais na adolescência e na primeira mocidade do autor (1918–1926).* 2 vols. São Paulo: Instituto Brasileira de Difusão Cultural, 1979.

————. *Tempo morto e outros tempos: trechos de um diário de adolescência e primeira mocidade 1915–1930.* Rio de Janeiro: Livraria José Olympio Editora S.A., 1975.

————. "Vida social no Nordeste: aspectos de um seculo de transição." In *Livro do Nordeste: commemorativo do primeiro centenario do Diario de Pernambuco, 1825–1925,* 75–90. Recife: Officinas do Diario de Pernambuco, 1925.

Freyre, Gilberto, et al. *Estácio Coimbra: homem representativo do seu meio e do seu tempo.* Recife: Instituto Joaquim Nabuco de Pesquisas Sociais, 1973.

————. *Estudos afro-brasileiros: trabalhos apresentados ao 1.o congresso afro-brasileiro realizado no Recife, em 1934.* Rio de Janeiro: Editora Ariel, 1935.

————. *Novos estudos afro-brasileiros (segundo tomo): trabalhos apresentados ao 1.o congresso afro-brasileiro do Recife.* Rio de Janeiro: Civilização Brasileira, S.A., 1937.

Fry, Peter. "Politics, Nationality, and the Meanings of 'Race' in Brazil." *Daedalus* 129:2 (2000): 83–118.

Fundação Guimarães Duque. *Memorial da seca.* Mossoró: Coleção Mossoroense, 1981.

Galloway, J. H. "The Last Years of Slavery on the Sugar Plantations of Northeastern Brazil." *HAHR* 51:4 (1971): 586–605.

————. "The Sugar Industry of Pernambuco during the Nineteenth Century." *Annals of the Association of American Geographers* 58:2 (1968): 285–303.

Gama, Lauro Lins. *Contribuição ao estudo da mortalidade infantil em Recife (causa-mortis e fatores determinantes).* Recife: Tipografia the Propagandist, 1938.

Garfield, Seth. *Indigenous Struggle at the Heart of Brazil: State Policy, Frontier Expansion, and the Xavante Indians, 1937–1988.* Durham: Duke University Press, 2001.

Giddens, Anthony. *The Consequences of Modernity.* Stanford: Stanford University Press, 1990.

Gilberto Freyre: sua ciência, sua filosofia, sua arte. Rio de Janeiro: José Olympio, 1962.

Gilman, Sander L. *Difference and Pathology: Stereotypes of Sexuality, Race, and Madness.* Ithaca: Cornell University Press, 1985.

————. *Disease and Representation: Images of Illness from Madness to AIDS.* Ithaca, NY: Cornell University Press, 1988.

Girard, René. *The Scapegoat.* Translated by Yvonne Freccero. Baltimore: Johns Hopkins University Press, 1986.

Goldstein, Jan. "Framing Discipline with Law: Problems and Promises of the Liberal State." *American Historical Review* 98:2 (1993): 364–75.

Gominho, Zélia de Oliveira. *Veneza americana x mucambópolis: o estado novo na cidade do Recife (décadas de 30 e 40).* Recife: Companhia Editora de Pernambuco, 1998.

Gould, Stephen Jay. *The Mismeasure of Man.* New York: Norton, 1996.

Graden. Dale T. "'So Much Superstition among These People!': Candomblé and the Dilemmas of Afro-Bahian Intellectuals, 1864–1871." In *Afro-Brazilian Culture and Politics: Bahia, 1790s–1990s,* edited by Hendrik Kraay, 57–73. Armonk, NY: M. E. Sharpe, 1998.

Graham, Richard. *Patronage and Politics in Nineteenth-Century Brazil.* Stanford: Stanford University Press, 1990.

Greenfield, Gerald Michael. "The Great Drought and Elite Discourse in Imperial Brazil." *HAHR* 72:3 (1992): 375–400.

————. "Migrant Behavior and Elite Attitudes: Brazil's Great Drought, 1877–1879." *The Americas* 43:1 (1986): 69–85.

———. *The Realities of Images: Imperial Brazil and the Great Drought.* Philadelphia: American Philosophical Society, 2001.

———. "Sertão and Sertanejo: An Interpretive Context for Canudos." *LBR* 30:2 (1993): 35–45.

Grinberg, Keila. *O fiador dos brasileiros: cidadania, escravidão e direito civil no tempo de Antonio Pereria Rebouças.* Rio de Janeiro: Civilização Brasileira, 2002.

Guimarães, Bernardo. *O garimpeiro.* Rio de Janeiro: H. Garnier, 1921 [1872].

Guimarães, Fábio de Macedo Soares. "Divisão regional do Brasil." *Revista Brasileira de Geografia* 3:2 (1941): 318–73.

Guy, Donna. *Sex and Danger in Buenos Aires: Prostitution, Family, and Nation in Argentina.* Lincoln: University of Nebraska Press, 1991.

———. *White Slavery and Mothers Alive and Dead: The Troubled Meeting of Sex, Gender, Public Health, and Progress in Latin America.* Lincoln: University of Nebraska Press, 2000.

Haberly, David T. *Three Sad Races: Racial Identity and National Consciousness in Brazilian Literature.* Cambridge: Cambridge University Press, 1983.

Hale, Charles A. "Political Ideas and Ideologies in Latin America, 1870–1930." In *Ideas and Ideologies in Twentieth Century Latin America,* edited by Leslie Bethell, 148–78. Cambridge: Cambridge University Press, 1996.

Hall, Anthony L. *Drought and Irrigation in North-East Brazil.* Cambridge: Cambridge University Press, 1978.

Hall, Stuart, David Held, Don Hubert, and Kenneth Thompson, eds. *Modernity: An Introduction to Modern Societies.* Oxford: Blackwell, 1996.

Hanchard, Michael George. *Orpheus and Power: The Movimento Negro of Rio de Janeiro and São Paulo, Brazil, 1945–1988.* Princeton: Princeton University Press, 1994.

Hecht, Tobias. *At Home in the Street: Street Children of Northeastern Brazil.* Cambridge: Cambridge University Press, 1998.

Hendricks, Howard Craig. "Education and Maintenance of the Social Structure: The Faculdade de Direito do Recife and the Brazilian Northeast, 1870–1939." PhD dissertation, State University of New York at Stony Brook, 1977.

———, and Robert M. Levine. "Pernambuco's Political Elite and the Recife Law School." *The Americas* 37:3 (1981): 291–313.

Herschmann, Micael M., and Carlos Alberto Messeder Pereira, eds. *A invenção do Brasil moderno: medicina, educação e engenharia nos anos 20–30.* Rio de Janeiro: Rocco, 1994.

Hirschman, Albert O. *Journeys toward Progress: Studies of Economic Policy-Making in Latin America.* New York: Twentieth Century Fund, 1963.

Hobsbawm, Eric. *Bandits.* Rev. ed. New York: Pantheon Books, 1969.

———. *Primitive Rebels: Studies in Archaic Forms of Social Movement in the 19th and 20th Centuries.* New York: Norton, 1965.

Hochman, Gilberto. *A era do saneamento: as bases da política de saúde pública no Brasil.* São Paulo: Editora Hucitec/Anpocs, 1998.

———, and Diego Armus, eds. *Cuidar, controlar, curar: ensaios históricos sobre saúde e doença na América Latina e Caribe.* Rio de Janeiro: Editora Fiocruz, 2004.

Hoffnagel, Marc Jay. "From Monarchy to Republic in Northeast Brazil: The Case of Pernambuco, 1868–1895." PhD dissertation, Indiana University, 1975.

Huggins, Martha Knisely. *From Slavery to Vagrancy in Brazil: Crime and Social Control in the Third World.* New Brunswick, NJ: Rutgers University Press, 1985.

Ianni, Octávio. *Raças e classes sociais no Brasil.* 3rd ed. São Paulo: Editora Brasiliense, 1987.

Ignacio, Luiz. "Electrocardiografia na educação física dos nossos escolares." *Archivos do Serviço de Anthropologia e Medicina Escolar* in *Boletim de Educação* (1936): 90–95.

Ignacio, Luiz, and Andrade Lima Júnior. "A capacidade vital entre os escolares do Recife." *RMP* 9:6 (1939): 165–72.

———. "Estatura dos escolares masculinos de Recife." *RMP* 8:7 (1938): 146–49.

———. "O indice ponderal." *RMP* 8:5 (1938): 111–16.

———. "O indice torace-pelvico nos escolares do Recife." *RMP* 8:1 (1937): 21–25.

———. "Relações fundamentais de Viola nos escolares do Recife." *RMP* 8:8 (1938): 169–75.

Inojosa, Joaquim. *O movimento modernista em Pernambuco.* 3 vols. Rio de Janeiro: Editôra Gráfica Tupy, 1968–1969.

Jameson, Fredric. *Postmodernism, or, The Cultural Logic of Late Capitalism.* Durham: Duke University Press, 1991.

Johnson, Adriana M. C. "Subalternizing Canudos." *Modern Language Notes* 120 (2005): 355–82.

Joseph, Gilbert M. "On the Trail of Latin American Bandits: A Reexamination of Peasant Resistance." *LARR* 25:3 (1990): 7–54.

———. *Revolution from Without: Yucatán, Mexico, and the United States, 1880–1924.* Durham: Duke University Press, 1988.

———, and Daniel Nugent, eds. *Everyday Forms of State Formation: Revolution and the Negotiation of Rule in Modern Mexico.* Durham: Duke University Press, 1994.

Kamin, Leon J. "The Pioneers of IQ Testing." In *The Bell Curve Debate: History, Documents, Opinions,* edited by Russell Jacoby and Naomi Glauberman, 476–509. New York: Times Books, 1995.

Karasch, Mary C. *Slave Life in Rio de Janeiro, 1808–1850.* Princeton: Princeton University Press, 1987.

Kelner, Salomão, et al. *História da Faculdade de Medicina do Recife, 1915–1985.* Recife: Universidade Federal de Pernambuco, Centro de Ciências da Saúde, 1985.

Kevles, Daniel J. *In the Name of Eugenics: Genetics and the Uses of Human Heredity.* Cambridge, MA: Harvard University Press, 1995.

King, Desmond. *In the Name of Liberalism: Illiberal Social Policy in the United States and Britain.* Oxford: Oxford University Press, 1999.

Kittleson, Roger A. *The Practice of Politics in Postcolonial Brazil: Porto Alegre, 1845–1895.* Pittsburgh: University of Pittsburgh Press, 2006.

Klein, Herbert S., and Francisco Vidal Luna. "Free Colored in a Slave Society: São Paulo and Minas Gerais in the Early Nineteenth Century." *HAHR* 80:4 (2000): 913–41.

Knight, Alan. "Racism, Revolution, and *Indigenismo*: Mexico, 1910–1940." In *The Idea of Race in Latin America, 1870–1940,* edited by Richard Graham, 71–113. Austin: University of Texas Press, 1990.

Koshar, Rudy. "Foucault and Social History: Comments on 'Combined Underdevelopment.'" *American Historical Review* 98:2 (1993): 354–63.

Kosminsky, Ethel Volfzon, Claude Lépine, and Fernanda Arêas Peixoto, eds. *Gilberto Freyre em quatro tempos*. Bauru, São Paulo: EDUSC, 2003.

Kraut, Alan. *Silent Travelers: Germs, Genes, and the "Immigrant Menace."* New York: Basic Books, 1994.

Lasso, Marixa. *Myths of Harmony: Race and Republicanism during the Age of Revolution, Colombia 1795–1831*. Pittsburgh: University of Pittsburgh Press, 2007.

Leão, Antônio Carneiro. "Conferencia proferida pelo sr. A. Carneiro Leão, na Associação Brasileira de Educação." In *Organização da educação no estado de Pernambuco (justificação, lei organica, explicação e commentarios, opinião associações e da imprensa)*, Pernambuco, 163–91. Recife: Imprensa Official, 1929.

———. *A sociedade rural: seus problemas e sua educação*. Rio de Janeiro: Editôra S.A. A Noite, [1937].

Leão, Laurindo. "Analogias sociaes." *RAFDR* 7 (1897): 69–115.

———. "A questão do criminoso nato, do seu typo e da sua interpretação." *RAFDR* 21 (1913): 67–138.

Leite, Edgar Teixeira. "O problema do cangaço no nordeste." *RIAHGP* 83:155–58 (1933–1935): 27–41.

Lenharo, Alcir. *Sacralização da política*. Campinas: Papirus, 1986.

Lessa, Origenes. "Rehabilitação do negro." *BMTIC* 11:126 (1945): 295–312.

Lesser, Jeffrey. *Negotiating National Identity: Immigrants, Minorities, and the Struggle for Ethnicity in Brazil*. Durham: Duke University Press, 1999.

———. *Welcoming the Undesirables: Brazil and the Jewish Question*. Berkeley: University of California Press, 1995.

Levine, Robert M. "The First Afro-Brazilian Congress: Opportunities for the Study of Race in the Brazilian Northeast." *Race* 15:2 (1973): 185–93.

———. "'Mud-Hut Jerusalem': Canudos Revisited." In *The Abolition of Slavery and the Aftermath of Emancipation in Brazil*, edited by Rebecca J. Scott et al., 119–66. Durham: Duke University Press, 1988.

———. *Pernambuco in the Brazilian Federation, 1887–1937*. Stanford: Stanford University Press, 1978.

———. *Vale of Tears: Revisiting the Canudos Massacre in Northeastern Brazil, 1893–1897*. Berkeley: University of California Press, 1992.

———. *The Vargas Regime: The Critical Years, 1934–1938*. New York: Columbia University Press, 1970.

Lewin, Linda. "The Oligarchical Limitations of Social Banditry in Brazil: The Case of the 'Good' Thief Antônio Silvino." In *Bandidos: The Varieties of Latin American Banditry*, edited by Richard Slatta, 67–96. New York: Greenwood Press, 1987.

———. *Politics and Parentela in Paraíba: A Case Study of Family-Based Oligarchy in Brazil*. Princeton: Princeton University Press, 1987.

Lima Júnior, Andrade. "Educação fisica nos escolares de Recife." *RMP* 8:2 (1938): 28–32.

———. "O indice de Froes." *RMP* 8:3 (1938): 57–60.

Lima Júnior, Andrade, and Luiz Ignacio. "O biotipo do escolar em Pernambuco." *Boletim de Educação* 5:7 (1936): 79–89.

———. "Os biotipos antagonicos e a nutrição entre os escolares do Recife." *RMP* 8:11 (1938): 288–293.

Lima, Eronides da Silva. *Mal de fome e não de raça: gênese, constituição e ação política da educação alimentar Brasil—1934–1946*. Rio de Janeiro: Editora Fiocruz, 2000.

Lima, Matheus de. "A hygiene do alietamento." *JMP* 24:7 (1928): 105–6.

Lima, Nísia Trindade. *Um sertão chamado Brasil: intelectuais e representação geográfica da identidade nacional*. Rio de Janeiro: Editora Revan/IUPERJ, 1999.

———, and Nara Britto. "Salud y nacíon: propusta para el saneamiento rural: un estudio de la revista Saúde (1918–1919)." In *Salud, cultura y sociedad en América Latina*, edited by Marcos Cueto, 147–56. Lima: IEP/Organización Panamericana de la Salud, 1996.

Lins, Meira. "Nos horizontes da pediatria." *RMP* 2:3 (1932): 89–99.

Lins e Silva, Augusto. "Eugenia e crime." *RMP* 1:12 (1931): 750–75.

———. "Influencia de clima e de molestia no typo anthropologico brasileiro (excerto da memoria apresentada ao 4.o Congresso Brasileiro de Geographia reunido em Pernambuco, em setembro de 1915)." *RAFDR* 29 (1921): 205–13.

———. "Lição inaugural de abertura de curso pelo livre-docente de medicina publica." *RAFDR* 26 (1918): 123–32.

Lôbo, Jorge. "Eugenica (conferencia realizada na sociedade de internos de Recife)." *JMP* 29:6 (1933): 99–114.

Lomnitz-Adler, Claudio. *Deep Mexico, Silent Mexico: An Anthropology of Nationalism*. Minneapolis: University of Minnesota Press, 2001.

———. *Exits from the Labyrinth: Culture and Ideology in the Mexican National Space*. Berkeley: University of California Press, 1992.

Lorenzo, Helena Carvalho de, and Wilma Peres da Costa, eds. *A década de 1920 e as origens do Brasil moderno*. São Paulo: Editora da UNESP, 1997.

Loreto, Galdino. "A psiquiatria de Pernambuco nos últimos cem anos." *Neurobiologia* 49:1 (1986): 17–36.

Love, Joseph L. *Rio Grande do Sul and Brazilian Regionalism, 1882–1930*. Stanford: Stanford University Press, 1971.

———. *São Paulo in the Brazilian Federation, 1889–1937*. Stanford: Stanford University Press, 1980.

Löwy, Ilana. "Representação e intervenção em saúde pública: vírus, mosquitos e especialistas da Fundação Rockefeller no Brasil." *História, Ciências, Saúde—Manguinhos* 5:3 (1998–1999): 647–77.

Lucena, José. "Characteristicas da escola psiquiatrica orientada pelo prof. Ulysses Pernambucano." In *Estudos pernambucanos dedicados a Ulysses Pernambucano*, 21–25. N.p., [1944].

———. "Os fumadores de maconha em Pernambuco." *RMP* 5:9 (1935): 255–365, 5:10 (1935): 391–404, 5:11 (1935): 429–41, 5:12 (1935): 467–83.

———. "Uma pequena epidemia mental em Pernambuco: os fanaticos dos municípios de Panelas." *Neurobiologia* 3:1 (1940): 41–91.

———, and Lourdes Pais Barreto. "Nivel de inteligencia e desenvolvimento fisico (Estudo experimental)." *AAPP* 2:1 (1932): 128–32.

Lunbeck, Elizabeth. *The Psychiatric Persuasion: Knowledge, Gender, and Power in Modern America*. Princeton: Princeton University Press, 1994.

Lutz, Adolpho, and Astrogildo Machado. "Viagem pelo rio S. Francisco e por alguns dos seus afluentes entre Pirapora e Joazeiro." *Memorias do Instituto Oswaldo Cruz* 7:1–2 (1915): 5–50.

Luz, Madel T. *Medicina e ordem política brasileira: políticas e instituições de saúde (1850–1930)*. Rio de Janeiro: Edições Graal, 1982.

Machado, Dulphe Pinheiro. "O conselho nacional de imigração e o amparo aos nordestinos." *BMTIC* 5:59 (1939): 297–307.

Machado, J. da Costa. "Contribuição ao estudo da assistencia ao doente mental no Rio Grande do Norte." *Neurobiologia* 1:2 (1938): 204–11.

Machado, Maria Helena Pereira Toledo. "From Slave Rebels to Strikebreakers: The Quilombo of Jabaquara and the Problems of Citizenship in Late-Nineteenth Century Brazil." *HAHR* 86:2 (2006): 247–74.

Maciel, Auryno. "Da necessidade das escolas domesticas: a emancipação da mulher não se realiza apenas com a capacidade political, com a simples conquista do direito do voto; na Escola Domestica a menina aprende a derramar em torno de si os beneficios da collaboração e do altruismo." *Boletim da Diretoria Technica de Educação* 2:1–2 (1932): 161–66.

Magalhães, Agamemnon. *O estado e a realidade contemporanea.* [Recife]: Officinas Graphicas do "Diario da Manhã," [1933].

———. *Idéias e lutas.* Recife: Editora Raiz, 1985.

———. "O nordeste brasileiro." *BMTIC* 2:19 (1936): 248–65, 2:20 (1936): 245–61; 2:21 (1936): 270–78.

———. *O nordeste brasileiro.* Recife: Governo de Pernambuco, Secretaria de Educação e Cultura, Departamento de Cultura, 1970 [1922].

Magalhães, Rosana. *Fome: uma (re)leitura de Josué de Castro.* Rio de Janeiro: Editora Fiocruz, 1997.

Magarinhos, José. "Povoamento." *BMTIC* 1:12 (1935): 287–97.

Maio, Marcos Chor, and Ricardo Ventura Santo, eds. *Raça, ciência e sociedade.* Rio de Janeiro: Fiocruz/CCBB, 1996.

Mamede, Jurandyr. "Esboçando um relatorio geral, já em principio de outubro deste anno havia a Secretaria da Justiça, Educação e Interior divulgado as seguintes siderações." *Boletim da Directoria Technica de Educação* 1 (1931): 7–13.

Maria Neto, José. "'O importante não é falar, mas ser ouvido': meios e entremeios da propaganda de Agamenon Magalhães em Pernambuco (1937–1945)." *Saeculum—Revista de História* 10 (2004): 47–64.

Mattos, Hebe Maria. *Escravidão e cidadania no Brasil monárquico.* Rio de Janeiro: Jorge Zahar Editor, 2000.

———. "Identidade camponesa, racialização e cidadania no Brasil monárquico: o caso da 'Guerra dos Marimbondos' em Pernambuco a partir da leitura de Guillermo Palacios." *Almanack Braziliense* 3 (May 2006): 40–46.

Mattoso, Kátia M. de Queirós. *To Be a Slave in Brazil, 1550–1888.* New Brunswick, NJ: Rutgers University Press, 1986.

McCann, Bryan. *Hello, Hello Brazil: Popular Music in the Making of Modern Brazil.* Durham: Duke University Press, 2004.

Meade, Teresa A. "'Civilizing Rio de Janeiro': The Public Health Campaign and the Riot of 1904." *Journal of Social History* 20:2 (1986): 301–22.

———. *"Civilizing" Rio: Reform and Resistance in a Brazilian City, 1889–1930.* University Park: Pennsylvania State University Press, 1997.

Medeiros, Amaury de. *Actos de fé: discursos.* Rio de Janeiro: Imprensa Medica, 1928.

————. *Saude e assistencia: doutrina experiencias e realizações, 1923–1926*. Recife: N.p., 1926.

Mello, Evaldo Cabral de. *O norte agrário e o Império, 1871–1889*. 2nd ed. Rio de Janeiro: Topbooks, 1999.

Mello, José Antônio Gonsalves de. *Gente da nação: cristãos-novos e judeus em Pernambuco, 1542–1654*. Recife: Fundação Joaquim Nabuco/Editora Massangana, 1989.

————. *Tempo dos flamengos: influência da ocupação holandesa na vida e na cultura do norte do Brasil*. Rio de Janeiro: Livraria José Olympio Editora, 1947.

Melo, Afonso Bandeira de. "O espírio de Genebra e a reconstrucão do mundo." *BMTIC* 11:132 (1945): 199–214.

Menezes, Djacir. *O outro nordeste: formação social do nordeste*. Rio de Janeiro: Livraria José Olympio Editora, 1937.

Merhy, Emerson Elias. *A saúde pública como política: um estudo de formuladores de políticas*. São Paulo: Editora Hucitec, 1992.

Merrick, Thomas W., and Douglas H. Graham. *Population and Economic Development in Brazil, 1800 to the Present*. Baltimore: Johns Hopkins University Press, 1979.

Meznar, Joan E. "Orphans and the Transition from Slave to Free Labor in Northeast Brazil: The Case of Campina Grande, 1850–1888." *Journal of Social History* 27:3 (1994): 499–515.

————. "The Ranks of the Poor: Military Service and Social Differentiation in Northeast Brazil, 1830–1875." *HAHR* 72:3 (1992): 335–51.

Milet, Henrique Augusto. *Os quebra-kilos e a crise da lavoura*. 2nd ed. São Paulo: Global, 1987 [1876].

Miranda, Maria do Carmo Tavares de. *Homem, terra e região tropical: anais do v encontro regional de tropicologia*. Recife: Fundação Joaquim Nabuco/Editora Massangana, 1990.

Miranda, Valdemir. "Exame pré-nupcial." *AAPP* 5:1–2 (1935): 208–11.

Monteiro Lobato, José Bento Renato. *Contos pesados: Urupês, Negrinha e o Macaco que se fez homem*. São Paulo: Companhia Editora Nacional, 1940.

Mosher, Jeffrey C. "Challenging Authority: Political Violence and the Regency in Pernambuco, Brazil, 1831–1835." *LBR* 37:2 (2000): 33–57.

————. "Pernambuco and the Construction of the Brazilian Nation-State, 1831–1850." PhD dissertation, University of Florida, 1996.

————. "Political Mobilization, Party Ideology, and Lusophobia in Nineteenth-Century Brazil: Pernambuco, 1822–1850." *HAHR* 80:4 (2000): 881–912.

————. *Political Struggle, Ideology, and State Building: Pernambuco and the Construction of Brazil, 1817–1850*. Lincoln: University of Nebraska Press, 2008.

————. "The Struggle for the State: Partisan Conflict and the Origins of the Praieira Revolt in Imperial Brazil." *LBR* 42:2 (2005): 40–65.

Nachman, Robert G. "Positivism and Revolution in Brazil's First Republic: The 1904 Revolt." *The Americas* 84:1 (1977): 20–39.

————. "Positivism, Modernization, and the Middle Class in Brazil." *HAHR* 57:1 (1977): 1–23.

Needell, Jeffrey D. "History, Race, and the State in the Thought of Oliveira Viana." *HAHR* 75:1 (1995): 1–30.

————. "Identity, Race, Gender, and Modernity in the Origins of Gilberto Freyre's Oeuvre." *American Historical Review* 100:1 (1995): 51–77.

————. *A Tropical Belle Epoque: Elite Culture and Society in Turn-of-the-Century Rio de Janeiro*. Cambridge: Cambridge University Press, 1987.

Neiva, Arthur, and Belisário Penna. "Viagem cientifica pelo norte da Bahia, sudoeste de Pernambuco, sul do Piauhí e de norte a sul de Goiaz." *Memorias do Instituto Oswaldo Cruz* 8:3 (1916): 74–224.

Novais, Stella. "O teste de 'Découpace' de Claparede e de Walther (aplicado aos alumnos das Escolas Profissionais do Recife)." *AAPP* 2:2 (1932): 178–83.

O'Brien, Michael. "On Observing the Quicksand." *American Historical Review* 104: 4 (1999): 1202–7.

Oliveira, Maria Leopoldina de. "Test de desenho de Miss Florence Goodenough (experimentação em Recife e Maceió)." *AAPP* 2:1 (1932): 70–78.

Oliveira, Waldemar de. "A educação em primeiro lugar." *Boletim de Educação* 3:3–4 (1933): 119–39.

————. "O exame medico pré-nupcial, tese de concurso á livre docencia de hygiene da Faculdade de Medicina do Recife." Recife: Officinas Graphicas da S.A. Revista da Cidade, 1928.

————. "A practica anthropometrica: como preencher, neste particular, a ficha de educação physica (para as monitoras de educação physical)." *Boletim da Diretoria Technica de Educação* 1 (1931): 27–41.

Outtes, Joel. "Disciplining Society through the City: The Genesis of City Planning in Brazil and Argentina (1894–1945)." *Bulletin of Latin American Research* 22:2 (2003): 137–64.

————. *O Recife: gênese do urbanismo 1927–1943*. Recife: Fundação Joaquim Nabuco/Editora Massangana, 1997.

Palacios y Olivares, Guillermo de Jesus. "Revoltas camponesas no Brasil escravista: a 'Guerra dos Marimbondos' (Pernambuco, 1851–1852)." *Almanack Braziliense* 3 (May 2006): 9–39.

"Palavras iniciaes." *RAFDR* 1:1 (1891): 5–8.

Pallares-Burke, Maria Lúcia Garcia. *Gilberto Freyre: um vitoriano dos trópicos*. São Paulo: Editora UNESP, 2005.

Pandolfi, Dulce Chaves. *Pernambuco de Agamenon Magalhães: consolidação e crise de uma elite política*. Recife: Fundação Joaquim Nabuco/Editora Massangana, 1984.

Pang, Eul-Soo. *Bahia in the First Brazilian Republic: Coronelismo and Oligarchies, 1889–1934*. Gainesville: University Presses of Florida, 1979.

————, and Ron L. Seckinger. "The Mandarins of Imperial Brazil." *Comparative Studies in Society and History* 14:2 (1972): 215–44.

Parahym, Orlando. *O problema alimentar no sertão*. Recife: Imprensa Industrial, 1940.

Peard, Julyan G. *Race, Place, and Medicine: The Idea of the Tropics in Nineteenth-Century Brazilian Medicine*. Durham: Duke University Press, 1999.

————. "Tropical Disorders and the Forging of a Brazilian Medical Identity, 1860–1890." *HAHR* 77:1 (1997): 1–44.

Penna, Belisário. *Saneamento do Brasil: sanear o Brasil é povoal-o; é enriquecel-o; é moralisal-o*. Rio de Janeiro: Typographia Revista dos Tribunaes, 1918.

Pernambucano, Ulysses. "A ação social do psiquiatria." *Neurobiologia* 6:4 (1943): 153–60.

————. *A Assistencia a Psicopatas em Pernambuco: idéas e realizações*. Recife: Imprensa Industrial, 1932.

————. "Estudo estatistico da paralisa geral." *AAPP* 3:2 (1933): 155–64.

————. "O trabalho dos alienados na Assistencia a Psicopatas de Pernambuco." *AAPP* 4:1 (1934): 19–25.

————, and Helena Campos. "As doenças mentais entre os negros de Pernambuco." *AAPP* 2:1 (1932): 120–27.

Pernambucano, Ulysses, and Arnaldo Di Lascio. "Estudo estatistico das doenças mentais encontradas em quatrocentos primeiros internados em casa de saúde particular." *Neurobiologia* 3:4 (1940): 497–504.

Pernambucano, Ulysses, Arnaldo Di Lascio, Jarbas Pernambucano, and Almir Guimarães. "Alguns dados antropologicos da população do Recife." *AAPP* 5:1–2 (1935): 40–45.

Perruci, Gadiel. "Introdução." In *Trabalhos do Congresso Agricola do Recife, outubro de 1878, edição facsimilar comemorativa do primeiro centenário*, compiled by Sociedade Auxiliadora da Agricultura de Pernambuco, i–xlii. Recife: Fundação Estadual de Planejamento Agrícola de Pernambuco, 1978.

Pessar, Patricia R. *From Fanatics to Folk: Brazilian Millenarianism and Popular Culture*. Durham: Duke University Press, 2004.

Pessôa, Ida Brandão de Sá. "Periódicos médicos de Pernambuco." In *História da Faculdade de Medicina do Recife 1915–1985*, edited by Salomão Kelner et al., 191–204. Recife: Universidade Federal de Pernambuco, Centro de Ciências da Saúde, 1985.

Pierson, Donald. "A distribuição espacial das classes e das raças na Baía." *BMTIC* 9:105 (1943): 287–297.

Pimenta, Joaquim. "Saúde e riqueza (conferencia que, por motivo de molestia, deixou de pronunciar o autor na sessão inaugural da Sociedade de Medicina e Hygiene Tropical, realizado no dia de julho de 1919)." *RAFDR* 27 (1919): 44–61.

Pinto, Estevão. "Como classificar os alunos?" *Boletim de Educação, Diretoria Técnica de Educação* 3:3 (1933): 47–50.

Pires, Nelson. "Estudo de um tipo de cidade—o malandro." *Neurobiologia* 1:1 (1938): 47–59.

————. "As manobras anti-conceptionais, as neuroses e o adulteiro." *Neurobiologia* 1:3 (1938): 287–311.

Plotkin, Mariano Ben. "The Diffusion of Psychoanalysis in Argentina." *LARR* 33:2 (1998): 271–77.

————. *Freud in the Pampas: The Emergence and Development of Psychoanalytic Culture in Argentina*. Stanford: Stanford University Press, 2001.

————. "Freud, Politics, and the Porteños: The Reception of Psychoanalysis in Buenos Aires, 1910–1943." *HAHR* 77:1 (1997): 45–74.

Pompeu Sobrinho, Thomaz. "O homem do nordeste." *BIFOCS* 1:6 (1934): 239–56; 2:1 (1934): 24–35; 2:2 (1934): 56–65.

————. "Terra das secas." *BIFOCS* 1:5 (1934): 210–19.

Porter, Roy. *The Greatest Benefit to Mankind: A Medical History of Humanity*. New York: Norton, 1997.

1.o Congresso Brasileiro de eugenia: actas e trabalhos. Rio de Janeiro: N.p., 1929.

Quelle, Otto. "Migraçõcs ethnicas no nordeste brasileiro." *BMTIC* 3:34 (1937): 279–92.

Quintas, Fátima, ed. *Evocações e interpretações de Gilberto Freyre*. Recife: Fundação Joaquim Nabuco/Editora Massangana, 2003.

Rago, Magareth. *Do cabaré ao lar: a utopia da cidade disciplinar; Brasil 1890–1930.* Rio de Janeiro: Paz e Terra, 1985.

Ramos, Arthur. *As culturas negras no novo mundo.* 2nd ed. São Paulo: Companhia Editora Nacional, 1946.

———. "A dinamica afetiva do filho mimado." *Neurobiologia* 1:3 (1938): 265–86.

———. *O folk-lore negro no Brazil: demopsychologia e psychanalyse.* Rio de Janeiro: Civilização Brasileira, 1935.

———. *O negro brasileiro: ethnographia religiosa e psychanalyse.* Rio de Janeiro: Civilização Brasileira 1934.

———, ed. *O negro no Brasil: trabalhos apresentados ao 2.o Congresso afro-brasileiro (Bahia).* Rio de Janeiro: Civilização Brasileira, 1940.

Reis, Jaime. "The Abolition of Slavery and Its Aftermath in Pernambuco (1880–1920)." PhD dissertation, University of Oxford, 1975.

Reis, João José. *Death Is a Festival: Funeral Rites and Rebellion in Nineteenth-Century Brazil.* Chapel Hill: University of North Carolina Press, 2003.

———. *Slave Rebellion in Brazil: The Muslim Uprising of 1835 in Bahia.* Baltimore: Johns Hopkins University Press, 1993.

Ribeiro, René. "Alguns resultados do estudo de 100 'mediuns': trechos de um trabalho em preparo organisado nos moldes das precedentes contribuições ao estudo das religiões do Recife." In *Estudos pernambucanos dedicados a Ulysses Pernambucano,* 73–83. N.p., [1944].

———. "As esquizofrenias: estudo estatistico e sua aplicação á higiene mental: tese para livre docente de clinica psiquiatrica na Faculdade de Medicina do Recife." Recife: N.p., 1937.

———. "Messianic Movements in Brazil." *LBR* 29:1 (1992): 71–81.

———, and Alvaro Ferraz. "Grupos ethnicos, areas naturais e mobilidade das populações de Pernambuco." *Neurobiologia* 9:1 (1946): 1–21.

Rivera-Garza, Cristina. "'She Neither Respected nor Obeyed Anyone': Inmates and Psychiatrists Debate Gender and Class at the General Insane Asylum La Castañeda, Mexico, 1910–1930." *HAHR* 81:3 (2001): 653–88.

Rocha, Leduar de Assis. "Aumento da mortalidade em Bom Jardim e causas determinantes." *RMP* 4:6 (1934): 202–14.

Rocha, Melchiades da. *Bandoleiros das catingas.* Rio de Janeiro: Francisco Alves, 1988 [1942].

Rodrigues, João. "Do Hospital Infantil Manoel S. Almeida e da sua actuação em 1933." In *Anuário do Departamento de Saúde Publica: Anno II, 1933,* Pernambuco, 247–65. Recife: Imprensa Industrial, 1934.

Rodrigues, Raymundo Nina. "A abasia choreiforme epidemica no norte do Brasil." In *As collectividades anormaes,* 23–49. Rio de Janeiro: Civilização Brasileira, 1939.

———. *O alienado no direito civil Brasileiro.* 3rd ed. São Paulo: Companhia Editora Nacional, 1939 [1901].

———. *O animismo fetichista dos negros bahianos.* Rio de Janeiro: Civilização Brasileira, 1935.

———. *Os africanos no Brasil.* 3rd ed. São Paulo: Companhia Editora Nacional, 1945.

———. *As collectividades anormaes.* Rio de Janeiro: Civilização Brasileira, 1939.

————. "A loucura das multidões: nova contribuição ao estudo das loucuras epidemicas no Brasil." In *As collectividades anormaes*, 86–91. Rio de Janeiro: Civilização Brasileira, 1939.

————. "A loucura epidemica de Canudos: Antonio Conselheiro e os Jagunços." In *As collectividades anormaes*, 50–77. Rio de Janeiro: Civilização Brasileira, 1939.

————. "Os mestiços brazileiros." *Gazeta Medica da Bahia* 21:9 (1890): 401–7.

Rodriguez, Julia. "South Atlantic Crossing: Fingerprints, Science, and the State in Turn-of-the-Century Argentina." *American Historical Review* 109:2 (2004): 387–416.

Rosen, George. *A History of Public Health*. Baltimore: Johns Hopkins University Press, 1993.

Rowe, William, and Vivian Schelling. *Memory and Modernity: Popular Culture in Latin America*. London: Verso, 1991.

Rufino, João. *Discurso proferido em memoriam do prof. Geraldo de Andrade, em sessão solene do Instituto Pernambucano de Historia da Medicina*. Recife: Divulgação do Laboratório Clímax, n.d.

Russell-Wood, A. J. R. *Fidalgos and Philanthropists: The Santa Casa da Misericórdia of Bahia, 1550–1755*. Berkeley: University of California Press, 1968.

Sá, João Marque de. *Contribuição ao estudo do quociente intelectual dos epiléticos, tese de concurso para o cargo de médico da assistência a psicopatas*. Recife: Typographia da Empresa Jornal do Commercio S.A., 1936.

————. "A organização do serviço de neuro-psiquiatria da Brigada Militar de Pernambuco." *AAPP* 5:1 (1935): 82–86.

Said, Edward W. *Orientalism*. New York: Vintage, 1979.

Sampaio, A. J. de. *A alimentação sertaneja e do interior do Amazonia: onomastica da alimentação rural*. São Paulo: Companhia Editora Nacional, 1944.

Sansone, Livio. *Blackness without Ethnicity: Constructing Race in Brazil*. New York: Palgrave Macmillan, 2003.

Santos, Martha Sofia. "'Sertões Temerosos (Menacing Backlands)': Honor, Gender, and Violence in a Changing World, Ceará, Brazil, 1845–1889." PhD dissertation, University of Arizona, 2004.

Santos, Ricardo Ventura. "Mestiçagem, degeneração e a viabilidade de uma nação: debates em antropologia física no Brasil (1870–1930)." In *Homo brasilis: aspectos genéticos, lingüísticos, históricos e socioantropológicos da formação do povo brasileiro*, ed. Sérgio D. J. Pena, 113–29. Ribeirão Preto, São Paulo: FUNPEC-RP, 2000.

Sarto, Ana del, Alicio Ríos, and Abril Trigo. *The Latin American Cultural Studies Reader*. Durham: Duke University Press, 2004.

Scheper-Hughes, Nancy. *Death without Weeping: The Violence of Everyday Life in Brazil*. Berkeley: University of California Press, 1992.

Schneider, Jane, ed. *Italy's "Southern Question": Orientalism in One Country*. Oxford: Berg, 1998.

Schwarcz, Lilia Moritz. *O espetáculo das raças: cientistas, instituições e questão racial no Brasil, 1870–1930*. São Paulo: Companhia das Letras, 1993.

————. *The Spectacle of the Races: Scientists, Institutions, and the Race Question in Brazil, 1870–1930*. New York: Hill and Wang, 1999.

Schwartz, Stuart B. *Slaves, Peasants, and Rebels: Reconsidering Brazilian Slavery*. Urbana: University of Illinois Press, 1996.

———. *Sugar Plantations in the Formation of Brazilian Society: Bahia, 1550–1835.* Cambridge: Cambridge University Press, 1985.

Schwartzman, Simon, Helena Maria Bousquet Bomeny, and Vanda Maria Ribeiro Costa. *Tempos de Capanema.* São Paulo: Editora Paz e Terra, 2000.

Schwarz, Roberto. *Misplaced Ideas: Essays on Brazilian Culture.* London: Verso, 1992.

Scott, James C. *Seeing Like a State: How Certain Schemes to Improve the Human Condition Have Failed.* New Haven: Yale University Press, 1998.

———. *Weapons of the Weak: Everyday Forms of Peasant Resistance.* New Haven: Yale University Press, 1985.

Scott, Rebecca J., Seymour Drescher, Hebe Maria Mattos de Castro, George Reid Andrews, and Robert M. Levine. *The Abolition of Slavery and the Aftermath of Emancipation in Brazil.* Durham: Duke University Press, 1988.

Sevcenko, Nicolau. *Literatura como missão: tensões sociais e criação cultural na primeira república.* São Paulo: Brasiliense, 1983.

———. *A revolta da vacina: mentes insanas em corpos rebeldes.* São Paulo: Editora Scipione, 1993.

Sicherman, Barbara. "The Quest for Mental Health in America, 1880–1917." PhD dissertation, Columbia University, 1967.

Silva, Arthur Lobo da. "A anthropologia no exercito brasileiro." *Archivos do Museu Nacional* 30 (1928): 9–299.

Silva, Denise Ferreira da. "Facts of Blackness: Brazil Is not (Quite) the United States . . . and Racial Politics in Brazil?" *Social Identities* 4:2 (1998): 201–35.

Silva, Leonardo Dantas, ed. *A abolição em Pernambuco.* Recife: Fundação Joaquim Nabuco/Editora Massangana 1988.

Silverstein, Leni. "The Celebration of Our Lord of the Good End: Changing State, Church, and Afro-Brazilian Relations in Bahia." In *The Brazilian Puzzle: Culture on the Borderlands of the Western World,* edited by David J. Hess and Roberto A. DaMatta, 134–51. New York: Columbia University Press, 1995.

Skidmore, Thomas E. *Black into White: Race and Nationality in Brazilian Thought.* Durham: Duke University Press, 1993 [1974].

———. "Racial Ideas and Social Policy in Brazil." In *The Idea of Race in Latin America, 1870–1940,* edited by Richard Graham, 3–36. Austin: University of Texas Press, 1992.

———. "Raízes de Gilberto Freyre." In *Gilberto Freyre em quatro tempos,* edited by Ethel Volfzon Kosminsky, Claude Lépine, and Fernanda Arêas Peixoto, 41–64. Bauru, São Paulo: EDUSC, 2003.

Sommer, Dorris. *Foundational Fictions: The National Romances of Latin America.* Berkeley University of California Press, 1991.

Souto Maior, Armando. *Quebra-quilos: lutas sociais no outono do império.* São Paulo: Companhia Editora Nacional, 1978.

Stein, Stanley J. *The Brazilian Cotton Manufacture: Textile Enterprise in an Underdeveloped Area, 1850–1950.* Cambridge, MA: Harvard University Press, 1957.

———. *Vassouras: A Brazilian Coffee County, 1850–1900; The Roles of Planter and Slave in a Plantation Society.* Princeton: Princeton University Press, 1985.

Stepan, Nancy Leys. *Beginnings of Brazilian Science: Oswaldo Cruz, Medical Research, and Policy, 1890–1920.* New York: Science History Publications, 1976.

————. "Eugenics in Brazil, 1917–1940." In *The Wellborn Science: Eugenics in Germany, France, Brazil, and Russia,* edited by Mark B. Adams, 110–52. New York: Oxford University Press, 1990.

————. *"The Hour of Eugenics": Race, Gender, and Nation in Latin America.* Ithaca, NY: Cornell University Press, 1991.

Stern, Alexandra Minna. "Buildings, Boundaries, and Blood: Medicalization and Nation-Building on the U.S.-Mexico Border, 1910–1930." *HAHR* 79:1 (1999): 41–81.

————. *Eugenic Nation: Faults and Frontiers of Better Breeding in Modern America.* Berkeley: University of California Press, 2005.

————. "Responsible Mothers and Normal Children: Eugenics, Nationalism, and Welfare in Post-revolutionary Mexico, 1920–1940." *Journal of Social History* 12: 4 (1999): 369–97.

Stoler, Ann Laura. *Race and the Education of Desire: Foucault's* History of Sexuality *and the Colonial Order of Things.* Durham: Duke University Press, 1995.

Taunay, Alfredo d'Escragnolle. *A retirada da Laguna: episodio da Guerra do Paraguay.* 10th ed. São Paulo: Companhia Melhoramentos de São Paulo, 1935 [1871].

Telles, Edward E. *Race in Another America: The Significance of Skin Color in Brazil.* Princeton: Princeton University Press, 2004.

Tomes, Nancy. *The Gospel of Germs: Men, Women, and the Microbe in American Life.* Cambridge, MA: Harvard University Press, 1998.

Torres, Alberto. *O problema nacional brasileira, introducção a um programma de organização nacional.* 2nd ed. São Paulo: Companhia Editora Nacional, Bibilotéca Pedagogica Brasileira, 1933.

Torres, Vasconcelos. *Condições de vida do trabalhador na agro-indústria do açúcar.* Rio de Janeiro: Edição do Instituto do Açúcar e do Álcool, 1945.

Valente, Waldemar. "Estácio Coimbra: a reforma Carneiro Leão e a sociologia na Escola Normal do Estado de Pernambuco." In *Estácio Coimbra: homem representativo do seu meio e do seu tempo,* edited by Gilberto Freyre et al., 57–60. Recife: Instituto Joaquim Nabuco de Pesquisas Sociais, 1973.

Van Young, Eric, ed. *Mexico's Regions: Comparative History and Development.* San Diego: Center for U.S.-Mexican Studies, University of California, San Diego, 1992.

Vargas, Getúlio. *A nova política do Brasil.* Vol. 2. Rio de Janeiro: Livraria José Olympio Editora, 1938.

Vasconcelos, Francisco de Assis Guedes de. "Fome, eugenia e constituição do campo de nutrição em Pernambuco: uma análise de Gilberto Freyre, Josué de Castro e Nelson Chaves." *História, Ciências, Saúde—Manguinhos* 8:2 (2001): 315–39.

Vasconcelos, José. *La raza cósmica: misión de la raza iberoamericana.* Madrid: Aguilar, 1966 [1925].

Vianna, Hermano. *The Mystery of Samba: Popular Music and National Identity in Brazil.* Chapel Hill: University of North Carolina Press, 1999.

"Vida educacional." *Boletim da Diretoria Technica de Educação* 1 (1931): 103–23.

Wade, Peter. *Blackness and Race Mixture: The Dynamics of Racial Identity in Colombia.* Baltimore: Johns Hopkins University Press, 1993.

————. *Music, Race, and Nation: Música Tropical in Colombia.* Chicago: University of Chicago Press, 2000.

————. *Race and Ethnicity in Latin America.* London: Pluto Press, 1997.

Weinstein, Barbara. *The Amazon Rubber Boom, 1850–1920.* Stanford: Stanford University Press, 1983.

———. "Brazilian Regionalism." *LARR* 17:2 (1982): 262–76.

———. *For Social Peace in Brazil: Industrialists and the Remaking of the Working Class in São Paulo, 1920–1964.* Chapel Hill: University of North Carolina Press, 1996.

———. "Slavery, Citizenship, and National Identity in Brazil and the United States South." In *Nationalism in the New World,* edited by Don Doyle and Marco Antonio Pamplona, 248–71. Athens: University of Georgia Press, 2006.

———. "Unskilled Worker, Skilled Housewife: Constructing the Working-Class Woman in São Paulo, Brazil." In *The Gendered Worlds of Latin American Women Workers: From Household and Factory to the Union Hall and Ballot Box,* edited by John D. French and Daniel James, 72–99. Durham: Duke University Press, 1997.

Wells, Allen, and Gilbert M. Joseph. *Summer of Discontent, Seasons of Upheaval: Elite Politics and Rural Insurgency in Yucatán, 1876–1915.* Stanford: Stanford University Press, 1996.

Williams, Daryle. *Culture Wars in Brazil: The First Vargas Regime, 1930–1945.* Durham: Duke University Press, 2001.

Williams, Steven C. "Nationalism and Public Health: The Convergence of Rockefeller Foundation Technique and Brazilian Federal Authority during the Time of Yellow Fever, 1925–1930." In *Missionaries of Science: The Rockefeller Foundation and Latin America,* edited by Marcos Cueto, 23–51. Bloomington: Indiana University Press, 1994.

Winant, Howard. "Rethinking Race in Brazil." *JLAS* 24:1 (1992): 173–92.

Wirth, John D. *Minas Gerais in the Brazilian Federation, 1889–1937.* Stanford: Stanford University Press, 1977.

Woodard, James P. "Coronelismo in Theory and Practice: Evidence, Analysis, and Argument from São Paulo." *LBR* 42:1 (2005): 99–117.

———. *A Place in Politics: São Paulo, Brazil, from Seigneurial Republicanism to Regionalist Revolt.* Durham: Duke University Press, 2009.

———. "Regionalismo paulista e política partidiária nos anos vinte." *Revista de História* 150:1 (2004): 41–56.

Zimmermann, Eduardo A. "Racial Ideas and Social Reform: Argentina, 1890–1916." *HAHR* 72:1 (1992): 22–46.

Zulawski, Ann. "New Trends in Studies of Science and Medicine in Latin America." *LARR* 34:3 (1999): 241–51.

INDEX

War of the Marimbondos, 24–25
women, 57, 120–21, 123, 125–27, 129, 181
workers: agricultural, 9, 29–30, 32–48, 117, 211; agricultural training of, 29–33; diet of, 141, 143–45; health of, 102–6, 115; industrial, 88, 118, 123, 128, 134–35, 156; racial characteristics of, 211, 213–14, 216, 220–21, 225–26

working conditions, 135, 146, 204

yellow fever, 37, 83, 87 90, 95, 97, 102, 147; control efforts, 85, 90, 94, 97; and Rockefeller Yellow Fever Commission, 103, 106–12

zona da mata, 33, 47